T0181260

Communications in Computer and Information Science 1999

Rationale

The CCIS series is devoted to the publication of proceedings of computer science conferences. Its aim is to efficiently disseminate original research results in informatics in printed and electronic form. While the focus is on publication of peer-reviewed full papers presenting mature work, inclusion of reviewed short papers reporting on work in progress is welcome, too. Besides globally relevant meetings with internationally representative program committees guaranteeing a strict peer-reviewing and paper selection process, conferences run by societies or of high regional or national relevance are also considered for publication.

Topics

The topical scope of CCIS spans the entire spectrum of informatics ranging from foundational topics in the theory of computing to information and communications science and technology and a broad variety of interdisciplinary application fields.

Information for Volume Editors and Authors

Publication in CCIS is free of charge. No royalties are paid, however, we offer registered conference participants temporary free access to the online version of the conference proceedings on SpringerLink (http://link.springer.com) by means of an http referrer from the conference website and/or a number of complimentary printed copies, as specified in the official acceptance email of the event.

CCIS proceedings can be published in time for distribution at conferences or as post-proceedings, and delivered in the form of printed books and/or electronically as USBs and/or e-content licenses for accessing proceedings at SpringerLink. Furthermore, CCIS proceedings are included in the CCIS electronic book series hosted in the SpringerLink digital library at http://link.springer.com/bookseries/7899. Conferences publishing in CCIS are allowed to use Online Conference Service (OCS) for managing the whole proceedings lifecycle (from submission and reviewing to preparing for publication) free of charge.

Publication process

The language of publication is exclusively English. Authors publishing in CCIS have to sign the Springer CCIS copyright transfer form, however, they are free to use their material published in CCIS for substantially changed, more elaborate subsequent publications elsewhere. For the preparation of the camera-ready papers/files, authors have to strictly adhere to the Springer CCIS Authors' Instructions and are strongly encouraged to use the CCIS LaTeX style files or templates.

Abstracting/Indexing

CCIS is abstracted/indexed in DBLP, Google Scholar, EI-Compendex, Mathematical Reviews, SCImago, Scopus. CCIS volumes are also submitted for the inclusion in ISI Proceedings.

How to start

To start the evaluation of your proposal for inclusion in the CCIS series, please send an e-mail to ccis@springer.com.

Abdalmuttaleb M. A. Musleh Al-Sartawi ·
Mohd Helmy Abd Wahab · Khaled Hussainey
Editors

Global Economic Revolutions: Big Data Governance and Business Analytics for Sustainability

Second International Conference, ICGER 2023
Sharjah, United Arab Emirates, February 27–28, 2023
Revised Selected Papers

 Springer

Editors
Abdalmuttaleb M. A. Musleh Al-Sartawi ⓘ
Ahlia University
Manama, Bahrain

Mohd Helmy Abd Wahab
Universiti Tun Hussein Onn Malaysia
Parit Raja, Malaysia

Khaled Hussainey ⓘ
University of Portsmouth
Portsmouth, UK

ISSN 1865-0929   ISSN 1865-0937 (electronic)
Communications in Computer and Information Science
ISBN 978-3-031-50517-1   ISBN 978-3-031-50518-8 (eBook)
https://doi.org/10.1007/978-3-031-50518-8

This Springer imprint is published by the registered company Springer Nature Switzerland AG
The registered company address is: Gewerbestrasse 11, 6330 Cham, Switzerland

Paper in this product is recyclable.

Foreword

"Big Data Governance and Business Analytics for Sustainability"

Digital transformation, widely acknowledged as the 4th industrial revolution, has seen exponential growth in the last few years. This expansion has continued, particularly throughout the COVID-19 pandemic. During the onset of the pandemic, although a large proportion of the global economy had come to a halt, many businesses managed to survive due to the digitalization initiatives that they had expedited. They recognized that organizations could continue to operate even if people were not physically located in one place [1].

The digital economy is a key breakthrough, and a hallmark of the 4th industrial revolution. Technological innovation has now become the key to sustainable economic growth and wealth creation by organizations. Technological innovation and economic development are inevitable necessities for sustainable development, whereby the digital economy has gradually become a new engine for enhancement and change. It has become an economy of new business models and new markets [2]. The digital economy can be described as the global network of economic activities, transactions, and professional interactions that are enabled by technology. It can be summed up as an economy based on digital technologies which has benefits vis-à-vis technological innovation ability, market expansion ability, and industrial integration ability.

Technological innovations have enabled higher levels of business effectiveness and efficiency at both the operational and strategic levels. Big data analytics is amongst the most vital digital innovations, yet very few firms have utilized its true potential for strategic purposes until recently [3]. Although the digital economy is fast becoming an important part of the world economy, research on this topic lags behind when compared to the dynamic development at the practical level and the significant attention at the policy level [4].

Thus, the International Conference on Global Economic Revolutions is a timely and much-needed event in terms of its focus on bringing together research, theory, and applications. It is hoped that this conference and its findings, conclusions, and recommendations will contribute to better decision making, improving on the well-being of mankind towards a more sustainable future. Accordingly, this book of proceedings provides a valuable platform for discussing a variety of viewpoints on a wide range of novel and important themes related to topical subjects such as big data analytics, artificial intelligence, the metaverse, sustainable technologies, and sustainability in general. This book offers salient knowledge to professionals, practitioners, scholars, managers, policymakers, and students.

Abdulla Yusuf Abdulwahab Al Hawaj

References

[1] Shah, T. R. (2022). Can big data analytics help organisations achieve sustainable competitive advantage? A developmental enquiry. Technology in Society, 68, 101801.

[2] Wang, Q., & Wei, Y. (2023). Research on the Influence of Digital Economy on Technological Innovation: Evidence from Manufacturing Enterprises in China. Sustainability, 15(6), 4995.

[3] Lin, C., & Kunnathur, A. (2019). Strategic orientations, developmental culture, and big data capability. Journal of Business Research, 105, 49-60.

[4] Ding, C., Liu, C., Zheng, C., & Li, F. (2021). Digital economy, technological innovation, and high-quality economic development: Based on spatial effect and mediation effect. Sustainability, 14(1), 216.

Preface

This book constitutes the revised and selected papers of the International Conference on Global Economic Revolutions (ICGER 2022) held in Sharjah City, United Arab Emirates, during February 27–28, 2023.

ICGER 2022 is the second conference in a series of conferences which aim to offer a platform for the exchange of ideas and information on technological advancements and developments in the era of digitalization. The conference brings together contributors from a variety of perspectives, disciplines, and communities seeking the advancement of knowledge regarding the digital economy. The scope of ICGER covers a wide range of interdisciplinary application fields of technology, particularly in the digital economy and society.

The 18 papers included in this book have been thoroughly selected and reviewed. The call for papers requested submissions centering around the theme of the digital economy. The submissions were accepted after a double-blind process with at least 3 reviews each.

This book offers insight on several important topics in the digital era. The papers present trendy and interdisciplinary topics related to data science and data centers, machine learning, sustainable technologies for a green economy, metaverse in healthcare education, predictive model analytics using data mining and machine learning, blockchain adoption and acceptance, narrow-band Internet of Things, and enhanced bubble sorting visualizer.

The success of the ICGER conference series depends on the efforts and support of various individuals, committees, and organizations. We would like to take this opportunity to thank the conference host, honorary chairs, scientific committee, organizers, strategic partners, and sponsors. We are grateful for the efforts of our keynote speakers, session chairs, and authors. Special thanks to our reviewers for refereeing the chapters, as well as their contributions towards the improvement of the quality and content of the chapters. I would also like to thank the *Communications in Computer and Information Science (CCIS)* editorial team for giving us the opportunity to be members of their family and for the support given in the production of this book.

November 2023

Abdalmuttaleb M. A. Musleh Al-Sartawi
Mohd Helmy Abd Wahab
Khaled Hussainey

Preface

Organization

Conference Executive Chair

Abdulmuttaleb M. A. Musleh Al-Sartawi — Ahlia University, Bahrain

Conference Honorary Chairs

Abdulla Y. Al Hawaj — Ahlia University, Bahrain
Saif Bin Rashid Al Gaberi — Arab Academics and Scientists Union, Jordan
Issa Saleh Al Hammadi — Educational Center for the Arabic Language for the Gulf States, UAE

Conference Chairs

Mansoor Alaali — Ahlia University, Bahrain
Eesa Mohammed Bastaki — University of Dubai, UAE
Allam Hamdan — Ahlia University, Bahrain
Khalid Al-Begain — Kuwait College of Science & Technology, Kuwait
Mohamed Dhiaf — Liwa College of Technology, UAE

Conference Executive Committee

M. Kabir Hassan — University of New Orleans, USA
Khaled Hussainey — University of Portsmouth, UK
Janice C. Sipior — Villanova University, USA
Talal Al-Hayale — University of Windsor, Canada
Cesario Mateus — Aalborg University Business School, Denmark
Khaled Guesmi — Paris School of Business, France
Mustafa Mohd Hanefah — Universiti Sains Islam Malaysia, Malaysia
Abdulnaser Ibrahim Nour — An-Najah National University, Palestine
Qasim Zureigat — Sulaiman Al Rajhi University, KSA
Ikhlas Altarawneh — Amman Arab University, Jordan
Ezz Hattab — International Computer Auditing Education Association, Canada

Programme Committee Chairs

Abdalmuttaleb M. A. Musleh Al-Sartawi	Ahlia University, Kingdom of Bahrain
Mohd Helmy Abd Wahab	Universiti Tun Hussein Onn Malaysia, Malaysia
Khaled Hussainey	Portsmouth University, UK
Abdulnaser Ibrahim Nour	An-Najah National University, Palestine

Programme/Scientific Committee

Agha Amad Nabi	Dow University of Health Sciences, Pakistan
Ahmad Alqatan	Arab Open University, Kuwait
Ahmad Mahmoud Ahmad Zamil	Prince Sattam Bin Abdulaziz University, KSA
Ahmed Elamer	Brunel University London, UK
Ahmed Elsayed	Durham University, UK
Araby Madbouly	Muscat College, Oman
Asma Salman	American University in the Emirates, UAE
Audil Rashid Khaki	American University of the Middle East, Kuwait
Azam Abdelhakeem Khalid Ahmed	Universiti Pendidikan Sultan Idris, Malaysia
Azzam Hannoon	American University in the Emirates, UAE
Elena Chatzopoulou	Athens University of Economics and Business, Greece
Elfindah Princes	University of Queensland, Australia
Essam Al-Husseini	Esraa University College, Iraq
Fadi Hassan Shihadeh	Technical University, Palestine
Gürdal Ertek	United Arab Emirates University, UAE
Habiba Al Mughairi	University of Technology and Applied Sciences, Oman
Hasan Ghura	Box Hill College Kuwait, Kuwait
Hassan Elhawary	Central Queensland University, Australia
Kalsoom Sumra	COMSATS University Islamabad, Pakistan
Karim Sorour	Northumbria University, UK
Liew Chee Yoong	UCSI University, Malaysia
Maged M. Gazar	Institute of Public Administration, KSA
Maha Radwan	University of Turin, Italy
Mayada A. Youssef	United Arab Emirates University, UAE
Nadia Mansour	University of Sousse, Tunisia, and University of Salamanca, Spain
Sergii Kavun	Interregional Academy of Personnel Management, Ukraine

Tord Häversjö — Nordic International Management Institute, Sweden

Waldemar Pfoertsch — Cyprus International Institute of Management, Cyprus

Willy Legrand — IU International University of Applied Sciences, Germany

Zenonas Turskis — Vilnius Gediminas Technical University, Lithuania

Hala Ismail Zaidan — University of Jordan, Jordan

Hazar Yasser Hmoud — University of Jordan, Jordan

Rand Hani Al-Dmour — University of Jordan, Jordan

Zainah Qasem — University of Jordan, Jordan

Farah Shishan — University of Jordan, Jordan

Ali Al-Moulani — Bahrain Economists Society, Bahrain

Nor Razinah Mohd. Zain — International Islamic University Malaysia, Malaysia

Oltiana Muharremi Pelari — Stonehill College, USA

Raed Ahmad Ibrahim Abueid — Al-Quds Open University, Palestine

Rohit Bansal — Rajiv Gandhi Institute of Petroleum Technology, India

Rui Dang — Westminster International University in Tashkent, Uzbekistan

Sebahattin Demirkan — Manhattan College, USA

Soumaya Askri — Canadian University Dubai, UAE

Stephen Aro-Gordon — Muscat College, Oman

Thouraya Snoussi — University of Sharjah, UAE

Vanja Piljak — University of Vaasa, Finland

Wafi Al-Karaghouli — Brunel University London, UK

Wajeha Awad — Albaraka Banking Group, Bahrain

Baker Al Serhan — Princess Sumaya University for Technology, Jordan

Cesario Mateus — Aalborg University, Denmark

Ikhlas Altarawneh — Amman Arab University, Jordan

Iqbal Thonse Hawaldar — Kingdom University, Bahrain

Janice C. Sipior — Villanova University, USA

Khaled Guesmi — Paris School of Business, France

Mustafa Mohd Hanefah — Universiti Sains Islam Malaysia, Malaysia

Qasim Zureigat — Sulaiman Al Rajhi University, KSA

Ravi Kumar Bommisetti — Amrita Sai Institute of Science and Technology, India

Talal Al-Hayale — University of Windsor, Canada

Muhammad Farrukh — Beijing Institute of Technology, China

Vincent Ribiere — Bangkok University, Thailand

Yalçın Kirdar	Maltepe University, Turkey
Khaled Dahawy	American University in Cairo, Egypt
Fadi Thabtah	Manukau Institute of Technology, New Zealand
Maria Manuela Cruz-Cunha	Polytechnic Institute of Cávado and Ave, Portugal
Laila Dahabiyeh	University of Jordan, Jordan
Hamzah Hussein Al-Mawali	University of Jordan, Jordan
Mohammad Tayeh	University of Jordan, Jordan
Adel Bino	University of Jordan, Jordan
Basheer Khamees	University of Jordan, Jordan
Ahmad L. Ahmad	University of Jordan, Jordan
Ali Mawlood Fadhil Al-Sammarraie	Al-Esraa College University, Iraq
Manaf Al-Okaily	Jadara University, Jordan
Myriam Aloulou	Liwa College of Technology, UAE
Sara Amar	Liwa College of Technology, UAE
Bedour Alboloushi	Kuwait College of Science & Technology, Kuwait
Hasan Ghura	Kuwait College of Science & Technology, Kuwait
Basil Alothman	Kuwait College of Science & Technology, Kuwait
Ismaeel Al Ridhawi	Kuwait College of Science & Technology, Kuwait
Murugappan Murugappan	Kuwait College of Science & Technology, Kuwait
Jaheer Mukthar K. P.	Kristu Jayanti College (Autonomous), India
Justin Nelson Michael	Kristu Jayanti College (Autonomous), India
Lijo P. Thomas	Kristu Jayanti College (Autonomous), India
Augustine George	Kristu Jayanti College (Autonomous), India
Mahmoud Mistarihi	Liwa College of Technology, UAE

Technical Committee

Amer Al Roubaie	Ahlia University, Bahrain
Wajeeh Elali	Ahlia University, Bahrain
Jasim Al Ajmi	Ahlia University, Bahrain
Sameh Reyad	Ahlia University, Bahrain
Adel Sarea	Ahlia University, Bahrain
Richard Cummings	Ahlia University, Bahrain
Rami Abu Wadi	Ahlia University, Bahrain
Sayed Mohamad Fadhul	Ahlia University, Bahrain
Zakeya Sanad	Ahlia University, Bahrain
Hooria Hafedh	Ahlia University, Bahrain
Maryam Althawadi	Ahlia University, Bahrain
Ali Mulla	Ahlia University, Bahrain
Bashar Matooq	Ahlia University, Bahrain

Hamad Almoajil	Ahlia University, Bahrain
Ebtisam AlMahari	Ahlia University, Bahrain
Reem Mansoor	Ahlia University, Bahrain

Program Review Committee

Abdulkrim Ziani	Umm Al Quwain University, United Arab Emirates
Abeer Abdelhalim	King Faisal University, Saudi Arabia, and Port Said University, Egypt
Aeshna Jain	Indira Gandhi Delhi Technical University for Women, India
Ahmed Sabek	Umm Al Qura University, Saudi Arabia
Alaa Makki Hadi	University of Sharjah, United Arab Emirates
Arushi Jain	Vellore Institute of Technology, India
Asal Alaa Alshammri	University of Sharjah, United Arab Emirates
Ashish Mathur	IGNTU, India
Azzeddine Nezai	University of Saida Dr. Moulay Tahar, Algeria
Carmen Olsen	Western Norway University of Applied Sciences (HVL), Norway
Chenguel Bechir	University of Kairouan, Tunisia
Dina Tahat	Al Ain University, Jordan
Gagan Kukreja	University of Bahrain, Kingdom of Bahrain
Raj Bahadur Sharma	University of Bahrain, Kingdom of Bahrain
Vandana Gupta	Lachoo Memorial College of Science and Technology, India
Easwaramoorthy Rangaswamy	Amity Global Institute, Singapore
Ebrahim Mansour	Hashemite University, Jordan
Enas Ahmed	Ain-Shams University, Egypt
Ghayur Ahmad	PMU, Saudi Arabia
Hamzeh Magableh	Amman Arab University, Jordan
Hanan Gunied	Cairo University, Egypt
Haneen Mohammad Shoaib	University of Business and Technology, Saudi Arabia
Islam Abdeljawad	An-Najah National University, Palestine
Jitesh Jassi	Delhi Technological University, India
Jolly Masih	PIEMR, Indore, India
Juma Khalifa Juma Aldarmaki	Universiti Utara Malaysia, Malaysia
Khalid AlDweri	Kuwait International Law School, Kuwait
Layth Dwaikat	An-Najah National University, Palestine
Maha Abdulmajeed Attia	Ajman University, United Arab Emirates

Maha Othman	Universiti Utara Malaysia, Malaysia
Mahendra Parihar	SVKM's NMIMS University, India
Manaf Alokaily	Jadara University, Jordan
Maryam Shadman	Teesside University, UK
Mayank Chugh	Delhi Technological University, India
Mohamed Ibrahim Mugableh	Irbid National University, Jordan
Mohammad Yousef Alghadi	Irbid National University, Jordan
Mohammed Habes	Yarmouk University, Jordan
Mohd Saiful Izwaan Saadon	Universiti Malaysia Terengganu, Malaysia
Mohiddin Shaw Shaik	Narasaraopeta Engineering College, India
Mokhtar Elareshi	Al Ain University, United Arab Emirates
Muhammad Saleem	Universiti Teknologi Malaysia, Malaysia
Nagaraju Dasari	Manipal University Jaipur, India
Nagwa Fahmy	Zayed University, United Arab Emirates
Nahla Etman	King Faisal University, Saudi Arabia
Nehad Shalaby	Qatar University, Qatar
Nidhi Arora	Indira Gandhi Delhi Technical University for Women, India
Harvinder Singh	Leaders Institute Pty., Australia
Jonathan Deutsch	Drexel University, USA
Manojkumar Deshpande	PIEMR, Indore, India
Saad Znad Darwish	Kingdom University, Bahrain
Rahima Aissani	Al Ain University, UAE
Rahul Shaw	Aliah University, India
Rana Taha	Hashemite University, Jordan
Saadia Anwar Pasha	Allama Iqbal Open University, Pakistan
Samar Shoaib	University of Business and Technology, Saudi Arabia
Seif Al Shbeil	Al al-Bayt University, Jordan
Umar Habibu Umar	Universiti Brunei Darussalam, Brunei
Vaishali Ojha	KES Shroff College of Arts and Commerce, India

Contents

Digitalization and Sustainable Technologies

Big Data Governance and Sustainability

The Critical Factors Affecting the Feasibility of the Construction and Operation of a Co-location Datacenter in Kuwait

Mohammed Harb[1], Wael Abdallah[2(✉)], and Arezou Haraf[2]

[1] Maastricht School of Management Kuwait, Dasma, Kuwait
[2] Box Hill College Kuwait, Abo Halifa, Kuwait
`w.abdallah@bhck.edu.kw`

Abstract. This study explores the critical factors affecting the construction and operation of the co-location data center in the Kuwaiti market. The study adopted the union model to collect and process data. The current research used a qualitative method, constructivism philosophy paradigm, inductive approach, and exploratory research type. Semi-structured interviews were used to collect and process data from nine research experts using purposeful sampling. The collected data were analyzed using the six thematic steps: becoming familiar with the data, generating initial codes, searching for themes, reviewing themes, defining themes, and writing up). This study reviews and discusses the thematic analysis of the data of the critical factors affecting the feasibility of establishing and operating co-location data centers in the Kuwaiti market. The results of constructing and operating a co-location data center showed two main themes, internal and external themes; under each theme, sub-themes clarify and explain the main themes—the internal theme, which includes the design of the location to ensure business continuity, operations of facilities, security, staff, and service level agreement operations, financial management, and company experience. At the same time, the external theme includes government regulations and standard certification.

Keywords: Co-location · Data Center · Uptime · Certification · Standards · Operations · Hosting · Qualitative Analysis · Kuwait

1 Introduction

The 1940s can be considered the beginning of the name data center. The first computers were manufactured, requiring huge server rooms to accommodate large computers. However, these vast rooms were no longer needed after the invention of microcomputers in the seventies of the last century. More modern servers were established with the development of information technology, which evolved into what we see today as cloud services. The development of data centers has become inevitable and very quick. The average life span of data centers is 12 years; they must be developed to keep pace with rapid technological development (Nazim et al. 2019). There are many definitions of a data center shown in Table 1 (Cisco, 2011) defines the data center as a center for storing applications and data of any organization or company. The data center design includes a network of computing and storage resources that handle many shared programs and data. The data center can be considered a centralized and reliable work environment for running and managing IT devices. The work environment includes cooling systems, primary and backup power, and a fire protection system with many supporting systems (Hoon and Yali 2014). While (Joshi and Kumar 2012) defined the data center as a large facility containing many information technology devices and equipment used to process, transmit, and store digital information. The data center can self-service to the center operator or other clients(Barroso et al. 2013). It is the definition adopted by the researcher, as it is comprehensive and contains all aspects of the data center. The data center contains(Barroso et al. 2013):

- communication devices,
- power equipment with all its booster devices (UPS, Batteries) that support its continuity and ensure non-stopping
- cooling devices, and
- environmental control equipment to maintain the appropriate operating conditions for the devices inside the center.

A simple definition of a *data center* is a permanent facility concerned with the long-term maintenance, storage, and processing of data (Arregoces and Portolani 2003). Moreover, many users, such as Internet service providers, banks, telecommunications companies, educational institutions, and government and private institutions, may exploit the data center.

Table 1. Data Center Definitions

Definition	Source
A center for storing applications and data of any organization or company	Cisco (2011)
A centralized and reliable work environment for running and managing IT devices. The work environment includes cooling systems, primary and backup power, and a fire protection system with many supporting systems	(Hoon and Yali 2014)
A large facility contains many information technology devices and equipment for processing, transmitting, and storing digital information. The data center can provide self-service to the center operator or other clients	(Barroso et al. 2013)
A permanent facility concerned with the long-term maintenance, storage, and processing of data	(Arregoces and Portolani 2003)

Source: (Authors)

The Co-location data center industry's market research predicts a CAGR of 15.87% with revenues of $161,089 million in 2028(*GLOBAL DATA CENTER COLOCATION MARKET FORECAST 2021–2028*, 2021). Several key factors are aiding the growth of

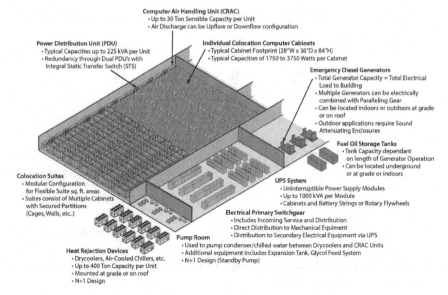

Fig. 1. Typical Data Center. Source: (Barroso et al. 2013)

the global Co-Location Data Center Market. With the increasing demand for cloud and hybrid services, the rising growth in the IoT and artificial intelligence industry, and thus the need for expansion and spread to reach the end customers quickly. In addition, government support, expertise, and financial viability are key factors supporting the Co-location data center market's growth(Hoon and Yali 2014) (Fig. 1).

Kuwait's co-location data center market began with ISPs (Internet Services Providers) such as Zajil Telcom, BOnline (Gulfnet Communications), and Quality net offering hosting services. However, their breadth of services was limited, and their price points were their crucial differentiator ("About Company" 2022). On the other hand, Telecom Companies such as Ooredoo Kuwait and Zain were late entrants and focused on customer value creation rather than price competition (*Kuwait Datacenter Assessment* 2020).

The benefit of the co-location data center industry affects the Kuwaiti market and economy. One of the essential pillars of Kuwait Vision 2035 is building a reliable infrastructure to keep pace with rapid regional and global technological development ("DEVELOPED INFRASTRUCTURE" 2022). The co-location data center project is a strategic project that serves the Kuwaiti market. The existence of such projects will be a magnet for global providers of cloud and data processing services(Al-Harbi 2022).

We found a gap in the co-location data center industry literature. The current research relied on a technical report of IDC (*Kuwait Datacenter Assessment*, 2020) and articles by (Tozzi 2021) and (Schafer 2016), which address the factors for the success of a data center in general, not the type of co-location site. Also, we did not find a practical study of these factors, especially in the Kuwaiti market. Therefore, this study enriches the literature on co-location data centers as it reviews essential factors that affect the data center industry and co-location data centers in the Arabian Gulf region and the Kuwaiti market. Moreover, this study reviews the benefits of co-location data centers in Kuwait (Fig. 2).

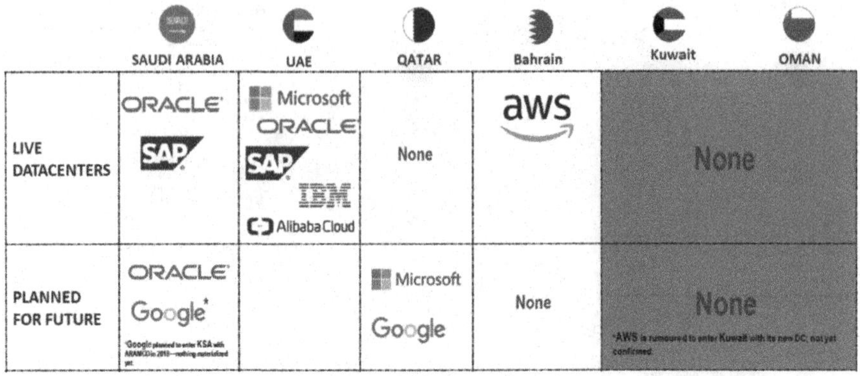

Fig. 2. Global Hyper-scalars' Investments within GCC Countries (Live/Planned DCs). *Source: (Kuwait Datacenter Assessment 2020)*

This paper contains the following parts: The second section will present the research methodology. At the same time, the third section discusses the research results. Finally, the paper reviews the conclusions and recommendations for constructing and operating co-location data centers in the Kuwaiti Market.

2   Methods

2.1   Research Design and Participants

A qualitative method, an interpretivism paradigm, an inductive reasoning approach that takes you from specific observation to general themes, and an exploratory research type were adopted in this research. Semi-structured in-depth interviews were conducted with several specialists in data centers to obtain the required data. The process of developing interview questions goes through several stages of research, reflection, and planning, which depend on reviewing the literature, the researcher's experience and knowledge of the research topic, and deciding what to ask and how to ask the question (Rubin and Rubin 2012). We divided each interview into several sections, starting with the introduction. All interviews began by thanking the participants for their time and mentioning the purpose and the expected duration of the interview (Boyce and Neale 2006). Then, the interview consent form was shared for each participant to be signed, emphasizing the confidentiality of any sensitive information and concealing the participant's identity if requested. The topic questions were pilot-studied by the specialized organization, ending with thanks and the end of the interview.

The purposive sampling technique was adopted for this study. The interviewees were selected based on clear criteria to obtain detailed information about the research topic (Saunders et al. 2009). One of the most important criteria was the number of experience years required in data centers, at least ten years and five years in a managerial position. Also, the interviewees were selected from various entities that may affect or be affected in the field of data centers, such as data center service providers, data center contractors (experience in the Kuwaiti market), cloud service providers, technology and information law legislators (government agencies), consulting service providers data center to avoid bias and ensure access to a valuable set of views on the establishment and operation of co-location data centers in Kuwait.

2.2 Data Collection

This study adopted the cross-sectional time frame. Therefore, semi-structured face-to-face interviews were organized from June to July 2022 with the relevant stakeholders of the research topic. First, we prepared the interview consent form, which included an explanation of the research topic, the purpose of the research, the reason for selecting the respondent, the duration of the interview (45–60 min), and the method of storing information. All the interview questions were developed based on the literature gaps in this field to obtain the required data for this research. The email was used to send invitations for the interview request, which included information about the research topic, research objectives, and the interview questions. Nine out of 13 interviews were conducted with the selected participants because we achieved data saturation, where enough data has been collected to draw necessary conclusions. Over-and-above data collection will not make value-added insights (Fusch and Ness 2015). All interviews were recorded and transcribed using software (Voice Text). All interviews were conducted in English.

2.3 Data Analysis

Using the framework approach, the thematic analysis of the interview transcripts was used to analyze the data. This method provides an organized guide of data analysis that seeks to draw exploratory conclusions aggregated conclusions about topics while maintaining links to the data (Smith and Firth 2011). Three main themes have been identified based on research propositions and literature review. Three main themes of the Co-Location Data Center Thesis are Critical factors affecting the feasibility of establishing and operating co-location data centers in the Kuwaiti market, the co-location data centers' benefits, and the solutions to ensure the success of co-location data center projects. All transcripts were saved into word files and then copied to Excel for easier use of the manual thematic analysis. The thematic analysis consists of six stages, as presented in Table 2.

3 Results

According to the results obtained through the interviews, two main themes must be addressed when building and operating a co-location data center in Kuwait. The two main themes are an internal theme and an external theme. In addition, each theme contains several sub-themes that have critical factors affecting the industry of co-location data centers in the Kuwaiti market.

Table 2. Thematic Analysis Phases

Phase	Description
1	Familiarizing yourself with the data
2	Generating initial codes
3	Searching for themes
4	Reviewing potential themes
5	Defining themes
6	Producing the report

Source: (Rozmi et al. 2020)

3.1 External

All factors related to third parties were collected under this primary theme. In addition, the **external** theme contains a factor: the **regulations**, which are divided into two sub-factors, namely, the **standards certificate** and **government regulations**. As one of the participants stated;

"Certifications are prime like certifications from uptime from TIA and all of that, and at the end is the quality of the construction because we suffer in Kuwait of quality of existing data center."

Some respondents were keen to mention the importance of government approvals and laws in influencing the co-location data center industry. For example, where one of them said:

"Legal and permit factors could also be influential and sometimes obstacles."

3.2 Internal

Through the Thematic Analysis, we collected all the factors affecting the co-location data center project, which depend on the organization itself, under the internal factor. The **Internal** factor contains sub-factors: **Design, Operations, Financial Management,** and **Company Experience**. These sub-factors have sub-sub-factors, as discussed below.

3.2.1 Design

The Internal theme of "Design" contains the sub-sub-themes: **Location** and **Business Continuity**.

The "Location" factor is considered critical, as it was mentioned by eight out of nine participants. One of the interviewees stated:

"The location of the data centers as if you are banks; this is part of the regulation. Suppose you are non-bank and do not have a regulation like a private entity; um. In that case, they might be interested in where is that from our head office, so location,

how far it is from head office, connectivity to that data center is important. It has to have multiple roads, And, you know, to that location, the closer the location to the head office is better."

However, Thematic analysis identified another sub-theme under the Location theme as "**Disaster Recovery,**" which was mentioned by four participants;

"Certain regulations like banking, for example, regulation by the central bank of Kuwait says: Every bank has to have the main and disaster recovery centers. Moreover, the distance between those two should not be less than 25 or 30 kilometers."

A new sub-factor was added by Thematic analysis under the **Location** factor is the **Latency**, which only one participant mentioned. However, he considered it an essential factor affecting the Location factor, as the less time to reach for the data stored in the data center is evidence of the correctness of the selected site to establish and operate a co-location data center;

"Latency is significant, So I would rather if I am if I want to host my server, probably going to a cloud service. I would rather be closer to the servers than, you know, far from the servers. Because latency matters those days and applications."

The second sub-sub-theme, '**Business Continuity,**' under the sub-theme '**Design**' is essential. This factor contains the element of "**Redundancy and Availability,**" which was mentioned by six respondents who indicated that it is a crucial element in ensuring the continuity of the service;

"The second critical factor is to build a state of the art data center with a high redundancy and availability."

The thematic analysis identified another element under the "**Business Continuity**" as "**Scalability,**" which was mentioned by five respondents. It works to ensure the easy expansion of the volume of services that can be provided to the customers of the co-location data center while not affecting the live environment of the business;

"And the scalability, so the design must be scalable and match all customer needs in Kuwait."

3.2.2 Operations

The Thematic Analysis identified the second internal factor, "**Operations.**" The "**Operations**" factor is an essential component of the operation of the co-location data center. This factor contains many sub-factors such as **Facilities, Security, Staff,** and **Service Level Agreement**.

The "**Facilities**" sub-sub-theme is an essential factor under the '**Operations**' theme, as one of the interviewees mentioned;

"The facility readiness means this data center is fit for the purpose. Whether it has enough capacity power, security, monitoring, and smart operations as required."

The second sub-sub-theme, "**Security**," is fundamental to data center operations. This factor has two main components: **physical security** and **cyber security**. Six respondents said the **physical security** component, while four respondents mentioned the **cyber security** component and its importance in the success of the co-location data center project;

> *"Physical security: Colocation centers must maintain high levels of physical security, including on-site security guards, 24x7x365 surveillance, and biometric authorization."*
> *"There are many factors like Improved network security."*

The Thematic analysis identified the sub-factor "**Staff**" as an essential factor in the operation of the data center. Four respondents mentioned the element "**Specialized Resources**." In comparison, two respondents said the element "**Remote Hands**.";

> *"Talent availability is also a prime because data centers are specialized buildings, and they need specialized resources certified data centers to run them."*
> *"if the data center provider provides any services on the IT layer. Money service or remote hands is also required, saving end users travel time and resources during emergencies."*

The last sub-factor under the "Operations" identified by thematic analysis is the "**Service Level Agreement**," which guarantees Customer Satisfaction and Reliability. One of the participants mentioned;

> *"And it has high SLA, uh, fewer readings, and this attracts, you know, Ah, someone, especially the international."*

3.2.3 Financial Management

The thematic analysis identified the third major internal sub-theme, "**Financial Management**." Several sub-sub-themes fall under this factor: **CapEx & OpEx Management, Market Study, and Marketing Strategy**.

The "**CapEx & OpEx Management**" contains three elements: OpEx, mentioned once and is considered by most of those interested in the co-location data center as a beneficial element in terms of savings. However, the eighth respondent specified that this element must be analyzed and studied well before starting the data center project. Many operations depend on having an adequate budget that covers all operating expenses. One of the interviewees stated:

> *"Also, the operation cost of the data center (OPEX) like electricity, management, and maintenance cost."*

The second element under the factor "CapEx & OpEx Management" is "Cost Efficiency," which studies how to spend effectively while achieving savings that do not affect the quality of data center services. Two respondents reported this element;

"And hence Cost effectiveness is the main factor and KPIs for the success of a colocation data center."

The last element under the "**CapEx & OpEx Management**" sub-theme is "**Budget**," which four respondents mentioned in the interviews where respondents indicated the importance of having an adequate budget to cover all the financial needs to establish and operate the required data center;

"So first of all, uh, definitely, uh, budget is the prime factor when we talk about data centers; data centers are capital-intensive facilities, different from residential or commercial buildings, so budget availability is prime."

The thematic analysis identified the sub-sub-theme "**Market Study**," which contains two elements: "**Business needs**" and "**Land**." Three respondents identified the importance of studying and identifying business needs before starting the co-location data center project. One respondent also identified the importance of the "land" element. He indicated that Kuwait's case is exceptional in the matter of available lands for data center projects, as well as the extent of the cost of these lands. Therefore, serious attention must be paid by the investors to the issue of the budget allocated to provide the necessary land for the data center project;

"Understanding business needs as it is critical to understand the goals of the local companies and how will the colocation service meets their needs."

"We have a big challenge in Kuwait as well as the availability of land."

Finally, the thematic analysis identified the third sub-sub-theme, "**Marketing Strategy**," under the "Financial management" sub-theme. This theme has three elements: "**Advertising**," "**Price**," and "**Offers**."

The fourth respondent mentioned the importance of making ads that show the quality of the co-location data center services and reviewing the strengths owned by the data center operator;

"The marketing will play a main role as a proper marketing plan must be performed to highlight the strength of the constructed facility."

While three respondents focused on the importance of the offered price for data center services, thus attracting the most significant possible number of customers and impacting the success of the data center project;

"Most important is the price. If the price is right. Then I think that is encouraging investors to invest in this technology, in this market."

The thematic analysis identified the "offers" as an essential element under the "marketing strategy" factor. Three respondents mentioned the importance of offering special offers that are appropriate to the needs of the co-location data center customers;

"Special offers can be a desirable factor for the co-location data center customers."

3.2.4 Company Experience

The success of any project depends on the extent of the company's experience in the required industry (Schafer 2016). Thematic analysis identified two sub-sub-themes under this factor: "Operation Excellence" and "Ownership." The thematic analysis identified the fourth major internal sub-theme, "Company Experience."

Five respondents mentioned the importance of the company's experience and reputation in the project's success in operating the co-location data center;

"Operation: Expert data center operators must be handling the facility."

In contrast, the seventh respondent mentioned the factor of ownership and its importance in highlighting the company's experience in the co-location data center industry;

"Data Center business and ownership

a. Who is the legal owner of the business

b? Are the data center, facility, and equipment wholly owned and operated by the business?

c. Is the building owned by the business?"

4 Discussion

The current study explores the critical factors affecting the feasibility of constructing and operating the co-location data center in the Kuwaiti market. The factors extracted from the literature review are similar to the research findings. In contrast, three factors derived from the literature review were excluded "Multiple and Flexible Billing Options," "Self-Service and Automated Provisioning Portal," and "Track Record.".

The study findings identified two main factors, Internal and external, that affect the feasibility of establishing and operating a co-location data center in Kuwait. The two main factors include a list of elements below:

Table 4 shows the mentioned factors under the central theme, "Internal." the "Internal" consists of four sub-factors: "Design," "Operations," "Financial Management," and "Company Experience." Two factors under the Design are "Location" and "Business Continuity." Three factors fall under the factor "Operations," which are "Facilities," "Security," "Staff," and "Service Level Agreement." Three sub-factors under the factor "Financial Management" are "CapEx & OpEx Management," "Market Study," and "Marketing Strategy." The last internal factor is "Company Experience," which contains two sub-factors, "Operation Excellence" and "Ownership."

The main factor "External" has been added, which contains a sub-factor "Regulations," under which two elements, "Standards Certificate" and "Government Regulations," fall. Table 3 shows the mentioned factors under the main theme, "External."

Table 3. Internal Factors

THEME	SUB-THEME	SUB-SUB-THEME
Internal	Design	Location
		Business Continuity
	Operations	Facilities
		Security
		Staff
		Service Level Agreement
	Financial Management	CapEx & OpEx Management
		Market Study
		Marketing Strategy
	Company Experience	Operation Excellence
		Ownership

Source: (Authors)

Table 4. External Factors

THEME	SUB-THEME	SUB-SUB-THEME
External	Regulations	Standards Certificate
		Government Regulations

Source: (Authors)

5   Study Recommendations

Based on the study findings, recommendations were presented that can be considered potential solutions to get the most out of the co-location data center project. Where the set of recommendations was classified according to their scope of work and in-charge person, as shown below:

The Director – Data Center should focus on standards certifications. Obtaining these certificates will enhance the confidence of potential customers in the standards that the operator has adhered to when designing and building the data center, in addition to emphasizing the standards that he adheres to in managing data center operations.

The design of the co-location data center is considered one of the fundamentals of the project's success. Therefore, the Director of – the Data Center and the specialized consultant must consider the achievement of Full Redundancy in addition to considering the future expansion by creating a Sufficient Scalability Plan and thus ensuring the continuity of providing services smoothly and immediately.

An effective project management method must ensure the co-location data center project's success from planning to implementation and commissioning. To achieve this, the assigned project manager must build a practical business plan that includes preparing the appropriate budget with clear objectives for the project.

The project manager of the co-location data center must prepare an appropriate project plan that contains all phases of the project while building strategic partnerships with specialists in the field of data centers.

The awarded vendor must also consider and study all matters related to local approvals and accreditations necessary to operate the co-location data center project.

For marketing, the Director of Marketing must design and prepare an effective marketing plan (4Ps), which includes four aspects: product, price, place, and promotion, to highlight the advantages and offers of the data center he manages.

The operating segment is at the core of the co-location data center's success. It reflects the extent of professionalism of the center's operator, thus ensuring business continuity. To achieve this goal, the Director of – the Data Center and HR department must be keen on employing skilled and experienced staff to operate the data center and providing all the intelligent tools and means to manage the center effectively.

References

Al-Harbi, M.: STC Kuwait - Data Center Opportunities and Challenges [Interview] (2022). 10 January 2022

Arregoces, M., Portolani, M.: Data Center Fundamentals. Cisco Press, Indianapolis (2003)

Barroso, L.A., Clidaras, J., Hölzle, U.: The datacenter as a computer: an introduction to the design of warehouse-scale machines. Synth. Lect. Comput. Archit. **8**(3), 1–154 (2013)

Boyce, C., Neale, P.: Conducting in-depth Interviews: A Guide for Designing and Conducting In-Depth Interviews for Evaluation input (Vol. 2). Pathfinder International, Watertown, MA (2006)

Cisco. Data Centre Power and Colling, s.l.: Cisco Public Information (2011). https://www.cisco.com/c/en/us/solutions/data-center-virtualization/what-is-a-data-center.html. Accessed 12 Oct 2022

Fusch, P.I., Ness, L.R.: Are we there yet? Data saturation in qualitative research. Qualit. Report **20**(9), 1408 (2015)

Hoon, C.C., Yali, T.: Data Centers. Fast growing, superior quality and high yielding asset class. s.l.:Alpha Watch (2014)

Joshi, Y., Kumar, P.: Energy Efficient Thermal Management of Data Centers. Springer Science & Business Media, London (2012)

Nazim, N.F.M., et al.: Data centre colocation: challenges and opportunities in private, public and hybrid cloud for businesses. Int. J. Acad. Res. Bus. Soc. Sci. **9**(6), 624–639 (2019)

Rozmi, A.N.A. et al.: Factors affecting SME owners in adopting ICT in business using thematic analysis. Int. J. Adv. Comput. Sci. Appl. **11**, 208–218 (2020)

Rubin, I., Rubin, H.J.: Qualitative Interviewing: The Art of Hearing Data. SAGE, Los Angeles (2012)

Saunders, M., Lewis, P., Thornhill, A.: Research Methods for Business Students. Prentice Hall, s.l. (2009)

Schafer, M.: Seven Critical Success Factors for Choosing a Reliable Data Center Provider, s.l.: Cyrus One (2016)

Smith, J., Firth, J.:. Qualitative data analysis: the framework approach. Nurse Res. **18**(2), 52–62 (2011)

Tozzi, C.: 5 factors to consider when choosing a colocation provider. Datacenter Knowledge (2021)

Effect of Socio-Demographic Factors on Consumer's Attitude Towards Artificial Intelligent Based Digital Voice Assistant

Meenu Mathur[✉] [iD], Yogita Mandhyana, and Madhulika Chaudhuri

Symbiosis University of Applied Sciences, Indore, India
mathur.meenu1@gmail.com, {meenu.mathur,yogita.mandhanya,
madhulika.chaudhuri}@suas.ac.in

Abstract. This paper aims to examine the role of socio-demographics in forming attitudes toward AI-based digital voice assistants. The study employs the quantitative approach to analyze the socio-demographic data of the study, descriptive statistical methods were applied. The differences in the attitudes towards AI-based digital voice assistants by various demographics were examined using one-way ANOVA statistics. The paper enhances understanding of AI-based digital voice assistants by highlighting the differences in consumer attitudes with regard to gender, age education, income, and occupation levels. Interestingly, the study also confirms a positive significant correlation between usage time and attitude towards the use of digital voice assistants. Utilizing this will surely allow businesses to carry out appropriate customized services/products for reaching the targeted consumers and formulates appropriate business strategies.

Keywords: Artificial Intelligence · Digital Voice Assistant · Age · Gender · Consumer Attitude

1 Introduction

There is a high growth of emerging technology devices like smartphones, tablets, smart TVs, and smart speakers, including digital voice assistants (DVA). DVAs are a type of voice-enabled artificial intelligence (AI) device that has revolutionized the way consumers use, and it has become a larger part of the social life of a consumer. Several companies are trying to apply conversational technology to enhance and widen their brands and maintain two-way interactions with consumers [1]. Digital Personal assistants use natural human language while processing/answering questions, making recommendations, and activating mobile applications [2]. It typically recognizes the user's voice and does information processing [3–5]. Users can make phone calls; they can send emails, and trace locations on the map with digital personal assistants [6]. Further, Google Duplex now books a hair salon or queries a restaurant over the smartphone [7]. Consumers are now shifting towards Omni channel shopping, as the process is driven by technology and artificial intelligence. There is a wide-ranging artificial intelligence-based technology being developed and one of which has progressively gained its presence is the AI-based DVA [8].

© The Author(s), under exclusive license to Springer Nature Switzerland AG 2024
A. M. A. Musleh Al-Sartawi et al. (Eds.): ICGER 2023, CCIS 1999, pp. 15–27, 2024.
https://doi.org/10.1007/978-3-031-50518-8_2

Currently, companies like Microsoft, Google, Amazon, and Facebook are engaging with their consumers frequently via voice recognition. There are many voice assistant devices and related smartphone applications like Google Now by Google, Siri by Apple, Cortana by Microsoft, and Alexa by Amazon. Amongst the various smartphones assistants, the major relative market share is captured by Apple's Siri at 45.1%, as per Kinsella [9] Google Assistant is in second position with 29.9%, Alexa by Amazon at 18.3%, and Bixby by Samsung at 4.7%. Large numbers of persons now make use of Siri, Alexa, and Google Assistants in everyday living, and the number is estimated to ascend dramatically. This is obvious as there is huge growth in voice technologies in the past few years. Voice-based instructions and inquiries that can range from weekly or off-order commands in the retail store such as calling an Uber car are traced and responded to by these digital devices [10]. Incorporating a gadget like Alexa with Amazon providing all the market information allows this DVA to promptly scan e-catalogs and offer personalized recommendations to users. Obviously, few companies will be able to ascertain their own digital voice assistant. Though, they can get on to acclimatize their product content to create it easier to recognize and comprehend by digital voice assistants and other equivalent devices [11].

There has been an increase in voice search inquiries in India by 270% each year. Being the highest populated country and the largest user of smartphones, India is the foremost and the world's largest voice-first internet market due to demographics and scale. Extant literature primarily focuses on the usage and acceptance of DVAs in particular contexts, like education, health, and the army, or amid explicit populations, including children, patients, and the elderly. While DVAs are progressively becoming more a part of day-to-day life definite consumer/user groups that may gain from this technology remains unexplored. Especially the categorical variables of gender, age, education, income, and user experience have prior been revealed to influence associations amid expectation confirmation theory and acceptance research [12, 13]. There is a need for developing an enhanced understanding of user/consumer attitudes towards newer technologies, especially where the technology can play a major role in the user experience (i.e., AI-based digital voice assistants). DVAs and their algorithms have been widely investigated to understand their influence on exchanges amid their users/consumers [14], perpetuate gendered and facilitate newer socio-technical familiarity or relationships. Given the fast growth of digital tools, it becomes imperative to reflect on the usage of DVAs as one of the capable tools for maintaining and enhancing social participation, purchasing/ordering, and spare time activities for a larger number of users/consumers. There remains a digital divide between the younger and older generations [15].

Therefore, it is important to practically and academically examine DVA users' attitudes against this background. Due to the demographic change, yet, there is huge potential for usage and sales for varied demographics. Many questions inevitably arise about whether such new voice-based technologies are accepted by consumers/users of all kinds similarly or differences in attitudes. This research is an effort to investigate how various socio-demographic factors influence the attitude toward the use of DVAs. The research strives to dwell on answering whether there are any differences amid the attitudes toward AI-based DVA among users according to varied socio-demographic variables including gender, age, education, occupation, annual family income, and user experience.

2 Literature Review

Artificial intelligence (AI) is the technology that facilitates machines to execute activities that entail human intellect [16] and it intends to build machines that act like humans [17]. Artificial intelligence (AI) can be seen everywhere and it has entered our work and private life. As per Amazon, DVA's fast-evolving existence is on the edge to be the upcoming most important technological disruption in humans–computer interface [18]. AI lets voice assistants study and understands human users' needs and give nearly all relevant responses in a particular situation [17]. This study uses the term AI-based Digital Voice Assistants (DVA).

AI-based digital assistants augment human task performance by using AI technologies (be it NLP, translation, recognition of speech, machine learning, or representation of knowledge) with higher possibilities of interactivity and intelligence than old-fashioned software applications. [17]. Most present-day AI-based digital assistants rely on speech-based or text-based conversational agents. Advanced AI-based digital assistants in the future could additionally use computer vision to identify visual input. These AI-based Digital Assistants may also process and represent the domain knowledge to learn and create novel understanding from the data that is collected by algorithms of machine learning [19–21]. Three major reasons for utilizing DVAs include "[a] convenience and ease of use with voice, [b] feelings of control with voice, and [c] positive emotion with voice" [22]. DVAs have been successfully implemented in smart home devices, smartphones, connected smart homes/cars, virtual reality headsets, and smart clothes [24]. Though such voice assistants are received and used for simple tasks in day-to-day life [23, 24]. More multifaceted scenarios such as voice shopping and searching are in process of development.

The use of DVAs is increasing significantly [25] and the commonly used DVA include home devices and mobile applications, for example, Siri by Apple, Alexa by Amazon, and Echo by Amazon as well as Kuri robots' companion and healthcare automation. He talks about the functional intelligence of VAs, creativity, and sincerity that improve the sense of power consumers observe throughout their voice interaction with virtual assistants, the concentration of the consumers while interacting with voice contributes towards consumer satisfaction and willingness to continue using the VA. Also, consumers become instantly fond of and are unwilling to give away digital services they have acquired [26] for instance services of DVAs.

Technology adoption model posits that the attitude towards technology is formed by perceived ease-of-use and perceived usefulness of technology and this formed attitude consequently persuades users' intentions and behavior to utilize a technology [27]. Attitude is a set of beliefs, emotions, and behavior toward digital voice assistants. Attitude consequences from a user/consumer's experience and can persuade their behavior. It is subject to change and is never constant. Understanding the consumer/user attitude towards the DVA has now become a dynamic research area, many studies have used diverse methods to evaluate subthemes of attitude including trust, disclosure, closeness, honesty, and smartness, [28, 29]. Another subtheme of attitude is Likeability which has been used to measure the trust, compatibility, and strength amid the consumers/users of DVAs [30] and the attitude towards the DVA is a well-researched area [31].

A current survey [32] established that consumers look for proactive product recommendations while purchasing via an online channel and using digital assistants. As per this survey, 88% of consumers insist businesses to integrate digital assistants to select the precise brand and product [32]. PWC also reported that digital assistants are used by consumers mainly to purchase groceries, books, homecare products, reservations of hotel rooms, and order food [33, 34] also highlighted that digital assistants will considerably impact business scenarios. It has turned out to be increasingly vital and essential to use DVAs. It is very imperative to realize the base of the voice technology's attitude first and then to understand the technology's effect on landing a sustainable decision [35, 36]. Digital voice assistants operate at diverse levels depending on their usage in different devices, supported by AI algorithms [37] and product providers. With such customized features, it is imperative to examine whether the consumers perceive DVA positively and if there are differences among gender, age, education, income levels, and occupation. Also, it is likewise significant to ascertain the relationship of attitude towards DVA with usage time patterns. Addressing the above following hypothesis are drawn.

H1: There is a significant difference between the gender of respondents and attitudes toward AI-based DVA
H2: There is a significant difference between the age of respondents and attitudes toward AI-based DVA
H3: There is a significant difference between the Occupation of respondents and their attitude toward AI-based DVA
H4: There is a significant difference between the education of respondents and their attitude toward AI-based DVA
H5: There is a significant difference between the Annual Income Level of the respondents and their attitude towards AI-based DVA
H6: There is a significant difference between Usage of Digital Voice Assistants by the respondents and attitude towards AI-based DVA

3 Research Methodology

The quantitative study involved the conduction of a survey and collected pertinent primary data using a structured questionnaire. The survey instrument is composed of three parts. The first part comprises of three categorical questions; (1) Do you know what digital voice assistants are? (Yes/No) (2) How long have you been using Digital Voice Assistant? (3) Have you purchased a product through DVA? The second part of the questionnaire consisted of socio-demographic variables (Gender, age, education, occupation, usage time, and purchase/order experience using DVA). The third part of the questionnaire measured the construct Attitude towards AI-based Digital Voice Assistants. The scale measurements are derived from the previous studies [27, 38] with five items on a seven-point Likert scale (Very Strongly Agree - 7 to Very Strongly Disagree -1).

3.1 Sampling Procedure

Online Google Survey method was adopted for the collection of primary data. A pilot study was conducted to check the understanding of the rationale of the study and understanding of the survey questions among respondents. No personal bias or distortions were observed. A convenient sampling method (being low cost and easy), following a non-probability sampling approach, was adopted to collect the responses in this research. The link to the Google survey was shared among friends, family, relatives, and students in geographical proximity and also shared on various social media platforms to seek responses. A total of 266 respondents answered yes to being aware of digital voice assistants and using them for more than six months. The used cases were 266 as they complete the criteria of being aware of AI-based DVA.

The primary data were collected from participants who resided in and around the Indore city of Madhya Pradesh. As the rationale of the research was the exploration, the sample was considered robust as it will symbolize the population of the Indore market- a tier two city in western India. The data collected was analyzed in agreement with the set objectives of the study using ANOVA statistical tool. Considering that artificial intelligence-based voice technologies are in their infancy stage in India, researchers specifically targeted only those consumers of digital voice assistants who have usage experience of minimum past six months.

3.2 Data Analysis

Data analysis was conducted using IBM SPSS Ver. 25.0. To analyze the socio-demographic data of the study, descriptive statistical methods were applied. The differences in Attitudes towards AI-based digital voice assistants by various demographics were examined using one-way ANOVA statistics. In order to examine the association amid usage patterns and attitude DVA among users, the Pearson correlation coefficient was calculated. For more details concerning statistical methods and studies the reader may refers to [39–41].

The sample profile is displayed in Table 1 reflecting the population usually engaged in the usage of AI-based digital voice assistants. There are in all 45% female and 55% male respondents wherein 51% of the respondents are in the age bracket 18–24 years, 55% are undergraduate, 30% are having annual family income above Rs 100000, and 22% in the range of Rs 500000 - Rs.100000. And 52% of respondents are students. Further 33% of the respondents have been using DVA for or more than 3 years, 40% are using it between 1–2 years. It shows the perfect profile for users of digital voice assistants who are well educated, and few in employment with a decent income to examine their attitude towards AI-based DVA.

4   Results

4.1 Demographic Characteristics and Differences for ATT Towards AI-Based DVA

Independent Sample T-Test: Independent sample t-test is used for testing the significance of two group means. The Leven's test result for equality of variances indicates that hypothesis H1 is accepted and there is a significant difference in variances of responses towards the Attitude (ATT) towards AI-based DVA across gender as P value (0.034) is less than 0.05 ($p < 0.05$) (Table 2).

Table 1. Socio-Demographic Profile of Sample

Variable	Characteristics	Frequency	Percentage
Gender	Male	147	55
	Female	119	45
Age	18 -24 years	161	61
	25–35 years	69	26
	36–45 years	24	9
	Above 45 years	12	4
Education	Undergraduate	172	65
	Graduate	41	15
	Postgraduate	40	15
	PhD	13	5
Annual Income (in INR)	Less than 200000	54	20
	200000–500000	49	18
	500000–10,00000	68	26
	Above 10,00000	95	36
Occupation	Student	164	62
	Service	23	9
	Self-employed / Business	33	12
	Professional	46	17
Usage Time	Less than 6 months	17	6
	More than 6 month and Less than 1 year	23	9
	1–2 years	34	13
	2–3 years	104	39
	More than 3 years	88	33

ANOVA Test: For testing the hypothesis ANOVA was conceded on the basis of income, age, & educational level, and occupation. Table 3 presents the number of users, mean scores, and standard deviations for all levels of each demographic variable, Attitude, usage time, and purchase/order categories. According to the differences in ATT, findings revealed that H2, H4, and H6 are accepted and there are statistically significant differences between respondents in terms of age educational level, and usage time ($p <$ 0.05) (Table 4). Further, it was found that there was no statistically significant difference regarding their Annual Income level and Occupation ($p >$ 0.05) and thus hypotheses H3 and H5 are not accepted.

Table 2. Independent samples t-test on Attitude (ATT) towards DVA across gender

		Levene's Test for Equality of Variances				t-test for Equality of Means
		F	Sig.	t value	dof	(2-tailed Sig.)
ATT	Equal variances assumed	4.519	.034	−2.209	264	.028
	Equal variances not assumed			−2.237	261.738	.026

Table 3. Descriptive Statistics

	N	Min	Max	Mean	Std. Deviation
Gender	266	0	1	.45	.498
Age	266	1	4	1.58	.836
Education	266	1	4	1.60	.915
Income	266	1	4	2.77	1.142
Occupation	266	1	4	1.85	1.190
ATT	266	5	35	24.84	7.524
Usage Time	266	1	5	3.84	1.166
Purchase Experience	266	1	5	4.10	1.273

Correlation: When the correlation between the Usage Time of DVAs and attitude towards DVA is established, a low positive correlation (0.219) was found to exist. The p-value (0.000) indicates that the association is significant (Table 5).

According to the results of our study, there is a positive significant correlation between ATT and Usage Time. In other words, whenever consumer enhances their usage time on AI-based DVA a significant promotion occurs in their attitude towards DVA. Several empirical studies have supported the idea and found that usage time and experience significantly moderate technology behavior [42, 43].

5 Discussion and Implications

The study examined the role of socio-demographic variables in forming attitudes toward AI-based Digital voice assistants. Though DVAs and conversational commerce's augmentation are apparent in a business scenario, less attention was given to empirical research background [44]. There are not many scholarly works to elucidate how consumers pose their attitudes toward DVAs from a socio-demographic perspective especially when the usage involves the understanding and acceptance of technology and

Table 4. One–way ANOVA results for differences based on Socio-demographics

		Sum of Squares	Df	Mean Square	F	p-value
Usage Time	Between Groups	56.026	26	2.155	1.694	.022
	Within Groups	304.023	239	1.272		
	Total	360.049	265			
Age	Between Groups	33.558	26	1.291	2.037	.003
	Within Groups	151.438	239	.634		
	Total	184.996	265			
Education	Between Groups	48.088	26	1.850	2.545	.000
	Within Groups	173.671	239	.727		
	Total	221.759	265			
Income	Between Groups	43.490	26	1.673	1.324	.142
	Within Groups	302.059	239	1.264		
	Total	345.549	265			
Occupation	Between Groups	48.648	26	1.871	1.369	.116
	Within Groups	326.634	239	1.367		
	Total	375.282	265			

Table 5. Correlation between Usage Time of DVAs and attitude towards DVA

		ATT	Usage Time
ATT	Pearson Correlation	1	.219**
	Sig. (2-tailed)		
	N	266	266
Usage Time	Pearson Correlation	.219	1
	Sig. (2-tailed)	.000	
	N	266	266

devices. DVA can be utilized throughout varied devices with several inquiries. Purchasing/ordering a product/service using DVAs could be one of its services. These rapidly changing market dynamics may pose a few risks. Voice shopping can bring severe consequences for retailers and brands. Knowing its immense utility along with its consumer involvement levels, it is crucial to appreciate consumer/users' attitudes towards it, particularly from a socio-demographic perspective. Given the fast extension of digital tools, it is essential to consider the attitude and usage of DVAs as a promising tool for day-to-day activities including purchasing/ordering. Though a digital divide amid older and younger generations remains [17], different kinds of users may gain to a less extent from the rewards of the latest technologies like DVAs. The study concludes that there is a difference between male and female DVA users in their attitude toward digital voice assistants. The results are in sync with the literature as in the review of around 50 articles it was, established that the consumer's attitude towards technology considerably differs across the female and male populations [45]. In our understanding no, particular scholarly work exists which has contradicted the gender differences with respect to attitudes toward technology, specifically relating to digital voice assistants. Additionally, men are keen to spend extra efforts to overcome varied constraints and complicatedness to follow their goals, while women tend to focus more on the scale of efforts involved and the course to attain their goals [15, 46]. Consequently, men are likely to rely lesser on facilitating conditions like the usage of new technology while women tend to put greater stress on external supporting factors. Another explanation partly is the cognitions associated with gender roles assigned by a society where men are likely to be more task-oriented [47].

In addition to this, our study found that there is no difference between users with varied Income levels and occupation groups in their attitude toward digital voice assistants. Hence it can be concluded that DVAs are being accepted by Indian consumers in recent years regardless of their personal backgrounds due to the attractiveness and increasing awareness and marketing campaigns for such devices. However, our study found there are differences among the demographic profiles on age, and education, level with regard to attitude towards AI-based DVA. The digital divide between the younger and older generations still exists [17] and older adults may leverage to an extent only from rewards of new technologies like DVAs. Older users with intellectual disabilities are at specific risk of digital exclusion and digital voice technology like DVAs have barely been assessed for this target group. Older users are likely to face more intricacies in processing newer or more difficult information, thus influencing their ability to learn newer technologies [48, 49]. This may be due to a decline in memory and cognitive abilities related to the aging process [50].

The study found a positive significant correlation between usage time and attitude towards the use of DVAs which is in alignment with the existing literature. As usage increases, users/consumers happen to be extra aware of DVAs' varied and astounding capabilities. They tend to practice newer features and gain experiences, unknown to them earlier besides practical features. During this journey of usage, their attitude towards DVAs is likely to be more positive. Greater experience can possibly lead to better familiarity with the technology including voice technology and improved knowledge structures ease user learning, thus dropping user dependence on peripheral support [51]. Similarly, a meta-analysis demonstrates that users/consumers with lesser experience or awareness will depend more on facilitating environment [52]. However, the challenge may also be to understand that as usage of DVAs enhances they would improve on learning user/consumer preferences and behavior, thus will more and more influence consumer behaviors [53] consequently the risk posed by DVAs is they may assume a vital relational role in the consumer marketplace and increasingly intervene market interactions. Continued use of DVAs time and again can enlighten whether consumers/users are experiencing the benefits of the technology. Positive initial experiences with new technology (like DVAs) were found among older users with continued usage [53]. Likewise, successful and useful voice interactions with DVAs can influence continued usage for consumers. Perhaps, an easy-to-follow tutorial as online customer support services can facilitate users of all ages [54].

In particular, user-related attitudinal differences amongst varied demographics can let businesses understand and gain knowledge of the varying preference of buyers groups (e.g., definite app users, consumers/users of different age groups, students, professionals, etc.), and how they react, utilize or relate with DVAs in a range of usage settings (e.g. education, entertainment, social interaction, productivity, etc.) and different types of AI-based conversant assistants (e.g. chatbots, digital avatars, embodied agents like robots, etc.). Yet again, context relevancy (e.g., education, entertainment, healthcare, service industry) is vital as the identical consumer/user segments may have varied expectations and preferences from DVA performance used for varying purposes. Importantly, this study analyzed herein recommends that demographic characteristics (such as gender and age, income, education, and occupation) should be considered by businesses as a basis for customization/personalization. Given these potential dynamics, the challenge would be to understand and comprehend the interplay among users/consumers, brands, and retailers' behaviors in response to the role of DVAs. Utilizing this will surely allow businesses to carry out appropriate and customized products/ services for reaching the targeted consumers and formulating appropriate business strategies.

6   Conclusion

Attitude plays a significant role in forming consumer/user beliefs as well as the way they are evaluating voice-based technology, especially which involves human-machine interaction. Digital voice assistants have the potential to assist consumers/users with day-to-day errands and leisure activities. Despite the lack of competence and limitations of consumers/users, digital voice assistants are by now being accepted and espoused by varied demographics, and their attitudes towards their usage were examined.

The current study has a few limitations too. The study relies on a sample from a limited geographical area in India leading to the limitation of a generalization of the results. In addition, the low sample size and convenience sampling approach adopted in this study also brings a few limitations of generalization of results. Few groups of users of DVAs are less represented as only those responses are considered who are aware of DVAs and have more than six months of usage experience. Further, the current study considers only demographic factors, however, there are numerous behavioral and psychographic factors impacting the users/consumers' attitude towards AI-based digital voice assistants which can possibly be considered in a similar context.

In summary, the study while examining the role of socio-demographic variables in forming attitudes toward AI-based Digital voice assistants concluded that there is a difference between male and female DVA users with regard to their attitudes toward digital voice assistants. In addition to differences among the demographic profiles on age, and education, the level was also found with regard to attitude toward AI-based DVA. However, results found that there is no difference between users with varied Income levels and occupation groups in their attitude toward digital voice assistants.

Interestingly, the study found a positive significant correlation between usage time and attitude towards the use of DVAs. Future research can possibly be socio-demographic studies in various settings which are highly context-dependent for more specific results.

References

1. Wilson, H.J., Daugherty, P.R., Bianzino, N.M.: When AI becomes the new face of your brand. Harvard Business Review, 27 June (2017). https://hbr.org/2017/06/when-aibecomes-the-new-face-of-your-brand. Accessed 20 July 2021
2. Iovine, A., Narducci, F., Semeraro, G.: Conversational recommender systems and natural language: a study through the ConveRSE framework. Decis. Support. Syst. **131**, 113250 (2020)
3. McLean, G., Osei-Frimpong, K.: Hey Alexa... examine the variables influencing the use of artificially intelligent in-home voice assistants. Comput. Hum. Behav. **99**, 28–37 (2019)
4. Aldayel, S.S.: The effectiveness of using mobile interactive voice assistant applications in developing academic self-efficacy of Saudi university students during the covid-19 pandemic. Inf. Sci. Lett. **11**(6), 2299–2311 (2022)
5. Resha, A.T., Razek, M.A.A., El-maghraby, E.E.: Enhancing authentication in online distant exams: a proposed method utilizing face and voice recognition. Inf. Sci. Lett. **12**(6), 2619–2628 (2023)
6. Moorthy, A.E., Vu, K.-P.L.: Privacy concerns for use of a voice-activated personal assistant in the public space. Int. J. Hum. Comput. Interact. **31**(4), 307–335 (2015)
7. Leviathan, Y., Matias, Y.: Google duplex: an AI system for accomplishing real-world Tasks over the Phone (2018)
8. Osman, N.A., Alshammar, M.M., Mohamed, T.I.: AI techniques for combating electronic crimes and enhancing cybersecurity: Kuwaits security services as a mode. Inf. Sci. Lett. **12**(7), 3339–3345 (2023)
9. Kinsella, B.: U.S. smart speaker ownership rises 40% in 2018 to 66.4 million and amazon echo maintains market share lead says new report from Voicebot. Voicebot.ai (2019)
10. Della Corte, V., Iavazzi, A., D'Andrea, C.: Customer involvement through social media: the cases of some telecommunication firms. J. Open Innov. Technol. Mark. Complex. **1**(1), 1–10 (2015)
11. Coyle, J.R., Smith, T., Platt, G.: I'm here to help: how companies' microblog responses to consumer problems influence brand perceptions. J. Res. Interact. Mark. **6**(1), 27–41 (2012)
12. Lankton, N.K., McKnight, D.H.: Examining two expectation disconfirmation theory models: assimilation and asymmetry effects. J. Assoc. Inf. Syst. **13**(2), 88–115 (2012)
13. Venkatesh, V., Thong, J.Y.L., Chan, F.K.Y., Hu, P.J.H., Brown, S.A.: Extending the two-stage information systems continuance model: incorporating UTAUT predictors and the role of context. Inf. Syst. J. **21**(6), 527–555 (2011)
14. Sciuto, A., Saini, A., Forlizzi, J., et al.: Hey Alexa, what's up? : a mixed-methods study of in-home conversational agent usage. In: Proceedings of 2018 Designing Interactive Systems Conference, Hong Kong, 9–13, pp. 857–868 (2018)
15. Anderson, M.: Mobile technology and home broadband (2019). https://www.pewresearch.org/internet/wpcontent/uploads/sites/9/2019/06. Accessed 8 Jan 2023
16. Kurzweil, R.: The Age of Intelligent Machines. MIT Press, Cambridge (1990)
17. Russell, S.J., Norvig, P.: Artificial Intelligence: A Modern Approach, 3rd edn. Pearson, Upper Saddle River (2010)
18. Kaplan, D.: Yelp's Chad Richard on the current state-and new future-of voice activation (2018). http://www.geomarketing.com/yelps-chad-richard-on-the-current-state-and-near-future-ofvoice-activation

19. Elbarougy, R., El-Badry, N.M., ElBedwehy, M.N.: An improved speech emotion classification approach based on optimal voiced unit. Inf. Sci. Lett. **11**(4), 1001–1011 (2022)
20. Alazzam, B.A., Alkhatib, M., Shaalan, K.: Artificial intelligence ChatBots: a survey of classical versus deep machine learning techniques. Inf. Sci. Lett. **12**(4), 1217–1233 (2023)
21. Parpoula, C., Drosou, K., Koukouvinos, C.: Large-scale statistical modelling via machine learning classifiers. J. Stat. Appl. Pro. **2**(3), 203–222 (2013)
22. Klaus, P., Zaichkowsky, J.: AI voice bots: a services marketing research agenda. J. Serv. Mark. **34**(3), 389–398 (2020)
23. Jones, V.K.: Voice-activated change: Marketing in the age of artificial intelligence and virtual assistants. J. Brand Strategy **7**(3), 233–245 (2018)
24. Novak, T.P., Hoffman, D.L.: Relationship journeys in the internet of things: a new framework for understanding interactions between consumers and smart objects. J. Acad. Mark. Sci. **47**(2), 216–237 (2019)
25. Poushneh, A.: 'Humanizing voice assistant: the impact of voice assistant personality on consumers' attitudes and behaviors. J. Retail. Consum. Serv. **58**, 102283 (2021)
26. Fritze, M.P., Eisingerich, A.B., Benkenstein, M.: Digital transformation and possession attachment: examining the endowment effect for consumers' relationships with hedonic and utilitarian digital service technologies. Electron. Commer. Res. **19**, 311–337 (2019)
27. Davis, F.D., Bagozzi, R.P., Warshaw, P.R.: User acceptance of computer technology: a comparison of two theoretical models. Manage. Sci. **35**(7), 972–1003 (1989)
28. Doyle, P.R., Edwards, J., Dumbleton, O., Clark, L., Cowan, B.R.: Mapping perceptions of humanness in intelligent personal assistant interaction. In: Proceedings of the 21st International Conference on Human-Computer Interaction with Mobile Devices and Services (MobileHCI 2019). 2019 (2019)
29. Kim, J.B.: An empirical study on consumer first purchase intention in online shopping: integrating initial trust and TAM. Electron. Commer. Res. **12**, 125–150 (2012)
30. Kontogiorgos, D., et al.: The effects of anthropomorphism and non-verbal social behavior in virtual assistants. In: Proceedings of the 19th ACM International Conference on Intelligent Virtual Agents (IVA 2019), pp. 133–140 (2019)
31. Pal, D., Vanijja, V., Zhang, X., Thapliyal, H.: Exploring the antecedents of consumer electronics IoT devices purchase decision: a mixed methods study. IEEE Trans. Consum. Electron. **67**(4), 305–318 (2021)
32. Linder, M.: Humanizing digital 2020- What consumers expect from you today (2020). https://zoovu.com/blog/ Accessed 9 Jan 2020
33. PWC. Consumer intelligence series: prepare for the voice revolution (2018). Accessed 09 Jan 2022
34. Mayer, R.D., Harrison, N.: As customers begin to shop through voice assistants, what can brands do to stand out? (2019). https://hbr.org/2019/08/ Accessed 5th Jan 2022
35. Wamba, S.F., Gunasekaran, A., Akter, S., Ren, S.J.F., Dubey, R., Childe, S.J.: Big data analytics and firm performance: effects of dynamic capabilities. J. Bus. Res. **70**, 356–365 (2017)
36. Akter, S., Wamba, S.F.: Big data analytics in e-commerce: a systematic review and agenda for future research. Electron. Mark. **26**(2), 173–194 (2016). https://voicebot.ai/2019/06/21/voice-assistant-demographic-data-young-consumers-more-likely-to-own-smart-speakers-while-over-60-bias-toward-alexa-and-siri/
37. Chattaraman, V., Kwon, W.S., Gilbert, J.E., Ross, K.: Should AI-based, conversational digital assistants employ social-or task-oriented interaction style? A task-competency and reciprocity perspective for older adults. Comput. Hum. Behav. **90**, 315–330 (2019)
38. Hsu, C.L., Lin, J.C.C.: Acceptance of blog usage: the roles of technology acceptance, social influence, and knowledge sharing motivation. Inf. Manag. **45**(1), 65–74 (2008)

39. Montshiwa, T.V., Botlhoko, T.: Modelling and predicting learners' numeracy test results using some regression and machine learning classifiers. J. Stat. Appl. Pro. **12**(3), 1345–1363 (2023)
40. Owolabi, A.T., Ayinde, K., Idowu, J.I., Oladapo, O.J., Lukman, A.F.: A new two-parameter estimator in the linear regression model with correlated regressors. J. Stat. Appl. Pro. **11**(2), 499–512 (2022)
41. Aljawawdeh, H.: Performance tracking e-learning model: a case study. J. Stat. Appl. Pro. **13**(1), 199–210 (2024)
42. Chang, H.H., Chen, S.W.: The impact of customer interface quality, satisfaction, and switching costs on e-loyalty: Internet experience as a moderator. Comput. Hum. Behav. **24**(6), 2927–2944 (2008)
43. Shi, S., Chow, W.S.: Trust development and transfer in social commerce: prior experience as a moderator. Ind. Manag. Data Syst. **115**(17), 1182–1203 (2015)
44. Bavaresco, R., et al.: Conversational agents in business: a systematic literature review and future research directions. Comput. Sci. Rev. **36**, 100239 (2020)
45. Cai, Z., Fan, X., Du, J.: Gender and attitudes toward technology use: a meta-analysis. Comput. Educ. **105**, 1–13 (2017)
46. Rotter, G.S., Portugal, S.M.: Group and individual effects in problem solving. J. Appl. Psychol. **53**(4), 338–341 (1969)
47. Lynott, P.P., McCandless, N.J.: The impact of age vs. life experience on the gender role attitudes of women in different cohorts. J. Women Aging **12**(2), 5–22 (2000)
48. Morris, M.G., Venkatesh, V., Ackerman, P.L.: Gender and age differences in employee decisions about new technology: an extension to the theory of planned behavior. IEEE Trans. Eng. Manage. **52**(1), 69–84 (2005)
49. Plude, D.J., Hoyer, W.J.: Attention and performance: identifying and localizing age deficits. In: Charness, N. (ed.) Aging and Human Performance, pp. 47–99. Wiley, London (1985)
50. Posner, R.A.: Aging and Old Age. University of Chicago Press, Chicago (1996)
51. Alba, J.W., Hutchinson, J.W.: Dimensions of consumer expertise. J. Consum. Res. **13**(4), 411–454 (1987)
52. Notani, A.S.: Moderators of perceived behavioral control's predictiveness in the theory of planned behavior: a meta-analysis. J. Consum. Psychol. **7**(3), 247–271 (1998)
53. Simms, K.: How voice assistants could change the way we shop. Harvard business review. Online version (2019). Accessed 1 Jan 2023. https://hbr.org/2019/05/how-voice-assistants-could-change-the-way-we-shop
54. Mitzner, T.L., et al.: Technology adoption by older adults: findings from the PRISM trial. Gerontologist **59**, 34–44 (2019)
55. Koon, L.M., McGlynn, S.A., Blocker, K.A., Rogers, W.A.: Perceptions of digital assistants from early adopters aged 55+. Ergon. Des. **28**(1), 16–23 (2020)

Fintech-Enabled Financial Inclusion for Rural Networking

P. Prasanna[✉]

Department of Management, Kristu Jayanti College, Bengaluru, India
cpprasanna@gmail.com

Abstract. To standardise rural development initiatives, many technological platforms are used. Financial technology [fintech] is a broad umbrella term for a variety of initiatives that provide this kind of vital data and support to the public. Indian farmers are yet to get benefits from agricultural technological development and fintech.

Most agricultural technology and fintech if used efficiently will significantly cut down on farming expenses. The promise of fintech in agriculture could not be realised since development agencies could not adequately deploy agricultural technology. Therefore, it is important to research how financial technology may enhance life in rural areas. Fintech paved the way for the expansion of banking services to rural areas. More than 20 million farmers who live in rural regions who have used this fintech banking system have benefitted. Farmers are increasingly making use of this service. Banking technology has contributed to reduced operating costs and improved corporate transparency, and fintech has aided in removing poverty from community frames. This research was conducted to assist institutional lenders, and more specifically banks, in determining the optimal scale at which to use fintech-enabled lending solutions in rural regions. Over 600 responses were gathered from 60 different villages in Tamil Nadu. The connection between fintech-enabled technology was studied using a conjoint analysis. The results of this research show that people in rural areas want access to financial services, including loans, that are based on their individual needs. This means that rural population must be the basis of the current system. It's estimated that 62% of people are resistant towards technology. To get rid of that amount of resistance, we need the 2.5x gearing effect. The purpose of developing the Rural Expertise Accomplishment System [REAS] was to bridge the gap between the financial technology sector and agricultural networks. Rural networking driven by demand may overcome the limitations of fintech-enabled financial services.

Keywords: Fintech · Microfinance · Rural Networking · Self-Help Groups · Gearing Effect

1 Introduction

The processes of integrating technology and society are challenging, but essential. It seems crucial to combine technological considerations with those of users and society at large. Comprehension, respect, and negotiation are all part of these inter-disciplinary

A. M. A. Musleh Al-Sartawi et al. (Eds.): ICGER 2023, CCIS 1999, pp. 28–38, 2024.
https://doi.org/10.1007/978-3-031-50518-8_3

procedures. Realizing that bridging disciplinary gaps requires the collaboration of many different professions is crucial, and so is identifying those fields for any socio-fintech initiative. There are many hurdles in bringing out such change.

Fintech in agriculture is a new area that aims to improve rural life in India. It entails novel applications of fintech in rural settings, with the ultimate goal of boosting farmers' incomes. Indian financial technology is only getting started. There is significant regional variation in the usage of outdated financial technology. Telecommunications, information, and people's efforts vary widely from one place to another. Using this technology, small businesses such as farms and agro-based outlets may be linked to sales channels. Implementation of supply chain networks based on technology is uncertain in rural India (Scott 2014). Greater economic openness and reduced costs are beneficial to small farmers (University of California 2012). One of the biggest problems in implementing financial technologies in rural regions is a lack of knowledge about how they work. Lack of relevant and localised material in native languages and lack of inexpensive access are two major factors contributing to this illiteracy. A further area of concern is the level of technological literacy and openness to change among rural residents. Farmers' reliance on people for the conveyance of information is a key component of the usage of fintech's by farmers and their associates, as shown in various examples. A major problem arises when there is a mismatch between the pace of technical advancement and the rate of basic development (Pal 2013). A third of rural income comes from the non-farm sector, which is also highly dependent on agriculture in times of economic stress (Peter 2000). Hundreds of failed financial technology initiatives are still used in agricultural sector which are meant to be used in developed industrial world, they are also documented on the World Bank's info Dev website. Most of these endeavours make use of mass-produced, industrialised world-oriented technologies (Kamala 2018). For a society that evaluates its progress and growth based on the quality of life it provides, banking is undeniably the backbone of the economic cycle. Installation of automated equipment in rural regions is helpful, but the wireless banking system is crucial for the development of outlying rural communities.

In addition, several commercial and state organisations provide microfinance fintech, which is essential for rural development. A low annual growth rate of 4.9% [Bharat Financial Inclusion Ltd., Annual Report, 2020] is indicative of microfinance's lack of popularity and acceptance in rural areas. Though efforts to spread awareness of the benefits of microfinance, such as the documentary "Pudhu Sakthi Pirakuthu" [Energizing new initiatives for economic integration], have been successful, this is not the case in all rural areas. Furthermore, the systemic failure is due to the absence of leadership and coordination among microfinance service organisations. Across the board, rural communities are struggling. Introducing microfinance to help stabilise their level of life is a good idea and incorporating fintech will make the process even more efficient.

To help close this digital divide between rural and urban locations, the current study set out to quantify how widely available and used fintech currently is. Using this data, regulators may also calculate the optimal leverage impact to speed up the adoption of financial technology.

2 Literature Reviews

The creation of financial technologies in outlying regions is now uncharted (Ricardo 2017). For rural regions of the third world to advance economically, they must have access to modern forms of communication. Cost-effectiveness (Abu-Serdaneh 2023) is heavily dependent on the technology used to do this (Raman 2017). The development of fintech presents both benefits and threats to small businesses in rural areas (Premkumar 2017). Experts in rural revitalization should push privately owned businesses in rural areas to embrace IT to boost regional transmission capacity and consumer demand (Joseph 2013). The key to the platform's quick uptake and widespread use was a methodical training programme (Kendal 2016). Tools for gathering data (Jahmani et al. 2023), (Ebiwonjumi et al. 2023) and identifying information gaps might provide a solution (Blattmen 2013). The potential for increasing centralization or decentralisation, as well as the appropriate use of fintech technology for indigenous growth, are all taken into account (Grimes 2018). Gyandoot, Madya Pradesh's official e-learning platform, has high satisfaction but little utilisation and is not reaching the state's poorest residents (Raina 2014).

Through improved access to healthcare, education, government services, and financial services, IT has the potential to significantly alleviate global poverty. Access to markets is a major challenge for small farmers and artisans, but IT may help with that, too (Meetha 2016). Following a thorough examination of the requirements of the target audience, the Gramya Vikas team developed a safe and fulfilling programme for a select group of rural customers (Rao 2012). For the much-heralded "new green revolution" to become a reality, it will be necessary to incorporate recently developed agricultural technologies into standard agricultural practises. (Trrip 2012). The agricultural credit is the lowest, and only with very optimistic assumptions about farm loan repayment rates does the output of the provisions exceed the cost of the plan (Khandker 2015).

Expanding India's telecommunications infrastructure significantly at the present cost per line and more recent innovations, many of which originated in India, have the potential to cut this cost by more than half (Ramamurthi 2018). IT could help primary healthcare providers in remote areas of developing nations have access to affordable communication and information technology. (Pozo 2017). Kiosks connected to the firm's ERP system provided access to corporate data as well as general information on agricultural methods, farm trade, weather, etc. (Gollakota 2018). Different and effective uses of ICT [especially financial technology] in India's quest for racial and economic equality (Singh 2016). In rural areas (Ahmed, H.A., et al. 2021), which have traditionally been economically and socially marginalised, the opportunities that IT [in particular fintech] offer individuals and communities to overcome the friction of distance and the constraints of materiality are seen as having particular significance (Holloway 2017). Having a reliable means of communication is crucial for fintech to reach their customers. As stated by (Mahapatra 2015).

Fintech-centric measurements, such as the expansion or contraction of the "digital gap," are at best substitutes for these deeper developments and the least resistant to adoption (Namara 2013). But rural poverty remains, and financial help is shrinking; a new story is needed to explain why? (Ashley 2012).

The success of a microfinance institution depends not only on its lending policies and pricing systems, but also on the nature and strength of the connections among its members

(Woolcock 2019). People living in poverty in India's rural areas have limited access to formal financial services. Microfinance initiatives aim to address this gap. Although SHGs have seen a significant growth in Bank Linkage, their impact on rural low-income families has been rather small (Srivastava 2015). Microcredit is a new kind of financing that may help solve problems in the credit market and reduce poverty (Bauer 2017). The anti-poverty mindset is also marginalised in microfinance. At now, this complex micro-business ecosystem is under the direction of the financial sustainability school (Olsen 2016). To further assist farmers, microlenders should lower lending rates and costs (Malcolm 2015) (Table 1).

Table 1. Knowledge gap in literature

Authors	Review	Fact	Knowledge
Simone & Scott (2016)	Rural Expertise	High resistance at low cost	Implementing trained professional
Crowder (2014)	Multi-Purpose Community Telecentres [MCT]	Resistance in the usage of wide available services	Improving awareness about the services to the people
Gopi Boddu (2018)	Implementation of Kiosk	Poor infrastructure in Kiosk settlement	Scientifically managing Kisok settlement
Rao (2012)	Collaboration	Inactive improvement in introducing technologies	Private Public Partnership should be practised
Mc Narma (2013)	Digital Divide	Low acceptance of technology	Increasing the conventional methods
Pichai (2018)	Wireless technology	Less advancement in IT enabled banking	Implementation of wireless Rural Banking [WRB]
Bowonder (2018)	e-Choupal	Wrong information designation through banking	Managing the IT network by trained corporate enterprises
Present study	Fintech as a tool of budding development in rural areas		Bridging the gap between rural and urban

A knowledge gap exists across the many fintech services, including Agriculture, Banking, Insurance, Education, and e-Commerce, as shown by the study above.

3 Objectives

For this study, the major goal is to explore how the usage of financial technology [fintech] enabled solutions might help eliminate the economic gap between rural and urban regions.

4 Methodology

Kongu belt which includes Coimbatore, The Nilgiris, Tiruppur, Erode, Namakkal, and Salem were among the six Tamil Nadu districts from which the total sample of 600 people was drawn. Respondents are identified using a snowball sampling technique. To achieve this goal, 10 residents of each village were selected to participate. The sample size of 600 was determined using the confidence interval technique. Primary data from 600 respondents was gathered using an interview schedule. After analysing data from the first survey of 30 participants, an interview plan was developed. To find out whether a set of brand variables forms a unidimensional scale, a scalogram analysis was performed. Respondents were divided into groups based on their use of financial technology with the use of a cluster analysis. Only responses from respondents with a greater resonance value were used for the subsequent study. Based on the findings, the sectors of banking, e-trading, agriculture, microfinancing, and education are all positioned to benefit from fintech. A conjoint analysis was carried out to determine the optimal combination of fintech activities that would maximise the value derived from their utilisation by fintech consumers (Table 2).

Table 2. Input Process Output Chart

Stage	Purpose	Input	Process	Output
I	To identify the fintech enabled technologies	12 rural technologies in India based in SR Chakravarthy	Modal value in ranking in rural villages if Tamil Nadu	Banking, Agriculture, Microfinance, Education & e-Trading
II	To identify commonly used banking fintech	8 variables in rural banking	Modal values in rural banking-bridging digital divide in Indian IT scenario (Subbarao 2005)	Rural Credit, VAS, EPS, Fund Transfer, Mobile Payments
III	Sampling	Confidentially mixed	Confidence interval approach	600 in 60 villages
IV	To find out the fintech acceptance level	Five fintech variables	Cluster analysis	38%
V	To find out the discriminating factor among the fintech enable variables	Five fintech variables	Discriminate analysis	Banking
VI	To find out the discriminating factor among the fintech enable banking technologies	Five fintech enabled banking variables	Discriminate analysis	Rural Credit
VII	To find out the penetration effect of fintech	Fintech usage variables	Time difference	3.7%
VIII	To find out the taxonomies of penetration effect	Output of above stages	Growth factor index	2.5 times

There is a substantial link between banks and microfinancing. It has the greatest effect (0.988) in microfinance and banking and the least effect (0.645) in the areas of education and agriculture. According to Table 3, most people are comfortable using banks and microloans.

Table 3. Correlation Among Fintech enabled Rural Initiatives

Correlation	Agri Accessibility	Agri Utilization	Edu Accessibility	Edu Utilisation	Banking Accessibility	Banking Utilization	Micro-Finance Accessibility	Micro-Finance Utilization	E-Trading Accessibility	E-Trading Utilization
Agri-Accessibility	1.000	0.780	0.971	0.762	0.780	0.762	0.971	0.780	0.681	0.672
Agri- Utilization	0.780	1.000	0.780	0.762	0.971	0.780	0.780	0.762	0.650	0.644
Edu Accessibility	0.645	0.762	1.000	0.971	0.762	0.780	0.971	0.762	0.971	0.780
Edu Utilisation	0.971	0.780	0.762	1.000	0.780	0.971	0.780	0.762	0.780	0.762
Banking Accessibility	0.780	0.762	0.971	0.762	1.000	0.762	0.988	0.780	0.762	0.780
Banking Utilization	0.971	0.780	0.780	0.780	0.971	1.000	0.780	0.762	0.971	0.761
Micro-Finance Accessibility	0.780	0.762	0.780	0.780	0.971	0.762	1.000	0.780	0.971	0.780
Micro-Finance Utilization	0.971	0.762	0.971	0.780	0.762	0.971	0.762	1.000	0.971	0.762
E- Trading Accessibility	0.971	0.780	0.762	0.750	0.780	0.762	0.780	0.971	1.000	0.780
E-Trading Utilization	0.780	0.762	0.780	0.780	0.971	0.780	0.971	0.762	0.780	1.000

Source: Primary Data.

Clusters Analysis

Cluster analysis has been performed despite widespread opposition to use of fintech. Because of the massive sample size, cluster analysis was utilised to stratify respondents [customers] who are reasonably similar in terms of their use of fintech. Three criteria for categorising fintech adoption were established in accordance with the degree to which they were generally accepted. The clusters are based on how widely used banking, farming, microfinancing, schools, and online shops are that make use of fintech. The clustering criteria used is Akanke's Information Criterion (AIC). Using a minimum of three centroids, we can discriminate across clusters and show that a certain number of centroids was used to establish the cluster size. Attitude factors are rated on a three-point Likert scale. Figure 1 show the cluster team based on fintech perception level.

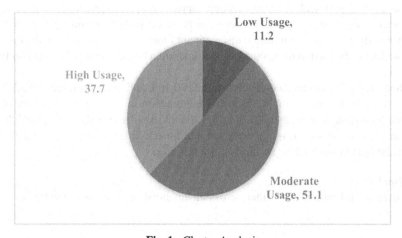

Fig. 1. Cluster Analysis

The values for all parameters of fintech-enabled consumption are rather high in Cluster 1. This led to the classification of "High Usage". The variables in Cluster 2 are all rather high, although not quite at the top. Because of this, it was given the moderate rating. The third-degree values for all four variables are greatest in cluster 3. Because of this, it was classified as "Low Usage". The cluster analysis' validity was examined by looking for differences between the attitude components and cluster variables.

5 Discriminate Analysis I

To see whether fintech-enabled use can be differentiated amongst banking, microfinance, agriculture, education, and e-commerce, a stepwise-multiple discriminant function is built. One function was created because all group means were the same. The results are shown in the table below (Table 4).

Table 4. Canonical Discriminant Function of Fintech.

Factors	Functions
Banking	0.883
Microfinance	−0.006
Agriculture	−2.04
Education	−0.297
E-Trading	−0.204

For this function, the eigenvalue is 0.29, and the canonical correlation is 0.176. As a result of using this model, we can account for all the observed variation in these metrics. Wilks's lambda for this function is 0.91. Therefore, rural inhabitants often use the banking services made possible by fintech.

6 Discriminant Analysis II

To assess whether fintech-enabled banking services may be segmented by geography [rural credit, electronic payment system, value-added service, mobile payments, and money transfer], a stepwise-multiple discriminant function is developed. On the basis of the equality established in the group a single function. Here is a rundown of the findings (Table 5).

The function's canonical correlation value is 0.169, and its eigen value is 0.33. This model accounts for every single observed phenomenon in the banking industry made possible by advances in financial technology. For Wilks, the corresponding lambda for this function is 0.78. So, it may be argued that fintech-enabled banking services face significant bias in the lending facilities of rural banks.

Gearing Effect
The analysis and ratings show that across all financial service domains, the leverage

Table 5. Canonical Discriminant Function of Fintech enabled Banking.

Factors	Functions
Rural Credit	0.826
Value Added Service	−0.544
Electronic Payment System	−0.54
Fund Transfer	0.113
Mobile Payments	−0.20

effect is 38% and the resistance level is 62%. Therefore, the acceptable threshold is used to establish the impact of gearing.

The acceptance rate was 34.27% when the trial started on September 1; by November 30, it had grown to 38%, an increase of 3.7% points. Even though it has already crossed 75% in urban areas like Navi Mumbai and Gurgoan, if the present rate of adoption continues, it will only reach 52.8%. The gearing effect must be increased by 2.5%, or four times the existing pace of development, in order to reach the same level as urban regions; this means that 2.5% × 14.8% = 37% can be reached, which, when added to the current level of acceptance, results in 75% of total growth.

The following formula may be used to calculate this influence:

$$Fintech\ Gearing\ Effect = \frac{Desired\ Level\ of\ Acceptance - Present\ Level\ of\ Acceptance}{Compounded\ Annual\ Growth\ Rate}$$

7 Findings

Banking, microfinance, agriculture, and e-commerce are just a few examples of where fintech is being used in rural communities. The rate of acceptance is greatest in the banking sector, followed closely by the microfinance sector. Value Added Service [VAS], Electronic Payment System [EPS], Mobile Pay, Fund Transfer, and Rural Credit are just few of the many banking services offered. The most helpful banking services for rural areas are the ones banks provide via their Rural Credit departments. It is through these departments that fintech may eventually make its way into rural life. With a larger pool of borrowers for rural lending, costs may be lowered, and the fintech-enabled banking industry can grow rapidly and profitably.

The adoption of financial technology in rural regions may be boosted by using it in banking and microfinance. With the help of SHGs, microfinance might become more widespread in these areas; however, the Public Private Partnership [PPP] framework is required to put this fintech-enabled microfinance into action. Clientele will increase thanks to the efforts of SHGs and PPP.

When all the aforementioned are put into effect, the acceptance rate will increase by a factor of 2.5% over what it is now, for a total acceptance rate of 75%. Because of this general agreement, rural and urban regions can only expand so far (Fig. 2).

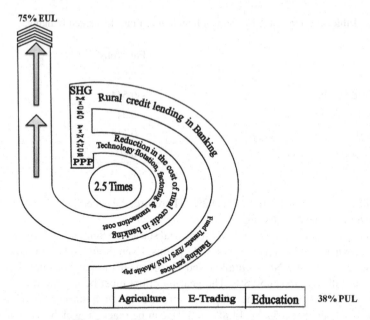

Fig. 2. Rural Expertise Accomplishment System

8 Conclusion

75% of people in metropolitan areas already use fintech, and the goal is to grow that number by 2.5 times in rural areas. This level of penetration would be a boon to rural areas since it would result in several advantages, not the least of which would be a complete absence of financial exclusion for the rural sector, which is still the primary focus of the study. It also makes it possible to create a centralised decision-making framework to increase national financial flexibility, which has the knock-on effect of decreasing urban concentration and increasing rural sector business prospects and entrepreneurs. When a balance is reached between the financial inclusions in rural areas and those in metropolitan centres, rural residents get the same economic agency as their urban counterparts.

To increase the system's popularity and, by extension, its user base, it's important to include a "pull" component into fintech-enabled microfinance, which may be done via Self Help Groups [SHG]. This kind of technology-enabled Microfinance may be done via a Public Private Partnership.

Value Added Service [VAS], Electronic Payment System [EPS], Mobile Pay, Fund Transfer, and Rural Credit are only few of the services provided by the rural bank. The rural credit programme is one of the most popular programmes provided. With an increased client base thanks to rural credit, fintech may join the market at the same time as expenses like factoring fees, transaction fees, floating fees, and technology costs are lowered. As a result, the implementation of fintech in banking in rural areas would gain greater traction than its counterparts in agriculture, e-commerce, and instruction.

9 Scope for Further Studies

The present study considered for inclusion of fintech with the help of self-help groups in the location considered for study. Other medium like co-operative banks, post-office which plays a vital role in day-to-day working of rural community may be considered. Similar studies can be conducted in bringing other technological services to the rural mass.

References

Abu-Serdaneh, J.: New insights of asymmetric cost behavior in non-financial MENA companies. Inf. Sci. Lett. **12**(1), 125–133 (2023)

Ahmed, H.A., Sery, M., Marzouk, O.I.A., Loatyif, M.S.M., Abdeldayem, M.M.: Characteristics of social and physical environment associated with and chest diseases of the circulatory system: a comparative study of different social strata in the rural and urban. Inf. Sci. Lett. **10**(2), 213–222 (2021)

Ashley. Rethinking rural development. Dev. Policy Rev. **19**, 395–425 (2012)

Bauer, M.: Behavioural foundations of microcredit : Rural India. IZA Discussion Paper No:4901 (2017)

Blattmen, C.: Assessing the need and potential of community networking for development in rural India. Inf. Soc. **19**, 349–364 (2013)

Ebiwonjumi, A., Chifurira, R., Chinhamu, K.: A robust principal component analysis for estimating economic growth in Nigeria in the presence of multicollinearity and outlier. J. Stat. Appl. Pro. **12**(2), 611–627 (2023)

Gollakota: ICT use by businesses in rural India. Int. J. Inf. Manage. **28**, 336–341 (2018)

Grimes: Exploiting information and communication technologies for rural development. J. Rural. Stud. **8**, 269–278 (2018)

Holloway: Rural children's use of information and communication technologies. J. Rural. Stud. **17**, 384–394 (2017)

Jahmani, A., Jawabreh, O., AL-Fahmawee, E.A., Almasarweh, M.S., Ali, B.J.A.: The impact of employee management on organizational performance in Dubai's five-star hotel sector. J. Stat. Appl. Pro. **12**(20), 395–404 (2023)

Joseph: Creating demand: influencing information technology diffusion in rural communities. Gov. Inf. Q. **20**, 135–150 (2013)

Kam. [National Development.]. The case for technology in developing regions. IEEE Comput. Soc. J. **38**, 25–38 (2005)

Kaushik. Information technology and broad-based development: preliminary lessons from North India. World Dev. Mag. **32**, 591–607 (2014)

Kendal, J.: Inter net kiosk in rural india. NET Inst. Workinh Paper No 6–5 (2016)

Khandker: The impact of formal finance on the rural economy of India. J. Dev. Stud. **32**, 234–262 (2015)

Mahapatra, A.: Modes of communication and effectiveness of agroforestry extension in Eastern India. Hum. Ecol. **29**, 285–305 (2015)

Malcolm, H.: Farm credit and Microfinanace - is there a critical mismatch? Small Entrep. Dev. **16**, 58–67 (2015)

Meetha, S.: ICT a bridge for social equity and sustainable growth in India. Int. Inf. Libr. Rev. **38**, 147–160 (2016)

Metha, S.: ICT a bridge for social equity and sustinable development in India. Int. Inf. Libr. Rev. **29**, 540–545 (2016)

Namara. ICT poverty and development: learning from experience . *info*Dev Annual Symposium, Economic Affairs of Switzerland, pp. 24–32 (2013)

The Report of National Urban Survey. Department of Indian Surveys. 2015/11.445, pp. 111–112 (2015)

olsen, E.: Paradigms and reality in micro-finanace. Prespectives Global Dev. Technol. 5(1-2), 31–54 (2016)

Pal, J.: Development promise of ICT in India. Am. Sociol. Rev. 10, 89 (2013)

Peter. [National Development]. Rural - urban growth linkages in India. Agriculture and Ruaral Development, World Bank, 430

Pozo. [National Development]. Rural telemedicine for primary healthcare in developing countries. Technol. Soc. Mag. IEEE 23(2), 13–22 (2004)

Premkumar: Adoption of new information technologies in rural small businesses. Omega 27, 467–484 (2017)

Rao, P.: Rural communication in India using cellular system. Commun. Mag. IEEE 32, 70–77 (2012)

Rao, S.: Bridiging digital divide in Indian ICT. Tele. Inf. 22, 370–375 (2015)

Raina: Electronic government and the rural poor: the case of gyandoot. Inf. Technol. Int. Dev. 2, 65–76 (2014)

Ramamurthi. The role of technology in telecom expansion in India. Commun. Mag. IEEE 36, 88–94 (2018)

Raman. Experiences in using WiFi for rural internet in India. J. Indian Inst. Technol. (2017)

Rao, S.S.: Social development in rural India. Int. J. Inf. Manage. 28, 478–482 (2012)

Recardo: A model for rural and remote information and communication technologies. Telecommun. Policy 25, 315–330 (2017)

Scott. (National Development). Can information and communications technology applications contribute to poverty reduction. Inf. Technol. Dev. 10, 73–84 (2003)

The Competitons of rural areas. Second International School of Rural Development, University College Galanway (2017)

Singh, N.: ICT & ruarl development. In: Paper for Hungarian Academy of Sciences Transitions V Conference vol. 2, (2016)

Srivastava, P.B.: Scalling-up microfinanace for India's rural poor. World Bank Policy Research, vol. 3646 (2015)

Bharat Financial Inclusion Annual Report. Bharat Financial Inclusion (2017–2020)

Trrip, R.: Agricultural technology policies for rural development. Dev. Policy Rev. 19, 479–489 (2012)

Woolcock, M.: Learning from failures in microfinanace. Am. J. Econ. Soc. 58, 17–42 (2019)

Distributed Denial of Service Attack Detection Using Sequence-To-Sequence LSTM

Anand Parmar[1]($\boxtimes$) (ID) and Hemraj Lamkuche[2] (ID)

[1] Symbiosis University of Applied Sciences (SUAS), Indore, India
anandparmar967@gmail.com
[2] School of Computing Science and Engineering, VIT Bhopal University, Kothrikalan, Sehore 466114, Madhya Pradesh, India
hemraj.lamkuche@gmail.com

Abstract. Log files are a great way to find out what's wrong with a system and how secure it is. They can be very large and have a complicated structure, which is why they are so useful. We use Machine Learning (ML) to find network anomalies and build different models that are driven by data to find DDoS attacks. The main goal of this article is to reduce the number of times that DDoS detection is wrongly labeled. In this paper, we describe a method for security analysis that uses Deep Learning techniques like simple LSTM, LSTM with embedding, and Seq-to-Seq LSTM on several systems log files to find and extract data that may be related to distributed denial of service (DDoS) attacks made by malicious users who want to break into a system. Through a process of learning, these data will help to find attacks, predict attacks, or find intrusions. In this study, we looked at how different optimizers, the size of the hidden state, and the number of layers affected the same architecture to find the best way to set it up. When compared to other models, the proposed model was able to correctly identify DoS/DDoS packets that had never been seen before with a 98.95% level of accuracy.

Keywords: DDoS Attack Detection · Cyber Physical System · LSTM · Deep Learning · Machine Learning

1 Introduction

Denial of Service (DoS) attacks aim to crash a network or service by overwhelming it with traffic/requests, causing it to become unavailable to intended users. They can result in financial loss, reputational damage, and loss of data [1]. They can be carried out by a single source or multiple sources (DDoS). DoS/DDoS attacks are a critical and rapidly evolving threat. This research has been conducted to analyze various DDoS attacks in different environments and setups. Some examples include, the study of the "ping of death" attack and its impact [2], the effect of such attacks on Software Defined Networking (SDN) [3], and the examination of how DDoS attacks can be executed and their impact on popular web servers such as Apache and IIS [4]. There have also been efforts to detect and counter DDoS/DoS attacks using Artificial Neural Networks

© The Author(s), under exclusive license to Springer Nature Switzerland AG 2024
A. M. A. Musleh Al-Sartawi et al. (Eds.): ICGER 2023, CCIS 1999, pp. 39–53, 2024.
https://doi.org/10.1007/978-3-031-50518-8_4

(ANNs) and Machine Learning techniques. Some works utilize Convolutional Neural Networks (CNNs) [5–7] to identify attacks, and others employ popular ML techniques [8] for detection and analysis. A few studies have employed Feed-Forward ANNs [9, 10] to detect DDoS attacks, and some examine the detection of DDoS/DoS attacks as a sequential problem and attempt to use Long-Short Term Memory [11](LSTM) or Recurrent Neural Network [12] (RNN) networks to achieve this [13].

The DoS/DDoS attacks are difficult to detect and lack a comprehensive solution despite being one of the earliest cyber threats. They closely resemble legitimate traffic, making traditional techniques inadequate. The largest recorded DDoS attacks to date were on Google (2.54 Tbps), AWS (2.3 Tbps), and GitHub (1.3 Tbps). Building on prior work, our new methodology for detecting DoS/DDoS attacks using ANN addresses various issues seen in previous studies such as data imbalance. We collect data in sessions, four sessions were recorded in our study. Unlike many previous studies, we also incorporate IP addresses as a feature by utilizing the Embedding technique. We use accuracy, precision, recall, and F1 score for performance measurement using an unseen dataset. For the classification technique, we present a novel approach to counter Dos/DDos attacks using ANN, utilizing a Sequence-to-Sequence architecture with LSTM and attention mechanism. This is a new approach in the field, as prior works have limited use of this technology. We chose the Sequence-to-Sequence model for its efficiency in processing sequential data, and LSTM for its ability to handle large data sets in the context of Dos/DDoS attacks. Our approach emphasizes utilizing underutilized features. We further improve our model by testing different configurations of hidden state, layer count, batch size, activation functions, and optimizers during training. Finally, we compare our approach against other methods. For more details about cybersecurity and attacks, refer to [14–19].

The paper is structured as follows: Sect. 2 reviews prior research in the field. Section 3 covers the data collection, preprocessing, analysis, and storage, as well as the description and comparison of our deep learning model architecture and its results. Section 4 looks at conventional DDoS detection methods, and Sect. 5 summarizes and concludes our work.

2   Literature Review

In the past, various solutions have been created to combat DoS/DDoS attacks on SDN and other types of networks. As noted in [3], most of these solutions as of 2021 have been tested using simulators. However, there are a few strategies that are focused on working under an attack, such as [16–20], while others are focused on mitigation or prevention. Some strategies typically involve using statistical analysis to identify the network's status, such as tracking resource usage and request volume. Additionally, a few solutions involve adding extra hardware to the network [16, 21], such as caches, middleboxes, and third-party servers.

Research has been conducted to assess the effects of DoS/DDoS attacks on cloud environments [22]. Specifically examining the impact of slow HTTP headers (slowloris), slow HTTP POST, and slow read attacks on the target virtual machine in terms of CPU, RAM, and network usage, as well as the impact on neighboring machines in terms of response time. The research found that even a small amount of low-rate traffic from a single attacker can negatively affect neighboring VMs and reduce web server response time by 2.09% and 11% when using a distributed DoS attack.

Further studies have been conducted to examine the use of machine learning algorithms such as Random Forests, Naive Bayes, and Support Vector Machines (SVMs) to detect DDoS attacks on cloud platforms [8]. SNORT was also utilized to detect all the attacks and provide data for the study. The study found that among the three algorithms used, SVM had the highest accuracy, recall, and precision. However, the study also highlights that the data used in the study was imbalanced.

Fekadu Yihunie et al. describe the effects of 'Ping of Death' DoS and DDoS attacks in their research [2]. Their work examined the effects of the respective attack in three different network topologies, 1) A well-functioning network serves as a reference point for comparing response time with the next two scenarios. 2) The first scenario is replicated and a malicious node is added to the network. 3) The second scenario is replicated and two more attacking machines are added, increasing the number of ping requests by the malicious nodes on the server.

Additionally, research has been conducted to examine the impact of DoS/DDoS attacks on web servers [4]. Rizgar et al. in their study compared the effects of SYN and HTTP flood on two web servers Apache 2 and IIS 10.0 using the HOIC [23] tool. The study shows that both servers were unable to function during the attack, but IIS was found to be more stable under both attacks. The study also focuses on the impact of SYN flood attacks, as there is limited research on this type of attack.

Recently, several proposals have been made to use neural networks for identifying DoS/DDoS attacks, one such example of the use of ANN for DDoS detection includes, Multi-layer perceptron (MLP) [10] on CharGen, DNS, and UDP attacks. Evaluated through computer simulation, this work has shown outcomes with higher accuracy of 95.6%.

Another research on the use of Artificial Neural Networks (ANN) for DDoS detection is the research work done by Shahzeb et al. [5]. Shahzeb et al. in their work proposes a CNN-based ensemble mechanism for the detection of different flow-based DDoS attacks in SDN. The CICIDS2017 dataset is used for evaluation, the dataset contains 40% DDoS and 60% normal traffic. The study concludes that the use of multiple CNN models in an ensemble-style architecture improves both detection accuracy and computational efficiency.

Jieren et al. [7] suggest a method for identifying DDoS attacks using a convolutional neural network to address the issue of high false and missing alarm rates in big data environments. They introduce the use of Gray Scale Matrix Features (GMF) to train the CNN model, and test it using SYN/SYN + ACK flood attacks from the CAIDA "DDoS Attack 2007" dataset. Their proposed method is reported to be more accurate than comparable detection techniques, it also shows lower rates of false alarms and missed alarms. Additionally, it can effectively detect DDoS attacks in big data environments.

Although most research proposals focus on detecting Application layer DDoS attacks, there is also a need for Network layer DDoS detection systems, particularly for IoT devices. The research [24] proposes a simple classifier utilizing a feedforward neural network with backpropagation, it is capable of distinguishing between normal and malicious traffic produced by IoT devices communicating with machines via the

MQTT protocol. The study covers TCP, UDP, ARP, and ICMP attacks [25]. The final model that uses 8 features was found to be superior to the same model using 10 features and an RNN using 10 features.

Another interesting study consisting of the use of DNN is the work done by Aanshi *et al.* [26]. Their work presents an architecture that utilizes a well-designed Autoencoder (AE) [27] to address the difficulties of efficient feature learning, dealing with noisy data, and avoiding overfitting. The proposed architecture is compared to ten other machine-learning techniques on NSL-KDD and CICIDS2017 datasets. As a result, the proposed methodology was able to classify DDoS/DoS traffic with an accuracy of 98.43% and 98.92% on the NSL-KDD and CICIDS 2017 datasets.

Another popular study "Detection of known and unknown DDoS attacks using Artificial Neural Networks" [9] aims to classify DDoS attacks and to evaluate the performance of an Artificial Neural Network (ANN) when it is trained with both old and recent datasets. Features such as IP address, TCP sequence number, and port numbers were used. The results indicate that the trained model classified 95% of unknown and 100% of known DDoS attacks when tested on old and recent datasets.

Another study that uses Recurrent Neural Networks (RNNs) for DDoS detection is the research by Xiaoyong *et al.* [13]. In their work, they tackle the issue of DDoS detection by treating it as a sequence classification problem and converting packet-based detection to window-based detection. The study trains various models including CNN, RNN, LSTM, and GRU [28], on the UNB ISCX dataset. The findings reveal a decrease in error rate by 39.69% when compared to the shallow machine learning methods on a small dataset, and a decrease in error rate from 7.517% to 2.103% on a larger dataset.

3   Proposed Methodology

Here we present our deep learning-based approach to classify DoS/DDoS attacks, we will detail its architecture and the methods used for data preprocessing, collection, storage, and analysis. We will then discuss the experiments conducted and the DDoS strategies employed.

3.1   Data Collection

We employ our solution using AWS cloud services, the lab setup is as follows:

I. 5 machines running bot-scripts to simulate benign traffic. These machines randomly send requests to random routes in our web server within random intervals.
II. Kali-Linux machine acting as the attacker.
III. The target web server running on PORT 80, which uses Flask, has five distinct routes that support both POST and GET requests along with authentication, as well as JavaScript, CSS, HTML, and image resources.

Our proposed method involves collecting and organizing data into sessions, as this approach addresses the issue of imbalanced data caused by the faster speed of DoS/DDoS packets compared to normal packets. It also allows for the capture of a wider range of features, such as variations in size, balance, addresses, and timestamps.

The following datasets were recorded as follows (Table 1):

Table 1. DDoS dataset captured on virtual machine

Dataset	Start Time	Attack Started	Stop Time	Length	Benign Count	DDOS Count
dataset-1	22:00	22:30	22:37	121784	70956 (59%)	50828 (41%)
dataset-2	23:17	23:50	23:55	60543	50663 (83%)	9880 (17%)
dataset-3	16:10	16:41	17:00	171296	89229 (53%)	82067 (47%)
dataset-4	9:30	10:05	10:17	267830	120292 (45%)	147538 (55%)

3.2 Data Processing

Our method uses TCP and IP properties of packets as captured in our datasets. It aims to make use of features, such as IP addresses, that are not commonly utilized.

We utilize Source and Destination IP addresses by Embedding them. Embedding, published in 2013 is a technique used for NLP tasks [29]. Embedding employs a neural network to discover associations, which we utilize to link various IP addresses. This approach allows our model to view the addresses as distinct but related entities instead of continuous values, and also aids in identifying addresses that belong to the same subnet. We input each octet of the IP address into the embedding process, converting it into a single value between 0 and 1. Finally, we concat the result of embedding all octets of the address. We repeat this process for every octet in both the Source and Destination IP addresses. For example: "127.0.0.1" becomes "0.98, 0, 0, 0.01". These values are learned during training. The same is done for destination and source PORT numbers. We also introduce the "direction" feature, which allows us to categorize packets as incoming or outgoing. This is a simple yet effective feature. Finally, TCP and IP flags, and their other properties were used as features.

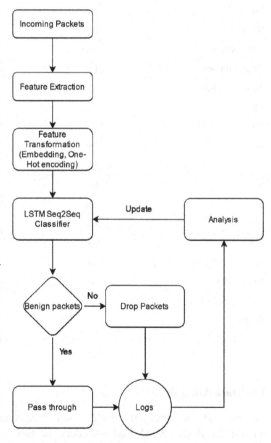

Fig. 1. Flow diagram of DoS/DDoS detection system

3.3 Data Storage

Our goal is to make the data easily accessible for various purposes. To achieve this, we store the data in a CSV format, which is widely supported. This allows for easy visualization and analysis using various tools and can also be easily consumed for various purposes (Table 2).

Table 2. List of features used in datasets

Field	Field Type	Field Example
SRC	String	"192.168.1.1"
DST	String	"192.168.1.2"
DIRECTION	Bool	[1,0]
IP_TOS	Int	[1,0]
DF	Int	[1,0]
IP_TTL	Int	64
TCP_SPORT	Int	80
TCP_DPORT	Int	4456
TCP_RESERVED	Int	[1,0]
FPA	Int	[1,0]
FA	Int	[1,0]
A	Int	[1,0]
S	Int	[1,0]
SA	Int	[1,0]
PA	Int	[1,0]
R	Int	[1,0]
RA	Int	[1,0]
TCP_WINDOW	Int	489
TCP_MSS	Int	1460
TCP_WSCALE	Int	7
TYPE	Int	[1,0]

3.4 Data Analysis

Our method for identifying DDoS/DoS attacks utilizes Deep Learning techniques, specifically RNN/LSTM, and considers the task as a sequence problem. We experiment with various architectures and evaluate their performance. We contrast models that do not incorporate Embedding with models that do and models that employ Seq2Seq architecture.

Our solution functions as a filter that examines each incoming packet, discards any suspicious packets, and records all transaction data for analysis and to retrain the classifier as shown in Fig. 1.

Based on previous studies using Encoder-Decoder architecture to detect DDoS/DoS attacks [26], we propose utilizing Seq2Seq architecture with attention for improved DDoS/DoS attack identification.

In the past Seq2Seq models [30] have shown success as generative models in various natural language processing tasks. In our approach, we aim to harness this generative capability of recurrent neural networks by using Seq2Seq architecture with an Attention mechanism.

We utilize an Encoder that condenses a batch of input data into a batch of outputs and a single Hidden State using LSTM, which is then passed to the Decoder mechanism that applies attention and generates its own output. This output, when processed through a feed-forward network, can predict the type of input.

We choose to employ LSTM in our proposed methodology because of its ability to handle longer sequences more effectively than traditional RNN and GRU models.

As illustrated in Fig. 2.

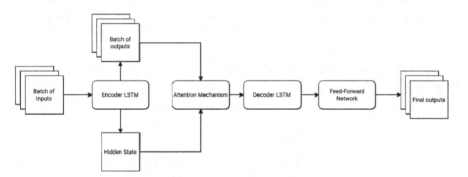

Fig. 2. Deep Learning based DDoS/DoS classifier

3.5 Results

As described before data used in this proposal is based on sessions. We recorded 4 datasets out of which datasets 1–3 are used for training and dataset 4 is used for validation. The study examines three distinct architectures, including Simple LSTM, LSTM with Embedding, and LSTM in the Seq2Seq technique.

The training approach involved, training and validating the model on different optimizers and learning rates and choosing the most optimal one. This was done for each architecture. A module was used to calculate the steepest gradient and use the findings to figure out the most optimal optimizer with the most optimal Learning rate. Figure 3, 4, and 5 shows the steepest gradient for three different optimizers.

After identifying the optimal set of hyperparameters, each architecture was evaluated, and the best one was chosen for additional fine-tuning. We show the performance

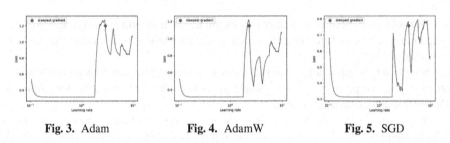

Fig. 3. Adam   **Fig. 4.** AdamW   **Fig. 5.** SGD

difference between the three architectures based on Accuracy, Precision, and Recall in Table 3.

Table 3. Model Comparison

Architecture Used	Accuracy	Precision	Recall	F1
Simple LSTM	94.80	0.923	0.963	0.942
LSTM with Embedding	97.80	0.923	0.974	0.982
Seq-to-Seq LSTM	98.95	0.992	0.983	0.974

Figure 6 shows a comparison of the three tested approaches in form of Taylor Diagram.

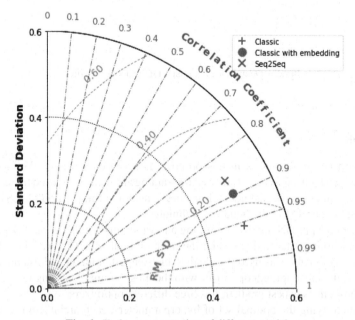

Fig. 6. Taylor representation of different models

Based on these results we selected Seq2Seq LSTM with Embedding as our final model architecture. We further re-evaluate the selected model for its best configuration. Figures 7, 8, 9 and 10 shows the results of training and evaluating different configurations for 10 iterations based on the different number of LSTM layers, Hidden state size, different activation functions, and different batch sizes.

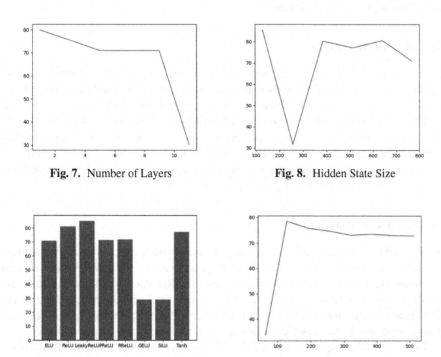

Fig. 7. Number of Layers   **Fig. 8.** Hidden State Size

Fig. 9. Activation Functions   **Fig. 10.** Batch Size

The finalized model was trained for 30 iterations and validated on dataset 4. The model was able to accurately identify previously unseen DoS/DDoS packets with an accuracy of 98.95%, which was the highest achieved with this approach.

In this study, we showed that log-based methodologies for detecting Dos/DDoS attacks are becoming obsolete and how the application of Artificial Neural Networks and Machine Learning Techniques is becoming more prominent in this field. This study also shows that there are still some gaps left for improvement in current work. We prove that by utilizing LSTM based Sequence-to-Sequence architecture for the said task and comparing it with other methodologies. Clearly the proposed method outperforms rest of the techniques, as it can be clearly seen in Table 3 and Fig. 6 above. This study also contributes new data collection and utilization techniques that could be used as a base for future studies.

4　DDoS Strategies

Our methodology is based on the TCP SYN Flood attack. The impact of the attack is recorded in all benign machines connected to the network in terms of Response time, Status codes, etc. Below we discuss the impact of DDoS attacks and a primitive technology to detect such attacks.

4.1　Bandwidth Analysis

Bandwidth analysis is a technique used to detect and mitigate DoS/DDoS attacks. During a DDoS attack, an attacker floods a network with traffic from multiple sources in an attempt to overload the system and disrupt service [34]. Bandwidth analysis can be used to identify the attack and the type of attack being used. This information can then be used to take appropriate countermeasures, such as blocking traffic from the identified sources or implementing rate limiting to mitigate the attack. Additionally, monitoring the traffic flow over time can also help identify patterns that may indicate an ongoing attack, allowing for early detection and preve2ntion [35].

4.2　Resource Consumption

During a DDoS attack, an attacker floods a network with traffic from multiple sources in an attempt to overload the system and disrupt service. One of the ways this is done is by consuming resources on the targeted system [31]. Resource consumption attacks are designed to consume resources such as CPU, memory, and network bandwidth, making the targeted system unavailable to legitimate users. There are several types of resource consumption attacks such as CPU, Memory, and bandwidth consumption attacks.

In our case, the impact of the attacks can be observed on non-malicious machines attempting to communicate with the targeted server.

As illustrated in Figs. 11, 12, 13 and 14, during an attack, the response time from the server increases due to the overload caused by excessive DoS/DDoS requests, resulting in the inability to promptly process legitimate requests.

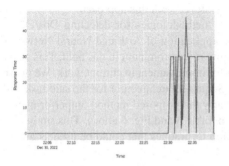

Fig. 11. Dataset 1 Response Time

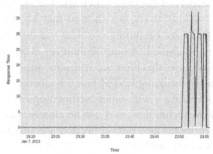

Fig. 12. Dataset 2 Response Time

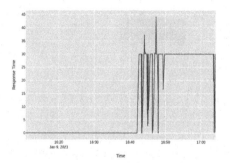

Fig. 13. Dataset 3 Response Time

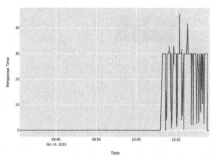

Fig. 14. Dataset 4 Response Time

Figures 15, 16, 17 and 18 shows that during an attack, a higher number of 500 status codes are returned, indicating that the server encountered an internal error and was unable to process the request and provide a valid response.

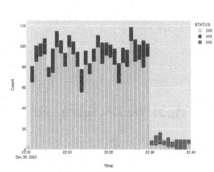

Fig. 15. Dataset 1 status count

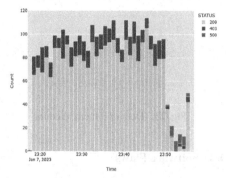

Fig. 16. Dataset 2 status count

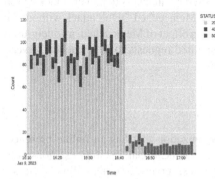

Fig. 17. Dataset 3 status count

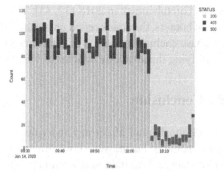

Fig. 18. Dataset 4 status count

Figures 19, 20, 21 and 22 illustrates a comparison of various HTTP methods in terms of the count and status codes returned by the server.

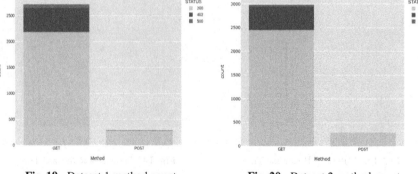

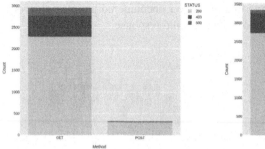

Fig. 19. Dataset 1 method count

Fig. 20. Dataset 2 method count

Fig. 21. Dataset 3 method count

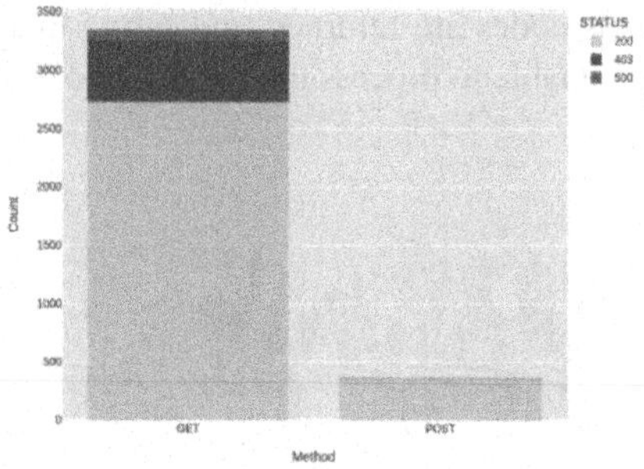

Fig. 22. Dataset 4 method count

4.3 Software Flaws

Software flaws, also known as vulnerabilities, can be exploited by attackers. These flaws can exist in a wide range of software, including operating systems, web servers, and application software. These flaws are often used by attackers to launch attacks, such as the GitHub attack in 2018 [32, 33]. This was a Memcached DDoS attack without the use of botnets, the attack relied on the amplification effect of Memcached, a widely-used database caching system. The attackers sent spoofed requests to Memcached servers, amplifying the attack by a factor of 50,000 times.

5 Conclusion

DDoS attacks can affect any individual or organization that has an online presence. This includes businesses, government agencies, educational institutions, non-profit organizations, and individuals who operate websites, servers, or other online services.

And that's why a robust protection mechanism is required to prevent such attacks. As we have seen before, the conventional methods for detecting DoS/DDoS attacks include log-based approaches which are not very efficient. While Modern approaches like Machine Learning and Artificial Neural Networks have been proven very effective for this task, they still have room for improvements. This research aims to fill those gaps while showing relevant results. To counter the imbalance issue seen in previous studies, this study proposes a novel data collection and data utilization approach. This study also shows comparison between various deep learning model architectures and their configurations on this task. The final trained model was able to accurately identify previously unseen DoS/DDoS packets with an accuracy of 98.95%, which was the highest achieved with this approach. For future work, we aim to propose a multi-model approach for classifying DoS/DDoS attacks in both TCP and UDP networks, as well as incorporating functionality to reduce load during attacks.

References

1. Almajali, M.H., Ghazwi, M., Alqudah, F.T., ALmahasnah, M.J., Alajarmeh, H.H., Masarweh, A.A.: The legal aspects and the enhanced role of cybersecurity in protecting the electronic voting process in the context of Jordan Parliament election law no. (4) of 2022. Inf. Sci. Lett. **12**(8), 2839–2848 (2023)
2. Yihunie, F., Abdelfattah, E., Odeh, A.: Analysis of ping of death DoS and DDoS attacks. In: 2018 IEEE Long Island Systems, Applications and Technology Conference, LISAT 2018 (2018). https://doi.org/10.1109/LISAT.2018.8378010
3. Eliyan, L.F., Di Pietro, R.: DoS and DDoS attacks in software defined networks: a survey of existing solutions and research challenges. Future Gener. Comput. Syst. **122**, 149–171 (2021). https://doi.org/10.1016/j.future.2021.03.011
4. Zebari, R.R., Zeebaree, S.R.M., Jacksi, K.: Impact ANALYSIS of HTTP and SYN flood DDoS attacks on apache 2 and IIS 10.0 web servers. In: ICOASE 2018 - International Conference on Advanced Science and Engineering (2018). https://doi.org/10.1109/ICOASE.2018.8548783
5. Haider, S., et al.: A deep CNN ensemble framework for efficient DDoS attack detection in software defined networks. IEEE Access **8**, 53972–53983 (2020). https://doi.org/10.1109/ACCESS.2020.2976908
6. Elbarougy, R., Aboghrara, E., Behery, G.M., Younes, Y.M., El-Badry, N.M.: COVID-19 detection on chest x-ray images by combining histogram-oriented gradient and convolutional neural network features. Inf. Sci. Lett. **12**(5), 2247–2260 (2023)
7. Cheng, J., Liu, Y., Tang, X., Sheng, V.S., Li, M., Li, J.: DDoS attack detection via multi-scale convolutional neural network. Comput. Mater. Continua **62**(3), 1317–1333 (2020). https://doi.org/10.32604/cmc.2020.06177
8. Wani, A.R., Rana, Q.P., Saxena, U., Pandey, N.: Analysis and detection of DDoS attacks on cloud computing environment using machine learning techniques. In: Proceedings - 2019 Amity International Conference on Artificial Intelligence, AICAI 2019 (2019). https://doi.org/10.1109/AICAI.2019.8701238
9. Saied, A., Overill, R.E., Radzik, T.: Detection of known and unknown DDoS attacks using Artificial Neural Networks. Neurocomputing **172**, 385–393 (2016). https://doi.org/10.1016/j.neucom.2015.04.101
10. Peraković, D., Periša, M., Cvitić, I., Husnjak, S.: Model for detection and classification of DDoS traffic based on artificial neural network. Telfor J. **9**(1), 26–31 (2017). https://doi.org/10.5937/telfor1701026P
11. Dar, S.A., Palanivel, S., Geetha, M.K., Balasubramanian, M.: Mouth image based person authentication using DWLSTM and GRU. Inf. Sci. Lett. **11**(3), 853–862 (2022)
12. Hussein, S., et al.: Diagnosis of COVID-19 from X-rays using recurrent neural network. Inf. Sci. Lett. **11**(6), 2279–2284 (2022)

13. Yuan, X., Li, C., Li, X.: DeepDefense: identifying DDoS attack via deep learning. In: 2017 IEEE International Conference on Smart Computing, SMARTCOMP 2017 (2017). https://doi.org/10.1109/SMARTCOMP.2017.7946998
14. Eltahir, M.E., Ahmed, O.S.: Cybersecurity awareness in African higher education institutions: a case study of Sudan. Inf. Sci. Lett. **12**(1), 171–183 (2023)
15. Alghenaim, M.F., Abu-Bakar, N.A., Abdul-Rahim, F.B.: Reviewing cybersecurity awareness training tools used to address phishing attack at the workplace. Inf. Sci. Lett. **11**(2), 391–398 (2022)
16. Wang, H., Xu, L., Gu, G.: FloodGuard: a DoS attack prevention extension in software-defined networks. In: Proceedings of the International Conference on Dependable Systems and Networks, vol. 2015-September (2015). https://doi.org/10.1109/DSN.2015.27
17. Singh, S., Khan, R.A., Agrawal, A.: Prevention mechanism for infrastructure based Denial-of-Service attack over software Defined Network. In: International Conference on Computing, Communication and Automation, ICCCA 2015 (2015). https://doi.org/10.1109/CCAA.2015.7148442
18. Al-Sherideh, A.S., et al.: Development of a secure model for mobile government applications in Jordan. J. Stat. Appl. Pro. **13**(1), 145–155 (2024)
19. Abuasal, S., Alsarayra, K., Alyabroodie, Z.: Designing a standard-based approach for security of healthcare systems. J. Stat. Appl. Pro. **13**(1), 419–434 (2024)
20. Bedi, H., Roy, S., Shiva, S.: Mitigating congestion-based denial of service attacks with active queue management. In: GLOBECOM - IEEE Global Telecommunications Conference (2013). https://doi.org/10.1109/GLOCOM.2013.6831276
21. Giotis, K., Androulidakis, G., Maglaris, V.: A scalable anomaly detection and mitigation architecture for legacy networks via an OpenFlow middlebox. Secur. Commun. Netw. **9**(13), 1958–1970 (2016). https://doi.org/10.1002/sec.1368
22. Yevsieieva, O., Helalat, S.M.: Analysis of the impact of the slow HTTP DOS and DDOS attacks on the cloud environment. In: 2017 4th International Scientific-Practical Conference Problems of Infocommunications Science and Technology, PIC S and T 2017 - Proceedings, vol. 2018-January (2017). https://doi.org/10.1109/INFOCOMMST.2017.8246453
23. Mahadev, Kumar, V., Kumar, K.: Classification of DDoS attack tools and its handling techniques and strategy at application layer. In: Proceedings - 2016 International Conference on Advances in Computing, Communication and Automation (Fall), ICACCA 2016 (2016). https://doi.org/10.1109/ICACCAF.2016.7749002
24. Ivanova, V., Tashev, T., Draganov, I.: Detection of IoT based DDoS attacks by network traffic analysis using feedforward neural networks. Int. J. Circuits Syst. Signal Process. **16**, 653–662 (2022). https://doi.org/10.46300/9106.2022.16.81
25. Lamkuche, H.S., Pramod, D., Onker, V., Katiya, S.A., Lamkuche, G.S., Hiremath, G.R.: SAL – a lightweight symmetric cipher for Internet-of-Things. Int. J. Innov. Technol. Explor. Eng. **8**(11), 521–528 (2019). https://doi.org/10.35940/ijitee.K1088.09811S19
26. Bhardwaj, A., Mangat, V., Vig, R.: Hyperband tuned deep neural network with well posed stacked sparse autoencoder for detection of ddos attacks in cloud. IEEE Access **8**, 181916–181929 (2020). https://doi.org/10.1109/ACCESS.2020.3028690
27. Lamkuche, H.S., Pramod, D.: CSL: FPGA implementation of lightweight block cipher for power-constrained devices. Int. J. Inf. Comput. Secur. **12**(2–3), 349–377 (2020). https://doi.org/10.1504/IJICS.2020.105185
28. Sarma, S.N.S., Lamkuche, H.H., Umamaheswari, S.: A review of secret sharing schemes. Res. J. Inf. Technol. 5(2) (2013). https://doi.org/10.3923/rjit.2013.67.72
29. Church, K.W.: Word2Vec. Nat. Lang. Eng. **23**(1) (2017). https://doi.org/10.1017/s1351324916000334
30. Sutskever, I., Vinyals, O., Le, Q.V.: Sequence to sequence learning with neural networks. Adv. Neural Inf. Process. Syst. **4**(January) (2014)

31. Ramesh, A., Pradhan, V., Lamkuche, H.: Understanding and analysing resource utilization, costing strategies and pricing models in cloud computing. In: Journal of Physics: Conference Series, vol. 1964, no. 4 (2021). https://doi.org/10.1088/1742-6596/1964/4/042049

32. Kumar, S., Kumar, D., Lamkuche, H.S.: TPA auditing to enhance the privacy and security in cloud systems. J. Cyber Secur. Mobility **10**(3), 537–568 (2021). https://doi.org/10.13052/jcsm2245-1439.1033

33. Lamkuche, H.S., Kondaveety, V.B., Sapparam, V.L., Singh, S., Rajpurkar, R.D.: Enhancing the security and performance of cloud for e-governance infrastructure: Secure E-MODI. Int. J. Cloud Appl. Comput. **12**(1) (2022). https://doi.org/10.4018/IJCAC.2022010108

34. Lamkuche, H.S., Singh, K., Shirkhedkar, K.: A lightweight block cipher for cloud-based healthcare systems. In Computing, Communication and Learning: First International Conference, CoCoLe 2022, Warangal, India, 27–29 October 2022, Proceedings, pp. 3–14. Springer, Cham (2023). https://doi.org/10.1007/978-3-031-21750-0_1

35. Agarwal, D., Gurele, S., Lamkuche, H.S.: SAILFISH-I: a lightweight block cipher for cloud-enabled fog devices. In 2022 IEEE 6th Conference on Information and Communication Technology (CICT), pp. 1–6. IEEE (2022)

Business Analytics, Blockchain, and IoT

Link Adaptation Performance in the Narrow Band Internet of Things

Raed S. M. Daraghma[1][✉], Hacene Fouchal[2], Yousef-Awwad Daraghmi[1],
Marwane Ayaida[2], and Eman Daraghmi[1]

[1] Department of Telecommunication Technology Engineering,
Faculty of Engineering and Technology, Palestine Technical, Tulkarm, Palestine
R.daraghmeh@ptuk.edu.ps
[2] Department of Mathematics, Mechanics and Computer Science, University de Reims, Reims,
France

Abstract. The aim of the paper was to explore the effectiveness of NB-IOT Narrowband Physical Downlink Shared Channel (NPDSCH), which the 3GPP released in version 13 to serve as a mobile communications feature. When compared to previous cellular technologies, NB-expanded IOT's coverage, data rate, latency, and battery lifetime are its key characteristics. These NB-IOT capabilities make it extremely useful for IOT manufacturing and enable the upcoming technology that may be applied in a variety of situations of deployments, including Agriculture, smart cities, and health, and WSNs. The primary goal of this survey is to evaluate the execution of various NB-IOT grid characteristics with acceptable rates of error in uplink and downlink connections. The effectiveness of the distinct approaches was estimated based on how well they met the requirements of IOT sector. In order to evaluate the various criterion sets and determine which options offer the optimal cost-efficiency trade-offs for building an NB-IOT grid, software simulations were employed. According to the findings, data that is sent in a reduced Transport Block Size (TBS) units experiences less errors than data that is sent in a bigger size units. The outcomes also reveal that, in the propagation channel model, the ER rises as the Doppler frequency rises. The findings also demonstrate that as the subject of modulation and coding scheme (IMCS) increases, the ER rises; finally, the results indicate that an increasing number of antennas is nearly optimal for all parameters.

Keywords: Transport Block Size · NBIOT · Doppler frequency · Modulation and coding index

1 Introduction

Since IEEE 802.11 is the standard used for most IOT connections, their range is constrained to a few meters. Cellular networks are ideal for this use since long-range connections are frequently needed in IOT applications. Depending on the mode of operation, NB-IOT is a technology that makes this kind of communication possible utilizing either GSM or LTE carriers. NBOT allows for long-range communications as well as a large

A. M. A. Musleh Al-Sartawi et al. (Eds.): ICGER 2023, CCIS 1999, pp. 57–68, 2024.
https://doi.org/10.1007/978-3-031-50518-8_5

number of connected devices in a small space, whereas IEEE 802.11 would be rendered useless in this situation due to excessive interference.

In paper [1], The performance of the recommended model of the system and its derivations is confirmed by the author's demonstration that the systematic expressions completely reflect the simulated ones. This paper's task offers helpful guidelines for NB-IoT system implementation and coexistence test.

The author addressed in article [2] 3 GPP LPWA technology criteria in Release 13 and its physical layer (PHY) method is being practiced. He focused on the benefits and incorporation of Physical communication routes exist at the NB-IOT base station (BS) and UE levels.

In paper [3], Over NB-IOT grids, the author mentioned the NPDCCH time change and the NB-IOT schedule issue. The goal is to reduce the amount of radio resource used. He showed that the issue with the timeframe is NP-hard and that it cannot be approximated with a percentage greater than 3/2.

The author introduced a type of coverage extension known as Narrow Band Timing Advance (NB-TA) in article [4], which can extend NB-IOT range coverage beyond 35 km, and the design's practicability was demonstrated by a practical calculation across a medium of the sea. The author of article [5] proposed a hybrid connection alternation technique based on all three merits, with the objective of achieving the greatest possible latency and coverage. He designed and solved an issue of optimization that calculates the ideal value of repetitions, bandwidth, and MCS to do this.

According to paper [6], NB-IOT and eMTC will be implemented. As a consequence, data rate, power dispersion, latency, and spectral efficiency are investigated in several coverage scenarios. Despite the fact that both technologies make use of the same power-saving strategies [7, 8] and repetitions to increase the connection area, the testing indicated differences in data size, rate, and coupling loss. In paper [9], to forecast the peak performance in a particular script with the specified settings of specific parameters for the purpose, the author devised an NB-IOT survey and a numerical pattern of network fit. The author of study [10] discussed typical smart grid implementations and determined the compatibility of NB-IOT. Additionally, Monte Carlo simulations [11, 12] are utilized to precisely predict how well NB-IOT will function in ideal smart grid communication environments, such as urban and rural areas.

In paper [13], The author examined NB-IOT event-triggered reporting in terms of time-to-live (TTL) communicate accuracy in outage demodulation and frequency using an example would be a smart parking lot application. In paper [14], The technical distinctions between Sigfox, LoRa, and NB-IoT at the MAC layer are presented and evaluated. The author used his simulation to assess how well various technologies performed in terms of of Packet error arte.

The author provided the preliminary empirical power consumption data on two NB-IOT units that are publicly accessible in article [15].

In paper [16], for the credibility of NB-IOT duties, the efficiency of the NB-IOT grid should be improved in both the downlink and the uplink. In terms of NB-IOT downlink call success rate, for calling in multicellular interference mediums, the author presented the modulation and coding schema (MCS) optimization states.

In paper [17], the author discussed the use of emerging NB-IOT radio technology that was recently confirmed by 3GPP, improvements to active strategies for fundamental wireless connectivity.

In paper [18], the procedure for receiving NB-IOT user equipment and the eNB employee policy were both taken into account when the author created a random arrival transit pattern. Then, he examined Latency in the network for the NB-IOT pattern of arrival using the stochastic network calculus (SNC).

In paper [19], NB-IOT with a single cell disseminated as part of the 5G Test Network (5GTN) and managed by a smart-campus micro-operator, and the author commented on its effective performance. The University of Oulu's vast, interconnected interior medium served as the setting for the collection of the empirical data used in this study.

The contribution of article [20] is the study, synthesis, and comparison of some of the important presenting schemes in terms of overcoming the obstacles of NB-IOT development. The author provided a smart parking method in article [21]. To transmit data from the sensor node, the proposed system employs the NB-IOT module, a revolutionary cellular technology developed for LPWA applications.

In paper [22], the author proposed an NB-IOT system in order to implement smart metering. The ratted number of UE that this equipment can enhance coverage in terms of LTE technology.

In paper [23], the author used exact in-field measurements under identical implementation settings to compare Lora WAN and NB-IOT performance in order to make an objective assessment of energy efficiency, longevity, service quality, and coverage.

The basic purpose of this study [24] is to establish the performance of unique NBIOT network characteristics with acceptable rates of error in uplink and downlink links. The performance of the distinct methods investigated in order to ascertain their effectiveness in respect to the requirements of the IOT sector.

Paper [25], the research analyzes several authentication techniques for boosting security while keeping calculation and transmission time to a minimum. On the three levels, several machine-learning methods, such as decision trees, logistic regression, and support vector machines, are employed for data analysis. The suggested architecture is tested on actual data made out of medical vital indicators utilizing CloudSim, iFogSim, and ns3-NBIOT.

In paper [26], the effect of various interference measuring approaches on the flexibility and throughput performance of Narrowband Internet of Things links is explored. Different interference measurement methodologies are defined and analyzed, as well as their key process concepts, including technique overhead features, and detailed performance evaluation and comparison is carried out. For more application for the IOT, kindly refer to [27, 28].In this paper, we examine the following simulation parameters: BLER to SNR with various coding schemes, resource units, number of repetitions, the transmit block size, channel estimator reference signal, and propagation channel mode, such as Doppler frequency, are all-important considerations.

The following is how the paper is organized. The deployment modes for NB-IOT are described in Sect. 2. Section 3 assessment and simulation result. In Sect. 4, a conclusion is presented.

2   NBIOT Deployment Modes

The NB-IOT technology is the best for LPWA implementation due to a number of intrinsic properties.

Additionally, about 80% of all LPWA use cases, including those for smart grid, wearables, smart meters, and smart parking, require low power consumption. Additionally, everything around us can become intelligent because to the accessibility of huge connections. It is preferable to have roughly 50K devices per cell to achieve this; this is feasible if there are 1500 households per sq. m and 40 devices each family. Additionally, NB-IOT promises 20 + dB coverage, 1000× connections, and a 10-year lifespan while use just 200 kHz of bandwidth, while additional technologies, such as eMTC and SigFox give far less performance (Fig. 1).

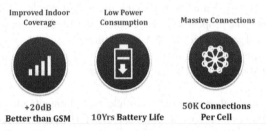

Fig. 1. NBIOT Inherent capabilities

Guard Band, In Band, and Stand Alone are the three deployment choices are provided by the recently 3GPP-agreed NB-IOT technology for LPWA deployment. Guard band deployment makes use of the bandwidth protected in the present LTE network's guard band, while standalone deployment primarily makes use of fresh capacity. Although in-band deployment employs the same, resource block in the LTE carrier of the current LTE network (Fig. 2).

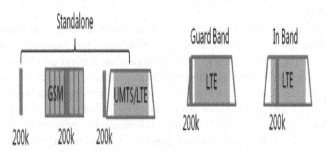

Fig. 2. Three deployment scenarios of NB-IOT

In conclusion, it is evident that FDMA (GMSK) deployment choices in the Standalone and Guard bands tend to provide the greatest results in terms of enhanced interior coverage, as well as cheaper cost and a 20% reduction in power usage.

3   Data Transmission Security and Challenges at NBIOT

It is useful to define specific security goals while discussing the security features of various NBIOT systems. Each frequency band at NBIOT presents its own set of operational challenges and benefits. The data transmission scheme governs how information is encoded as a continuous stream of bits. The modulation technique governs how that stream of bits is sent between the tag and the reader. To transmit the baseband code, in most cases, RF communications modify a high frequency carrier signal. The massive difference in power between the signal emitted by the reader and the signal emitted by the tag is a trouble in data transmission systems. In some cases, the difference may be in the 80–90 dB range, making the return signal is undetectable. To avoid this problem, the reflected signal is sometimes modulated onto a sub-carrier before being modulated onto the carrier. Although universally deploying NBIOT tags may provide various possible security advantages, it may also reveal new privacy dangers. However, NBIOT systems can enable intrusive or time-consuming security techniques like airline passenger and luggage tracking.

4   Applications and Future of NBIOT

Palestine has one of the Asian region's fastest-growing economies. Its economy is growing by the day. It is a country with a population of nearly 5 million people. It has grown in recent years in industries such as clothing, industry, and infrastructure, transportation, farming, information technology, and so on. Technology is constantly improving, and its application is expanding at a rapid pace. Because of the use of modern technology, everyday tasks are getting lot simpler. And faster. That is why we must act immediately consider the right use of technology to improve our daily lives, which will lead to greater national development. The NBIOT is a recently created IOT technology based on LTE-A systems that has the potential to be extremely valuable in the context of Palestine, which will use 4G in future. NBIOT is an appropriate technology in this case because of its low cost and compatibility with earlier network technologies like as GSM, WCDMA, and so on, as well as decrease installation and maintenance complexity and expense, as previously noted. Palestine is currently deploying technology-based livelihood improvement solutions. It is paving the way for the creation of a smart city system, a smart grid system, an intelligent home automation system, an intelligent agricultural system, an intelligent industrial automation system, and so on.

5   Analysis and Simulation

The outcomes of our simulations are presented in this part. The following four collections of simulation findings have been created:

- Doppler frequency versus block ER simulation.
- Block ER simulation vs. Antenna Count.
- Block ER simulation of various coding and modulation schemes.
- Block ER simulation of different repetitions vs SNR.

Block ER simulation of different Transport Block Size.

The next subsections display and analyze the outcomes according to the timing noted above. The SNR, also known as the desired signal power to undesirable signal power ratio, is shown on the horizontal axis and is represented by the following form:

$$SNR = \text{power of the signal/power of the noise} \tag{1}$$

Higher SNR levels indicate a flawless signal type with minimal interference. The horizontal axis is the BER, defined as the relationship between BE and the total amount of bits transmitted and expressed in the following form:

$$BER = \text{Number of BE/Total amount of bits sent} \tag{2}$$

Utilizing NPDSCH scheduling, we create an adaptation technique for 200 kHz bandwidth in the NBIOT network. It is necessary to implement the link adaptation for NBIOT networks in three dimensions:

The level of coding and modulation that is chosen:

1) The calculation of the repetition number
2) Configuration of the channel estimator

By selecting the right number of repetitions (NRS) and Doppler frequency, it is necessary to achieve a trade-off between transmit validity and system throughput when using the link modification design.

Figure 3 shows a block ER versus Transport Block Size (TBS), the SNR was chosen to be 0 dB with one repetition rate, the results demonstrate that even under poor channel conditions, we can accurately decode the message when we employ a large number of Transport Block Sizes (large block ER), the primary method proposed by NBIOT to provide strengthened coverage with low complexity and significant throughput results is the number of transmitted blocks.

Figure 4 displays a block ER versus TBS with an SNR of -6 dB and 32 repetitions per second. This figure demonstrates that even though the BLER does not necessarily increase when we use more transport blocks, it is still necessary to get a tradeoff between SNR and BLER in the link modification design.

We can infer from Fig. 5 that the probability of error increases when data is conveyed with a greater modulation and coding scheme. To reduce the ER, NB-IOT operators using modulation and coding values of fewer than four should deliver information (IMCS 4). By lowering the Modulation and Coding Scheme Index (IMCS) by one, we were able to remedy this issue.

From Figs. 6, 7, we compare the error performance of the NB-IOT system using distinct number of antennas in the downlink with different number of repetitions. Figures 6, 7 show the results of this simulation, number of repetitions (exactly one and 32) with one and two antennas, the results show that when the SNR increases, the ER shrinks significantly. In other hand, increasing number of repetitions is preferable in this case for instants if we compare the error at value SNR -4 dB, the error at this value is zero when we used 32 repetitions and 0.25 when we used one repetition, also increasing the number of antennas is needed to decrease the block rate error.

The purpose of the final two simulations was to contrast how the NB-IOT system performed in terms of errors when employing various Doppler frequencies in the downlink. Figures 8 and 9 display the simulation's outcome. The result shows that the error rate becomes comparably extremely tiny with a reduced number of Doppler frequencies. A lower Doppler frequency value (5Hz) was used.

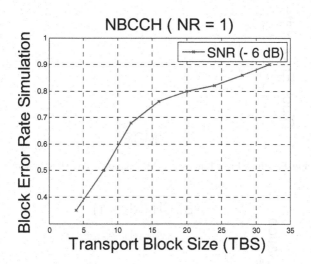

Fig. 3. Block Error Rate versus Transport Block Size.

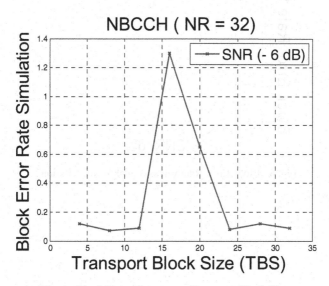

Fig. 4. Block Error Rate versus Transport Block Size.

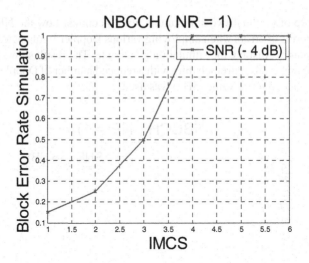

Fig. 5. Block Error Rate versus Modulation and Coding Scheme

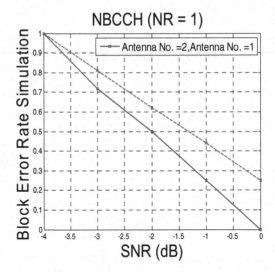

Fig. 6. Block Error Rate versus Signal to Noise Ration.

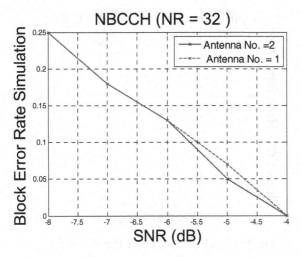

Fig. 7. Block Error Rate versus Signal to Noise Ration.

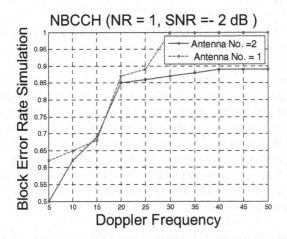

Fig. 8. Block Error Rate versus Doppler Frequency

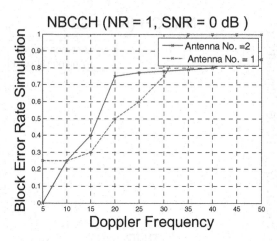

Fig. 9. Block Error Rate versus Doppler Frequency.

6   Conclusion

When it comes to deployment, NBIOT is a flexible technology that supports three different types of deployment (namely: standalone, in-band and guard band). It is simple for NB-IOT to be compatible with long-term evolution because the technology's framework and uplink and downlink pathways are identical to those of long-term evolution. This paper's main goal was to analyze NB-IOT's performance. The outcomes showed that the main NB-IOT coefficient settings are what determine the error performance. The performance of errors improves as the transport block size decreases. Technically, the likelihood of an error when sending data decreases the more frequently the same data is delivered. The likelihood of error increases with the amount of data you send instantly while using the Antenna number and TBS. The more sub frame repetitions there are. Lower Doppler frequency results in improved error performance, which is inversely correlated with error performance.

Acknowledgements. This research is supported by the Al Maqdisi initiative, a French-Palestinian cooperation organized by the French Ministries of Europe and Foreign Affairs (MEAE) and the French Ministry of Higher Education, Research and Innovation (MESRI), and by the Consulate General of France in Jerusalem.

References

1. Yang, B., Zhang, L., Qiao, D., Zhao, G., Imran, M.A.: Narrowband Internet of Things (NBIOT) and LTE systems co-existence analysis. In: IEEE Global Communications Conference (GLOBECOM), pp. 9–13. Enlighten Publications, Abu Dhabi (2018)
2. Kanj, M., Savaux, V., Le Guen, M.: A tutorial on NBIOT physical layer design. IEEE Commun. Surv. Tutor. **22**(4), 2408–2446 (2020)
3. Yu, Y.J.: NPDCCH period adaptation and downlink scheduling for NBIOT networks. IEEE Internet Things J. **8**(2), 962–975 (2021)

4. Ha, S., Seo, H., Moon, Y., Lee, D., Jeong, J.: A novel solution for NBIOT cell coverage expansion. In: Global Internet of Things Summit (GIOTS), pp. 1–5. IEEE, Bilbao (2018)
5. Ravi, S., Zand, P., El Soussi, M., Nabi, M.: Evaluation, modeling and optimization of coverage enhancement methods of NBIOT. In: IEEE 30th Annual International Symposium on Personal, Indoor and Mobile Radio Communications (PIMRC), pp. 1–17. Cornell University, Istanbul (2019)
6. Jörke, P., Falkenberg, R., Wietfeld, C.: Power consumption analysis of NBIOT and eMTC in challenging smart city environments. In: IEEE Globecom Workshops (GC Wkshps), pp. 1–6. IEEE, Abu Dhabi (2018)
7. Reda, I., Elzefzafy, H., Al-Rawi, O.Y.M.: Effect of luminaries' arrangement and type on visual comfort and energy consumption. Inf. Sci. Lett. **10**(3), 417–426 (2021)
8. Ismail, F.B., Randhawa, G.S., Al-Bazi, A., Alkahtani, A.A.: Intelligent optimization systems for maintenancescheduling of power plant generators. Inf. Sci. Lett. **12**(3), 1319–1332 (2023)
9. Feltrin, L., Condoluci, M., Mahmoodi, T., Dohler, M., Verdone, R.: NBIOT: performance estimation and optimal configuration. In: 24th European Wireless Conference, pp. 1–6. VDE VERLAG GMBH, Catania (2018)
10. Li, Y., Cheng, X., Cao, Y., Wang, D., Yang, L.: Smart choice for the smart grid: narrowband Internet of Things (NBIOT). IEEE Internet Things J. **5**(3), 1505–1515 (2018)
11. Nkechi, E.M., Chekwube, B.D., Paul, O.C., Chizoba, K.L.: A monte carlo simulation comparison of methods of detecting outliers in time series data. J. Stat. Appl. Pro. **11**(3), 819–834 (2022)
12. Singh, U., Singh, S.K., Yadav, A.S.: Bayesian estimation for extension of exponential distribution under progressive type-II censored data using markov chain monte carlo method. J. Stat. Appl. Pro. **4**(2), 275–283 (2015)
13. Lin, Y., Tseng, H., Lin, Y., Chen, L.: NBIOTtalk: a service platform for fast development of NBIOT applications. IEEE Internet Things J. **6**(1), 928–939 (2019)
14. Mroue, H., Nasser, A., Hamrioui, S., Parrein, B., Motta-Cruz, E., Rouyer, G.: MAC layer-based evaluation of IoT technologies: Lora, SigFox and NBIOT. In: IEEE Middle East and North Africa Communications Conference (MENACOMM), pp. 1–5. IEEE, Jounieh (2018)
15. Lauridsen, M., Krigslund, R., Rohr, M., Madueno, G.: An empirical NBIOT power consumption model for battery lifetime estimation. In: IEEE 87th Vehicular Technology Conference (VTC Spring), pp. 1–5. IEEE, Porto (2018)
16. Chung, H., Lee, S., Jeong, J.: NBIOT optimization on paging MCS and coverage level. In: 15th International Symposium on Wireless Communication Systems (ISWCS), pp. 1–5. IEEE, Lisbon (2018)
17. Petrov, V., et al.: Vehicle-based relay assistance for opportunistic crowd sensing over narrowband IoT (NBIOT). IEEE Internet Things J. **5**(5), 3710–3723 (2018)
18. Chen, X., Li, Z., Chen, Y., Wang, X.: Performance analysis and uplink scheduling for QoS-aware NBIOT networks in mobile computing. IEEE Access **7**(1), 44404–44415 (2019)
19. Yasmin, R., Pouttu, A., Mikhaylov, K., Niemelä, V., Arif, M., Liinamaa, O.: NBIOT micro-operator for smart campus: performance and lessons learned in 5GTN. In: IEEE Wireless Communications and Networking Conference (WCNC), pp. 1–6. IEEE, Seoul (2020)
20. Migabo, E.M., Djouani, K.D., Kurien, A.M.: The Narrowband Internet of Things (NBIOT) resources management performance state of art, challenges, and opportunities. IEEE Access **8**(1), 97658–97675 (2020)
21. Shi, J., Jin, L., Li, J., Fang, Z.: A smart parking system based on NBIOT and third party payment platform. In: 17th International Symposium on Communications and Information Technologies (ISCIT), pp. 1–5. IEEE, Cairns (2017)
22. Pennacchioni, M., Di Benedette, M., Pecorella, T., Carlini, C., Obino, P.: NBIOT system deployment for smart metering: evaluation of coverage and capacity performances. In: AEIT International Annual Conference, p. 1–6. IEEE, Cagliari (2017)

23. Ballerini, M., Polonelli, T., Brunelli, D., Magno, M., Benini, L.: NBIOT versus Lora WAN: an experimental evaluation for industrial applications. IEEE Trans. Ind. Inf. **16**(12), 7802–7811 (2020)
24. Daraghma, R.S.M: Performance of link adaptation in narrow band internet of things. J. Commun. **17**(3), 210–215 (2022)
25. Daraghmi, Y.-A., Daraghmi, E.Y., Daraghma, R., Fouchal, H., Ayaida, M.: Edge–fog–cloud computing hierarchy for improving performance and security of NBIOT-based health monitoring systems. Sensors **22**(22), 1–17 (2022)
26. Daraghma, R.S.M.: Effect of number of interference on long-term evolution throughput with minimum mean square error-interference rejection combining receiver. Int. J. Commun. Ant. Propagat. (IRECAP) **12**(2), 120–127 (2022)
27. Karar, M.E., Al-Rasheed, M.F., Al-Rasheed, A.F., Reyad, O.: IoT and neural network-based water pumping control system for smart irrigation. Inf. Sci. Lett. **9**(2), 107–112 (2020)
28. Karar, M.E., Alotaibi, F., Al-Rasheed, A., Reyad, O.: A pilot study of smart agricultural irrigation using unmanned aerial vehicles and IoT-based cloud system. Inf. Sci. Lett. **10**(1), 131–140 (2021)

Enhanced Bubble Sorting Visualizer with Sound

Shubham Tiwari, Neha Gupta$^{(\boxtimes)}$, Devendra Chouhan, Ishwarlal Rathod,
and Harsh Vaja

Symbiosis University of Applied Sciences Indore, Indore, India
{neha.gupta,devendra.chouhan,Ishwarlal.rathod}@suas.ac.in

Abstract. In this research paper we are proposing a sorting visualizer with sound is a tool that can assist users in comprehending and learning about different sorting algorithms. It enables them to see in real-time the process of sorting a set of data, such as a list of numbers. The visualizer animates the movement of the data as the algorithm sorts it, making it easy to see how the algorithm works and how the order of the data changes. Sound effects, such as beeps or chimes, can also help the user understand the sorting process by providing an auditory cue for the algorithm's various actions. When the algorithm compares two elements, for example, a beep may be heard, or a chime may be heard when elements are swapped. Sorting visualizers with sound can be used for educational purposes, such as teaching students about different sorting algorithms and how they work. They can also be used by programmers to better understand how specific sorting algorithms work, and to compare the efficiency of different algorithms. Additionally, sorting visualizers can be used to debug sorting code, and to ensure that the algorithm is sorting the data correctly. Overall, sorting visualizers with sound is a powerful tool for understanding, learning, teaching and debugging sorting algorithms. It offers a visual and auditory representation of the algorithm's behavior, making it easy for users to understand the process and identify any errors. This tool can be used to improve understanding of sorting algorithms and to help developers write efficient code.

Keywords: Sorting · Data Structure and Algorithm · JavaScript · Visualizer · beep sound · Bubble Sort

1 Introduction

Sorting algorithms are a fundamental concept in computer science with numerous applications in areas such as data analysis and information retrieval. Understanding and comparing the performance of different sorting algorithms, on the other hand, can be a difficult task, especially for students and practitioners who are new to the field. We propose a novel approach to sorting algorithm visualization in this paper by incorporating sound into the process [1]. We present a sorting visualizer tool that not only visually displays the sorting process but also generates distinct sounds for each sorting step. The tool allows users to choose from a number of sorting algorithms and compare their performance on various input data sets visually and audibly. This research looks

A. M. A. Musleh Al-Sartawi et al. (Eds.): ICGER 2023, CCIS 1999, pp. 69–77, 2024.
https://doi.org/10.1007/978-3-031-50518-8_6

at the design, implementation, and evaluation of the visualizer with sound integration in an educational setting. We also present student and instructor feedback on the tool's effectiveness in improving understanding of sorting algorithms [2, 3]. The goal of this research is to develop a powerful and engaging educational resource that can improve learning experience and sorting algorithm retention.

2 Literature Review

Algorithms and Data Structures are essential components of computing education for any computer professional. In recent years, there has been an increase in the amount of technical schools introducing new methods to help students learn and comprehend algorithms. One proposed system focuses on using visualizations to assist students in understanding concepts. Visualizations have proven to be effective in enhancing comprehension, as students need to understand algorithms at a low level to fully grasp their power. However, current learning methods do not allow for this level of understanding. With the rise of online education through the pandemic, there is a necessity for a platform where teachers can teach procedures easily and assess students at all.

To design actual software, software engineers need to have a thorough considerate of DSA. Algorithm visualizers have been developed over the past few years to provide useful information to enhance understanding. Some examples of algorithm visualizers include an artificial intelligence search algorithm visualizer established by Abu Naser et al. in 2008, a platform named JHAVEPOP created by Furcy David in 2009, and a platform named Visual go designed by Dr. Steven Halim in 2011. These platforms allow students to visualize algorithms step by step and offer explanations of various concepts. A platform for algorithm visualization was also designed by Shaffer C. et al. in 2011, which promotes group learning through forums and discussions.

Learning about algorithms and data structures can be time-consuming as information is scattered across various sources. Algorithm visualizers offer a way for students to access and understand the logic of various algorithms efficiently.

Algorithms and data structures are central components of computer science and should be included in the training of every computer scientist. Extensive knowledge of the subject in recent decades, with an increase in the number of students enrolling in technical institutes that introduce approaches to support and enrich their education [6]. The proposed system focuses on learning and understanding algorithms through visualization. Pictures help students understand concepts. To better understand and grasp the power of algorithms, students need to understand algorithms at a low level, which is not possible with today's learning methods. With the development of the online education system during the pandemic [7], a suitable platform was needed where teachers could easily teach algorithms and assess students remotely. In order to design effective software, every software developer must have a thorough understanding of DSA. Viewers have a proven track record of providing useful information to understand the user. The different algorithm viewers that have been developed so far in the past few years are: Algorithm Finder.

The algorithm viewer was developed historically by Abu Nasser et al. in 2008 [8].

3 Motivation

In unprecedented times like Covid-19, where online education is critical, there is a need for a platform for teachers to effectively teach students. DSA is at the heart of computer engineering and understanding it is critical. Visualization of any topic provides a clear understanding of the topic and aids the learner in quickly grasping the concept. This algorithm was created with the goal of assisting learners in easily grasping and understanding any data structure or algorithm concept, as well as bringing teachers and students together to provide a collaborative platform to facilitate remote learning. The project was created with the goal of assisting students, scholars, and professionals in learning and understanding the concepts of Algorithms through visualization and sound. It also offers a synergetic.

4 Research Methodology

The research methodology for this study on the sorting visualizer with sound integration can be divided into the following steps:

Design and Implementation: The sorting visualizer tool will be designed and implemented using programming languages such as JavaScript and Python. The tool will allow users to select from a variety of sorting algorithms and input data sets. The visualization of the sorting process will be displayed on the screen, while the sound will be generated using a library such as the Web Audio API.

Evaluation: The effectiveness of the sorting visualizer with sound integration will be evaluated in an educational setting. This will involve conducting user studies with students and instructors to gather feedback on the tool's usability, engagement, and effectiveness in improving understanding of sorting algorithms.

Data Collection: Data on the users' interaction with the visualizer will be collected, such as the time taken to sort the data, the amount of swaps made, the number of comparisons made and the number of clicks made on the visualizer.

Data Analysis: The composed data will be analyzed to control the efficiency of the tool in improving understanding of sorting algorithms. This analysis will involve comparing the performance of different sorting algorithms and evaluating the impact of sound integration on user engagement and understanding.

Conclusion and future work: Based on the results of the study, conclusions will be drawn on the effectiveness of the sorting visualizer with sound integration as an educational tool. Suggestions for future work will also be provided, such as the integration of more sorting algorithms, or the addition of more interactive features to the visualizer.

The methodology for this research study on the sorting visualizer with sound integration will consist of several key stages. First, the design and implementation of the sorting visualizer tool will be undertaken. This process will involve utilizing programming languages such as JavaScript and Python to create a user-friendly interface for selecting sorting algorithms and input data sets. The visualization of the sorting process will be displayed on the screen, while unique sounds will be generated for each sorting step, using a library such as the Web Audio API.

Next, the effectiveness of the sorting visualizer with sound integration will be evaluated in an educational setting through user studies with students and instructors. This will involve collecting feedback on the tool's usability, engagement, and effectiveness in enhancing understanding of sorting algorithms.

Data collection will also be a critical aspect of the study, where information on users' interactions with the visualizer will be gathered, such as the time taken to sort the data, the amount of swaps made, the number of comparisons made, and the number of clicks made on the visualizer.

The composed data will then be analysed to regulate the impact of the visualizer with sound integration on users' understanding of sorting algorithms. This analysis will include comparing the performance of different sorting algorithms, and evaluating the effect of sound integration on user engagement and understanding.

Finally, founded on the results of the study, conclusions will be drawn on the effectiveness of the sorting visualizer with sound integration as an educational tool. Furthermore, recommendations for future work will be provided, such as the integration of more sorting algorithms, or the inclusion of more interactive features to the visualizer, in order to further improve its effectiveness as an educational tool.

This bubble sort algorithm is a basic sorting algorithm that compares each next to pair of items in a list and swaps them if they are not in the correct order. This process is repeated until no more swaps are necessary, indicating that the list is sorted. This algorithm, which is a comparison sort, is called "bubble sort" because smaller or larger elements gradually rise to the top of the list as the sorting process continues. Bubble sort has a time complexity of O(n^2).

```
myCanvas.width=500;
myCanvas.height=400;
const margin=30;
const n=15;
const array=[];
let moves=[];
const cols=[];
const spacing=(myCanvas.width-margin*2)/n;
const ctx=myCanvas.getContext("2d");

const maxColumnHeight=200;

init();

let audioCtx=null;

function playNote(freq,type){
    if(audioCtx==null){
        audioCtx=new(
            AudioContext ||
            webkitAudioContext ||
            window.webkitAudioContext
        )();
    }
    const dur=0.2;
    const osc=audioCtx.createOscillator();
    osc.frequency.value=freq;
    osc.start();
    osc.type=type;
    osc.stop(audioCtx.currentTime+dur);

    const node=audioCtx.createGain();
    node.gain.value=0.4;
    node.gain.linearRampToValueAtTime(
        0, audioCtx.currentTime+dur
    );
    osc.connect(node);
    node.connect(audioCtx.destination);
}
```

```javascript
function init(){
    for(let i=0;i<n;i++){
        array[i]=Math.random();
    }
    moves=[];
    for(let i=0;i<array.length;i++){
        const x=i*spacing+spacing/2+margin;
        const y=myCanvas.height-margin-i*3;
        const width=spacing-4;
        const height=maxColumnHeight*array[i];
        cols[i]=new Column(x,y,width,height);
    }
}

function play(){
    moves=bubbleSort(array);
}

animate();

function bubbleSort(array){
    const moves=[];
    do{
        var swapped=false;
        for(let i=1;i<array.length;i++){
            if(array[i-1]>array[i]){
                swapped=true;
                [array[i-1],array[i]]=[array[i],array[i-1]];
                moves.push(
                    {indices:[i-1,i],swap:true}
                );
            }else{
                moves.push(
                    {indices:[i-1,i],swap:false}
                );
            }
        }
    }while(swapped);
    return moves;
}

function animate(){
    ctx.clearRect(0,0,myCanvas.width,myCanvas.height);
    let changed=false;
    for(let i=0;i<cols.length;i++){
        changed=cols[i].draw(ctx)||changed;
    }

    if(!changed && moves.length>0){
        const move=moves.shift();
        const [i,j]=move.indices;
        const waveformType=move.swap?"square":"sine";
        playNote(cols[i].height+cols[j].height,waveformType);
        if(move.swap){
            cols[i].moveTo(cols[j]);
            cols[j].moveTo(cols[i],-1);
            [cols[i],cols[j]]=[cols[j],cols[i]];
        }else{
            cols[i].jump();
            cols[j].jump();
        }
    }

    requestAnimationFrame(animate);
}
```

```
# styles.css
1   body {
2       display: flex;
3       flex-direction: column;
4       align-items: center;
5       color: rgb(24, 31, 51);
6       background-color: #74E8D5;
7       background-image: linear-gradient(110deg, #74E8D5 0%, #0FACE6 100%);
8       font-family: system-ui, -apple-system, BlinkMacSystemFont, 'Segoe UI', Roboto, Oxygen, Ubuntu, Cantarell, 'Open Sans', 'Helvetica Neue', sans-serif;
9   }
10  img{
11      height: 600px;
12      position: relative;
13      left: -500px;
14      top: -700px;
15      border: black;
16      border: solid;
17      border-radius: 20px;
18  }
19  button {
20      /* padding: 5; */
21      border: none;
22      border-radius: 30px;
23      height: 40px;
24      background-color: #37459c;
25      width: 200px;
26      color: white;
27      font-size: 24px;
28      font-weight: 600;
29      margin: 10px;
30      font-family: system-ui, -apple-system, BlinkMacSystemFont, 'Segoe UI', Roboto, Oxygen, Ubuntu, Cantarell, 'Open Sans', 'Helvetica Neue', sans-serif;
31  }
32  hr{
33      color: black;
34
35  }
```

5 Conclusion

A successful implementation of a "sorting algorithm with visualizer and sound" has been achieved. The system has been designed meticulously, ensuring it is free from errors and is both effective and time-saving. With practical experience using this algorithm, we believe that it helps to improve our understanding of the DSA concept, particularly the bubble sort algorithm. This work contributes to solving some problems with similar algorithms.

Our strong mindset has enabled us to research and develop animations that can enhance learning in the classroom. Through this work, we can easily comprehend the sorting process through visualization and sound, as well as explanations. It is simple to understand the efficiency and effectiveness of the bubble sort algorithm with this tool (Figs. 1, 2 and 3).

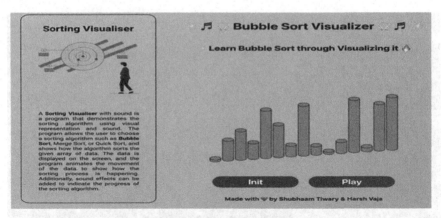

Fig. 1. Bubble Sort Visualizer

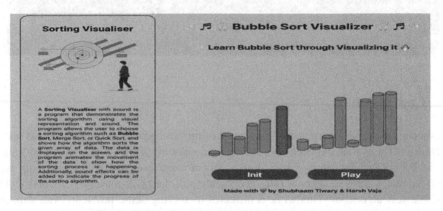

Fig. 2. Bubble Sort Visualizer during sorting Process

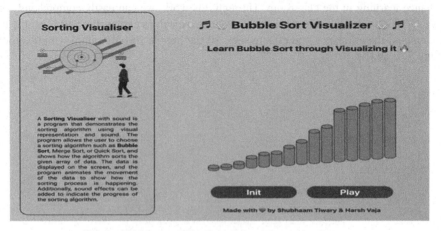

Fig. 3. Bubble Sort Visualizer during after sorting Process

References

1. Storer, Tarjan, R.E.: "A Visualization Tool for Sorting Algorithms" by This paper describes the design and implementation of a visualization tool for sorting algorithms and evaluates its effectiveness in improving understanding of sorting algorithms (1993)
2. Berry, M.W., Kernighan, B.W.: "Visualization of Sorting Algorithms: An Empirical Study" by This study presents a visualization tool for sorting algorithms and evaluates its effectiveness in an educational setting (1991)
3. Storer, Tarjan, R.E.: "A Visualization Tool for Sorting Algorithms" This paper describes the design and implementation of a visualization tool for sorting algorithms and evaluates its effectiveness in improving the understanding of sorting algorithms (1994)
4. Storer, Tarjan, R.E.: "Sorting Algorithm Visualization" by This study presents a visualization tool for sorting algorithms and evaluates its effectiveness in an educational setting (1995)
5. Berry, M.W., Kernighan, B.W.: "Visualizing Sorting Algorithms" by This paper presents a visualization tool for sorting algorithms and evaluates its effectiveness in improving understanding of sorting algorithms (1998)
6. Urquiza-Fuentes, J., Velázquez-Iturbide, J.N.: A survey of successful evaluations of program visualization and algorithm. Animation systems. ACM Trans. Comput. Educ. 9(2), 1–21 (2009). https://doi.org/10.1145/1538234.1538236
7. Mishra, L., Gupta, T., Shree, A.: Online teaching-learning in higher education during the lockdown period of COVID-19 pandemic. Int. J. Educ. Res. Open 1, 100012 (2020). https://doi.org/10.1016/j.ijedro.2020.100012
8. Abu Naser, S.S.: Developing visualization tool for teaching AI searching algorithms. Inf. Technol. J. 7(2), 350–355 (2008). https://doi.org/10.3923/itj.2008.350.355
9. Furcy, D.: JHAVEPOP: visualizing linked-list operations in C++ and Java. J. Comput. Sci. Coll. 25, 32–41 (2009)
10. Halim, S.: Visual go visualising data structures and algorithms through animation. VisuAlgo (2011). https://visualgo.net/en
11. Halim, S., Halim, F.: Competitive Programming 2: this increases the lower bound of programming contests (2011). http://www.lulu.com
12. Shaffer, C.A., Akbar, M., Alon, A.J.D., Stewart, M., Edwards, S.H.: Getting algorithm visualizations into the classroom. In: Proceedings of the 42nd ACM Technical Symposium on Computer Science Education - SIGCSE 2011, p. 121 (2011). https://doi.org/10.1145/1953163.1953204
13. Dozed, A.: Data Structures and Algorithms in Java, 2nd edn. Thomson Publications. Shane, S.: Data Structures, Algorithms, and Applications in Java. McGraw

Machine-Learning Holistic Review in Tourism and Hospitality

Rashed Isam Ashqar[2,3]([✉]) [iD] and Célia M. Q. Ramos[1,2] [iD]

[1] ESGHT, University of Algarve, Faro, Portugal
cmramos@ualg.pt
[2] CinTurs, Faro, Portugal
riashqar@ualg.pt
[3] Al Zaytona University of Science & Technology (ZUST), Salfit, Palestine

Abstract. Artificial intelligence (AI) has been used as an innovative and developing big data analytics technique, and AI has been a significant consideration in hospitality and tourism, as a result of the recent world which is wealth in data and implies the need to consider big data analysis to achieve some insights about the tourism and hospitality business, mainly to know their customer, in terms of preferences and what contributes to their satisfaction. This paper aims to present a holistic view of Machine Learning in tourism and hospitality research and discover the challenges and gaps that need to be focused on by forthcoming investigation. This research found that the holistic literature reviews on this subject are yet limited, restricting our understanding of the historical advancement of Machine learning investigation and its potential prospects. Future research can be extended to a systematic literature review to offer a more comprehensive review of how Machine learning has high light on tourism and hospitality research and suggest the newest growth in this subject.

Keywords: Machine Learning · Big data · Artificial Intelligence · Tourism · Hospitality

1 Introduction

Big data and artificial intelligence (AI) have been receiving important consideration from academics in different fields involving hospitality and tourism (Kwon et al., 2020; Li et al., 2018). However, the research in these areas is still in its early stage (Alazzam et al., 2023; Parpoula et al., 2013). Nowadays, these topics have played a gradually significant part in transforming the whole industry procedures and how businesses evaluate client and marketplace trends (Lv et al., 2022). Moreover, Big data analytics lets investigators and businesses obtain hidden patterns and explore new knowledge and understanding from big data (Medhat et al., 2023; Sayed el al., 2023; Ahmed el al., 2023). Even though AI is one of the developing big data analytics methods, hospitality, and tourism studies have demonstrated slight attempts to manage and investigate 'big hospitality data' through AI (Lee et al., 2021).

In a recent study, Lv et al. (2022) reviewed 270 journal papers published from 2007 to 2020 about big data and AI studies. They showed the application of AI in big data analytics has begun to go into the domain of hospitality and tourism, primarily involving AI methods such as machine learning, deep learning, and AI techniques such as neural networks, fuzzy logic, and heuristic search method (Mwitondi el al., 2016). Also, they stated that researchers primarily studied attitude and behavior at the individual level; performing assessments and marketing administration at the business level; and predicting and business development at the industry level.

Furthermore, AI occasionally known as machine learning (ML), indicates intelligence displayed by machines or computer systems, in distinction to humans' natural intelligence (Lee et al., 2021). Therefore, AI improves technical, analytics, instinctive, and sympathetic duties in the service setting (Huang & Rust, 2018).

The objective of this paper is to present a holistic review of Machine Learning in Tourism and Hospitality research and discover the challenges and gaps that need to be focused on by forthcoming investigation and also identify several datasets used in the research in ML. This paper is structured as follows. Section two presents the related literature about using machine learning in Tourism and Hospitality. Section three reports the data used in the previous studies. Section four presents the discussions and section five concludes the paper.

2 Literature Review

Some studies focused on using artificial neural networks. For example, Sánchez-Medina & Eleazar (2020) used machine learning methods and artificial neural networks optimized with genetic algorithms to forecast hotel booking cancellations. Also, Aakash et al. (2021) examined the features connected to customer satisfaction through the text content of online reviews of Electronic-word-of-mouth (eWOM) and used these features for forecasting the satisfaction levels of customers by integrating text analytics, feature extraction, and Artificial Neural Networks (ANN).

Moreover, Zhao & Tsai (2021) investigated the scale development strategy of high-star hotels and infer the key influencing factors using principal component analysis and partial relationship analysis. Moreover, they used Back Propagation (BP) to create a forecast model for the growth scale of hotels with high stars.

On the other hand, other studies used different techniques of Machine-Learning. For example, Ku et al. (2019) showed using visual analytics and machine learning techniques by 40 hotels in London with 91,051 reviews and 70,397 observations, that 72.5% of hotels have no predilection to react to positive and negative reviews. Sun et al. (2019) used machine learning and internet search indexes to predict travelers to trendy destinations in China and assessed their forecasting performance with the search results generated by Google and Baidu. They showed using the kernel extreme learning machine (KELM) models might enhance the forecasting performance significantly in the forecasting accuracy and robustness analysis.

In addition, Yadegaridehkordi et al. (2021) examined tourists' option behavior regarding green hotels using online travel reviews of Malaysian on TripAdvisor. They found using the Technique Order of Preference by Similarity to Ideal Solution (TOPSIS) that sleep quality is a very crucial element for eco-hotel selection for the most of groups. Besides, Castelli et al. (2022) focused on a tree-based pipeline optimization tool (TPOT) to assess and forecast data accuracy by automated machine learning (AutoML). They showed from the TPOT findings using data to transform key hospitality variables such as customer satisfaction and loyalty to revenue.

Moreover, Alsayat (2023) analyzes the influence of social data on tourists in hotels in Saudi Arabia based on a hybrid method consisting of supervised learning, text mining, and segmentation machine learning methods. They used support vector regression with sequential minimal optimization (SMO), latent Dirichlet allocation (LDA), and k-means methods to improve the mixture technique. Also, they found that this method is efficient for hotels in Mecca.

On the other side, some research developed models using artificial intelligence and machine learning. For example, Sánchez et al. (2020) developed a model for addressing cancellations made in a short using AI techniques to identify people likely to cancel near the moment of service based on their characteristics and the historical reasons for changing their minds. Also, Lee et al. (2021) developed and assessed expectation models for review helpfulness using ML algorithms to investigate restaurant data. They inferred that extreme gradient boosting (XGBoost) is the greatest model to forecast review helpfulness along with others. Moreover, they concluded that elements concerning a reviewer's credibility were essential elements influencing a review's helpfulness.

3   Data Used in the Literature

The use of ML techniques applied to tourism and hospitality implies the need to have access to large datasets to enable investigation of an empirical nature. However, this task is not always easy, as they are sensitive, and from the owners that it is sometimes difficult to make them aware of the need to share them with researchers, guaranteeing their confidentiality, which is why this present article intends to identify the sources of data considered in other studies as a starting point in the process of identifying our forms of information and how it can be obtained. In this sense, Table 1 presents the data and methods used for the previous studies.

As can be seen in Table 1, most of the datasets come from social media or are made available online and constituted by reviews generated by tourists, which express the testimonies of the experiences lived during the trip or the stay at the hotel, as guests.

Table 1. Data and methods used for the previous studies. Source: Own elaboration.

Literature	Region(s)	Data source(s)	Process of data collection	Objective	Modeling and forecasting method(s)
Castelli et al. (2022)	Branches operating across Europe and America	284,229 observations from customers who were in the hotel	Survey data	Valuation and expect data accuracy in hospitality through AutoML	The tree-based pipeline optimization tool
Yadegaridehkordi et al. (2021)	Malaysia	Online travel reviews on TripAdvisor	TripAdvisor	Examined travelers' choice behavior towards green hotels	TOPSIS
Sánchez-Medina & Eleazar (2020	Spain	Booking data from a hotel partner in Gran Canaria (Spain)	Hotel chain	Forecast hotel booking cancellations	Artificial neural networks optimized with genetic algorithms
Sánchez et al. (2020)	Spain	Booking data from a hotel partner in Gran Canaria (Spain)	Hotel chain	Developed a model for addressing cancellations made	AI techniques based on PNR
Ku et al. (2019)	UK	40 hotels with 91,051 reviews in London	TripAdvisor	Examine if hotel managers act in response to positive and negative reviews in a different way	Visual analytics and ML techniques
Lee et al. (2021)	11 states in North America	1,483,858 observations from restaurant reviews	Yelp.com	Developed and assessed models for review helpfulness	Machine learning

(*continued*)

Table 1. (*continued*)

Literature	Region(s)	Data source(s)	Process of data collection	Objective	Modeling and forecasting method(s)
Aakash et al. (2021)	10 highly visited cities in the world	Online reviews of 36,560 eWOM	TripAdvisor	Examined the features associated with client satisfaction	Text analytics, feature extraction, and Artificial Neural Networks
Alsayat (2023)	Saudi Arabia	Online reviews of who were staying in Mecca hotels	TripAdvisor	Analyzes big social data on travelers in the hotels	Supervised learning, text mining, and segmentation machine learning
Sun et al. (2019)	China	Google Trends, Baidu Index, and Wind Database	Wind Database (http://www.wind.com.cn)	Forecast tourist arrivals for popular destinations	Kernel extreme learning machine models

4 Discussion

The potential of ML for hotels and tourism will still be the target of many researchers since these studies show the benefits obtained for companies in this sector of economic activity in terms of analyzing consumer behavior, that is, tourists.

In the investigation of consumer behavior with ML techniques, these can help to identify the characteristics of the tourists' profile, what attracts them to a certain tourist destination or hotel, which can lead to their retention or repetition as a customer., and even can contribute to improving and developing the relationship between the hotel and the customer in a satisfactory way for both, by offering personalized products according to their preferences and lifestyle.

In scientific terms, the combination of the two areas could help to develop innovative business models and identify new performance identifiers and new trends for future potential customers. The academy will be able to relate the concepts of society 5.0, which places the human being at the center of the development of society, with the economic and social balance, in a relationship that meets the sustainability objectives, through the tourist sector, which contributes to the economy of locations, by obtaining intelligence and patterns in the data obtained through ML algorithms.

5 Conclusions

Given that Machine learning has had an important influence on many sides of hospitality and tourism investigation, an examination of the application of Machine learning is vital for insight into the status of Machine learning in this field.

Some recent studies used artificial neural networks for specific issues in hospitality and tourism, such as forecast hotel booking cancellations (Sánchez-Medina & Eleazar, 2020), examining the features associated with client satisfaction (Aakash et al., 2021), and creating a model for the growth measurement of high-star hotels (Zhao & Tsai, 2021). Also, recent research used different Techniques of Machine Learning such as visual analytics (Ku et al., 2019), kernel extreme learning machine (Sun et al., 2019), TOPSIS (Yadegaridehkordi et al., 2021), tree-based pipeline optimization tool (Castelli et al., 2022), supervised learning, text mining, and segmentation machine learning (Alsayat, 2023), real Personal Name Records (Sánchez et al., 2020), and machine learning algorithms (Lee et al., 2021). This research found that literature reviews on this subject are limited, restricting our understanding of the advancement of Machine learning investigation and its potential capabilities. Future research can be extended to a systematic literature review to offer a more comprehensive review of how Machine learning has high light on tourism and hospitality research and suggest the newest growth in this subject.

Acknowledgment. This paper is financed by National Funds provided by FCT-Foundation for Science and Technology through project UIDB/04020/2020 and project Guest-IC I&DT nr. 047399 financed by CRESC ALGARVE2020, PORTUGAL2020 and FEDER.

References

Aakash, A., Tandon, A., Gupta Aggarwal, A.: How features embedded in eWOM predict hotel guest satisfaction: an application of artificial neural networks. J. Hosp. Market. Manag. **30**(4), 486–507 (2021). https://doi.org/10.1080/19368623.2021.1835597

Alazzam, B.A., Alkhatib, M., Shaalan, K.: Artificial intelligence chatbots: a survey of classical versus deep machine learning techniques. Inf. Sci. Lett. **12**(4), 1217–1233 (2023)

Alsayat, A.: Customer decision-making analysis based on big social data using machine learning: a case study of hotels in Mecca. Neural Comput. Appl. **35**, 4701–4722 (2023). https://doi.org/10.1007/s00521-022-07992-x

Castelli, M., Pinto, D.C., Shuqair, S., Montali, D., Vanneschi, L.: The benefits of automated machine learning in hospitality. Emerg. Sci. J. **6**(6), 1237–1254 (2022). https://doi.org/10.28991/ESJ-2022-06-06-02

Huang, M.-H., Rust, R.T.: Artificial intelligence in service. J. Serv. Res. **21**(2), 155–172 (2018). https://doi.org/10.1177/1094670517752459

Ku, C.H., Chang, Y.-C., Wang, Y., Chen, C.-H., Hsiao, S.-H.: Artificial intelligence and visual analytics: a deep-learning approach to analyze hotel reviews & responses. In: 52nd Annual Hawaii International Conference on System Sciences (HICSS) (2019)

Kwon, W., Lee, M., Back, K.-J.: Exploring the underlying factors of customer value in restaurants: a machine learning approach. Int. J. Hosp. Manag. **91**, 102643 (2020). https://doi.org/10.1016/j.ijhm.2020.102643

Lee, M., Kwon, W., Back, K.-J.: Artificial intelligence for hospitality big data analytics: developing a prediction model of restaurant review helpfulness for customer decision-making. Int. J. Contemp. Hosp. Manag. **33**(6), 2117–2136 (2021). https://doi.org/10.1108/IJCHM-06-2020-0587

Li, J., Xu, L., Tang, L., Wang, S., Li, L.: Big data in tourism research: a literature review. Tour. Manage. **68**, 301–323 (2018). https://doi.org/10.1016/j.tourman.2018.03.009

Lv, H., Shi, S., Gursoy, D.: A look back and a leap forward: a review and synthesis of big data and artificial intelligence literature in hospitality and tourism. J. Hosp. Market. Manag. **31**(2), 145–175 (2022). https://doi.org/10.1080/19368623.2021.1937434

Medhat, M., Bayomy, W.A.: Big data analytics impact transformation. Inf. Sci. Lett. **12**(4), 1901–1911 (2023)

Mwitondi, K., Khorsheed, E.: A parameter leveraging method for unsupervised big data modelling. J. Stat. Appl. Probab. **5**(2), 203–211 (2016)

Parpoula, C., Drosou, K., Koukouvinos, C.: Large-scale statistical modelling via machine learning classifiers. J. Stat. Appl. Pro. **2**(3), 203–222 (2013)

Sayed, A., Gomaa, M.M., Nazier, M.M.: Sentiment analysis on twitters big data against the covid-19 pandemic using machine learning algorithms. Inf. Sci. Lett. **12**(8), 2747–2756 (2023)

Sánchez-Medina, A.J., Eleazar, C.: Using machine learning and big data for efficient forecasting of hotel booking cancellations. Int. J. Hosp. Manag. **89**, 102546 (2020). https://doi.org/10.1016/j.ijhm.2020.102546

Sánchez, E.C., Sánchez-Medina, A.J., Pellejero, M.: Identifying critical hotel cancellations using artificial intelligence. Tour. Manag. Perspect. **35**, 100718 (2020). https://doi.org/10.1016/j.tmp.2020.100718

Sun, S., Wei, Y., Tsui, K.-L., Wang, S.: Forecasting tourist arrivals with machine learning and internet search index. Tour. Manag. **70**, 1–10 (2019). https://doi.org/10.1016/j.tourman.2018.07.010

Yadegaridehkordi, E., et al.: Customers segmentation in eco-friendly hotels using multi-criteria and machine learning techniques. Technol. Soc. **65**, 101528 (2021). https://doi.org/10.1016/j.techsoc.2021.101528

Zhao, N., Tsai, S.-B.: Research on prediction model of hotels' development scale based on BP artificial neural network algorithm. Math. Probl. Eng. **2021**, 1–12 (2021). https://doi.org/10.1155/2021/6595783

Does Blockchain Technology Adoption Affect Decision-Making Performance: Evidence from Jordan

Seif Obeid Al Shbeil[1]([✉]), Hashem Alshurafat[2], Marah Al-Safadi[1], and Rakan Alshbiel[1]

[1] Department of Accounting, School of Business, Al al-Bayt University, Mafraq, Jordan
seifobeid1980@aabu.edu.jo
[2] Department of Accounting, Faculty of Economics and Administrative Sciences, The Hashemite University, Zarqa, Jordan

Abstract. In many developing countries, such as Jordan, the use of blockchain technology is in its infancy. In this study, the decision-making performance of audit firms in Jordan is examined together with the factors impacting the intention to adopt blockchain technology. This article offers a model for the adoption of blockchain technology that combines essential factors from prior research with additional, unstudied factors. 104 decision-makers from different Jordanian audit firms provided data that was used to evaluate the model of blockchain technology adoption and identify the factors linked to blockchain technology adoption. The factor, intention to use blockchain technology, was significantly influenced by infrastructure, system quality, and trust. The factor, intention to adopt blockchain technology, has been found to have a positive link with decision-making performance. These findings can be utilized by decision-makers to expand the adoption of blockchain technology systems in Jordan.

Keywords: Blockchain technology · decision-making performance · trust · infrastructure · system quality

1 Introduction

A number of research papers have noticed the potential of blockchain technology for the accounting system, and it has recently emerged as a crucial technology in the digital revolution of the accounting and auditing sectors [1]. It is prepared to change the way that firms and traditional accounting systems have operated in the audit sector over the past few decades [2–4]. The decentralization and digitalization of audit institutions will be facilitated by information and communication technologies (ICTs) and blockchain, which are important enabling technologies. Recent studies on the blockchain [5, 6], which was first developed by [7], have mostly concentrated on financial transactions and distributed ledger technologies [1]. Cryptocurrencies are where blockchain technology is most frequently discussed and deployed, although there are a much wider range of potential uses. It can be used for any data sharing, including contract negotiations,

A. M. A. Musleh Al-Sartawi et al. (Eds.): ICGER 2023, CCIS 1999, pp. 85–95, 2024.
https://doi.org/10.1007/978-3-031-50518-8_8

shipment tracking, and financial transactions (payments). The system is transparent since each activity is recorded in a block and the data is dispersed among numerous nodes (computers). Benefits for accounting are even more promising because blockchain will offer a triple entry accounting system with immutable, time-stamped, real-time, encrypted transactions [8]. Additionally, Blockchain can enhance the performance of decision-making [9, 10], leading to a more fulfilling service for the customer [11]. Likewise, it would be advantageous for the decision-making procedures of these end users of blockchain to understand the implied factors connected with blockchain. We should utilize a system like this to record every choice we make as a community and as individuals. By doing this, we will be able to retain an accurate record of all decisions that would be hard to forge. From this record, we can use artificial intelligence software to learn the optimal course of action for each problem and extract the best suggestions from prior data to inform future decisions. This applies to every person as well as the governance structures we employ in every type of organization, such as accounting, auditing, the economy, etc.

Today, the relationship between blockchain technology and decision support is more obvious [1]. Research studies have therefore mostly been undertaken to evaluate the advantages and pros of blockchain on decision-making [1]. According to [12], the adoption of blockchain technology by enterprises will result in decentralized, reliable, trusted, and automated decision-making. According to [1], the main purpose of implementing blockchain technology is to eliminate inconsistent data, which causes operational problems. To improve the overall effectiveness of information in the organization, however, blockchain technology is commonly used.

Various drivers of the adoption of blockchain have been covered in a number of studies. It is critical for enterprises that want to use blockchain technology to recognize these factors in order to minimize risks and promote careful assessment, implementation, adoption, and deployment of the technology. Unfortunately, there aren't many comprehensive studies or analyses that summarize the crucial factors, how they affect the adoption of blockchain technology, and how they affect decision-making abilities. Despite these numerous organizational advantages, prior research has identified a number of instances where adoption rates for blockchain technology are low and failure rates for implementation are high. The organization's several attempts to deploy blockchain technology failed before they could reach their full potential [13]. Understanding the factors that could affect how well blockchain technology is adopted in the organization is vital. The intention to adopt new technology depends on the infrastructure, system quality, and trust, according to published studies [14–16].

The rest of this article is organized as follows. In Sect. 2, the research hypotheses and some relevant past papers are examined. Section 3 presents the study's design and methods. In Sect. 4, the outcomes of the data analysis are displayed. Section 5 contains the conclusions.

2 Literature Review and Hypotheses Development

2.1 Trust and Blockchain Technology Adoption

Trust has been highlighted as one of the main factors influencing acceptance of digital applications facilitated by the internet in the adoption process of technology. There is evidence that trust is a crucial advantage and adoption motivator in the domain of technology adoption [17]. The adoption and exchange of technology and information depend heavily on trust. According to [18, 19], trust is a key element that improves inter-organizational connections and is, therefore, a critical element that significantly influences the adoption of block chain technology. Additionally, trust functions as a precondition for usage behavior by fostering positive expectations for the system and as a precondition for controllability by lowering uncertainty [20]. Numerous studies support the notion that trust present an important factor for people accepting technology when it comes to internet banking [21]. Furthermore, it is believed that trust plays a multi-faceted role in the adoption of new technologies and is closely related to three antecedents: perceived privacy, perceived security, and perceived trustworthiness. The adoption of social platforms and systems is proven to be positively impacted by trust in the social media contexts [22]. In the same context, [23] argues that adoption of blockchain technology and applications is significantly influenced by trust. This led to the development of the following hypothesis;

H1: The intention to adopt blockchain technology is positively impacted by trust.

2.2 Infrastructure and Blockchain Technology Adoption

The requirement for infrastructure including transport, secure decentralized storage, ICT protocols, network administrator, archival and address management, is another reason to embrace blockchain [24]. Effective technological infrastructure is required, according to [25], for enterprises to fully reap the rewards of such technology. For instance, having reliable, fast Internet and energy are essential. In addition, an effective IT infrastructure is essential [26]- [28] for the adoption of new technologies. Companies and employees consistently need the infrastructure required for them to effectively utilize blockchain technology. Despite having many benefits, investing in technology is useless if a company cannot take advantage of it owing to a lack of resources and expertise [29, 30]. This led to the development of the following hypothesis;

H2: The intention to adopt blockchain technology is positively impacted by infrastructure.

2.3 System Quality and Blockchain Technology Adoption

System quality is a key feature, a driver of information systems success, and a criterion for attaining performance targets [31]. The technological attributes of the data system and quality of the system that provide information output were characterized as system quality [32]. An IS user's desire to use a system is significantly impacted by design quality, accessibility, and reaction time [32]. A vital crietria for the adoption of blockchain technology is the quality of the system. It has a favorable effect on further organizational adoption antecedents as well. System quality is a representation of an information system's processing power and operational features. A blockchain technology's system quality is defined as its platform's capacity to let users complete upstream to downstream tasks [33]. The quality of the system has a significant positive effect on behavioral intention, according to the study by [32]. Such factors, in particular, affect how users use the system. Users will be more inclined to use a system if they think it has excellent system quality [34]. This led to the development of the following hypothesis;

H3: The intention to adopt blockchain technology is positively impacted by system quality.

2.4 Blockchain Technology and Decision-Making Performance

Although cryptocurrencies are where blockchain technology is most frequently discussed and deployed, there are a much wider range of potential uses. Blockchain is a sort of distributed archive made up of a series of blocks combined with cryptographic data that each include a batch of transactions [1]. One of the key benefits of adopting a blockchain is its capacity to enable anyone to independently and transparently check the veracity of the combined database without needing a reliable tertiary party. Blockchain technology makes it possible to boost security and transparency while also accelerating the flow of information, money, and other goods and services [35]. Decision-making can be enhanced via tracking the flow using blockchain [1]. According to earlier studies, blockchain technology has a lot of potential, but decision-making frameworks must be developed to scale the costs and advantages of using this technology. Blockchain can be viewed as a "institutional technology" to decentralize governance structures utilized for the coordination of individuals and the making of economic decisions, claims [36]. According to [37]'s study, the blockchain technology has significantly improved decision-making. Given the positive correlation between the adoption of blockchain technology and effective decision-making, the following hypothesis may be put forth;

H4: Intention to adopt blockchain technology has a positive impact on decision-making performance.

3   Method

3.1   Data Design and Collection

For the purpose of acquiring data, this study used a cross-sectional research design. Hand-delivered questionnaires were distributed to 150 decision-makers at audit firms (Big 4 and Non-Big 4). Our survey received feedback from 119 decision-makers in total. Due to incomplete or missing information, 15 responses were eliminated after content analysis. Further statistical analysis was conducted using 104 questionnaires, with a response rate of 69.3%.

This survey questionnaire was created using the questions of prior related investigations [1, 16, 32]. Both the demographic information and the answers to the questions are recorded in the questionnaire. Answers to these inquiries are given on a seven-point

Likert scale (5: Strongly agree to 1: Strongly disagree). After this survey questionnaire had been pre-tested on a group of four accounting professors, a pilot test with 25 participants was carried out to identify instrument concerns, such as language, substance, and ambiguity. Following that, the questionnaire was adjusted in light of the results.

3.2 Common Method Bias

The fact that the data collection was primarily done in cross-sectional settings may enhance the likelihood of a commsectional design, which is a problem with common method bias (CMB). Therefore, it is crucial to look into the CMB issue. Utilizing the variance inflation factor (VIF) [38], we conducted a complete collinearity assessment [39, 40]. The results revealed that every VIF value was under the 3.3 threshold (see Table 1). The results showed that CMB was not a problem for this study.

4   Results

In this study, we want to understand how different constructs are related [41]. For this reason, we tested our model using SmartPLS and the PLS SEM method [42]. PLS-SEM has been utilized in the context of Blockchain in a number of research [1]. In two steps [43–46], the model's validity is evaluated. The first is concerned with the measurement model's quality, while the second is an evaluation of the structural model's prediction ability.

4.1   Measurement Model

The model was initially verified in order to evaluate the outer model, since all of the elements were reflective (see Fig. 1). This requires assessing the validity of measurements, both at the construct level and at the individual item level (indicator reliability), according to [41]. (internal consistency reliability). Additionally, convergent and discriminant validity were both evaluated.

Indicator loadings should be monitored in order to evaluate indicator reliability (i.e., the percentage of each indicator's variance that is explained by the construct, which should be at least 50%) [47, 48]. Because this number shows that the construct explains 50% of the indicator variation, it is advised that indicator loadings be larger than or equal to 0.708 (see Fig. 1) [49, 50]. All indicator loadings were higher than 0.708, as indicated in Table 1, suggesting sufficient indicator reliability. On the other hand, the composite reliability (CR) and Dijkstra and Henseler's rho_A were computed to investigate the internal consistency reliability [41, 51, 52]. According to Table 1, the CR was greater than 0.7 for all constructions [41, 53]. In every instance, the rho_A was also more than 0.7 [54]. As a result, the proposed outer model's internal consistency dependability was satisfactory.

To confirm discriminant validity, the heterotrait-monotrait (HTMT) ratio and Fornell-Larcker criterion were looked at. As a fresh strategy to get over the previous traditional approach limitation, the HTMT ratio was discovered [45]. Table 2 shows that the criteria for discriminant validity were met because the square root of the AVE value for each

Table 1. Construct Reliability and Validity

Construct	Code	Loadings	VIF	C. alpha	rho_A	CR	AVE
Trust	TRU.1	0.913	2.573	0.847	0.882	0.906	0.764
	TRU.2	0.799	1.751				
	TRU.3	0.905	2.267				
Infrastructure	INF.1	0.819	1.305	0.770	0.787	0.817	0.599
	INF.2	0.756	1.390				
	INF.3	0.744	1.257				
System quality	SYQ.1	0.712	1.323	0.790	0.792	0.826	0.613
	SYQ.2	0.823	1.385				
	SYQ.3	0.810	1.324				
Intention to adopt blockchain technology	BCT.1	0.793	1.981	0.815	0.819	0.871	0.575
	BCT.2	0.795	1.768				
	BCT.3	0.730	1.610				
	BCT.4	0.730	1.651				
	BCT.5	0.741	1.601				
Decision-making performance	DMP.1	0.902	2.960	0.871	0.877	0.912	0.722
	DMP.2	0.810	2.004				
	DMP.3	0.894	3.118				
	DMP.4	0.787	1.857				

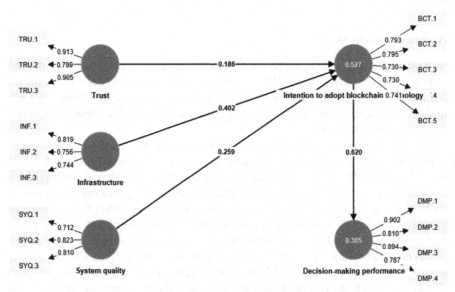

Fig. 1. Item loadings, path coefficient and R^2 values

variable was larger than the sum of all correlations between each pair of variables. Additionally, the HTMT ratio value for each construct has to be below 0.9 as a general rule [41, 56]. All of the HTMT values met this requirement, according to the analysis's findings in Table 3. As a result, the findings showed that all constructs had strong evidence of good discriminant validity.

Table 2. Discriminant validity-Fornell-Larcker criterion

Construct	1	2	3	4	5
Decision-making performance	**0.850**				
Infrastructure	0.595	**0.774**			
Intention to adopt blockchain technology	0.620	0.663	**0.758**		
System quality	0.493	0.593	0.602	**0.783**	
Trust	0.646	0.578	0.564	0.562	**0.874**

Table 3. Discriminant validity-HTMT criterion

Construct	1	2	3	4	5
Decision-making performance	-				
Infrastructure	0.762	-			
Intention to adopt blockchain technology	0.725	0.835	-		
System quality	0.595	0.824	0.778	-	
Trust	0.744	0.752	0.657	0.706	-

4.2 Assessing the Structural Model

The structural model evaluation comes next. This entails analyzing the inflation invariance factor (VIF) and the statistical significance of the impacts of the route coefficients to determine the collinearity of the structural model. Table 1's VIF values are less than 3.3 [1], ruling out issues with this indication.

Table 4 demonstrates that the main effects of trust, infrastructure, and system quality have a positive impact on the intention to adopt blockchain technology (H1, H2 and H3: $\beta = 0.186, 0.402$ and 0.259; $p < 0.05$, respectively). A positive and significant influence was found in the relationship between intention to adopt blockchain technology and decision-making performance (H4: $\beta = 0.620$; $p < 0.001$). R^2 obtains a values of 0.527 (intention to adopt blockchain technology) and 0.385 (decision-making performance), which indicates a moderate impact. Stone-Geisser (Q^2 values)'s of 0.364 (intention to adopt blockchain technology) and 0.217 (decision-making performance), as a measure of predictive relevance, show that the model has predictive power.

Table 4. Structural model results

Structural path	β and t-values	Conclusion	R^2	Q^2
H1: Trust - > Intention to adopt blockchain technology	0.186 (1.985)	*Supported*		
H2: Infrastructure - > Intention to adopt blockchain technology	0.402 (3.407)	*Supported*		
H3: System quality - > Intention to adopt blockchain technology	0.259 (2.194)	*Supported*	0.527	0.364
H4: Intention to adopt blockchain technology - > Decision-making performance	0.620 (9.181)	*Supported*	0.385	0.217

5 Discussion and Conclusion

The goal of the study was to develop a model for the factors that influence Jordanian audit firms' adoption of blockchain technology. The study also sought to assess the impact of blockchain adoption on the decision-making performance of audit companies. According to the report, the adoption of blockchain technology is significantly impacted by trust, infrastructure, and system quality. The results of the study are anticipated to help Jordanian audit companies adopt blockchain technology, and the factors for adoption that were highlighted would raise awareness of blockchain technology adoption among the owners and investors of the firm. Furthermore, these findings would help company management concentrate on the key drivers that would encourage the acceptance and adoption of blockchain technology.

Instead of examining the effects of every potential factor, the current study examined the effects of the key drivers of the adoption of blockchain technology. Future research should study additional factors and how effective they are at influencing people's acceptance of blockchain technology. The findings might not apply to just any other developing country because the study's environment is Jordanian audit companies. In addition, the study's data collection was based on the respondents' perceptions, experiences, and understanding, which may not represent an objective perception, even though the study's data quality is appropriate for exploratory research. Last but not least, the sample chosen was quite small, and future research can study the constructs in a more generic and extensive sample.

References

1. Alshurafat, H., Al-Mawali, H., Al Shbail, M.O.: The influence of technostress on the intention to use blockchain technology: the perspectives of Jordanian auditors. Development and Learning in Organizations: An International Journal, 2022(ahead-of-print)
2. Bonyuet, D.: Overview and impact of blockchain on auditing. Int. J. Digit. Account. Res. **20**, 31–43 (2020)
3. Desplebin, O., Lux, G., Petit, N.: To be or not to be: blockchain and the future of accounting and auditing. Accounting Perspectives **20**(4), 743–769 (2021)

4. Bonsón, E., Bednárová, M.: Blockchain and its implications for accounting and auditing. Meditari Accountancy Research (2019)
5. Khatwani, R., Mishra, M., Bedarkar, M., Nair, K., Mistr, J.: Impact of blockchain on financial technology Innovation in the Banking, Financial Services and Insurance (BFSI) sector. J. Stat. Appl. Pro. **12**(1), 181–189 (2023)
6. Al-jabra, A.A., AlNuhait, H., Almanasra, S., Al-Khawaja, H.A.: A vision towards the future of cryptocurrencies rooting, its financial significance, and legal challenges in its use. Inf. Sci. Lett. **12**(8), 2545–2557 (2023)
7. Nakamoto, S., Bitcoin: A peer-to-peer electronic cash system. Decentralized Business Review, p. 21260 (2008)
8. Alarcon, J., Ng, C.: Blockchain and the future of accounting. Pennsylvania CPA J. **88**(4), 26–29 (2018)
9. Alsheek, M.A., Al-Sammarraee, A.E., Alshareeda, N.: The role of accounting information systems in supporting privatization program (an empirical study in bahrain airport company, cars puplic transportation company and al hidd power company). Inf. Sci. Lett. **10**(S1), 151–179 (2021)
10. Abdel-Aleem, N.: The effectiveness of a program based on blended learning in developing business management and decision-making skills among female students of Samtah University College. J. Stat. Appl. Pro. **12**(3), 1321–1344 (2023)
11. Tijan, E., et al.: Blockchain technology implementation in logistics. Sustainability **11**(4), 1185 (2019)
12. Belotti, M., et al.: A vademecum on blockchain technologies: When, which, and how. IEEE Commun. Surv. Tutorials **21**(4), 3796–3838 (2019)
13. Dagher, G.G., et al.: Ancile: Privacy-preserving framework for access control and interoperability of electronic health records using blockchain technology. Sustain. Cities Soc. **39**, 283–297 (2018)
14. Janssen, M., et al.: A framework for analysing blockchain technology adoption: integrating institutional, market and technical factors. Int. J. Inf. Manage. **50**, 302–309 (2020)
15. Saurabh, S., Dey, K.: Blockchain technology adoption, architecture, and sustainable agri-food supply chains. J. Clean. Prod. **284**, 124731 (2021)
16. Shrestha, A.K., Vassileva, J.: User acceptance of usable blockchain-based research data sharing system: an extended TAM-based study. In: 2019 First IEEE International Conference on Trust, Privacy and Security in Intelligent Systems and Applications (TPS-ISA). IEEE (2019)
17. Pavlou, P.A., Fygenson, M.: Understanding and predicting electronic commerce adoption: an extension of the theory of planned behavior. MIS quarterly, p. 115–143 (2006)
18. Supranee, S., Rotchanakitumnuai, S.: The acceptance of the application of blockchain technology in the supply chain process of the Thai automotive industry (2017)
19. Istaitih, Y., Alsadi, S., Elrashidi, A., Kanan, M., Al-Sartawi, A., Asad, J.: Socio-economic assessing of researcher's perceptions and farmer's willingness to adopt silage technology in palestine-west bank. Inf. Sci. Lett. **12**(9), 2241–2253 (2023)
20. Jaradat, Z., et al.: Factors influencing business intelligence adoption: evidence from Jordan. J. Decision Syst., 1–21 (2022)
21. Dimitriadis, S., Kyrezis, N.: The effect of trust, channel technology, and transaction type on the adoption of self-service bank channels. Serv. Ind. J. **31**(8), 1293–1310 (2011)
22. Ng, M.: Factors influencing the consumer adoption of Facebook: a two-country study of youth markets. Comput. Hum. Behav.. Hum. Behav. **54**, 491–500 (2016)
23. Fleischmann, M., Ivens, B.: Exploring the role of trust in blockchain adoption: an inductive approach. In: Proceedings of the 52nd Hawaii International Conference on System Sciences (2019)
24. Swan, M.: Blockchain: Blueprint for a new economy. 2015: O'Reilly Media, Inc. (2015)

25. Choi, D., et al.: Factors affecting organizations' resistance to the adoption of blockchain technology in supply networks. Sustainability **12**(21), 8882 (2020)
26. Zailani, S., et al.: Determinants and environmental outcome of green technology innovation adoption in the transportation industry in Malaysia. Asian J. Technol. Innov.Innov. **22**(2), 286–301 (2014)
27. Alshurafat, H., et al.: Factors affecting online accounting education during the COVID-19 pandemic: an integrated perspective of social capital theory, the theory of reasoned action and the technology acceptance model. Educ. Inf. Technol. **26**(6), 6995–7013 (2021)
28. Abuaddous, H.Y., Otair, M.A., Awad, M.: The impact of information systems management elements on human resource development: the case of jordan commercial bank. Inf. Sci. Lett. **11**(6), 2241–2250 (2022)
29. Alsetoohy, O., et al.: Intelligent agent technology: what affects its adoption in hotel food supply chain management? Journal of Hospitality and Tourism Technology (2019)
30. Alshurafat, H., Al Shbail, M., Almuiet, M.: Factors affecting the intention to adopt IT forensic accounting tools to detect financial cybercrimes. Int. J. Bus. Excellence (2021)
31. DeLone, W.H., McLean, E.R.: Measuring e-commerce success: applying the DeLone & McLean information systems success model. Int. J. Electron. Commer.Commer. **9**(1), 31–47 (2004)
32. Al Shbail, M., et al.: Individual and technological factors affecting the adoption of enterprise resource planning systems in the Jordanian banking sector. Int. J. Business Information Systems, 2022. In press
33. Alazab, M., et al.: Blockchain technology in supply chain management: an empirical study of the factors affecting user adoption/acceptance. Clust. Comput.. Comput. **24**(1), 83–101 (2021)
34. Al Shbail, A., Al Shbail, M., Al-Shbiel, S.: Adoption of enterprise resource planning (ERP) Systems and Impact on decision-making performance in Jordanian manufacturing SMEs Int. J. Bus. Inf. Syst. (2023). In press
35. Chang, S.E., Chen, Y.: When blockchain meets supply chain: a systematic literature review on current development and potential applications. IEEE Access **8**, 62478–62494 (2020)
36. Tasca, P.: Digital currencies: principles, trends, opportunities, and risks. Trends, Opportunities, and Risks (2015)
37. El Khatib, M., Al Mulla, A., Al Ketbi, W.: The Role of Blockchain in E-Governance and Decision-Making in Project and Program Management. Advances in Internet of Things 12(3), 88–109 (2022)
38. Ebiwonjumi, A., Chifurira, R., Chinhamu, K.: A robust principal component analysis for estimating economic growth in nigeria in the presence of multicollinearity and outlier. J. Stat. Appl. Pro. **12**(2), 611–627 (2023)
39. Kock, N.: Common method bias in PLS-SEM: A full collinearity assessment approach. International Journal of e-Collaboration (ijec) **11**(4), 1–10 (2015)
40. Al Shbail, M.O., et al.: The moderating effect of job satisfaction on the relationship between human capital dimensions and internal audit effectiveness. Cogent Business & Manage. **9**(1), 2115731 (2022)
41. Aburumman, O.J., et al.: How to Deal with the Results of PLS-SEM? In: International Conference on Business and Technology. 2023. Springer
42. Fazel, H.: Digital marketing and sustainability in the era of climate change: PLS-structural equation modeling approach. J. Stat. Appl. Pro. **13**(1), 491–505 (2024)
43. Taha, N., et al.: The impact of different intellectual capital dimensions on banks operational and financial performance. In: International Conference on Business and Technology. Springer (2023)

44. Alshurafat, H., et al.: An instructional project: compliance with IASB conceptual framework by the listed companies. In: International Conference on Business and Technology. Springer (2023)
45. Shbail, A., et al. The Impact of Job Stressors and Burnout on Internal Auditors' Satisfaction. in International Conference on Business and Technology. 2023. Springer
46. Alshurafat, H., et al.: Forensic Accounting Education Within the Australian Universities. in International Conference on Business and Technology. Springer (2023)
47. Shbail, A., et al. Factors Affecting the Adoption of Remote Auditing During the Times of COVID-19: An Integrated Perspective of Diffusion of Innovations Model and the Technology Acceptance Model. in International Conference on Business and Technology. Springer (2023)
48. Al-Hazaima, H., et al.: Dataset for integration of sustainability education into the accounting curricula of tertiary education institutions in Jordan. Data Brief **42**, 108224 (2022)
49. Hair, J., et al.: When to use and how to report the results of PLS-SEM. Eur. Bus. Rev. **31**(1), 2–24 (2019)
50. Al Shbail, M., et al.: Dataset of Factors affecting online cheating by accounting students: The relevance of social factors and the fraud triangle model factors. Data in Brief, 2022. 40
51. Alserhan, H., Shbail, M.: The role of organizational commitment in the relationship between human resource management practices and competitive advantage in Jordanian private universities. Manage. Sci. Lett. **10**(16), 3757–3766 (2020)
52. Shbail, M., Shbail, A.: Organizational climate, organizational citizenship behaviour and turnover intention: Evidence from Jordan. Manage. Sci. Lett. **10**(16), 3749–3756 (2020)
53. Al Shbail, M., Salleh, Z., Nor, M.: The effect of ethical tension and time pressure on job burnout and premature sign-off. Journal of Business and Retail Management Research, 2018. 12(4)
54. Dijkstra, T., Henseler, J.: Consistent partial least squares path modeling. MIS Q. **39**(2), 297–316 (2015)
55. Henseler, J., Ringle, C., Sarstedt, M.: A new criterion for assessing discriminant validity in variance-based structural equation modeling. J. Acad. Mark. Sci. **43**(1), 115–135 (2015)
56. Obeid, M., Salleh, Z., Nor, M.: The mediating effect of job satisfaction on the relationship between personality traits and premature sign-off. Acad. Accoun. Financial Stud. J. **21**(2), 1–17 (2017)

Quantifying the Dynamic Enablers of Blockchain Technology to Achieve Operating Performance: A Conceptual Framework

Gaurav Kumar Singh[1], Manish Dadhich[1(✉)], and Kamal Kant Hiran[2(✉)]

[1] Sir Padampat Singhania University, Udaipur, India
{gaurav.singh,manish.dadhich}@spsu.ac.in
[2] Symbiosis University of Applied Sciences, Indore, India
kamalkant.hiran@suas.ac.in

Abstract. The evolution of Blockchain has revolutionized supply chain activities and has impacted numerous organizational functions. This research investigates the applications of Blockchain in the supply chain management of Indian cement industry. A sample of 285 retail industry suppliers (Delhi/NCR) was taken. The information is gathered using a structured questionnaire based on a five-point Likert scale and convenience sampling. Eight constructs with 34 manifests were discovered from previous studies, hypotheses are evaluated using factor analysis, and the model fit is achieved using confirmatory factor analysis (CFA) and structural equation modelling (SEM). Applications of blockchain technology will have a favorable impact on the supply chain of the cement industry because it offers better transparency in the supply chain, flexibility, sustainable process & transportation, effective utilization, and various relative benefits. The proposed model is the first to empirically substantiate and evaluate the multimodal framework in which applications of Blockchain act as a mediator to achieve operational performance. As a result, blockchain models should be implemented throughout the supply chain, which will benefit all stakeholders.

Keywords: Blockchain Technology (BoT) · Sustainable Supply Chain Management · Operational Performance (OP) · PLS-SEM

1 Introduction

Blockchain technology (BoT) has been regarded as the next invention that would transform the structure and scale of enterprises and how they perform economic activity (Paliwal et al., 2020). A plethora of monitoring requirements and a diverse spectrum of cultural and human behavior in supply chain operations make analyses of data complicated (Tribis et al., 2018). In the words of (Treiblmaier, 2018), ineffective operations, fraud, and failing supply chains are all factors that lead to a lack of trust and the need for greater information interchange and verifiability. Tracing of goods and process flow are very demanding in supply chain sectors, including the cement industry. A sustainable supply chain will use blockchain technology to streamline interactions between suppliers, merchants, and purchasers and various types of paperwork such as purchase orders, invoice payments, and financing (Al-Rawashdeh et al., 2023), (Ali et al., 2022). In the present chaotic scenario, no human effort can run without using supply chain management. Further, using BoT-SCM in the building industry has considerable financial advantages (Mukri, 2008). BoT enables real-time improvement and monitoring of products and passengers from their inception to the end of the supply chain management process. One of the most direct benefits of it is reliable identity management systems. Even though Blockchain is primarily viewed as a general-purpose technology that increases productivity, some authors believe BCT will revolutionize the industrial structure (K. Mathiyazhagan and Sarthak Ahuja, 2021).

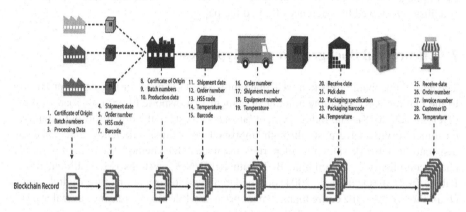

Fig. 1. Process flow of BoT-SCM.

Figure 1 depicts the comprehensive process of BoT-SCM operation, which starts from the certificate of origin to the final identity and order number of goods. Each transaction is recorded in a different block or folder that is unalterable, but the BoT experts need to be acquainted with the SCM optimization technique. When deploying Blockchain or any other technology to improve efficiency and accuracy in business operations, organizations must review the application to help create correct data (Mahtab Kouhizadeh, Sara Saberi, 2021). According to market watch research published in 2019, the global market for blockchain-enabled supply chains will reach $9.8 billion by 2025. The global contribution of BoT to the supply chain industry is estimated to reach $424 million by 2023 (Garay-Rondero et al., 2020). Since every blockchain transaction is simpler, more reliable, traceable, and efficient, supply-chain stakeholders must include BoT in their operations (Kshetri, 2018).

Certain Indian banks, conglomerates, and stock exchanges (AlRowaiei et al., 2021) were early adopters of blockchain technology in India. There are now many more participants in a typical supply chain as a result of increased competition, globalization, and outsourcing (Srivastava et al., 2023). This technology makes it possible to measure critical SCM activities' performance and results validly and reliably. Walmart, the world's largest retailer, recently teamed up with IBM to boost supply chain transparency and explore the use of blockchain technology (Carlos Alberto Schettini Pinto; Augusto

Da Cunha Reis; Marco Braga, 2020). Scholars would investigate the blockchain phenomenon and its potential repercussions from various theoretical perspectives. It will help answer two main research issues.

RQ1: What best way to understand a supply chain that incorporates blockchain technology?

RQ2: Can blockchain technology improve operating performance by forming more flexible, transparent, and sustainable supply chains?

The theoretical foundation of this study, which informs its hypotheses and research framework, is covered in the next section of this essay. The methodology and statistical results are presented in the next part. Further, the detailed discussion and theoretical implications have also been incorporated. Eventually, limitation, future scope, and conclusion followed by references framed the paper.

2   Theoretical Background and Hypotheses

The term blockchain refers to a DLT that emphasized the need for the plant's proximity to the market, a considerable amount of cement is transported by rail or road in India (Treiblmaier, 2018). The Indian cement business invests in the organization to improve customer service, save costs through improved operational efficiency, and make the distribution network safer for all parties involved. One method for reducing supply chain complexity is to combine BoT with RFID/NFC systems (M. Dadhich, M. S. Pahwa, 2021a). (Öztas et al., 2004) outlined that the transformation of the digital supply chain should affect the entire management process while also increasing several aspects of sustainability. In this regard, Industry 4.0 efforts aim to use emerging technologies like IoT, RFID, and Blockchain to digitize a range of processes. (Calvo-Mora et al., 2015) studied the practical models for understanding the effects of SCM and logistics-related systems in the corporate world.

(Baird et al., 2011) stated that the supply chain has numerous problems, including delivery effectiveness and efficiency, continuous monitoring, and strong partnerships. According to (Kumar Naresh, Dadhich Manish, 2014), and (Dadhich, Poddar, & Kant, 2022), information easily accessible to end-users and enterprises in the supply chain is referred to as transparency in the supply chain. Every company may have its digital BoT system, giving all major stakeholders instant product information. Access to a product can be restricted via security measures, allowing only those having the appropriate digital keys to use it. Transparency includes user freedom of information without active participation in the supply chain system (Anil et al., 2016). Transparency in the supply chain improves customer satisfaction and aids business growth by providing helpful feedback, increasing sales, and launching more successful projects (Mueller & Carter, 2005; Sharma & Dadhich, 2014). (Dadhich, Purohit, et al., 2021b; Wang & Wu, 2021) believed that supply chain function is very dynamic and uncertain in the business context than ever before.

In the words of (Dadhich, Hiran, Rao, Sharma, et al., 2022a; Mendoza-Fong et al., 2019), using a distribution system, a network of facilities known as the supply chain manages the process of producing raw materials, turning them into intermediate goods, and finally into finished items. (Shrimali & Patel, 2021) studied the main goal of supply chain management, which encompasses procurement, production, and distribution in order to optimize chain performance to create as much value as feasible for the least cost possible. (Casino et al., 2019; Gaurav Kumar Singh, 2022) assessed that enhanced supply chain productivity provides the most benefits to all parties involved, it strives to connect all agents in the supply chain to work together as a team within the company. These publications critically evaluate changes in supply management theory and practice and define the concept, guiding principles, nature, and evolution of SCM. (Dadhich, Hiran, Rao, & Sharma, 2022b; Shrimali & Patel, 2021) expanded the scope of SCM to include aspects of Total Quality Management such as managerial commitment, organizational structure, training, and behavioral difficulties in addition to material management, partnerships, and information technology. A thorough understanding of the integration process is a crucial component of SCM since integration is essential to a firm's sustainability. Also, it is noted that research employs increasingly sophisticated methods for decision-making in SCM, including simulation, artificial neural networks, and fuzzy logic. (Shokouhyar et al., 2020) demonstrated how the concepts of collaborative agents and artificial neural networks (ANNs) can work together to enable collaborative supply chain planning. They used the principles of fuzzy logic for analyzing and monitoring the performance of suppliers based on the criteria of product quality and delivery time (SCP). According to a survey of the literature, supply chain management has either been examined from a system perspective or the systemic character of interactions between supply chain actors is evident. Even though many studies analyze SCM from various angles, this research provides a deeper knowledge of supply chain activities (Fig. 2).

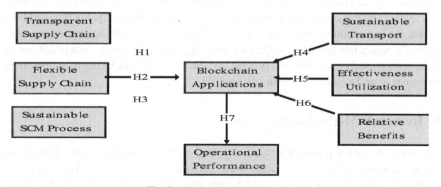

Fig. 2. Conceptual Framework

In the words of (Sabella et al., 2014), smart contract management and process rules in a blockchain-based distribution network may regulate actor accreditation and authorization. They are permitted to access and which are required for execution. Changes to actor data may occur based on the supply chain category, location, and event defined by a blockchain network. Provenance-related apps may increase accessibility and accountability in the construction supply chain. Because every transaction in the blockchain ecosystem is available, it is straightforward to follow the supply chain of any product or service in terms of conformity or quality assurance (Bouranta et al., 2019; Purohit et al., 2022). Due to the need for more efficient cross-border operations, the demand for blockchain in transport and logistics applications has grown in lockstep with other sophisticated technologies. (Dadhich & Kant, 2022; S. Kumar & Singh, 2021) covered a variety of cutting-edge technologies created and used for managing cross-border transportation. Face detection, artificial intelligence (AI), fingerprints, robotics, and laser and infrared methods are all examples of technology. From the results of the literature review, the following hypotheses were developed:

H1: BoT improves the transparency of supply chains.

H2: BoT aids in the creation of a more adaptable and flexible supply chain management system. H3: BoT significantly impacts a long-term supply chain process system.

H4: Blockchain has a significant impact on sustainable transportation.

H5: Adopting blockchain application augments effectiveness utilization of practices of SCM. H6: Using blockchain technology in supply chain management provides relative benefit.

H7: Blockchain application has a favorable and mediating relationship with the operating performance of the cement industry (Table 1).

Gap and Novelty

The recent study has begun to justify using technology in SCMs and its potential opportunities along with BoT. According to a literature review, much of the research focuses on major firms, and the cement industry has got very little attention in emerging economies (AL-Nawaiseh et al., 2022). Previous research, such as (Benzaquen & Charles, 2020; Calvo-Mora et al., 2015), has emphasized the relevance of SCM-BoT in determining sustainability but is unable to propose a conceptual framework to be followed by industry experts. The cement sector is one of the most critical drivers of SD in the worldwide market, as it promotes value creation and innovation. By allowing improving expertise in the topic, this research bridges a knowledge gap in research. As a result, supply chain professionals must follow a precise BoT-SCM framework to improve operational performance and ensure long-term sustainability.

3   Research Methodology

Exhaustive literature research yielded valid and well-structured criteria reframed in a detailed questionnaire. All responses were classified on a 5-point Likert scale, with 1 indicating strong disagreement and 5 indicating strong agreement. There were 32 manifests filled with the opinions of 285 cement industry respondents. Furthermore, responses from various functional units of cement manufacturing plants were collected using non-probabilistic convenient sampling strategies. In addition, the researchers took explicit steps to eliminate frequent procedure bias. Respondents initially provided no clear or proper answer to each manifest, instead suggesting that they answer the question based on their experience, working knowledge, and so on.

Second, the data is subjected to a single test, which enumerates only 31% of the total variance, indicating that CMB is not present in the data set (Aguirre-Urreta, 2019). The statements in the questionnaire were written to be concise, plain, and clear. There have been concerns raised about the validity of the CMB single-factor approach (Kenny D.A. & Baron R.M., 1986). The study, therefore, used a different method to check CMB.

Table 1. Summary of Codes & Constructs

Blockchain Applications	BLA_1: BoT records transaction data as products enter the system BLA_2: BoT improves partner information systems BLA_3: BoT reduces expenses related to complex supply chain transactions BLA_4: BoT improves privacy and suitability BLA_5: BoT enhances information of supply chain partners. BLA_6: BoT improves efficiency	(Dutta P, Choi TM, Somani S, 2020; Qu et al., 2019; Saxena et al., 2021)
Transparent Supply Chain	TSC_1: Informed supply chain partners and customers TSC_2: Materials Flows from Suppliers to Production Unit TSC_3: Easily determine the materials required from SCP TSC_4: Verify the materials utilized in continuous production	(Marco Remondino, 2020; Tribis et al., 2018)
Flexible Supply Chain	FSC_1: Changes in the number of orders to suppliers in real-time FSC_2: Changes in the times of orders submitted with suppliers FSC_3: Variations in production capacity FSC_4: Changes in the production blend as orders in the manufacturing unit change	(Addis, 2019; Das, 2018; Dubey et al., 2015; Sinha & Dhall, 2020)
Sustainable SCM Process	SSP_1: Enhancements to demand-driven process SSP_2: Reduced order-to-delivery period SSP_3: Increased Supply Chain Integration SSP_4: Shorter and more effective response time to supply chain problems	(Agrawal & Agrawal, 2019; Mueller & Carter, 2005)

(*continued*)

Table 1. (*continued*)

Sustainable Transport	STT_1: Optimize real-time ramp allocation and sequencing STT_2: Scheduled delivery per customer requirements STT_3: Cost modelling from the ground up STT_4: Make dynamic routing easier	(Anil et al., (2016); Das, 2018) (Dadhich, Rao, et al., 2021)
Effectiveness Utilization	EFU_1: Improvement in the firm's overall capacity deployment EFU_2: Advancement in product and service quality EFU_3: Increasing the firm's competitive advantage by providing a differentiated product mix EFU_4: Keeping updated supply chain and client base	(Akanksha Jain, 2014; Cantele, S., Zardini, 2018)
Relative Benefit	RLB_1: BoT-SCM improves company operations RLB_2: In BoT-SCM, the cost of confirming transactions is cheap RLB_3: BoT-SCM can boost a company's earnings RLB_4: BoT-SCM is favorable to operations and SCM	(Das, 2017; Wali et al., 2003)
Operating Performance	OP_1: Upgraded Quality OP_2: Trustworthiness and sustainability in terms of delivery OP_3: Cost efficiency of operation OP_4: Productivity & optimum resource utilization	(Das, 2018; Hietschold et al., 2014; Tortorella et al., 2019)

Afterward, CMB was examined using the Common Latent Factor (CLF) in the SEM model. The standard of standardized regression weights with and without a common factor were also estimated by the researcher; the CLF is significant if the difference between the two values is greater than 0.20.

4   Data Analysis and Discussion

The above Table 2 depicts that 66.67% of actors were male, and the share of female respondents was 33.33%. The employee size of the organization outlines 47.40% of the respondent working where several employees in the department were less than 50. 22.80% denotes 50–100 employee size. The rest, 29.8%, worked where the firm's size was above 100 employees. Similarly, 34.60% of the respondent had job experience of above five years, 26.50% for 5–10 years and 38.90% were highly experienced employees. The respondents have been brought from distinct roles like 27.40% from first-line managers, 42.10% from middle managers, and 30.50% from the senior section. For more accurate data, respondents considered who have BDA experience, 30.90% of respondents have less than 05 years of experience followed by 27.70 % between 5–10 years and 41.40% having more than ten years of experience (Table 3).

Each component's CR and AVE values were more than 0.7 and 0.5, respectively. The AVE was less than the CR for each construct, indicating convergent validity. Similarly, the AVE for each idea was higher than the MSV, indicating that discriminant validity was present. Before determining validity, the CFA model was determined to be a good fit. By comparing the actual values of the model fit indices to the threshold limits, a proper fit was established (Hair et al., 2010; LT & PM, 1999). Table 4 shows the findings of model fit indices.

Convergent validity is defined as (i) composite reliability (CR) of more than 0.700; (ii) average variance extracted (AVE) greater than 0.5 for each construct; and (iii) CR greater than AVE for each construct (Hair et al., 2010). According to (Fornell and Larcker,

Table 2. Respondents' Demographic Profile

Particulars	Measure	Freq	%
Gender	Male	190	66.67
	Female	95	33.33
Employee size	<50	135	47.40
	50–100	65	22.80
	>100	85	29.80
Job Experience	<5 Yrs.	98	34.60
	5–10 Yrs.	76	26.50
	>10 Yrs.	111	38.90
Position	First line managers	78	27.40
	Middle managers	120	42.10
	Senior managers	87	30.50
Experience of Blockchian	<5 Yrs.	88	30.90
Analytics	5–10 Yrs.	79	27.70
	>10 Yrs.	118	41.40

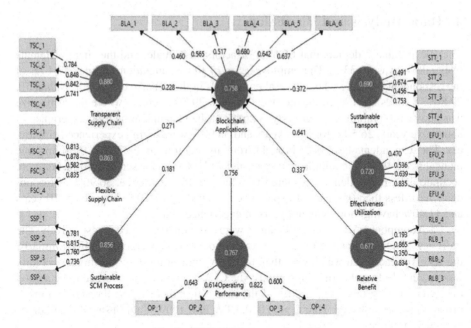

Fig. 3. BTU-SCM structural model

Table 3. Reliability and Convergent Validity

Scale	Code	Chron.α	rho_A	CR	AVE	MSV
Blockchain Applications	BLA	0.758	0.706	0.768	0.504	0.151
Transparent Supply Chain	TSC	0.880	0.807	0.714	0.572	0.566
Flexible Supply Chain	FSC	0.863	0.748	0.626	0.664	0.692
Sustainable SCM Process	SSP	0.856	0.810	0.768	0.494	0.565
Sustainable Transport	STT	0.690	0.731	0.632	0.584	0.486
Effectiveness Utilization	EFU	0.720	0.805	0.740	0.615	0.515
Relative Benefit	RLB	0.677	0.672	0.591	0.582	0.486
Operating Performance	OP	0.767	0.850	0.625	0.459	0.458

1981), DV is satisfied when the AVE of a latent variable exceeds the mean shared variance (MSV) and average variance shared (ASV) of the latent variables (Table 5).

Discriminant validity is also confirmed using HTMT, which shows that items load higher on the hypothesized criteria (Hair Jr, Joseph F., G. Tomas M. Hult, Christian Ringle, 2016). If the structures under consideration are conceptually similar, the HTMT coefficient should be smaller than 0.90. In Smart-PLS, SEM was employed to test six hypotheses. CFA and route analysis are included in the SEM. According to (Hair, J. F., Ringle, C. M., Sarstedt, 2018), SEM is an approach for dealing with various problems

Table 4. Fornell-Larcker Criterion

Constructs	BLA	TSC	FSC	SSP	STT	EFU	RLB	OP
Blockchain Applications	0.886							
Transparent Supply Chain	0.737	0.551						
Flexible Supply Chain	0.663	0.488	0.765					
Sustainable SCM Process	0.657	0.499	0.460	0.694				
Sustainable Transport	0.797	0.463	0.449	0.633	0.685			
Effectiveness Utilization	0.626	0.536	0.433	0.591	0.592	0.562		
Relative Benefit	0.866	0.631	0.615	0.487	0.557	0.599	0.519	
Operating Performance	0.625	0.529	0.589	0.425	0.455	0.570	0.498	0.425

Table 5. Heterotrait-Monotrait Ratio (HTMT)

Particular	BLA	TSC	FSC	SSP	STT	EFU	RLB	OP
Blockchain Applications	0.784							
Transparent Supply Chain	0.697	0.564						
Flexible Supply Chain	0.799	0.416	0.796					
Sustainable SCM Process	0.691	0.419	0.518	0.535				
Sustainable Transport	0.597	0.337	0.538	0.472	0.488			
Effectiveness Utilization	0.884	0.392	0.431	0.446	0.429	0.662		
Relative Benefit	0.718	0.412	0.492	0.469	0.489	0.569	0.554	
Operating Performance	0.718	0.456	0.526	0.658	0.701	0.685	0.688	0.513

with regression models, such as measurement error and decrement correction. As a result, we tested all hypotheses using SEM with maximum likelihood. Figure 3 depicts the BTU-SCM diagram (Table 6).

Supply chain transparency is observed to favorably stimulate BLA (t = 13.05, p-0.003, F_2-0.351). As a result, the null hypothesis, which is unwavering and supported by past research, is acknowledged. The initial finding of the study was that BoT would

Table 6. Path Coefficient

S.N.	Structural Pathway	Original Sample	Sample Mean	95% Conf. It. (LB, UB)	T- Stat. P. val F2	P. val	F2
H_1	Transparent Supply Chain → BLA	0.756	0.762	(0.129, 0.367)	13.05	0.003	0.351
H_2	Flexible Supply Chain → BLA	0.271	0.263	(0.183, 0.246)	4.93	0.020	0.311
H_3	Sustainable SCM Process → BLA	0.337	0.317	(0.297, 0.346)	3.86	0.020	0.388
H_4	Sustainable Transport → BLA	0.756	0.773	(0.262, 0.262)	3.94	0.011	0.469
H_5	Effectiveness Utilization → BLA	0.303	0.323	(0.219, 0.340)	2.86	0.005	0.321
H_6	Relative Benefit → BLA	0.815	0.826	(0.384, 0.391)	11.23	0.002	0.413
H_7	Blockchain Applications → OP	0.756	0.773	(0.292, 0.262)	5.35	0.003	0.556

augment SCM transparency. This observation is in line with what has been discovered in the literature (Jyoti et al., 2017). According to the literature, transparency enables proactive communication and collaboration in supply chains (Dadhich, 2017; Marco 2020). Transparency can also help firms improve their practices for including customers in product design. Supply chain transparency is becoming increasingly important for cement companies that want to meet consumer demand, mitigate risk, improve efficiency, meet regulatory requirements, and support sustainability goals. By embracing transparency and implementing robust supply chain management practices, companies can position themselves for long-term success in a rapidly changing business environment.

Similarly, BoT applications augment supply chain flexibility (t = 4.93, p-0.020, F_2-0.311). BoT-SCM will enable real-time data sharing and elasticity in the cement manufacturing process. Because the corporate environment is more complicated than ever, blockchain application is utilized to integrate all supply chain operations simultaneously, and the same has been found in previous studies (Jun et al., 2004; Singh, 2021). Flexible supply chain and BoT are essential for companies that want to remain competitive, responsive, and sustainable in today's business environment. By embracing flexibility and adopting supply chain management practices that prioritize agility, companies can position themselves for long-term success and growth.

The findings also revealed that BoT applications might be employed in the SCM process to increase supply network assurance (t = 3.86, p-0.020, F^2-0.388). The findings were also similar to those (Pambreni et al., 2019), who noted that better integration across the supply chain reduces resource waste and improves response time to supply chain issues. The findings of this investigation corroborate similar results in the literature (Garay-Rondero et al., 2020). Implementing a sustainable SCM process can bring significant benefits to a cement company, including reducing carbon emissions, ensuring ethical sourcing, improving efficiency, enhancing reputation, and meeting regulatory requirements. By adopting sustainable SCM practices, cement companies can position themselves for long-term success and sustainability in a rapidly changing business environment.

The fourth hypothesis suggests that BoT application promotes a sustainable carrying system in the cement industry (t = 3.94, p-0.011, F^2-0.469). The use of BoT increases real-time routing and ramp allocation for continuous supply. Furthermore, a proper transport system is favorable to a delivery schedule by client requirements and is based on a clean-sheet cost modelling approach. This type of dynamic routing is compatible with past studies (N. Kumar & Dadhich, 2014). Sustainable transport is crucial for the cement industry to reduce its carbon footprint, save costs, improve its reputation, comply with regulations, and meet the growing demand for sustainable operations.

The fifth hypothesis states that BoT augments the effectiveness utilization of supply chain competitiveness and is closely related to operating devices (t = 2.86, p-0.005, F^2-0.321). Effectiveness denotes an improvement in the degree of a firm's overall capacity utilization and upgrading in its products and services quality. The findings were consistent with those of (Das, 2017), who proposed and agreed on the concept of effective utilization of the current SCP and client base. Effective utilization of supply chain competitiveness can help companies to improve efficiency, reduce costs, improve quality, and manage risks. By adopting collaboration, technology, lean principles, risk management, and talent development practices, companies can optimize their supply chain operations and enhance their competitiveness.

According to the findings of the sixth hypothesis, the relative benefit was a crucial external factor in explaining BoT applications (t = 11.23, p-0.002, F^2-0.413). This is consistent with a prior study on BoT adoption factors that confirm the profound effect of new technology in SCM (K. Mathiyazhagan and Sarthak Ahuja, 2021) It has been proposed that Blockchain might be a game-changer in the supply chain business. Further, the potential benefit of developing a networked ledger of information that everyone on the network can access and process the real-time supply chain. The use of blockchain in the supply chain can provide a range of benefits, including increased transparency, security, efficiency, trust, and compliance. However, it is important for companies to carefully consider the potential challenges and limitations before implementing blockchain solutions in their supply chain operations.

The last hypothesis is acknowledged due to the statistical significance value (t = 5.35, p-0.003, F^2-0.556). These findings contradict earlier work (Joash Mageto; Gerrie Prinsloo; Rose Luke, 2020), which did not get a significant relationship between BoT and the operational performance of an organization. It has also been examined that BoT applications in the conceptual frame act as a mediator to achieve the operational performance of SCM in the cement industry. However, these findings are again consistent and in line with past work (Das, 2017; Rathore et al., 2020) that confirmed the role of BoT to attain sustainable development, hence augmenting the company's overall performance. The use of blockchain can have a significant impact on a company's operational performance by improving transparency, efficiency, security, collaboration, and innovation. By leveraging the capabilities of blockchain technology, companies can enhance their operational performance and gain a competitive advantage in the marketplace.

5 Theoretical Implications

This study addresses a need identified by (Paliwal et al., 2020), who said that empirical evidence is urgently needed to augment the current state of blockchain research, which is primarily experimental. The key reason for using BoT in the sustainable supply chain is to promote trust, accountability, and transparency. Implementing BoT expertise is pricey and fraught with danger, but many cement companies can overcome the associated challenges by embracing technology know-how. Furthermore, the logistics-BoT community should become acquainted with methodological knowledge to consider the research objectives derived and assessed in this study in an organized manner. The findings would undoubtedly benefit logistic managers seeking a well-structured and in-depth understanding of how BoT reports for sophisticated SCM networks work.

6 Limitations and Future Scope

The data is restricted to a single production, namely the cement industry. The researcher recommends using a more extensive pan-industry database for the full adjudication of the metaheuristic framework. Based on top executives of cement companies, the report gives recommendations. However, all relevant elements dealing with human resources, marketing, and societal issues have been ignored. These could be studied further by combining stratified sampling with other variables such as R&D unit, industry kind, governance, profit, and so on, resulting in even more incredible innovations. The consequences of this study may apply to other industries. However, obtaining more refined results will necessitate an in-depth and intense work plan. Furthermore, the cultural and behavioral challenges confronting cement industry companies must be examined thoroughly, as they may threaten the successful application of BLA in the face of adversity. Future studies may evaluate, change, or extend the proposed framework by considering the constructs of this research.

7 Conclusion

Blockchain, like AI, is one of the most technological innovations that disrupt and transform the supply chain. According to the findings, exploratory Blockchain behaviors steer the business toward a transitional approach to sustainability, but proactive experimental methods guide the organization toward a revolutionary process. A transparent supply chain, flexibility in SCM process, sustainable transportation, effective utilization, and relative gain are indisputably favorable and significant features for BoT applications. As a result, current BoT usage would positively impact the cement industry's SCM because it provides privacy, security, scalability, and a smooth production line without delay. Like artificial intelligence (AI), BoT is a technological innovation disrupting and revolutionizes the supply chain. Decentralized accounting is increasingly important in the cement industry's materials supply networks and logistical systems. As in previous industrial advances, new entrants can benefit from growing alliances, establishing standards, and boosting Blockchain adoption. Given the topic's novel nature and scarcity of literature, the study enables practitioners to assess its various elements by directing them to relevant data sources and Blockchain implications. This study also defines a fresh approach to assembling research questions, ideas, and conceptual models requiring logistics research and Blockchain in the academic and industry. Blockchain technology has the potential to transform many industries by enabling secure and efficient transactions without the need for intermediaries. It has the potential to significantly improve operating performance, but its success depends on a comprehensive strategy that considers these key enablers. By embracing blockchain technology and investing in the necessary infrastructure organizations can position themselves for long-term success in the digital economy.

References

Ali, B.J.A., et al.: Integration of supply chains and operational performance: the moderating effects of knowledge management. Inf. Sci. Lett. 11(4), 1069–1076 (2022). https://doi.org/10.18576/isl/110407

AL-Nawaiseh, K., Alawamleh, H., Al-Shibly, M., Almari, M.: The relationship between the enterprise resource planning system and maintenance planning system: an empirical study. Inf. Sci. Lett. 11(5), 1335–1343 (2022). https://doi.org/10.18576/isl/110502

Al-Rawashdeh, O.M., Jawabreh, O., Ali, B.J.A.: Supply chain management and organizational performance: the moderating effect of supply chain complexity. Inf. Sci. Lett. 12(3) (2023). https://doi.org/10.18576/isl/120351

Addis, S:. Study on the application of statistical quality control techniques in shoe manufacturing for quality improvements. Eur. J. Eng. Technol. 7(6) (2019)

Agrawal, N., Agrawal, N.M.: Modeling Deming's quality principles to improve performance using interpretive structural modeling and MICMAC analysis. Int. J. Qual. Reliab. Manag. 36(7), 1159–1180 (2019). https://doi.org/10.1108/IJQRM-07-2018-0204

Aguirre-Urreta, M.I.: Detecting common method bias: performance of the Harman's single-factor test. Adv. Inf. Syst. 50(2), 45–70 (2019). https://doi.org/10.1145/3330472.3330477

Jain, A.: The concept of triple bottom line reporting and India's perspective. Indian J. Appl. Res. 4(5), 128–130 (2014)

AlRowaiei, W.A., Oudat, M.S., Ali, J.A.: The relationship between non-performing loans and the performance of commercial banks listed on bahrain stock exchange: empirical study. Inf. Sci. Lett. 10(S1), 55–70 (2021). https://doi.org/10.18576/isl/10S10

Anil, A., Technology, K.S.-P.: Investigating the relationship between TQM practices and Firm's performance: a conceptual framework for Indian organizations. Elsevier (2016)

Baird, K., Hu, K.J., Reeve, R.: The relationships between organizational culture, total quality management practices and operational performance. Int. J. Oper. Prod. Manag. 31(7), 789–814 (2011). https://doi.org/10.1108/01443571111144850

Benzaquen, J., Charles, V.: A stratified bootstrapping approach to assessing the success of TQM implementation in Peruvian companies. Total Qual. Manag. Bus. Excell. **33**, 1–24 (2020). https://doi.org/10.1080/14783363.2020.1816165

Bouranta, N., Psomas, E., Suárez-Barraza, M.F., Jaca, C.: The key factors of total quality management in the service sector: a cross-cultural study. Benchmarking **26**(3), 893–921 (2019). https://doi.org/10.1108/BIJ-09-2017-0240

Calvo-Mora, A., Picón-Berjoyo, A., Ruiz-Moreno, C., Cauzo-Bottala, L.: Contextual and mediation analysis between TQM critical factors and organisational results in the EFQM excellence model framework. Int. J. Prod. Res. **53**(7), 2186–2201 (2015). https://doi.org/10.1080/002 07543.2014.975859

Cantele, S., Zardini, A.: Is sustainability a competitive advantage for small businesses? An empirical analysis of possible mediators in the sustainability financial performance relationship. J. Clean. Prod. **182**, 166–176 (2018). https://doi.org/10.1016/j.jclepro.2018.02.016

Pinto, C.A.S., Reis, A.D.C., Braga, M.: The supply chain as part of knowledge management in organisational environments. Int. J. Logistics Syst. Manag. **36**(3), 385–398 (2020). https://doi.org/10.1504/IJLSM.2020.108693

Casino, F., Dasaklis, T.K., Patsakis, C.: A systematic literature review of blockchain-based applications: current status, classification and open issues. Telematics Inform. **36**, 55–81 (2019). https://doi.org/10.1016/j.tele.2018.11.006

Dadhich, M.: An analysis of volatility of macro economic variables on gold price. Pac. Bus. Rev. Int. **9**(12), 21–25 (2017)

Dadhich, M., Hiran, K.K., Rao, S.S., Sharma, R.: Impact of Covid-19 on teaching-learning perception of faculties and students of higher education in Indian purview. J. Mob. Multimedia **18**(4), 957–980 (2022). https://doi.org/10.13052/jmm1550-4646.1841

Dadhich, M., Hiran, K.K., Rao, S.S., Sharma, R., Meena, R.: Study of combating technology induced fraud assault (TIFA) and possible solutions: the way forward. In: Balas, V.E., Sinha, G.R., Agarwal, B., Sharma, T.K., Dadheech, P., Mahrishi, M. (eds.) Emerging Technologies in Computer Engineering: Cognitive Computing and Intelligent IoT, pp. 715–723. Springer, Cham (2022). https://doi.org/10.1007/978-3-031-07012-9_59

Dadhich, M., Kant, K.: Empirical investigation of extended TOE model on corporate environment sustainability and dimensions of operating performance of SMEs: a high order PLS-ANN approach. J. Clean. Prod. **363**, 1–16 (2022). https://doi.org/10.1016/j.jclepro.2022.132309

Dadhich, M., Poddar, S., Kant, K.: Antecedents and consequences of patients' adoption of the IoT 4.0 for e-health management system: a novel PLS-SEM approach. Smart Health **25**(5), 1–14 (2022). https://doi.org/10.1016/j.smhl.2022.100300

Dadhich, M., Purohit, H., Bhasker, A.A.: Determinants of green initiatives and operational performance for manufacturing SMEs. Mater. Today Proc. **46**(20), 10870–10874 (2021). https://doi.org/10.1016/j.matpr.2021.01.889

Dadhich, M., Rao, S.S., Sethy, S., Sharma, R.: Determining the factors influencing cloud computing implementation in library management system (LMS): a high order PLS-ANN approach. Libr. Philos. Pract. **6281** (2021). https://digitalcommons.unl.edu/libphilprac/6281

Das, D.: Development and validation of a scale for measuring sustainable supply chain management practices and performance. J. Clean. Prod. **164**, 1344–1362 (2017). https://doi.org/10.1016/j.jclepro.2017.07.006

Das, D.: The impact of sustainable supply chain management practices on firm performance: lessons from Indian organizations. J. Clean. Prod. **203**, 179–196 (2018). https://doi.org/10.1016/j.jclepro.2018.08.250

Dubey, R., Gunasekaran, A., Samar Ali, S.: Exploring the relationship between leadership, operational practices, institutional pressures and environmental performance: a framework for green supply chain. Int. J. Prod. Econ. **160**, 120–132 (2015). https://doi.org/10.1016/j.ijpe.2014.10.001

Dutta, P., Choi, T.M., Somani, S., Butala, R.: Blockchain technology in supply chain operations: applications, challenges and research opportunities. Transp. Res. Part E Logistics Transp. Rev. **142**, 102607 (2020)

Garay-Rondero, C.L., Martinez-Flores, J.L., Smith, N.R., Caballero Morales, S.O., Aldrette-Malacara, A.: Digital supply chain model in Industry 4.0. J. Manuf. Technol. Manag. **31**(5), 887–933 (2020). https://doi.org/10.1108/JMTM-08-2018-0280

Gaurav Kumar Singh, M.D.: Assessment of multidimensional drivers of blockchain technology (BoT) in sustainable supply chain management (SSCM) of Indian cement industry: a novel PLS-SEM approach. Int. J. Logistics Syst. Manag. (2022). https://doi.org/10.1504/IJLSM. 2022.10045308

Hair, J., Ringle, F., C.M., Sarstedt, M., Ringle, C.M.: Advanced issues in partial least square structural equation modeling (PLS-SEM). SAGE Publications Ltd. (2018)

Hair, J.F., Hult, G.T.M., Ringle, C.M., Sarstedt, M.: A primer on partial least squares structural equation modeling (PLS-SEM) (2016)

Hair, J.F., Black, W.C., Babin, B.J., Anderson, R.E.: Multivariate Data Analysis. 7th edn. (2010)

Hietschold, N., Reinhardt, R., Gurtner, S.: Measuring critical success factors of TQM implementation successfully-a systematic literature review. Int. J. Prod. Res. **52**(21), 6254–6272 (2014). https://doi.org/10.1080/00207543.2014.918288

Jun, M., Cai, S., Peterson, R.T.: Obstacles to TQM implementation in Mexico's maquiladora industry. Total Qual. Manag. Bus. Excell. **15**(1), 59–72 (2004). https://doi.org/10.1080/147 8336032000149108

Jyoti, J., Kour, S., Sharma, J.: Impact of total quality services on financial performance: role of service profit chain. Total Qual. Manag. Bus. Excell. **28**(7–8), 897–929 (2017). https://doi.org/ 10.1080/14783363.2016.1274649

Mathiyazhagan, K., Ahuja, S.: Modelling the sustainable supply chain management practices in Indian industries: a business model using the fuzzy TOPSIS approach. Int. J. Oper. Res. **41**(3), 324–351 (2021)

Kenny, D.A., Baron, R.M.: The moderator-mediator variable distinction in social psychological research: conceptual, strategic, and statistical considerations. J. Pers. Soc. Psychol. **51**(6), 1173 (1986)

Kumar, N., Dadhich, M.: Risk management for investors in stock market. EXCEL Int. J. Multidisc. Manag. Stud. **4**(3), 103–108 (2014)

Kumar, S., Singh, M.: Environmental dynamism, industry 4.0 and performance: mediating role of organizational and technological factors. Ind. Mark. Manage. **95**, 54–64 (2021). https://doi. org/10.1016/j.indmarman.2021.03.010

Dadhich, M., Pahwa, M.S., Goswami, S., Rao, S.S.: Analytical study of financial wellbeing of selected public and private sector banks: a CAMEL approach. In: IEEE Explore Emerging Trends Industry 4.0 (ETI 4.0), pp. 1–6 (2021). https://doi.org/10.1109/ETI4.051663.2021.961 9424

Kouhizadeh, M., Sara Saberi, J.S.: Blockchain technology and the sustainable supply chain: theoretically exploring adoption barriers. Int. J. Prod. Econ. **231**, 107831 (2021). https://doi.org/ 10.1016/j.ijpe.2020.107831

Kshetri, N.: 1 Blockchain's roles in meeting key supply chain management objectives. Int. J. Inf. Manag. **39**, 80–89 (2018)

Luke, R.: The impact of COVID-2019 on transport in South Africa. J. Transp. Supply Chain Management **14**(1), 1–5 (2020)

Remondino, M.: Augmented reality in logistics: qualitative analysis for a managerial perspective. Int. J. Logistics Syst. Manag. **36**(1), 1–15 (2020). https://doi.org/10.1504/IJLSM.2020.107218

Rathore, H., Sahay, S.K., Thukral, S., Sewak, M.: Detection of malicious android applications: classical machine learning vs. deep neural network integrated with clustering. In: InInternational Conference on Broadband Communications, Networks and Systems, pp. 109–128, 11 December 2020

Mendoza-Fong, J.R., García-Alcaraz, J.L., Díaz-Reza, J.R., Jiménez-Macías, E., Blanco-Fernández, J.: The role of green attributes in production processes as well as their impact on operational, commercial, and economic benefits. Sustainability 11, 1–23 (2019). https://doi.org/10.3390/su11051294

Mueller, F., Carter, C.: The scripting of total quality management within its organizational biography. Organ. Stud. 26(2), 221–247 (2005). https://doi.org/10.1177/0170840605049466

Mukri, B.: Blockchain technology in supply chain management: a review. Int. Res. J. Eng. Technol. 5(6), 2497–2500 (2008)

Öztas, A., Özbay, E., Yeğinobali, A.: Current status of total quality management implementation in the Turkish cement industry. Total Qual. Manag. Bus. Excell. 15(7), 985–999 (2004). https://doi.org/10.1080/14783360410001681881

Paliwal, V., Chandra, S., Sharma, S.: Blockchain technology for sustainable supply chain management: a systematic literature review and a classification framework. Sustainability (Switzerland) 12(18), 1–39 (2020). https://doi.org/10.3390/su12187638

Pambreni, Y., Khatibi, A., Ferdous Azam, S.M., Tham, J.: The influence of total quality management toward organization performance. Manag. Sci. Lett. 9(9), 1397–1406 (2019). https://doi.org/10.5267/j.msl.2019.5.011

Purohit, H., Dadhich, M., Ajmera, P.K.: Analytical study on users' awareness and acceptability towards adoption of multimodal biometrics (MMB) mechanism in online transactions: a two-stage SEM-ANN approach. Multimedia Tools Appl. 1, 1–25 (2022). https://doi.org/10.1007/s11042-022-13786-z

Feng, Q., He, D., Zeadally, S., Khan, M.K., Kumar, N.: A survey on privacy protection in blockchain system. J. Netw. Comput. Appl. 126, 45–58 (2019)

Qu, Q., Nurgaliev, I., Muzammal, M., Jensen, C.S., Fan, J.: On spatio-temporal blockchain query processing. Future Gen. Comput. Syst. 98, 208–218 (2019)

Sabella, A., Kashou, R., Omran, O.: Quality management practices and their relationship to organizational performance. Int. J. Oper. Prod. Manag. 34(12), 1487–1505 (2014). https://doi.org/10.1108/IJOPM-04-2013-0210

Saxena, S., Bhushan, B., Abdul, M.: Blockchain based solutions to secure IoT: background, integration trends and a way forward. J. Netw. Comput. Appl. 181, 103050 (2021). https://doi.org/10.1016/j.jnca.2021.103050

Sharma, N., Dadhich, M.: Predictive business analytics: the way ahead. J. Commerce Manag. Thought 5(4), 652 (2014). https://doi.org/10.5958/0976-478x.2014.00012.3

Shokouhyar, S., Seddigh, M.R., Panahifar, F.: Impact of big data analytics capabilities on supply chain sustainability. World J. Sci. Technol. Sustain. Dev. 17(1), 33–57 (2020). https://doi.org/10.1108/WJSTSD-06-2019-0031

Shrimali, B., Patel, H.B.: Blockchain state-of-the-art: architecture, use cases, consensus, challenges and opportunities. J. King Saud University – Comput. Inf. Sci. (2021). https://doi.org/10.1016/j.jksuci.2021.08.005

Singh, G.K.: Impact execution of total quality management (TQM) on operational performance of Indian cement manufacturing industry: a comprehensive SEM approach. Des. Eng. 8, 13538–13562 (2021). http://thedesignengineering.com/index.php/DE/article/view/6476

Sinha, N., Dhall, N.: Mediating effect of TQM on relationship between organisational culture and performance: evidence from Indian SMEs. Total Qual. Manag. Bus. Excell. 31(15–16), 1841–1865 (2020). https://doi.org/10.1080/14783363.2018.1511372

Srivastava, S., Bhadauria, A., Dhaneshwar, S., Gupta, S.: Supply chain management system in Indian pharmaceutical industries: strategies and best practices. J. Stat. Appl. Probab. **12**(3) (2023). Article 30. https://doi.org/10.18576/jsap/120330

Tortorella, G., Giglio, R., Fogliatto, F.S., Sawhney, R.: Mediating role of learning organization on the relationship between total quality management and operational performance in Brazilian manufacturers. J. Manuf. Technol. Manag. **31**(3), 524–541 (2019). https://doi.org/10.1108/JMTM-05-2019-0200

Treiblmaier, H.: The impact of the blockchain on the supply chain: a theory-based research framework and a call for action. Supply Chain Manag. **23**(6), 545–559 (2018). https://doi.org/10.1108/SCM-01-2018-0029

Tribis, Y., El Bouchti, A., Bouayad, H.: Supply chain management based on blockchain: a systematic mapping study. MATEC Web Conf. **200**. https://doi.org/10.1051/matecconf/201820000020

Wali, A.A., Deshmukh, S.G., Gupta, A.D.: Critical success factors of TQM: a select study of Indian organizations. Prod. Plann. Control **14**(1), 3–14 (2003). https://doi.org/10.1080/0953728021000034781

Wang, R., Wu, Y.: Application of blockchain technology in supply chain finance of Beibu gulf region. Math. Problems Eng. **1**, 1–10 (2021). https://doi.org/10.1155/2021/5556424

Factors Affecting Behavioral Intention to Use Digital Currency in the Kingdom of Bahrain

Fahad Mohamed Alyahya[✉] and Sameh M. Reda Reyad

Ahlia University, Al-Hoora 310, Gosi Complex, Manama, Kingdom of Bahrain
fahad_alyahya_1@hotmail.com

Abstract. The rapid technological development in our lives has created a new form of currency called digital currency. It can be defined as a form of virtual currency that is electronically created and stored. This study investigates issues that affect an individual's behavioral intention to use digital currency. Factors influencing behavioral intention by individuals in the Kingdom of Bahrain, such as perceived usefulness, perceived ease of use, trust, social influence, and security, are investigated. A questionnaire was distributed to citizens and residents to collect primary data, and 396 responses were acknowledged, bringing the study's sample size to the required level. The study's conceptual framework and primary hypothesis were developed using a quantitative research methodology. The data was checked for errors and validity, and a regression analysis was performed to check the study's hypothesis. The findings of the study proved a significant level of behavioral intention toward using digital currency in the Kingdom of Bahrain, where perceived usefulness, perceived ease of use, social influence, and trust were found to significantly affect behavioral intention to use digital currency, while security, on the contrary, did not significantly affect behavior.

Keywords: Digital currency · Behavioral Intention · Usefulness · Ease of Use · Trust · Social Influence · Security

1 Introduction

Currencies are an integral part of our lives in terms of managing our lives and purchasing our main needs, such as foods and clothes. Almost every single day of our lives doesn't end without using money. Money and currencies evolved through several stages before becoming what they are today in our lives. And with the rapid technological development of recent years, digital currency has risen as a novel method of payment. Digital currency is the new trend in our society, and as per Rose (2015), it can be defined as a form of virtual currency that is electronically created and stored. Some, but not all, digital currencies are cryptocurrencies Al-jabra (2023). According to CoinMarketCap (2022), the most-referenced website for crypto assets, presently there are more than 21,000 cryptocurrencies in the market, led by Bitcoin, which has the largest market cap overall.

In 2008, Satoshi Nakamoto introduced the first digital currency, "Bitcoin," as an alternative currency to what is traded in the banking system (Nakamoto, 2022). Since

A. M. A. Musleh Al-Sartawi et al. (Eds.): ICGER 2023, CCIS 1999, pp. 114–130, 2024.
https://doi.org/10.1007/978-3-031-50518-8_10

then, Bitcoin has gained widespread popularity year after year. All digital currency transactions are maintained on a distributed public ledger, called the blockchain, rather than a centralized body, like a bank, to track the balance and develop assurance in the currency (Wu, Fan, Wang, & Zou, 2019). The benefits of digital currencies are numerous, in addition to the fact that they are beneficial not only to businesses or entrepreneurs but also to consumers. Some of those advantages are: they are simple to use, payments are quick, it is less expensive, it is secured, you can maintain your anonymity, your personal information is kept private, there will be no chargebacks, and there will be no third-party involvement. However, the benefits do not imply that there are no risks associated with dealing in digital currencies; it has limitations, such as being difficult to understand, requiring insufficient knowledge, not being widely accepted, you could lose your money, there is no way to reverse the payment, and it is unpredictable (Khan & Hakami, 2021).

Major internet companies and enterprises, like Microsoft, Expedia, Rakuten Japan, and Amazon, have started adopting digital currencies for payment, either directly or indirectly, for practical purposes. Even though Bitcoin is becoming more popular, many underdeveloped nations remain ignorant of it. Most SMEs retail merchants avoid digital currency transactions due to their complexity or because they are completely unaware of their existence in other situations (Ter Ji-Xi, Salamzadeh, & Teoh, 2021).

Bahrain Financial Services has been ranked the first cryptocurrency asset platform in the Arabian Gulf (Shaikh, Wadi, & AlMahari, 2021), (Jasim et al., 2021), (Abdul-rahman et al., 2021). And according to Dempere (2019), Bahrain and the United Arab Emirate (UAE) are racing to become the hubs of digital currency in the Gulf territory. Furthermore, the Central Bank of Bahrain approved the Bahrain-based digital currency exchange called "Rain" to become the first fully regulated digital currency exchange in the Middle East and North Africa (MENA) region.

People often prefer to pay for things without cash these days. With the push of a button, mobile phones and internet services have simplified and made life easier. This in turn increases customer requirements and expectations. Therefore, cashless payments have almost completely replaced physical cash transactions in the contemporary environment (Yuvaraj & Sheila Eveline, 2018).

Recently, there has been a lot of talk about digital currencies, whether among people or on social media platforms; thus, it has become the talk of the town, and several currencies have arisen and started in the Kingdom of Bahrain. However, so far, there has been no study conducted in Bahrain that measures people's intentions regarding the use of these currencies. Furthermore, there is no study that identifies the factors that affect behavioral intentions to use digital currency.

Since the past, the Kingdom of Bahrain has been a key financial center (Al-Alkawi et al., 2020), (Adnan, 2022). There are now more than 400 licensed financial institutions in Bahrain, which represent a wide range of international, regional, and local brands. They specialize in wholesale banking, insurance, and fund and asset management. With almost 27% of GDP, the financial sector has become the most significant sector of the economy. Bahrainis account for almost 80% of the workers in the financial sector (eGovernment Portal, 2022).

Recently, the Central Bank of Bahrain took a big step in regulating the work of digital currencies by issuing licenses to companies providing crypto-asset services and crypto-asset exchanges. So, with the emergence of these institutions and the announcement of their establishment in the Kingdom of Bahrain, Bahraini citizens and non-Bahraini residents are the main drivers for them. Thus, it is necessary to know what behaviors will encourage them to use these currencies. Therefore, this research study will contribute to understanding the behavioral intention level to use digital currency and the factors driving them to use digital currencies through perceived usefulness, perceived ease of use, trust, social influence, and security.

2 Literature Review

2.1 Digital Currency

Nowadays, digital currency has become part of wider society and is having a huge influence in developing countries. This evidence indicates how alternative financial systems can significantly improve the well-being of societies and groups of people, so it's a strong endorsement for the need for various monetary methods beyond the traditional banking systems that primarily use fiat currencies as a medium of exchange. It's worth noting that, while Bitcoin was the first crypto currency to attain widespread acceptance, it wasn't the first crypto currency. However, it was the first digital currency to enable a truly decentralized system that works on a global scale (Ateniese, Magri, Venturi, & Andrade, 2017), while simultaneously preventing double spending through the use of encryption (Swammy, Thompson, & Loh, 2018). And since its inception in 2008, bitcoin has been lauded by some as being free of any third-party supervision, such as that of any government legislature or a central bank (Baldwin, 2018). Moreover, bitcoin was introduced for circulation in 2009 when the first block was created at that time (Raskin & Yermack, 2018).

Consumers were exposed to digital money as a financial innovation and as an alternate payment mechanism. Because it can improve financial efficiency by ensuring safe, quick, and low-cost transactions. The use of digital currency (such as bitcoin) as a universal means of exchange, on the other hand, undermines the central bank's dominance in currency supply. While the value of fiat money is supported by the government's and the country's central bank's trustworthiness, the price of digital currency is determined solely by demand and supply with the anticipation that it will be utilized and appreciated by the currency holders (Hanafi & Rahman, 2019).

In addition, as per Hossain (2021), the primary goal of digital currencies is to make transactions and transfers easier while maintaining safety through the use of either an internal or external network key. This approach allows consumers to avoid charges that are mandated by traditional banking institution rules, allowing them to complete transactions with minimum transaction fees.

2.2 Blockchain

It is also necessary to know about the technology that operates the digital currencies, which is called the blockchain. As per Bakar & Rosbi (2018), the blockchain is a distributed public ledger of transactions that is transmitted via safe encryption. Each block uses a secure hash code from a computer language to store prior transaction data, timestamps, and any new transaction requests. Also, it allows people to easily share their transaction ledger. Furthermore, the history of all transaction activities is sent to all network users, who can then authenticate the transactions using their computer devices, eliminating the need for any 3rd party intermediary such as banks and financial institutions. The information in the blockchain can never be deleted once it's been recorded, giving a full audit trail of all linked events and activities, and that information can only be updated by most of the system's members.

Based on the above, we can notice that the ability of the blockchain to move cash from one jurisdiction to another for a cheap price is among the key benefits of this technology. Transactions on the blockchain are inexpensive, quick, accessible, and safe. And it is an encrypted, decentralized network that ensures confidentiality and safeguards it from unauthorized access and change (Mazanec, 2021).

The fast growth of blockchain and fintech has influenced the global industrial structure in the last few years. Simultaneously, blockchain and fintech are slowly but steadily altering the whole economic structure. Nations have also started to investigate the possibility of their countries advancing into the digital currency era. This demonstrates that the introduction of the Internet and digital currency based on cryptographic algorithms has marked a significant shift in fintech development. Transactions and payment patterns have altered because of these financial technology advancements, and the regular banking firms' roles are changing as well (Hsu & Tsai, 2021).

Zalan (2018) draws our attention to the fact that research and development for the blockchain are considered open source, where any individual with a PC and Internet connectivity may contribute a part of the code or any other specific learning from anywhere in the world. Also, he added, nearly every major banking institution in the world, including government central banks, is researching blockchain technology, and most of the largest countries have an exchange platform for digital currency. Furthermore, he explains how the blockchain and its smart contract technology enable so-called "decentralized autonomous organizations" (DAOs), where companies can exist just on the internet with no physical presence and whose contracts of establishment and association exist only as smart contracts on the blockchain.

2.3 Definition of the Digital Currency

It is important to have a proper definition for the digital currency in order for all of society, whether they are individuals or businesses, to align with it and to unify it in a proper way. However, currently there are a variety of technical definitions being used for this terminology. At the moment, there is no widely accepted definition (Jayawardhana & Colombage, 2020). Hence, we will consolidate in this section the most commonly used definitions in order to have an appropriate and comprehensive one that we are going to adopt in this research.

According to FATF (2014), they defined digital currency as a "digital representation of either virtual currency (non-fiat) or e-money (fiat) and thus is often used interchangeably with the term virtual currency." And by "virtual currency," they meant any digital form of value that can be exchanged electronically and can be used as a medium of exchange, a unit of account, or a store of value, but it has no legal status in any country.

Bakar & Rosbi (2018) define cryptocurrency as a "digital currency in which encryption techniques are used to regulate the generation of units of currency and verify the transfer of funds, operating independently of a central bank." Moreover, Mora, López, Tello, & Morales (2019) agree with them in their research paper in terms of its consideration as a digital representation of money, in that it is not distributed by the country's central bank and its value is not maintained by the government itself.

Baldwin (2018) defined it as "a digital coin that is constructed and structured as a chain of digital signatures." It has no physical value and is nothing more than a digital ledger entry. Making their transactions entirely peer-to-peer, without the use of a middleman. It also makes use of encryption to verify and secure the transactions. In a simple way, Shou, Wang, Li, & Zhou (2020) define it as "an alternate currency in the form of electronic money."

According to Jayawardhana and Colombage (2020), they gathered and reviewed numerous articles and resources before arriving at the following definition: "a sustainable digital asset with the potential to transform business interactions, place, and the direction of the economy and environment."

From the above definitions, we can see that the majority has agreed that the digital currency is also known as "cryptocurrency," and those two terminologies can be clearly used interchangeably. Hence, it can be well-defined as the comprehensive term to describe all electronic money, which includes virtual currencies and cryptocurrencies that are available in electronic and digital form, unlike paper or coin currencies, which are considered intangible. It does, however, have the same characteristics as fiat currencies, such as instant transactions and unlimited ownership transfer; it can even be used to purchase various goods and services.

2.4   Types of Digital Currencies

The digital currencies on the market are divided into several types. In this section, we will talk about its details. In general, we can have 3 main categories of them: first, we have the "coins," which are crypto currencies that are based according to their own blockchain platform and independently operated; second, we have the "tokens," which are also crypto currencies, but rely on the blockchain technology platform of another coin to function (Cennamo, Marchesi, & Meyer, 2020). And lastly, we have the "central bank digital currencies," or "CBDC," as they are established and controlled sovereignly by the country's central bank (Bordo & Levin, 2017).

- Cryptocurrency "Coins"

A coin is a digital currency that has been mainly used as a means of exchange in peer-to-peer networks to transfer value for users. Moreover, those cryptocurrencies are built from scratch, they work independently, and they have their own standalone blockchain network (Schellinger, 2020).

According to Pillai, Biswas, and Muthukkumarasamy (2019), in order to generate, trade, and verify the transaction in a decentralized way, those coins are recorded on a blockchain ledger, which uses methods such as encryption, peer-to-peer networks, distributed consensus, and smart contracts. In addition, they agreed with many other researchers that by referring to the term "coin" in cryptocurrency, it meant a cryptographic asset used as a medium of exchange in principle.

An example of cryptocurrency coins in the market are Bitcoin and Ethereum, which also have the largest market caps in terms of the value of their circulating supply in the overall market (CoinMarketCap, 2022). So, for example, the Ethereum blockchain is used whenever any Ether transactions take place. Every transaction in this network is encrypted, and only the members of the network have access to it. Whereas Bitcoin transactions, on the other hand, are processed on their own blockchain as well. The blockchain for a specific coin record all its related transactions, and there are also a variety of ways to mine coins. Each blockchain has its own limited coin number; thus, there will be a limited number of circulated supplies in the market. Individuals can mine for coins in two ways, according to another feature owned by those coins. The first method is to mine using the Proof of Work technique. Another option is to use "proof of stake," which is a newer technique of earning coins by mining. What distinguishes this method is that it uses less energy and has a more straightforward process (Nahar, 2022).

- Cryptocurrency "Tokens"

Token is a digital currency that depends on third-party blockchain infrastructures to function (Cennamo, Marchesi, & Meyer, 2020). Nahar (2022) confirmed the same point in his article that tokens don't have their own standalone blockchain; however, they work on other cryptocurrency coin blockchains. Many tokens, for example, operate on Ethereum. This category also includes stablecoins, which are generally fixed to the US dollar. They also depend on the "smart contract," which is a set of codes that makes trading between two people easier. According to Schellinger (2020), the introduction of so-called "smart contracts" on the Ethereum blockchain, which are described in the Ethereum project's white paper, was one of the main reasons for the growth in token sales. Smart contracts automate the execution of predetermined contract conditions and are critical to the advancement of digital contracts in both the financial and nonfinancial sectors.

According to Gandal, Hamrick, Moore, & Vasek (2021), tokens are commonly used to get access to a product or service. On the one hand, this means that tokens are more likely to capture (possible) genuine economic activity in the industry, and on the other, tokens have the profitable chance to acquire capital from investors through the initial coin offerings (ICOs). And Schellinger (2020) added to this point by noting that the launch of initial coin offerings (ICOs), also known as token sales, created whole new avenues for funding blockchain-related initiatives and start-ups through the issue of tokens.

- Central Bank Digital Currencies (CBDC)

The Federal Reserve Board (2022) defined the CBDC as a digital liability that a central bank has that is broadly accessible to the public. Today in the US, the only type of central bank money that the general public can use is Federal Reserve notes, which are physical cash. A CBDC, like other types of money, would let people make digital payments like they can with other types of money. A CBDC would be the least risky digital money available to the general public. There would have been no credit or cashflow risk with it.

Unlike reserves or settlement balances kept by commercial banks at central banks, CBDCs are a new type of digital central bank currency that is being developed. To keep pace with the increasing increase of digital payments in place of cash, as well as the advent of commercial global stablecoins, most central banks are presently exploring or actively creating CBDCs as an "alternative secure, resilient, and convenient payment mechanism." In accordance with the Bank for International Settlements, 86% of central banks throughout the world are now conducting comprehensive studies on CBDCs (Foster, Blakstad, Gazi, & Bos, 2021).

According to Bordo & Levin (2017), CBDC would be set in nominal terms, be available to everyone, and be the medium of exchange for all public and private transactions, making it a good way to pay for everything. As a result, CBDC is very different from other forms of digital currencies that have been made by private businesses and whose prices have changed a lot in recent years (such as Bitcoin, Ethereum, and Ripple). They concluded their research paper by saying that CBDC can be used as a cheap medium of exchange, a safe store of value, and a stable measure of value.

3   Research Methodology

This research will adopt a mono methodological choice by having a quantitative research design to achieve our key goals and objectives. Our research is experimental, and the hypotheses are determined to be tested; thus, our aim is to quantify the effect of the results using statistical data that will be collected through a questionnaire circulated by electronic means to the citizens and residents of the Kingdom of Bahrain.

3.1   Study Conceptual Model

The conceptual model built for this research study is illustrated below. The conceptual model tests the relationships between 5 independent variables and 1 dependent variable. Each relationship is represented by a hypothesis. The variables include perceived usefulness, perceived ease of use, trust, social influence, and security. The dependent variable is defined as the behavioral intention to use digital currency (Fig. 1).

3.2   Research Hypothesis

The following are the research hypotheses intended to address which factors affect individuals' behavioral intention to use digital currency in the Kingdom of Bahrain:

- **H1:** Perceived usefulness is a factor that has a significant effect on behavioral intention to use digital currency in the Kingdom of Bahrain.
- **H2:** Perceived ease of use is a factor that has a significant effect on behavioral intention to use digital currency in the Kingdom of Bahrain.
- **H3:** Trust is a factor that has a significant effect on behavioral intention to use digital currency in the Kingdom of Bahrain.
- **H4:** Social influence is a factor that has a significant effect on behavioral intention to use digital currency in the Kingdom of Bahrain.
- **H5:** Security is a factor that has a significant effect on behavioral intention to use digital currency in the Kingdom of Bahrain.

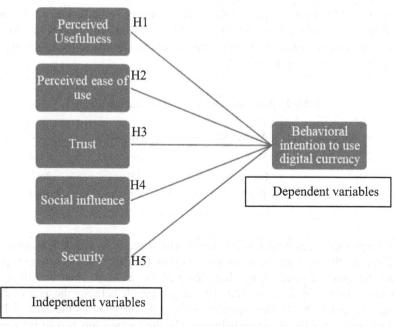

Fig. 1. Research Conceptual Model of factors that affect behavioral intention to use digital currency in the Kingdom of Bahrain

3.3 Research Population and Research Sample

Through data analysis, we will look at the potential relationships between our dependent variable and the independent variables. The research population, targeted population, and sample size are shown in the Table 1 below.

Table 1. Research Population, Targeted Population, and Sample Size.

Population	1,504,365 (as per iGA data, 2021 population of the kingdom of Bahrain)
Targeted Population	1,131,648 (as per iGA data, 2021 population age of 20 and above in the Kingdom of Bahrain)
Sample Size	384

4 Data Analysis and Findings

4.1 Descriptive Analysis of Demographic Data

The gender of the respondents was the first question in the demographic section of the survey's data collection. Those who identify as male and those who identify as female are naturally separated into two categories. The first category is the male gender, which accounts for 74.7% of the total, and the second category is the female gender, which accounts for 25.3% of the total. In addition, we can suppose from the large difference between the ratio of males and females that men are more interested in dealing with digital currency than women (Table 2).

Table 2. Participants Responses to Gender Question

No.	Question	Answer Selected	Frequency	Percent
1	Gender	Male	296	74.7%
		Female	100	25.3%
		Total	**396**	**100%**

The respondents' age ranges were detailed in the survey's second demographic question. There are five distinct age brackets defined by the data. The first group is people between the ages of 20 and 29, which made up 24.7% question. There are five distinct age brackets defined by the data. The first group is people between the ages of 20 and 29, which made up 24.7%. The second group was people between the ages of 30 and 39, which made up 47% of the participants. The third group was people between the ages of 40 and 49, which made up 16.4% of the participants. The fourth group was people between the ages of 50 and 59, which made up (6.6%) of the participants, and the fifth group was people between the ages of 60 and 69, which made up (5.3%) of the participants. Those between the ages of 20 and 39 made up the bulk of the survey's respondents, making their participation a clear indication of their generation's interests. It's possible that this means that the younger generation is more interested in digital currency and adopting innovative technology. Obviously, this assumption has to be tested and confirmed in further study (Table 3).

Table 3. Participants Responses to Age Question

No.	Question	Answer Selected	Frequency	Percent
2	Age	20–29 years old	98	24.7%
		30–39 years old	186	47%
		40–49 years old	65	16.4%
		50–59 years old	26	6.6%
		60–69 years old	21	5.3%
		Total	**396**	**100%**

The third and last piece of demographic information from the survey questions was the level of education of the people who took it. There are five groups based on the level of education of the participants. The first group was made up of people with a high school diploma, which accounted for 12.1% of the participants. The second category was for people with a bachelor's degree, which made up 68.7% of the participants. The third category was for people with a master's degree, which made up 15.7% of the participants. The fourth category was for people with a PhD, which made up 0.8% of the participants. The fifth and final category was for people with any other type of certification, which made up 2.8% of the participants. Based on the statistics shown above, it's reasonable to assume that most of the participants have a bachelor's degree. This might explain why most of the participants were in the 20- to 39-year-old age group (Table 4).

Table 4. Participants Responses to Education Question

No.	Question	Answer Selected	Frequency	Percent
3	Education	High School Diploma	48	12.1%
		Bachelor's Degree	272	68.7%
		Master's Degree	62	15.7%
		PhD	3	0.8%
		Others	11	2.8%
		Total	**396**	**100%**

4.2 Research Hypothesis Testing

In this section, the interpretation of the multiple regression analysis for our identified variables in the conceptual model is discussed, and it is hypothesized to show and understand the relationship between independent variables and the dependent variable in order to determine the final results.

Table 5. Output of Model Summary for the Multiple Regression Analysis

Model Summary				
Model	R	R^2	Adj R^2	Std. Error of the Estimate
1	0.827	0.684	0.680	0.665

As shown in Tables 5 and 6, the results show that 68% of the variance in behavioral intention to use digital currency can be accounted for by the five independent variables, collectively, $F(5, 390) = 168.960$, P 0.001, which indicates that the overall model is significant.

Looking at the unique individual contributions of the independent variables as shown in Table 7, the results show that perceived usefulness (b = .631, t = 11.717, P = 0.000), perceived ease of use (b = .185, t = 3.515, P = 0.000), trust (b = .218; t = 3.835, P

Table 6. Output of ANOVA for the Multiple Regression Analysis

ANOVA

Model	SS	df	MS	F	Sig.
Regression	373.722	5	74.744	168.960	0.000
Residual	172.528	390	0.442		
Total	546.250	395			

Table 7. Output of Coefficients for the Multiple Regression Analysis

Coefficients

Model	B	SE	t	Sig.
(Intercept)	−0.636	0.159	−4.009	0.000
Perceived Usefulness	0.631	0.054	11.717	0.000
Perceived Ease of Use	0.185	0.053	3.515	0.000
Trust	0.218	0.057	3.825	0.000
Social Influence	0.099	0.040	2.485	0.013
Security	0.095	0.058	1.636	0.103

= 0.000), and social influence (b = .099, t = 2.485, P = 0.013) significantly impact behavioral intention to use digital currency. However, the findings showed that security (b = .095, t = 1.636, P = .103) had no effect on behavioral intention to use digital currency.

The result of multiple regression stated above is taken into consideration for the hypothesis results. With a significance level (p-value) of less than 0.05 for four variables, the regression analysis results demonstrated a definitive conclusion that perceived usefulness, perceived ease of use, trust, and social influence had a significant relationship with the dependent variable. Furthermore, security had a p-value greater than 0.05, indicating that this factor does not have a relationship with the dependent variable. Results from a regression analysis test performed for this study are displayed and summarized in Table 8.

Table 8. Summary of all factors linear regression results

Hypothesis	Path	Sig.	Result
H1: Perceived usefulness is a factor that has a significant effect on behavioral intention to use digital currency in the Kingdom of Bahrain	PU → BI	0.000	Accepted
H2: Perceived ease of use is a factor that has a significant effect on behavioral intention to use digital currency in the Kingdom of Bahrain	PE → BI	0.000	Accepted
H3: Trust is a factor that has a significant effect on behavioral intention to use digital currency in the Kingdom of Bahrain	T → BI	0.000	Accepted
H4: Social influence is a factor that has a significant effect on behavioral intention to use digital currency in the Kingdom of Bahrain	SI → BI	0.013	Accepted
H5: Security is a factor that has a significant effect on behavioral intention to use digital currency in the Kingdom of Bahrain	S → BI	0.103	Rejected

5 Conclusion

This research focuses on measuring the level of individual behavioral intention that leads toward using digital currency in the Kingdom of Bahrain and the factors that affect this behavior. In this research, a quantitative methodology was used by conducting an online survey. As a result, the 396 participants in this study represent a representative sample of the Kingdom of Bahrain's population. The hypothesis of this research is to test the impact of "perceived usefulness," "perceived ease of use," "trust," "social influence," and "security" on individuals' behavioral intention to use digital currency and determine whether they are affected significantly by them or not. Descriptive analysis, validity analysis, and linear regression analysis used in this research all helped to verify or disprove the five examined hypotheses. The findings show the following:

- Our findings support the conclusion of Ter Ji-Xi, Salamzadeh, & Teoh (2021) that perceived usefulness is a critical factor in determining individuals' behavioral intentions toward using digital currency. In their study of Malaysian consumers, they found that perceived usefulness was the most important factor in determining intention, implying that consumers prefer technologies that allow them to do their activities easily and effectively. Our findings are consistent with these results and extend them to the context of the Kingdom of Bahrain. Our study found that perceived usefulness significantly affects individuals' behavioral intentions toward using digital currency, indicating the high advantages of this new technology and its usefulness in people's lives.

- Our findings are consistent with the study conducted by Saleh, Ibrahim, Noordin, & Mohadis (2020) which investigated the relationship between ease of use and behavioral intentions toward using digital currency in the Malaysian market. They found that ease of use has a direct impact on behavioral intentions to use digital currency and that the relationship showed a significant positive influence. Our study extends these findings to the context of the Kingdom of Bahrain, where we found that individual behavioral intentions toward using digital currency are significantly influenced by the factor ease of use. This indicates that people in Bahrain are aware of and understand digital currency and that it is easy for them to use it.

- The finding in the Kingdom of Bahrain, that trust has a big effect on individuals' behavioral intentions towards using digital currency, is in line with the results of previous studies. In the study by Gupta, Gupta, Mathew, & Sama (2020), it was found that perceived trust had a medium impact on the intention to invest in digital currency. Similarly, Soomro, Shah, & Abdelwahed (2022) found that trust had a strong positive impact on the intention to adopt digital currency among potential investors in Pakistan. These studies support the conclusion that trust is a crucial factor in determining individuals' behavioral intentions towards digital currency. Moreover, the results of this study in the Kingdom of Bahrain indicate that the sophisticated cryptographic system and decentralization of digital currency contribute to making it a trustworthy option for individuals, which in turn affects their behavioral intentions towards using it.

- The findings of my study align with previous literature on the impact of social influence on individuals' behavioral intentions towards using digital currency. This is similar to the findings of the study conducted by Arias-Oliva, de Andrés-Sánchez, & Pelegrín-Borondo (2021), which found that social influence combined with other factors, such as effort expectancy, positively influenced behavioral intentions to use digital currencies in Spanish populations. On the other hand, the study conducted by Mazambani & Mutambara (2019) found a non-significant negative relationship between social influence and behavioral intention to adopt digital currency in South Africa. This difference could be due to cultural differences and privacy concerns in financial matters. Nevertheless, my study highlights the importance of social influence in shaping individuals' behavior intentions towards using digital currency in the Kingdom of Bahrain.

- The findings of my study are in line with previous literature on the impact of security on individuals' behavioral intentions towards using digital currency. The study conducted by Guych et al. (2018) in Taiwanese hotels found that security risk related to digital currency payments was not shown to significantly affect the usefulness of digital currency. Similarly, the study by Alaklabi & Kang (2021) found that there was insufficient evidence to support the notion that users' behavior was significantly negatively impacted by security risk in Saudi Arabia. My study adds to this body of literature by demonstrating that in the Kingdom of Bahrain, security does not play a significant role in shaping individual behavior towards using digital currency.

In conclusion, this research has shown that individuals in Bahrain are utilizing digital currencies, and four of the factors identified have a significant impact on their intentions to use digital currencies in the Kingdom of Bahrain. Moreover, the results of this study have important implications for the economy, policy, and businesses in the Kingdom of Bahrain. With a significant level of behavioral intention toward the use of digital currency in the country, there is an opportunity for the government and businesses to tap into the potential of this innovative technology. For example, the government can consider promoting and regulating digital currencies, thereby boosting the country's digital economy. Policymakers can also use the findings of this study to develop appropriate policies that would enhance the growth of the digital currency market, thereby fostering economic development. Businesses, on the other hand, can take advantage of the high level of acceptance for digital currency to offer innovative products and services that cater to the needs of the local population. By doing so, they can increase their competitiveness, profitability, and customer satisfaction in the market. The results of this study provide valuable insights that can help the government, policymakers, and businesses to make informed decisions about the future of digital currency in the Kingdom of Bahrain.

Appendix: Survey

Section 1: General Information.
   Section 2: Measuring research study factors:

1. Strongly Disagree
2. Disagree
3. Not certain
4. Agree
5. Strongly Agree

Part 1: *Measuring Perceived Usefulness*	1	2	3	4	5
I think that owning Digital Currency has its benefits					
I think that trading in Digital Currency would be useful in my life					
I think that trading in Digital Currency makes it easier to improve my financial situation					
I think that with Digital Currency, I can instantly transfer money					
I think that with Digital Currency, I do not have to deal with any third party (such as Bank)					

Part 2: *Measuring Perceived Ease of Use*	1	2	3	4	5
I think that Digital Currency is easy to use					
I think that it is easy to learn how to trade in Digital Currency					
I think that trading in Digital Currency is clear and understandable					
I can easily convert Bahraini Dinars into Digital Currency and vice versa					

Part 3: *Measuring Trust*	1	2	3	4	5
Digital Currency can be trusted completely					
I feel safe when using Digital Currency					
The decentralization of Digital Currency makes it a safe Currency					
Digital Currency has sophisticated cryptographic system which makes it forgery-proof					

Part 4: *Measuring Social Influence*	1	2	3	4	5
People who can influence my behavior would think that I should use Digital Currency					
People who are important to me (family, friends, colleagues etc.) would probably suggest that I should use Digital Currency					

Part 5: *Measuring Security*	1	2	3	4	5
Digital Currency allows me to transfer money securely					
Digital Currency enables me to control my money					
Money is considered safe in transactions using Digital Currency					

Section 3: Measuring behavioral intention to use Digital Currency.

1. Strongly Disagree
2. Disagree
3. Not certain
4. Agree
5. Strongly Agree

Measuring behavioral intention to use Digital Currency	1	2	3	4	5
I intend to continue using digital currency in the future					
I expect my use of Digital currency to continue in the future					
I plan to use digital currency in the future					

References

Al-Fehani, N.A., Al-Alkawi, T., Al-Dulaimy, S., Binshams, F.: The effect of valontery disclouser on the financial performance of commertial banks sector on Bahrain bourse: an empirical study. Inf. Sci. Lett. **10**(4), 111–127 (2021)

Saifi, R.A., Hatamleh, I.M.: Electronic management requirements and their role in improving job performance. J. Stat. Appl. Pro. **11**(1), 353–376 (2022)

Al-Alkawi, T., Al-Qallaf, A.J.: Feasibility of investment in HR training to develop employee performance - applied study in the ministry of education in the Kingdom of Bahrain. J. Stat. Appl. Pro. **9**(3), 495–505 (2020)

Alaklabi, S., Kang, K.: Perceptions towards cryptocurrency adoption: a case of Saudi Arabian Citizens. J. Electron. Bank. Syst. **2021** (2021)

Al-jabra, A.A., HendAlmanasra, H., Al-Khawaja, H.A.: A vision towards the future of cryptocurrencies rooting, its financial significance, and legal challenges in its use. Inf. Sci. Lett. **12**(8), 2545–2557 (2023)

Arias-Oliva, M., de Andrés-Sánchez, J., Pelegrín-Borondo, J.: Fuzzy set qualitative comparative analysis of factors influencing the use of cryptocurrencies in Spanish households. Mathematics **9**(4), 324 (2021)

Ateniese, G., Magri, B., Venturi, D., Andrade, E.: Redactable blockchain–or–rewriting history in bitcoin and friends. In: 2017 IEEE European Symposium on Security and Privacy (EuroS&P), pp. 111–126 (2017)

Bakar, N.A., Rosbi, S.: Robust framework diagnostics of blockchain for bitcoin transaction system: a technical analysis from Islamic Financial Technology (i-FinTech) perspective. Int. J. Bus. Manag. **2**(3), 22–29 (2018)

Baldwin, J.: In digital we trust: bitcoin discourse, digital currencies, and decentralized network fetishism. Palgrave Commun. **4**(1), 1–10 (2018)

Bordo, M.D., Levin, A.T.: Central bank digital currency and the future of monetary policy. National Bureau of Economic Research (2017)

Cennamo, C., Marchesi, C., Meyer, T.: Two sides of the same coin? Decentralized versus proprietary blockchains and the performance of digital currencies. Acad. Manag. Discoveries **6**(3), 382–405 (2020)

CoinMarketCap: All cryptocurrencies I CoinMarketCap. Retrieved from CoinMarketCap, 8 August 2022. https://coinmarketcap.com/

Dempere, J.M.: Factors affecting the return and volatility of major cryptocurrencies. In: 2019 Sixth HCT Information Technology Trends (ITT), pp. 104–109 (2019)

eGovernment Portal: Kingdom of Bahrain - eGovernment Portal, 8 August 2022. https://www.bahrain.bh/wps/portal/

FATF: FATF report, virtual currencies – Key definitions and potential AML/CFT risks. Paris Cedex 16, France: FATF/OECD (2014)

Federal Reserve Board: Central Bank Digital Currency (CBDC), 30 June 2022. Federal Reserve Board. https://www.federalreserve.gov/central-bank-digital-currency.htm

Foster, K., Blakstad, S., Gazi, S., Bos, M.: Digital currencies and CBDC impacts on least developed countries (LDCs). The Dialogue on Global Digital Finance Governance Paper Series (2021)

Gandal, N., Hamrick, J.T., Moore, T., Vasek, M.: The rise and fall of cryptocurrency coins and tokens. Decisions Econ. Finan. **44**(2), 981–1014 (2021)

Gupta, S., Gupta, S., Mathew, M., Sama, H.R.: Prioritizing intentions behind investment in cryptocurrency: a fuzzy analytical framework. J. Econ. Stud. **48**(8), 1442–1459 (2020)

Guych, N., Anastasia, S., Simon, Y., Jennet, A.: Factors influencing the intention to use cryptocurrency payments: an examination of blockchain economy. In: TOURMAN 2018 Conference Proceedings, pp. 303–310. Munich Personal RePEc Archive, Rhodes, Greece (2018)

Hanafi, S.F., Rahman, S.A.: Regulating digital currency: taming the unruly. In: Emerging Issues in Islamic Finance Law and Practice in Malaysia. Emerald Publishing Limited (2019)

Hossain, M.: What do we know about cryptocurrency? Past, present, future. China Finan. Rev. Int. **11**(4), 552–572 (2021)

Hsu, J., Tsai, L.: An alternative monetary system reimagined: the case for central bank digital currency. California Western Int. Law J. **51**(2), 13 (2021)

Harban, F.J.M.J., Ali, B.J., Oudat, M.S.: The effect of financial risks on the financial performance of banks listed on Bahrain bourse: an empirical study. Inf. Sci. Lett. **10**(4) 71–89 (2021)

Jayawardhana, A., Colombage, S.: Does blockchain technology drive sustainability? An exploratory review. Governance Sustain., 17–42 (2020)

Khan, R., Hakami, T.: Cryptocurrency: usability perspective versus volatility threat. J. Money Bus. **2**(1), 16–28 (2021)

Mazambani, L., Mutambara, E.: Predicting FinTech innovation adoption in South Africa: the case of cryptocurrency. Afr. J. Econ. Manag. Stud. **11**(1), 30–50 (2019)

Mazanec, J.: Portfolio optimization on digital currency market. J. Risk Finan. Manag. **14**(4), 160 (2021)

Mora, H., López, F.A., Tello, J.C., Morales, M.R.: Chapter 12 virtual currencies in modern societies: challenges and opportunities. Polit. Technol. Post-Truth Era, 171–185 (2019)

Nahar, P.: Crypto class: difference between crypto coin & token, 17 2022 January. The Economic Times. https://economictimes.indiatimes.com/markets/cryptocurrency/crypto-class-difference-between-crypto-coin-token/articleshow/88947666.cms

Nakamoto, S.: Bitcoin: a peer-to-peer electronic cash system, 8 August 2022. https://bitcoin.org/bitcoin.pdf

Pillai, B., Biswas, K., Muthukkumarasamy, V.: Blockchain interoperable digital objects. In: International Conference on Blockchain, pp. 80–94 (2019)

Raskin, M., Yermack, D.: Digital currencies, decentralized ledgers and the future of central banking. In: Research Handbook on Central Banking, pp. 474–486 (2018)

Saleh, A.H., Ibrahim, A.A., Noordin, M.F., Mohadis, H.M.: Factors influencing adoption of cryptocurrency-based transaction from an Islamic perspective. Glob. J. Comput. Sci. Technol. **20**(4) (2020)

Schellinger, B.: Optimization of special cryptocurrency portfolios. J. Risk Finan. **21**(2), 127–157 (2020)

Shaikh, Z., Wadi, R.A., AlMahari, E.: The impact of Fintech phenomenon on economic development: the case of Bahrain. In: The International Conference on Global Economic Revolutions, pp. 129–138 (2021)

Shou, M.-H., Wang, Z.-X., Li, D.-D., Zhou, Y.-T.: Forecasting the price trends of digital currency: a hybrid model integrating the stochastic index and grey Markov chain methods. Grey Syst.: Theor. Appl. **11**(1), 22–45 (2020)

Soomro, B., Shah, N., Abdelwahed, N.: Intention to adopt cryptocurrency: a robust contribution of trust and the theory of planned behavior. J. Econ. Adm. Sci. (2022)

Swammy, S., Thompson, R., Loh, M.: History of money. In: Crypto Uncovered, pp. 1–16. Palgrave Macmillan, Cham (2018)

Ter Ji-Xi, J., Salamzadeh, Y., Teoh, A.P.: Behavioral intention to use cryptocurrency in Malaysia: an empirical study. Bottom Line **34**(2), 170–197 (2021)

Wu, Y., Fan, H., Wang, X., Zou, G.: A regulated digital currency. Sci. China Inf. Sci. **62**(3), 1–12 (2019)

Yuvaraj, S., Sheila Eveline, N.: Consumers' perception towards cashless transactions and information security in the digital economy. Int. J. Mech. Eng. Technol. **9**(7), 89–96 (2018)

Zalan, T.: Born global on blockchain. Rev. Int. Bus. Strategy **28**(1), 19–34 (2018)

New Retail Format, Sales Management Applications for Business Using AI and Wireless Network

Shweta Ajay Mishra[✉] and Kapil Rokade[✉]

Symbiosis University of Applied Sciences, Indore, India
samishra3009@gmail.com, kapilsds@gmail.com

Abstract. Cloud computing, the Internet of Things (IoT), big data, and general-purpose machine learning algorithms (GPML) can manage a number of data sources, including audio, video, and text, to increase the accuracy of product demand projections. Enterprise sales are distinct from other technology sales categories. It refers to the acquisition of large contracts with lengthy sales cycles, several decision-makers, and a higher amount of risk than typical sales. It has an unique decision-making method. Nearly every firm in the current Internet age has included or improved Artificial Intelligence (AI) technologies. In a similar vein, contemporary technology is used to business sales to simplify the work of sales representatives. The jobs of the personnel have not changed, but they are much simplified. The idea of selling things by fusing online and physical venues is known as the "new retail format." Business-to-business (B2B) product sales management is another aspect of enterprise sales management. This research shows how effective marketing strategies and current retail AI integration are significantly impacted.

Keywords: AI · Marketing · sales · retail · wireless

1 Introduction

AI is popular in business, health, vehicles, and education (Aldawsari 2022). Marketing employs AI. This article discusses AI and marketing. How does AI affect marketing managers? AI-based marketing samples and secondary data analysis solved these problems. AI is commonly used in marketing, but not operationally. Careful experimental technology utilisation may explain this. AI's unpredictability makes implementation cautious. Artificial intelligence has an impact on consumer value, marketing organization, and management.Integrating AI into marketing, innovating, and hiring tech-savvy marketers have commercial ramifications. AI, robots, and machine learning are transforming marketing. Marketing will change quickly. Marketers require ongoing training and field supervision. Robots and AI are becoming prevalent (and may be a necessity for survival). Sales and marketing personnel must supplement AI and robotics (rather than the other way around). They must do tasks that machines cannot, such as creativity, design, and invention, which will become less important. Our period is exciting, challenging, and dangerous.

© The Author(s), under exclusive license to Springer Nature Switzerland AG 2024
A. M. A. Musleh Al-Sartawi et al. (Eds.): ICGER 2023, CCIS 1999, pp. 131–141, 2024.
https://doi.org/10.1007/978-3-031-50518-8_11

Prior to the present epidemic, the significance of digitization and innovation in digitization processes had expanded dramatically (Butschan et al., 2019; Schallmo et al., 2020). Due to the application of artificial intelligence for various commercial reasons, such as forecasting the future success of innovations, guaranteeing the viability of strategies with management choices, etc., the efficacy of these processes has increased dramatically (Bencsik, 2021). Nevertheless, mostly as a result of the current situation, everything has accelerated even more. In reality, digitalization may stimulate economic growth and increase the competitiveness of goods and services (Goker and Ayar, 2020). In light of the magnitude and pace of contemporary digital transformations, the speed with which significant trends are handled constitutes a significant competitive advantage.

AI will change sales and marketing (Siau and Yang, 2017). Low-level marketing and sales positions might be eliminated. AI will change marketing and sales. Organizational change theories will explain such changes in this investigation. Lewin (1951) suggested defreezing, altering, and refreezing. Defrosting prepares for change. Refreezing fixes new behaviours. AI will change marketing, business models, sales, customer service, and consumer behaviour. Three industry examples may explain these developments. Real-time AI assistants will aid teleconferences. An AI agent may apply in-depth audio analysis to deduce from a customer's tone that an unstated problem remains a concern and provide immediate feedback to assist the salesperson. Hence, AI may improve salespeople's talents, but if customers are uncomfortable with AI monitoring conversations, it might have unintended consequences. In the future, sales prospects may be contacted by AI bots1. Consumers may react negatively if they discover they are conversing with a bot. The shopping-then-shipping method is used by internet retailers.—Agrawal et al. (2018); Gans et al. (2017).

The AI anticipates customer preferences. Consequently, firms will use AI to identify consumers' preferences and ship items without orders, allowing customers to return undesirable purchases (Agrawal et al. 2018; Gans et al. 2017). Changes would occur for marketers, companies, and consumers (e.g., information search). Using AI, Birchbox, Stitch Fix, and Trendy Butler predict customer preferences with unpredictable results. Academics and practitioners believe AI will revolutionise marketing and consumer behaviour. Salesforce predicts AI to be the most popular marketing tool in 2019 (Columbus). "This precise second is the great turning moment in history," thus artificial intelligence may help (Reese 2018, p. 38). It's debatable. First, technology can't implement earlier events. Self-driving vehicles cannot manage adverse weather (Lowy, 2016). Shipping-then-shopping to minimise product returns requires better predictive analytics.

Marketing managers and academics must understand AI's potential and development path. Marketing, business, psychology, sociology, computer science, and robotics literature and practitioner interviews address these challenges. Second, past instances concentrated on AI's advantages without addressing valid worries about its usage. Musk thinks AI is "hazardous" (Metz 2018). Data protection, computational biases, and ethics may prohibit AI from delivering (Larson 2019).

Marketing should be at the forefront of AI concerns, since it stands to gain the most. McKinsey & Company stated that AI has the greatest potential value in marketing and sales (Chui et al., 2018) through impacts on marketing activities such as next-best offers to customers, programmatic acquisition of digital ads, and predictive lead scoring (Davenport et al. 2011). CPG, retail, banking, and travel marketing are most affected by AI. These businesses collect massive consumer transaction and attribute data and engage customers. Social media and data broker reports may be included. AI can then analyse this data and provide real-time suggestions about what to purchase, pricing, etc. (Mehta et al. 2018). Since AI marketing literature is rare, our paradigm describes AI's current state and expected future. Marketers want AI for segmentation, analytics, messaging, personalization, and consumer behaviour prediction (Columbus 2019).

2   Literature Review

Luo et al. (2021) Mobile communication and wireless network systems have increased. This article develops a cloud-based wireless network solution for smart online product marketing. Cloud services and wireless network technologies are used. Intelligent products share information with consumers through the Internet. As smart goods become more popular, corporations are producing more. Marketing anything produced is difficult due to significant competition. Marketing may be done on the cloud. Data, servers, software, databases, and networking are accessed online in cloud computing. Data from a remote server doesn't need a hard disc. Data centres are needed for large clouds. Computer and data services are on-demand. This article uses SWOT analysis to investigate smart product marketing in cloud service wireless network systems. S, W, O, and T are recognised in a technical assessment. A hybrid algorithm for Smart Product Marketing Crisis Prediction is created using SWOT analysis and smart product marketing (SPMCP). With 99.54% accuracy, the proposed smart product marketing plan exceeds Ant Colony Optimization (ACO).

E-commerce marketing incorporates artificial intelligence technologies, according to Cao (2021). This essay claims that urban green space is crucial to every urban ecosystem in our country, enhancing urban economies and growth. E-commerce sales links may benefit from artificial intelligence. Plant community organisation, landscape pattern, and the link between plant ecological factors inside and outside the community are examined in this article. Nowadays, major companies compete for data and information. Using Internet big data technology to better corporate marketing may establish a new network marketing management model, which is crucial for maximising my country's e-commerce items' worth. Internet big data domestic e-commerce has grown significantly as well. Online shopping has changed. E-commerce has gradually increased the economy's size.Logistics development is still behind e-commerce in my nation. Logistics improves electronic commerce's competitiveness. Researchers and organisations are increasingly concerned about whether an enterprise's logistics model can be used for long-term growth.

Digitalization is accelerating commercial communication. 2021). Digitalization requires new revenue opportunities to amortise large investments (Frohmann, 2018). Schubach/Schumann, 2020). Multi-channel marketing operations are also important for marketing communication competitiveness and digital agility. The perspective is conventional marketing and its communication options.. Despite the pandemic, contemporary buyers demand more. So, demand has increased. Customers may be more comfortable and learn faster with digital marketing solutions. Customer value recognition must be accelerated. Hollebeek et al. (2017); Colton (2018). Individualized approach and quick response are its main benefits. Customers value their time, therefore they need fast responses and personalised service (Shpak et al., 2020; Dzupina and Dzupinova, 2019).

2.1 AI and Marketing Strategy

Predictability AI's capacity to estimate client purchases may improve prediction. Predictive accuracy may help companies provide goods and services. Thus, marketing and client buying behaviour research abound. The accuracy of AI-driven prediction systems in gauging demand for really new items may be worth studying. AI-predicted RNPs are worrisome. AI can predict future items. Machine learning techniques for AI algorithms to recognise RNPs need data. RNP forecasting and AI-human collaboration may be researched. AI will forecast client purchases, pricing, and discounts (Shankar 2018). Pricing and promotions affect sales, thus marketing scholars must study them (Biswas et al., 2013; Guha, 2018). Thus, future studies should explore how artificial intelligence predicts optimum pricing and whether price promotions are essential. Advertising resource allocation is also crucial. Advertising promotes research and awareness.

AI may affect prospecting, pre-approach, presentation, and follow-up (Singh et al. 2019; Syam and Sharma 2018). Research concerns: Can AI analyse customer dialogue and other data like social media postings to develop more engaging communications? Can AI help salespeople enhance presentations with real-time customer feedback? How can AI anticipate repurchases by utilising text, voice, consumer behaviour, and other data (e.g., comparable customers)? Cells 2–6 need non-numerical data. How can businesses employ Luo et al.'s (2019) AI sales bots? These questions may boost AI-optimized sales. Sales and innovation processes must be examined and reorganised. These points are not in Fig. 1 cells. Sales process AI-powered salespeople require what skills? First, how AI bots and humans should organise a sales team How might the company reconcile AI's emphasis on customers' stated demands with salespeople's better customer stewardship skills?

AI innovation AI's unpredictability necessitates company development. Stitch Fix's senior management told us data scientists may work autonomously and attempt new projects (Colson, 2018). A Stitch Fix data scientist designed Style Shuffle, a Tinder-like app for choosing clothes. This strategy taught stylists client preferences and matched them with individual customers, an unexpected advantage data scientists are encouraged to work autonomously (Colson, 2018) and attempt new project ideas. A Stitch Fix data scientist designed Style Shuffle, a Tinder-like app for choosing clothes. Unexpectedly, this strategy taught hairdressers client preferences and connected them with individual customers. "Swiped" stylists sold more ensembles and got better ratings (i.e., both qualitative feedback about the stylist and increased sales of clothes curated by that stylist). Hence, AI-using companies may profit from data scientists working on "pet projects," a 3M research and development strategy (Shum and Lin 2007). (2007).

AI research should focus on how to maximise anticipated and unforeseen benefits. "Short-term, AI will deliver evolutionary advances; long-term, it will likely be revolutionary," so companies must moderate expectations (Davenport 2018, p. 7). (2018). Gartner's hype cycle suggests that AI's short-term benefits may be overestimated and its long-term benefits understated (Dedehayir and Steinert 2016; Shankar 2018also see van Lente et al. 2013). Shankar (2018). Top management said this. Will AI's rise follow this paradigm or Roger's or Bass's innovation models? Discover which innovation model forecasts AI development. Consumption AI, like other new technology, will change consumer behaviour (e.g., Giebelhausen et al. 2014; Groom et al. 2011; Hoffman and Novak 2018; Longoni et al. (2019) feel that letting customers tweak the AI may make them choose personalization over originality. This may also reduce such worries. Robots with AI applications increase our uneasiness with AI. UVH makes humanlike robots unpleasant to customers. Concerns about AI adoption should be investigated. If customers see AI as a collaborator, UVH impacts may be stronger. Research other ways to reduce such consequences. Early efforts focused on triggering empathy by convincing customers that robots can see things from their viewpoint and feel sorry for them if they are suffering (Castelo 2019). (2019). Anthropomorphizing the AI may persuade customers that it is more empathetic (although this must be balanced with UVH issues). Sociologists focus on how robots with integrated.

AI could get into people's lives (Boyd and Holton 2018, p. 338). "When cultural choices about whether a person or a machine should provide a personal service are looked at, complications arise." Customers like robots that are social? Researchers can look at how different cultures see robots (Li et al. 2010). (2010). Aside from cultural factors, it may be important to find out if there are other personality traits that affect whether people will let robots cut their hair or take care of them (Pedersen et al. 2018Research should be done to find out what other ways AI may change people's minds, such as making them care more about safety. Since communication works best when it fits the person's state of mind, relevant insights would change how the AI application talks to customers.

Robots with artificial intelligence are meant to be service workers, friends, babysitters, and pets (Wirtz et al., 2018). Several studies suggest that interacting with robots, including AI, can cause pain and make people act in ways that try to make up for the pain (Mende et al. 2019). (Mende 2019). It's important to find out if people dislike robots with AI and if they might change their minds. Lastly, if a customer's ideal preferences are different from what they've done in the past (for example, if they're trying to avoid unhealthy meals), AI may make it harder for them to find and get closer to their ideal choices by only showing them options that are similar to what they've done in the past. "Retargeting" digital ads shows this problem. How can we teach AI to figure this out? The effects of adopting AI after the fact suggest other research topics. If AI can accurately predict what people will do, they may lose their freedom.

(Schrift et al. 2017; André et al. 2018) If an AI system can guess what a customer wants, they may choose something they don't want to regain control. This brings up a number of research questions. How do customers feel about their ability to make decisions when AI is involved? In this situation, it may be helpful to know if customers see AI as a servant or a partner. Because they affect customers' identities in different ways, hedonic and utilitarian products may seem to give them less freedom than hedonic ones. People worry that they will lose human connections if they connect with machines that are powered by AI. Popular media in March 2019 warns that robots with AI will have more partners than humans. Harmony from Realbotix has potential because it can show emotion and have different personalities. But these robots could hurt society by making people feel more alone, making it harder for people to get married, or lowering birth rates, which is especially important for countries like Japan with low birth rates.

Since there isn't much written about marketing AI, our paradigm explains how it works now and what we think it will do in the future. Marketers want AI to help them with things like segmentation, analytics, messaging, personalization, and predicting how customers will act (Columbus 2019). So, we suggest a research agenda that includes AI, marketing, and consumer behaviour. We meet the needs for AI research of computer scientists.

Model:

The importance of enterprise sales agents continues to increase. AI sales assistants enhance sales representatives and leads. Nowadays, sales rely on these AI helpers. AI sales assistants provide numerous essential functions:

(1) Communication - leads and salespeople: The AI assistant qualifies leads prior to delivering them to salespeople. Sales managers interact with prospects. The AI sales assistant teaches salespeople and provides sales-related emails, chats, and videos to prospects.
(2) Prioritize leads for salespeople: The AI sales assistant monitors each lead and chooses qualified prospects. These follow-ups save time for the sales team. This AI has advantages. With our AI sales assistant method, salespeople can concentrate on qualifying leads.
(3) Assessment and closing the deal: The artificial intelligence sales assistant analyses lead sales and generates a comprehensive report for salespeople. It concludes the transaction after examination. Sales processes in corporations rely largely on AI. It facilitates the sales process. Without an AI sales assistant, sales organisations suffer. By facilitating the sales process, AI technology has reduced sales representatives' burden. The competitive intelligence-driven AI sales assistant analyses several online sources and informs sales people through wireless sensor networks (WSN).

Having information on a competitor's behaviour may assist the sales team in developing more effective sales techniques. The artificial intelligence self-updates and generates fresh sales techniques. Smart wireless networks update themselves automatically. Consequently, AI is essential for the changing retail formats of modern companies.

3 Objective

To investigate the effect of AI implementation on marketing strategy.

To analyze the customer perspective on AI and wireless apps as tool for marketing.

4   Research Methodology

Nowadays, Artificial Intelligence (AI) is in a strong position to compete with Industry 4.0. Artificial intelligence has defeated difficult board games, such as chess and Chinese games. AI can now write poetry, make judgements, interact with people, analyse billions of data points, and respond in milliseconds. Artificial intelligence affects CRM the most. This article discusses AI-CRM. Academics created a method for assessing product quality, performance, and AI-enabled technology commitment. AI will likely change marketing and customer behaviour.Hence, primary data is acquired to comprehend the viewpoint of the client on the AI marketing plan. The data is gathered from 300 members of the public from June 2022 to January 2023 using a basic random sample approach. Journals, periodicals, and newspaper articles are utilised as sources for secondary data.

Table 1. Descriptive Study

	N	Min	Max	Mean	STD
Gender	300	1	2	1.53	.500
Age	300	1	3	1.35	.540
Education	300	1	4	1.20	.567
Work experience	300	1	3	1.35	.541
AI Personalized and relevant messages	300	1	3	1.01	.126
Cost savings	300	1	3	2.24	.631
Streamlines marketing efforts	300	1	5	2.18	.685
Personalization of products...	300	1	5	1.84	.852
Customers don't always like chatbots or even talking to computers on the phone	300	1	5	1.96	.823
Computers can't do it without humans	300	1	5	2.29	1.399
Increased efficiency	300	1	4	2.25	.650
make faster business decisions based on outputs from cognitive technologies	300	1	5	2.28	.706
You can target your audience at the right time	300	1	5	1.93	.788
Marketing allows you to know customers better...	300	1	2	1.03	.165
It lets the customer come to you...	300	1	5	1.88	.794
Digital marketing can increase your revenue	300	1	2	1.91	.284
Lack of trust, ethical issues	300	1	5	1.93	.842
The self-improving AI systems can become so mighty than humans that could be very difficult to stop from achieving their goals, which may lead to unintended consequences	300	1	5	1.85	.738
Overall AI is positively improving the marketing strategy	300	1	4	1.82	.727
Valid N (listwise)	300				

For a comprehensive understanding, the acquired data is analysed using SPSS Software utilising descriptive and regression analysis (Tables 1 and 2).

Table 2. Reliability Statistics

Reliability Statistics	
Cronbach's Alpha	N of Items
.764	15

The main data has a Cronbach's alpha rating of 0.764, which indicates that the data are trustworthy and consistent across all 15 items (Tables 3 and 4).

Hypothesis:
H1: There is significant positive impact of AI on marketing strategy resulting in productivity H0: AI doesn't impact on marketing strategy in the future.

Regression

Table 3. Variables Entered/Removeda

Variables Entered/Removed[a]			
Model	Variables Entered	Variables Removed	Method
1	AL – Marketing strategy[b]		Enter

[a]Dependent: Productivity Retail Business.
[b]All requested variables entered.

Table 4. Model Summary

Model Summary				
Model	R Value	R Square-Value	Adjusted R Square -Value	Std. Error of the Estimate
1	.767[a]	.668	.587	.468

[a]Predictors: (Constant), WLB Stratagies.

Due to the fact that the R value is 0.767 and the R-square value is $= 0.668$, it is feasible to arrive at the conclusion that the model is significant and demonstrates a degree of fit that is appropriate. This is because the R value and the R-square value both equal 0.668. Artificial intelligence has a major and beneficial influence on the marketing methods employed by retail establishments, which ultimately leads to greater levels of productivity. This may be attributed to the rise in overall levels of workforce productivity (Table 5).

Table 5. Anova

ANOVA Table

Model		Sum Squares	Df Value	Mean Square	F Value	Sig.
1	Regression	77.33	1	77.373	363.181	.000[b]
	Residual	54.11	237	.219		
	Total	131.52	248			

[a]Dependent: Productivity Retail Business.
[b]Predictors: (Constant), AL – Marketing strategy.

Since the R value is 0.767 and the R-square value is $= 0.668$, we may conclude that the model is both significant and accurately fits the data. The effectiveness of retail marketing is improved by artificial intelligence's ability to influence it.

The model is important and relevant since AlphaP is 0.00, less than 0.05 (Table 6).

Table 6. Coefficient

Coefficients Table

Model		Unstandardized-Coefficients		Standardized-Coefficients	T	Sig.
		B	Std. Error	Beta		
1	(Constant)	−.53	.12		−4.172	.000
	WLB Stratagies	.12	.007	.766	19.73	.000

This illustrates that the model is significant and that there is a meaningful relationship between the variables that are dependent on one another and those that are independent of one another due to the fact that the value of alpha p is 0.00, which is less than 0.05. Artificial intelligence has a major and favourable influence on the marketing tactics employed by retail organisations, which ultimately leads to greater levels of operational efficiency. This may be attributed to the fact that the usage of AI has led to increased levels of operational effectiveness (Table 7).

Since the value of Chi square is 414.871, the value of p is equal to 0.0000.05, and 81.3% of the cells have an anticipated count of less than 5, the hypothesis H1 is accepted while the hypothesis H0 is rejected. AI has a big and favourable influence on the marketing strategy of retail businesses, which results in improved levels of efficiency (Table 8).

Understanding customer needs and preferences is crucial in modern society. Current marketing significantly relies on it, and this knowledge may facilitate prompt and effective response. Moreover, AI helps marketing stakeholders make data-driven decisions in real time. Nevertheless, marketing teams are adept at integrating AI into campaigns and operations. Consequently, AI technology applications are still in their infancy. It raises a number of hurdles. So, some issues for AI in marketing. Following are the 10

Table 7. Chi Square

Chi-Square Tests

	Value	Df	Asymp. Sig. (2-sided)
Pearson Chi-Square	414.871[a]	56	.000
Likelihood Ratio	392.496	56	.000
Linear-by-Linear Association	72.804	1	.000
N of Valid Cases	249		

[a]61 cells (81.3%) have expected count less than 5. The Min expected count is .02.

Table 8. Symmetric Measures

Symmetric Measures

		Value	Asymp. Std. Error[a]	Approx. T[b]	Approx. Sig.
Interval by Interval	Pearson's R	.542	.069	10.131	.000[c]
Ordinal by Ordinal	Spearman Correlation	.572	.055	10.973	.000[c]
N of Valid Cases		249			

[a]Not assuming the null hypothesis.
[b]Using the asymptotic standard error assuming the null hypothesis.
[c]Based on normal approximation.

largest Challenges for AI in Marketing: Training duration and data accuracy Privacy and statutes Acceptance Obtaining development best practises Changing with the marketing climate. Inadequate IT infrastructure Lack of high-quality or sufficient data Lack of trust in AI software Inadequate funding Lack of in-house expertise.

5   Conclusion

This article gives a framework for understanding how artificial intelligence (AI) might affect marketing in the future, especially how AI might change marketing strategy and how people act as customers. We use both research that has already been done and our large network of professional connections. The first thing we do is build a framework with many levels for developing artificial intelligence. In this framework, we show how important factors are that relate to different levels of intelligence, different types of tasks, and whether or not the AI is built into a physical robot. This is the first time that a building has been built that uses all three dimensions at once. Besides that, we also make two (warning-related) comments. To start, it's possible that the media will exaggerate how big the effects of artificial intelligence will be in the short- to medium-term. Second, we think that the best way to use artificial intelligence will be to combine it with human management instead of letting it run on its own. To study AI's full effects, we propose a research agenda that focuses on three important areas: 1) how firms' marketing strategies will change, 2) how consumers' behaviours will change, and 3) data privacy, bias, and moral problems. Academics, businesses, and policy experts should look into this research agenda, keeping in mind that AI has already had some effect on marketing, but will have a much bigger effect in the future. There is, therefore, a lot to learn. We hope that this research plan will inspire and guide AI research in the future. AI has a big positive effect on retail marketing strategies, which makes them more effective. Since AlphaP $= 0.00$, which is less than 0.05, the model is significant and there is a meaningful relationship between the dependent and independent variables.

Practical Contribution and Its Impact
It is vital to locate qualities that are acceptable in order to successfully create an effective Smart Product Marketing Crisis Prediction (SPMCP) approach (features). The performance of a classifier might be improved by finding a solution to a "attribute selection issue," which is a frequent problem that arises in machine learning. [Case in point:] [Case in point:] [Case in point:] [Ca Marketing professionals in this day and age of artificial intelligence (AI) should make the most of the technological possibilities afforded by AI in order to maximise their effectiveness. Changing the current state of the marketing industry, making traditional marketing activities more effective and relevant, realising the customised and intelligent design of goods, and achieving the personalised and correct marketing of products to consumers are all goals that need to be accomplished in order for these objectives to be considered successful. On a basic level, you should work to improve the economic advantages that firms have and the viability of the commodities they sell. AI's applicability to the marketing industry is still in its infancy. While using AI technology, businesses must take a sensible approach. We should not only recognise the benefits of data analysis and correct identification that AI brings to business marketing, but also the technological pitfalls, user privacy concerns, and other issues that AI applications provide. Obviously, the use of AI technology in the sphere of marketing will continue to evolve in the future, and businesses must also conduct timely investigation and study.

Reference

Aldawsari, S.: Employing AI applications to authenticate people through neural networks. Inf. Sci. Lett. **11**(6), 1871–1878 (2022)

Digitalization and Sustainable Technologies

The Role of Industry 4.0 Technologies in Enabling Knowledge Management Practices: United Arab Emirates Perspective

Ibrahim A. Abu-AlSondos[1]([⊠]) [iD], Abeer F. Alkhwaldi[2] [iD], Maha Shehadeh[3] [iD],
Basel J. A. Ali[4] [iD], and Mohammad Rustom Al Nasar[5] [iD]

[1] College of Computer Information Technology, American University in the Emirates (AUE),
503000 Dubai, United Arab Emirates
Ibrahim.abualsondos@aue.ae
[2] Department of Management Information Systems (MIS), College of Business,
Mutah University, Karak 61710, Jordan
abeerkh@mutah.edu.jo
[3] Department of Finance and Banking Sciences, Faculty of Business, Applied Science Private
University, Amman 11931, Jordan
ma_shehadeh@asu.edu.jo
[4] Department of Arts in Economics, College of Economics and Management (CoEM), Al
Qasimia University, Sharjah, United Arab Emirates
bali@alqasimia.ac.ae
[5] College of Computer Information Technology, American University in the Emirates (AUE),
Dubai 503000, United Arab Emirates
mohammad.alnasar@aue.ae

Abstract. The purpose of this study is to discuss the role of Industry 4 (I4) technologies in Knowledge Management (KM). Industry 4 has the ability to enhance business processes and industrial operations. This study recognizes and discusses the opportunities for enterprises using I4 technology. Data was gathered from peer-reviewed academic publications found in databases like Scopus and Google Scholar. Moreover, the study highlights the roles of artificial intelligence, internet of things, cloud computing, and blockchain technology in KM. These technologies have the potential to enhance KM activities such as data collection and gathering, storage, knowledge exchange, and application. Third, this paper presents an overview of KMin the UAE and the potential use of industry 4 technology in this area. Future research should concentrate on different implementation issues and techniques to overcoming them. Evaluating case studies of Industry 4 technology can assist us in better understanding the problems.

Keywords: Knowledge Management (KM) · Industry 4.0 · AI · Internet of Things (IoT) · Cloud Computing · Blockchain Technology

A. M. A. Musleh Al-Sartawi et al. (Eds.): ICGER 2023, CCIS 1999, pp. 145–156, 2024.
https://doi.org/10.1007/978-3-031-50518-8_12

1 Introduction

Organizational workflows and management structures have been revolutionized by Industry 4.0, the fourth industrial revolution. The ways in which businesses handle and use their knowledge resources are a crucial aspect of this evolution. The United Arab Emirates (UAE) has been at the forefront of this technological shift, investing heavily in Industry 4.0 technology [1]. The purpose of this research is to determine the degree to which Industry 4.0 technologies have facilitated the adoption and implementation of KM methods in UAE enterprises. The UAE has a fast-rising economy and is noted for its investments in technology and innovation. The government has set lofty ambitions for the adoption of Industry 4.0 technology, with the goal of becoming a worldwide leader in this [2]. However, the influence of these technologies on the country's companies and their capacity to manage their knowledge resources is not fully recognized [3, 4]. This research seeks to address this void by offering insight into the adoption and implementation of KM methods in UAE enterprises, as well as the role that Industry 4.0 technologies play in this process.

This research will benefit both academics and practitioners. It will help academics better understand the interaction between Industry 4.0 technology and KM techniques [5, 6]. It will give practitioners with assistance on how to successfully adopt and apply KM approaches in their businesses, specifically in the UAE setting. The study's results will also be of interest to policymakers in the UAE, since they will give insight into the country's progress toward its aim of being a worldwide leader in Industry 4.0. The Industry 4.0 transition has the potential to improve industrial practices and procedures much farther than earlier transformations. The transition introduces advanced technology including IoT, simulations, cloud computing, simulations, and Augmented Reality (AR). These have a huge impact on our lives. According to [7], Industry 4.0 technologies enhance business processes by boosting productivity, conserving resources, enhancing process transparency, establishing viable business models, and delivering high-quality work conditions. Furthermore, intelligent surveillance offers businesses with a continual overview and updates on their operations, enabling them to adapt rapidly to changes in the business environment. These technologies have also proven critical in the Kprocess. KM is the most effective method of managing data and resources in order to increase the firm's [8]. Superior knowledge enables organizations to make critical choices about situations they face. As a result, is necessary to identify and understand the role of the major Industry 4.0 technologies in the KM process and recommending measures to help organizations benefit from digital transformation [9].

2 Background of Knowledge Management (KM)

According to researchers, knowledge is the most important competitive advantage in a business [11, 12]. According to [8, 10] knowledge is the practical and theoretical understanding of a certain topic. In enterprises, KM is used to manage, produce, and improve intellectual assets. Organizations use established strategies to collect information in its whole, organize, store, distribute, and analyze it [13]. Furthermore, the KM process has numerous phases, including data capture and creation. Organizations' principal data gathering techniques include regular recordkeeping, online analytics like Google Analytics, pop-up quizzes, surveys, interviews, and focus groups. The next level is knowledge organization, in which businesses arrange the information they produce or generate for simple access and retrieval [8, 15]. Data retrieval is further aided by categorization and indexing systems. The third level is knowledge storage, which includes capturing, transcribing, and coding information. Documents containing embedded or filtered information are safely kept for later retrieval. The next stage in knowledge sharing is the exchange of gained concepts, data, information, and experiences between individuals or businesses [15]. The final phase is utilizing existing knowledge to address issues or fill gaps. Nonetheless, the appropriate knowledge application techniques must be communicated effectively to users to guarantee that the entire process is successful. ICT and data platforms assist KM in supporting management activities [16]. As a result, KM necessitates collaboration between managers and workers in order to achieve goals linked to knowledge application in a company [8, 17].

3 Background on Industry 4 Technologies

The term "Industry 4" or I4 refers to a novel degree of organization and control that is applied to the entire value chain (VC) over the life cycle of a product. Companies' approaches to making, developing, and distributing their wares have been fundamentally altered as a direct result of the wave. Additionally, the revolution brought on by Industry 4.0 aims to transform standard machinery used in industries into self-aware and self-learning equipment in order to improve both the performance of these machines and the maintenance of them [18]. The transition intends to establish a manufacturing platform that is both open and intelligent, and it will utilize data from networked industrial sources. According to [19] I4.0 is supported by technologies like Big Data, the laborious process of acquiring, gathering, cleaning, and analyzing massive volumes of data to extract actionable insights. By acquiring, gathering, cleaning, and analyzing massive volumes of data, Big Data may be converted from raw data to actionable insights. In addition, autonomous robots carry out their missions with as little assistance from humans as possible. In reproductions, model-based system designs are studied and tested to see whether or not they can allow computers to duplicate the attributes of models that have been implemented. In addition, I4.0 is backed by cybersecurity solutions, which protect networked industrial systems from being hacked by cybercriminals. Intelligent sensors that can store information, interpret it, analyze it, and exchange it with other devices are another component of the IoT. The technology of cloud computing is characterized by the leasing of technologies, such as storage through the internet. Issues including the slow speed of the IWN networks, that restrict the transmission of data sets and raise the number of cyberattacks, make the use of I4 technologies difficult [18]. The current systems used in smart manufacturing are not independent, which hinders the process of making intelligent decisions. However, the I4.0 technologies have brought about considerable change in the industrial sector via the use of digitalization.

4 Opportunities to Improve Business Results with Industry 4.0 Technologies

The technologies of Industry 4.0 make it possible for companies operating inside communities and organizations to improve their productivity and product quality while simultaneously lowering their operational expenses. [20] believe that I4.0 technologies have the potential to reduce the amount of time it takes for online businesses to meet the requirements of their customers [21], therefore, the businesses gain a competitive advantage [22–25]. Additionally, the use of technology associated with Industry 4.0 has the potential to enhance the manufacturing process. Reducing a company's dependency on humans throughout the manufacturing process may be accomplished by methods such as using autonomous robots and machine learning technology. The technologies of machine learning may also be beneficial to corporations and institutions since they enable these entities to comprehend the behavior of customers and participate actively in marketing endeavors [20]. In addition, businesses have the opportunity to expand their storage capacities and expand their capabilities. The usage of cloud computing makes processing power readily available to businesses [26]. Additionally, there is the possibility that institutions may combine both vertical and horizontal systems in their operations [8, 17, 23, 27, 28]. Through this kind of integration, engineering systems might be connected with those of the production and sales departments. Additionally, companies produce and receive a significant quantity of data on a daily basis. Technology from the fourth industrial revolution, known as Industry 4.0, enables businesses and other organizations to carry out predictive maintenance and make decisions based on actual data. The careful monitoring of a variety of corporate operations is also made possible by augmented reality. Therefore, the technologies of Industry 4.0 provide various prospects for improvement in the operations of businesses, such as improved accessibility to computing capabilities and enhanced quality of equipment maintenance.

5 Artificial Intelligence (AI) and Knowledge Management (KM)

AI technology in the KM process may assist institutions in learning from prior errors and avoiding making similar mistakes [8, 29–32]. According to [33] AI-based Information Technology systems are essential for innovation, greater efficiency, and effectiveness. According to the authors, AI and Machine Learning facilitate the sharing of environmental data from cars and trading market procedures, boosting business cooperation [34]. According to [3], AI systems are useful in knowledge generation since they detect previously undiscovered patterns and lead to the development of new declarative information. Artificial intelligence-based technologies aid in the analysis and filtering of various content channels throughout the knowledge organization stage. The systems may also help teams reuse knowledge [8]. AI facilitates knowledge sharing across silos by coordinating and connecting systems and allowing real-time data flow across marketing and sales channels [4]. People and organizations working on similar causes are also linked. Furthermore, AI systems facilitate the application of information via natural and intuitive system interfaces such as voice assistants [24, 35]. The systems also search for and prepare knowledge sources. As a result, AI technologies enhance KM procedures via tactics such as the accessible application of knowledge through voice assistants [34].

6   The Internet of Things (IoT) and the Knowledge Management Process

The IoT offers companies a chance to enhance customer experiences by providing them with the ability to collect extensive volumes of data. Users are able to acquire data in the field of KM thanks to the IoT, which is connected to goods, customer assets, and the working environment [36, 37] For instance, the installation of intelligent sensors in automobiles enables the collection of data about fuel consumption, driver safety, and the need for vehicle maintenance. The data that is acquired is also useful for the knowledge application stage since it enables businesses to benefit from the behavioral data of their clients. In addition, the information that is gathered gives firms the ability to improve their efficiency and adapt to difficult circumstances. It has been suggested by [38] that the implementation of IoT in businesses has made it easier for employees to share their expertise and has opened up new doors via which various company objectives may be achieved. The data that is gathered regarding the everyday interactions of employees and stakeholders may be accessed by a variety of different organizations. The writers also note that the successful development of businesses in the Middle East is due, in part, to the exchange of information across different companies [38]. Systems based on the IoT make it possible to conduct analyses and share information and knowledge in real time. As a result, the IoT guarantees that enterprises have access to data of a high quality, which enables enhanced decision-making processes [9].

7   Cloud Computing's Role in Knowledge Management (KM)

The use of cloud computing has become more common as a result of its many advantages, which include the pooling of resources, the provision of services on demand, and the provision of network connectivity [39–42]. During the process of knowledge management, the use of technology enables organizations to manage substantial volumes of data without negatively impacting the efficiency of the system [43]. During periods of high data collection activity, companies may examine the data by renting extra processing capacity. In addition, cloud computing guarantees the confidentiality of the information that is gathered. Using private cloud designs, for instance, ensures that sensitive data is well safeguarded against illegal access [16, 32, 44]. Community and hybrid architectures make it possible for companies to work together by enabling institutions to pool their available resources. In addition to this, the technology guarantees that information is easily accessible by allowing workers to get it over the Internet regardless of where they are located. It has been argued that cloud computing may minimize the costs of KM systems since there are no installation expenses associated with cloud computing and institutions only pay for the services that they actually utilize. Cloud computing guarantees that information may be easily comprehended and leads to compatibility since the information is readily available from a variety of departments [8, 39]. The use of cloud computing makes it possible to store and later retrieve vast amounts of data that have been gathered via the process of knowledge management. In the event that data is lost, the cloud may also serve as a backup. Computing in the cloud thus plays an important part in KM by contributing to the facilitation of activities such as analysis and sharing.

8 Blockchain's Role in Knowledge Management (KM)

Blockchain technology (BCT) refers to highly developed databases that provide open and transparent data exchange through networks [45]. Extracting data from the KM process and submitting it to databases might be one way for researchers to generate new knowledge with the help of BCT. In addition, Blockchain has the potential to facilitate the storage of data by introducing novel approaches to the recording, maintenance, and dissemination of data [46]. In addition, since one of BCT's primary qualities is that it enables users to access data from a variety of locations, it makes it possible for KM Systems to circumvent the difficulties associated with the sharing of information. The movement of data at a fast speed, instantaneous access to information, and high levels of security that are all hallmarks of BCT all contribute to making the sharing of knowledge between individuals and organizations possible. According to [47], Blockchain-based KM systems automatically produce knowledge blocks and handle all of the data that is created. These systems also manage intellectual assets efficiently by limiting illegal access to stored data in order to keep that data secure. In addition, the use of encryption, which is a feature of BCT technology, helps to ensure that the knowledge application process is carried out accurately. In addition to this, statistical analysis might be performed using blockchain technology in order to get the data ready for use [48]. As a result, BCT will make it possible for small and middle-sized businesses to reap the benefits of industrial data, which will boost their development.

9 Methodology

This study utilized a review of peer-reviewed academic publications found in databases such as Scopus and Google Scholar to examine the impact of Industry 4.0 technologies on Knowledge Management (KM). The study discussed the results of previous studies and analyzed the role of AI, IoT, cloud computing, and blockchain technology in KM. The aim was to explore how these technologies can enhance KM activities such as data collection, storage, knowledge exchange, and application. The study also presented an overview of KM in the UAE and the potential use of Industry 4.0 technology in this area. The data collected was analyzed to provide insights into the impact of Industry 4.0 technologies on KM and to discuss the results of previous studies.

10 United Arab Emirates: Knowledge Management and Industry 4.0 Technologies

In both industrialized and developing nations throughout the globe during the last twenty years, there has been a rise in the amount of attention given to KM, both from a theoretical and practical point of view. At the organizational level, formal information systems (ISs) have been deployed for the efficient management of knowledge stock and also to develop new knowledge to confront business issues utilizing emerging technologies and capabilities [49]. KM is currently increasingly considered an origin of competitive advantage [50]. In addition, an increasing number of business corporations are realizing the significance of KM strategies and initiatives for acquiring, sharing, and leveraging knowledge [51].

The United Arab Emirates (UAE) is one of the leading countries in the region of the Middle East (ME) where the government's national programs support raising awareness regarding the strategic value of KM for economic and social development. This makes the UAE one of the leading countries in the region [2]. With a variety of first-of-their-kind initiatives, the Emirate of Dubai has emerged as a driving force in advancing the KM thinking process. One of the noteworthy initiatives was the founding of several free zones such as Media City, Knowledge Village, and Internet City, with the goal of attracting overseas universities and institutes, media businesses, and information technology and software development corporations to serve the increasing desires of the commercial community. The Dubai Knowledge Park, which was formerly known as Knowledge Village, is possibly "the world's only free zone." It has brought together higher education institutions (HEIs), human resources (HR), and consulting organizations "to develop the region's talent pool and establish the UAE as a knowledge-based economy." The 'Knowledge and Human Development Authority' (KHDA), which was established in the Emirate of Dubai in 2006, is one of the most important official bodies in the United Arab Emirates. Its purpose is to serve as the quality assurance authority in monitoring the growth of the education and human resources (HR) sectors in the UAE. Another government program is called the Digital knowledge hub, and it is described as "a pioneering knowledge platform that gathers, organizes, and makes accessible digital and knowledge information material in a complete and integrated framework."

The nation has come to the realization that economic development in the modern era can only be attained through the implementation of the concept of the knowledge economy, which contributes to the offering of innovative and distinctive products and services through the utilization of state-of-the-art technologies ((IoT), cloud computing (CC), and Artificial Intelligence (AI)). In addition, the United Arab Emirates (UAE) assigned particular indicators guaranteeing the commitment to its application. These indicators include attaining a high ranking in the Global Innovation Index (GII) and improving the rates of "knowledge field employees" relative to the total number of employees in the UAE [7]. The government initiatives are planned to inspire and motivate both public and private establishments to pursue KM from both theoretical and practical perspectives in order to build up their competitive positions in the UAE's business environments, which are becoming more and more globalized, with innovative products and services. It is expected that UAE organizations will be actively involved in KM practices in order to acquire, improve, and share knowledge in order to build and refine their knowledge resources and capabilities. This expectation is based on the UAE's explicit interest in building intellectual and human capital.

It is increasingly essential that information and knowledge be widely shared in order to cognitively assist work on all levels, including the individual, the commercial, and the governmental. More information and knowledge needs to be shared among the parties involved in order to effectively manage the growing complexity that is a direct result of the proliferation of big data around the world. This is especially true for governments and large corporations that offer a wide range of products and services. Recent advancements in technology, such as the (IoT), have made a contribution to such KM approaches, and demonstrations that serve as proofs of concept have been developed. The business sector and national governments throughout the world are going in this direction, and the United Arab Emirates is not an exception. In this context, the Ministry of Industry and Advanced Technology of the UAE is using the 4th Industrial Revolution Readiness Index to measure the level of digital maturity of various processes, technologies, and organizations. The index also indicates priority areas for improvement, which prompts the design of digital transformation initiatives [8, 16]. This would have a strong connection to the incorporation of digital technologies connected to Industry 4.0 for the objectives of knowledge management.

11 Conclusion

In conclusion, the purpose of this research was to investigate the degree to which technologies related to Industry 4.0 have made it possible for enterprises in the UAE to adopt and put into practice KM procedures. The results of this study have offered scholars, practitioners, and policy makers in the UAE with significant insights, which they may use in their work. The research underscores the significance of technologies related to Industry 4.0 in allowing efficient KM and the need for businesses in the UAE to embrace these technologies in order to maintain their position as market leaders. In addition to this, it contributes to the understanding of the link between the technologies of Industry 4.0 and the practices of knowledge management, therefore supplying businesses with information on how to adopt and apply KM practices in an efficient manner. Technology developed for Industry 4.0 has the potential to greatly advance KM procedures. The use of KM in businesses allows for the development, management, and improvement of intellectual assets. The procedure requires businesses to make use of various tools and strategies in order to collect, organize, store, and analyze information. In addition, the process of KM consists of several phases, including the following: data collecting and creation; organization; storage; knowledge sharing; storage; and application. IoT, artificial intelligence (AI), cloud computing, blockchain technology, and autonomous robotics are examples of technologies that drive Industry 4.0, which may enhance business results. These technologies provide up options, such as shortening the amount of time required for internet firms to cater to the requirements of their customers. The technologies also make the manufacturing process more efficient by lowering the amount of dependence placed on people. Artificial intelligence is essential to the process of knowledge development because it enables systems to identify previously unseen patterns. In addition, IoT devices gather information about items and the needs of customers. Cloud computing makes more information more readily available, while blockchain technology makes it possible to share data. This research provides baseline data on the current state of KM in the UAE as well as the advantages associated with using industry 4.0 technology for the purposes of KM. Therefore, in order to better their KM operations, such as data analysis and information storage, governments and businesses should integrate technologies from the Industrial IoT (I4.0).

As this is a literature review, the previous empirical findings will be based on the studies reviewed in the existing literature. Previous empirical findings related to the role of Industry 4.0 technologies in knowledge management have shown that these technologies have the potential to significantly enhance knowledge management processes. For example, AI and machine learning algorithms can be used to support data collection, analysis, and interpretation, making knowledge management more efficient and effective. IoT and cloud computing can also be used to enhance knowledge sharing and collaboration among different stakeholders. Blockchain technology has been shown to have the potential to improve the security and reliability of knowledge management systems, enabling secure knowledge exchange and storage. However, the implementation of Industry 4.0 technologies in knowledge management is not without challenges. Some of the challenges identified in the literature include data privacy and security concerns, a lack of standardization and interoperability, and a need for new skills and competencies among knowledge management professionals.

Overall, previous empirical findings suggest that the integration of Industry 4.0 technologies into knowledge management processes has the potential to significantly enhance these processes, but also highlights the need for careful consideration of the challenges and limitations involved.

12 Recommendations

Additional study on knowledge enhancers that assist corporations in improving their decision-making would be beneficial to businesses. Additional research has to be done on the workforce, management, and executive KM roles in order to facilitate the adoption of Industry 4.0 technology. In addition, the use of I4.0 technologies in a variety of different businesses should be the primary subject of case studies. These will assist in the understanding of the obstacles experienced throughout the implementation and application, which will allow for the creation of models to prevent and overcome these issues. For instance, researchers might explore the challenges related with IoT, such as integration, to assess the usefulness of the technology in KM (Rot & Sobinska, 2018). Researchers could also compare KM based on different I4.0 technologies. According to (foud Ali, Zowayed, Showaiter, Khder, & Ali, 2022) and (Saleh, Jawabreh, Al Om, & Shniekat, 2121), there is a need for more study on the scalability, security, and decentralization challenges associated with BCT. I4.0 technologies are vulnerable to cyberattacks as well. Therefore, future research should concentrate on the obstacles of deploying technologies associated with I4.0 and provide suggestions to handle them in order to assist businesses in benefiting from I4.0 prior to the arrival of Industry 5.0.

Acknowledgements. The authors are grateful to American University in the Emirates (AUE), Mutah University, Applied Science Private University, Jordan, Applied Science University (ASU), Bahrain, for the financial support granted to cover the publication fee of this article.

References

1. Bahlooq, S.A., Omar, M.A., Mezher, T.: Analyzing the United Arab emirates manufacturing sector and its readiness for industry 4.0. In: 2020 IEEE International Conference on Technology Management, Operations and Decisions (ICTMOD). IEEE (2020)
2. Rahman, N.S.F.A., et al.: The adoption of industry 4.0 practices by the logistics industry: a systematic review of the gulf region. Cleaner Logistics and Supply Chain, p. 100085 (2022)
3. Alawadhi, S.A., et al.: Impact of artificial intelligence on information security in business. In: 2022 ASU International Conference in Emerging Technologies for Sustainability and Intelligent Systems (ICETSIS). IEEE (2022)

4. foud Ali, A., et al.: Artificial intelligence's potential on Bahrain's labour market. In: 2022 ASU International Conference in Emerging Technologies for Sustainability and Intelligent Systems (ICETSIS). IEEE (2022)
5. Abualwafa, I., Ahmad, K., Mokhtar, U.A.: A conceptual framework for knowledge management implementation in organizations. Inf. Sci. Lett. **12**(5), 1547–1560 (2023)
6. Ali, B.J.A., Alawamleh, H.A., Allahham, M.I.O., Alsaraireh, J.M., AL-Zyadat, A.T., Badadwa, A.A.H.: Integration of supply chains and operational performance: the moderating effects of knowledge management. Inf. Sci. Lett. **11**(4), 1069–1076 (2022)
7. Zheng, T., et al.: The applications of Industry 4.0 technologies in manufacturing context: a systematic literature review. Int. J. Product. Res. **59**(6), 1922–1954 (2021)
8. Ali, B.J., et al.: Integration of supply chains and operational performance: the moderating effects of knowledge. Inform. Sci. Lett. **11**(04), 1069–1076 (2022)
9. Alawadhi, et al.: Internet of Things (IoT) security risks: challenges for business. In: 2022 ASU International Conference in Emerging Technologies for Sustainability and Intelligent Systems (ICETSIS). IEEE (2022)
10. Gao, T., Chai, Y., Liu, Y.: A review of knowledge management about theoretical conception and designing approaches. Int. J. Crowd Sci. (2018)
11. Chakrabarti, D., Arora, M., Sharma, P.: Evaluating knowledge quality in knowledge management systems. J. Stat. Appl. Pro. **7**(1), 75–83 (2018)
12. Al-Sharjabi, A.M., Al-Dhobaibi, A.A.M., Al-abidi, S.N.: Strategic intelligence and its impact on knowledge management governance: a field study on the university of science & technology-yemen. J. Stat. Appl. Pro. **13**(1), 323–337 (2024)
13. Abu-AlSondos, I.A., Khder, M.A., AlFudhala, F.: Proposed Knowledge Management Systems (KMS) for public sector organizations in Bahrain (2020)
14. Alaghbari, M.A., Al-Dubai, M.M., Arishi, N.A.: The relationship between total quality management and organizational performance. Inf. Sci. Lett. **11**(1), 199–207 (2022)
15. AlSondos, I.A.A., Salameh, A.A.M., Engineer, M.: Organizing event ubiquitous with a proposed event mobile application in bahrain. Int. J. Manage. **11**(6) (2020)
16. Alawamleh, H.A., et al.: The challenges, barriers and advantages of management information system development: comprehensive review. Acad. Strateg. Manag. J. **20**(5), 1–8 (2021)
17. Thuneibat, N.S.M., et al.: The mediating role of innovation on the relationship between information technologies and reducing tax evasion. Inform. Sci. Let. **11**(2), 13–23 (2022)
18. Vaidya, S., Ambad, P., Bhosle, S.: Industry 4.0–a glimpse. Procedia Manufac. **20**, 233–238 (2018)
19. Suleiman, Z., et al.: Industry 4.0: clustering of concepts and characteristics. Cogent Eng. **9**(1), 2034264 (2022)
20. Ali, N., Mohamed Isa, Z., Abu Bakar, S., Ahmad@ Ahmad Jali, F., Shaharruddin, S.: Industrial Revolution (IR) 4.0: opportunities and challenges in online business. In: Proceedings 2022, 82, 85. in International Academic Symposium of Social Science 2022. 2022. s Note: MDPI stays neutral with regard to jurisdictional claims in published (2022)
21. Abu-AlSondos, I., et al.: Customer attitudes towards online shopping: a systematic review of the influencing factors. Int. J. Data Network Sci. **7**(1), 513–524 (2023)
22. Bataineh, A., et al.: A structural equation model for analyzing the relationship between enterprise resource planning and digital supply chain management. Uncertain Supply Chain Manage. **10**(4), 1289–1296 (2022)
23. Shniekat, N., et al.: Influence of management information system dimensions on institutional performance. Inform. Sci. Let. **11**(5), 435–1443 (2022)
24. Jawabreh, O., et al.: The strategic deployment of information systems attributes and financial performance in the hospitality industry. Inform. Sci. Let. **11**(5) (2022)

25. Alqaraleh, M.H., et al.: The mediating role of organizational culture on the relationship between information technology and internal audit effectiveness. Corporate Govern. Organ. Behav. Rev. **6**(1) (2022)
26. Kumar, A., Kumar, S.: Industry 4.0: evolution, opportunities and challenges. Int. J. Res. Bus. Stud. **5**(1), 139–148 (2020)
27. Shan, R., et al.: The influence of accounting computer information processing technology on enterprise internal control under panel data simultaneous equation. Appl. Math. Nonlinear Sci. (2022)
28. Alkhodary, D., et al.: Visitor management system design and implementation during the covid-19 pandemic. Inform. Sci. Let. **11**(04) (2022)
29. Alshirah, M., et al.: The relationship between tax knowledge and compliance: an empirical study. Inform. Sci. Let. **11**(5), 393–1401 (2022)
30. Osman, N.A., Alshammari, M.M., Mohamed, T.I.: AI techniques for combating electronic crimes and enhancing cybersecurity: Kuwait's security services as a model. Inf. Sci. Lett. **12**(7), 3339–3345 (2023)
31. Aldawsari, S.: Employing AI applications to authenticate people through neural networks. Inf. Sci. Lett. **11**(6), 1871–1878 (2022)
32. Ali, B.J., Oudat, M.S.: Accounting information system and financial sustainability of commercial and islamic banks: a review of the literature. J. Manage. Inform. Decision Sci. **24**(5), 1–17 (2021)
33. Pai, R.Y., et al.: Integrating artificial intelligence for knowledge management systems–synergy among people and technology: a systematic review of the evidence. Economic Research-Ekonomska Istraživanja, pp. 1–23 (2022)
34. Hassan, W.M., et al.: Utilization of artificial intelligence and robotics technology in business. In: 2022 ASU International Conference in Emerging Technologies for Sustainability and Intelligent Systems (ICETSIS). IEEE (2022)
35. Saleh, M.M.A., et al.: Artificial Intelligence (AI) and the impact of enhancing the consistency and interpretation of financial statement in the classified hotels in Aqaba, Jordan. Acad. Strat. Manage. J. 2121 **20**
36. Rot, A., Sobinska, M.: The Potential of the Internet of Things in Knowledge Management System. in FedCSIS (Position Papers) (2018)
37. Alkhwaldi, A.F., et al.: Towards an understanding of FinTech users' adoption: intention and e-loyalty post-COVID-19 from a developing country perspective. Sustainability **14**(19), 12616 (2022)
38. Buja, A.G., et al.: Enhancing a mobile application with contextual information delivery using proximity beacon: a preliminary study at a tourist destination. Int. J. Adv. Technol. Eng. Explor. **8**(78), 662 (2021)
39. Al-Okaily, M., et al.: Cloud-based accounting information systems usage and its impact on Jordanian SMEs' performance: the post-COVID-19 perspective. J. Finan. Report. Account. (2022) (ahead-of-print)
40. Jalamneh, A.A., Khder, M.A.: Challenges of implementing cloud computing in the arab libraries environment. Inf. Sci. Lett. **10**(1), 81–91 (2021)
41. Jebreen, I., Alqaisi, M., Al-Qerem, A., Abu-Salem, A.: Challenges of cloud computing in Jordanian Govt.: insights from Telcos, J. Stat. Pro. **13**(1), 547–557 (2024)
42. Alkhwaldi, A.F.: Jordanian citizen-centric cloud services acceptance model in an e-Government context: security antecedents for using cloud services. University of Bradford (2019)
43. Gupta, C., Fernandez-Crehuet, J.M., Gupta, V.: Measuring impact of cloud computing and knowledge management in software development and innovation. Systems **10**(5), 151 (2022)

44. Shibly, M., et al.: The relationship between administrative empowerment and continuous improvement: an empirical study. Revista Geintec-Gestao Inovacao E Tecnologias **11**(2), 1681–1699 (2021)
45. Alkhwaldi, A.F., Aldhmour, F.M.: Beyond the Bitcoin: analysis of challenges to implement blockchain in the jordanian public sector. In: Convergence of Internet of Things and Blockchain Technologies, pp. 207–220. Springer (2022)
46. Akhavan, P., et al.: Developing a block-chained knowledge management model (BCKMM): beyond traditional knowledge management. In: Peyman, A., Maryam, P., Lila, R., Namvar, M. (eds.) Developing a Block-Chained Knowledge Management Model (BCKMM): Beyond Traditional Knowledge Management, The 19th European Conference on Knowledge Management (ECKM 2018), September, Italy (2018)
47. Akhavan, P., Namvar, M.: The mediating role of blockchain technology in improvement of knowledge sharing for supply chain management. Management Decision (2021)
48. Abdulrahman, M.S.A., et al.: How can blockchain revolutionize the health sector during Health Pandemics (Covid-19) in Kingdom of Bahrain. In: 2022 ASU International Conference in Emerging Technologies for Sustainability and Intelligent Systems (ICETSIS). IEEE (2022)
49. Ashok, M., et al.: How to counter organisational inertia to enable knowledge management practices adoption in public sector organisations. J. Knowl. Manage. (2021)
50. Alkhodary, D., et al.: Visitor Management System Design and Implementation during the Covid-19 Pandemic (2022)
51. Venkitachalam, K., Schiuma, G.: Strategic knowledge management (SKM) in the digital age–insights and possible research directions. J. Strateg. Manag. **15**(2), 169–174 (2022)

The "Metaverse Mania" in Healthcare Education: Students' Technology Acceptance

C. Nagadeepa[1] ⓘ, K. P. Jaheer Mukthar[1](✉) ⓘ, Edwin Ramirez-Asis[2] ⓘ,
Laura Nivin-Vargas[3] ⓘ, Jorge Castillo-Picon[3] ⓘ, and Rolando Saenz-Rodriguez[4] ⓘ

[1] Kristu Jayanti College Autonomous, Bengaluru, India
jaheer@kristujayanti.com
[2] Universidad Señor de Sipán, Chiclayo, Peru
[3] Universidad Nacional Santiago Antunez de Mayolo, Huaraz, Peru
[4] Universidad Cesar Vallejo, Huaraz, Peru

Abstract. The Covid 19 pandemic broke down the barriers between classroom teaching and online teaching, enabling people to study at any time and from any location. The next evaluation in online is VR and AR which is more technology oriented. The future of the internet may be the metaverse, which would expand the virtual universe. The present research is intended to serve as a resource for the changes in medical education pedagogy in the coming digital era. A survey was conducted to determine the level of awareness and acceptance of the new technology-driven education. Further, there was an attempt made to know the student's opinion about the difficulties they may face when they get into the virtual education world. The finding of the research was that 48% of the students are early adopters of the new education mode, and they are happy to accept and intend to use the technology. The study found that students were aware of the metaverse while learning but were not experienced in metaverse learning, although most of them were interested in metaverse learning.

Keywords: Metaverse · Early Adopters · Laggards · Healthcare Education

1 Introduction

During the pandemic, working and living online has become the social norm. As a result, virtual technologies like 5G, cloud computing, digital twins, virtual reality (VR), augmented reality (AR), mixed reality (MR), and artificial intelligence (AI) have developed quickly (AI). People can now pursue a greater level of e-learning social life scenarios, entertainment experiences, productivity, and life efficiency thanks to online study and blockchain. Technologies related to the metaverse are emerging as means of facilitating connections, community discovery, and company growth. Through the use of technologies like VR, AR, and MR as well as by giving digital interactions a more realistic appearance (Avila. S 2017), Metaverse is erasing the distinction between the real world and the virtual one (Zhang et al. 2022). It ushers in what the 5G era has in store for us. Through its transformative model of engagement, the metaverse has the potential to significantly modify how we interact with our surroundings.

A. M. A. Musleh Al-Sartawi et al. (Eds.): ICGER 2023, CCIS 1999, pp. 157–174, 2024.
https://doi.org/10.1007/978-3-031-50518-8_13

The larger potential of the platform has not been fully investigated, despite the fact that the potential of the metaverse has been widely probed in the corporate realm. Its careful application has the potential to have a favourable impact on other industries, such as healthcare services, education, and training. The metaverse has the potential to create workers who are more trained and talented, and who are better able to thrive in the real world. It is predicted that the market for metaverse in education will grow from USD 4.9 billion in 2021 to USD 94.9 billion by 2030, with a CAGR of more than 39.58%. The usage of XR in education has a bright future, and EdTechs have an intriguing possibility to develop in the metaverse. Leading market companies are transforming their businesses and integrating new technologies, which is propelling the market's expansion. Though still young, it has already found useful uses in teaching and learning.

1.1 Metaverse in Medical Education

The covid epidemic brought home to us the importance of distance learning (Ben 2023; Abdellatif et al. 2023). Every classroom was moved online. Additionally, the use of numerous technologies in educational platforms, such as virtual reality and the metaverse, was acknowledged (Salah et al. 2023). However, such online learning had a lot of disadvantages (Muammar and Alnaim 2023; Rabbani et al. 2023).

- There was poor student involvement.
- Even teachers and students reported feeling disengaged. The solitude grew.
- For teachers, maintaining control over a class was a major challenge and responsibility.

These difficulties indicated the want for an alternative educational strategy. The metaverse is right here! Many of the aforementioned problems are addressed by Metaverse. Engagement rises as a result. Additionally, it encourages students' active participation. Additionally, it provides a platform built on virtual reality (Casino et al. 2019). The metaverse offers several benefits to different educational paths.

1.1.a. Student Education
Healthcare experts can teach students about medicine in a simulated setting in the healthcare metaverse. Through the use of metaverses, they may train students more effectively by simulating actual medical operations. This enables students to engage with various medical scenarios and learn how to react. In a secure and realistic setting, students can observe healthcare professionals, receive instruction from knowledgeable teachers, and gain clinical experience. It provides a realistic and engaging online environment. You have the option to study at your own pace and finish the modules whenever it's convenient for you. You will have an immersive experience with the modules that will aid in your understanding of the ideas. It is a fantastic way to receive medical education online and cost-wise it is affordable also (Sonnenwald et al. 2001).

1.1.b. Education for Healthcare Professionals
In the metaverse, healthcare practitioners can build an avatar and study different medical conditions and treatments. Healthcare workers can observe and gain knowledge from other healthcare providers' patient care while they are being shadowed. The healthcare

metaverse can also be used to simulate medical operations, giving medical practitioners a chance to hone their abilities before putting them to use on actual patients (Ning et al. 2021). It can also be used by healthcare practitioners to teach new hires. Both the employer and the employee may benefit from this. The employee can gain a better grasp of the job before to starting work, and the company can make sure that the person is adequately trained. It may also be employed in research. Researchers can learn more about human behaviour by seeing how people respond to various medical circumstances. The treatments and processes utilised in healthcare can then be improved using this information. Healthcare in the metaverse has the potential to transform medical training and healthcare delivery.

1.1.c. Metaverse Education of Patients

Healthcare specialists have been considering how they may offer medical care to users of the metaverse. Additionally, it would enable them to communicate with patients in the metaverse and offer instruction and healthcare to people all around the world. In a 3D virtual setting, healthcare professionals can collaborate to treat patients. In addition, medical facilities can employ metaverses to give prospective patients virtual tours. Patients can gain a better understanding of the facility and what to anticipate before they even enter this manner.

1.2 Metaverse Applications in Medical Training

Medical school has always been a high-stakes game, especially surgical school. In other words, it's challenging to become comfortable with the body without access to real bodies. When patient lives are at stake, that isn't always easy to do (Mesko 2022).

Students studying medicine are frequently obliged to dissect cadavers in addition to studying medical diagrams. For the medical facility, this is expensive, and for the student, it is graphic. In the future, aspiring surgeons will have to learn by doing, with all the associated risk of medical error.

However, a new prospect has surfaced in recent years. Medical institutions have been moving toward simulation-based training based on virtual and augmented reality, taking cues from the aviation sector (VR and AR). In the future, it's likely that a brand-new learning environment will be introduced that is situated in the so-called "metaverse."

According to Rupantar Guha, an analyst at Global Data, "Without a common definition yet, the metaverse means different things to different people depending on the nature of their business." Global Data characterizes the metaverse, however, as a virtual environment where users can communicate in real time while participating in simulations of real-world situations. This entails mapping the body in 3D with exact anatomical information for medical training, which is very different from the traditional 2D representations that students had to learn. Giving surgeons a place to practise their techniques before applying them to actual patients is another aspect of it.

Few possibilities exist for medical residents who want to specialise in interventional cardiology to gain practical experience. Additionally, many medical students feel at ease using VR programmes when they first start their study (Parmaxi 2020). They are more familiar with video games and how to control an avatar than the elder generation. By selling their medical data, patients and doctors can interact in 3D and generate virtual assets. People will be able to visit the entirely virtual metaverse hospital and consult with medical professionals using their avatars. Here, doctors will be able to consult with patients, evaluate them, and keep an eye on them remotely. There will also be chances for innovative research methods and professional training.

1.3 Benefits of Metaverse Education

- By imitating real-life circumstances, it strengthens on-the-job and classroom training and enables students to pick things up more quickly and with greater assurance. Additionally, it measures skill growth and offers comments.
- The use of digital twin technologies to test dummies can provide information about a patient's reaction to treatments, the results of surgeries, potential issues with medical devices, etc. XR makes it possible for medical students to receive intense surgical training in a simulated environment for a much less money than it would cost to perform surgery on cadavers (Ramesh et al. 2022).
- You can utilise the customised content that is filmed with XR as you choose. Real-time interaction with lecturers may be possible during live webcast.
- Using VR to complete practical tasks that are risky or expensive to realistically model will be helpful. Also, it. It promotes accurate conceptual understanding while maintaining a risk-free environment.
- By letting doctors to videotape themselves executing medical operations, XR revolutionises invasive surgery. By superimposing AR and VR-based models on the patient, surgeons can visualise the patient's anatomy, including their bones and tissue, before making an incision.
- Decision-making will be aided and cognitive burden will be decreased by a sizable amount of data gathered in the metaverse.

1.4 Features of a Metaverse in Education

According to what we've been saying, the metaverse is a third realm that provides real-world experiences Javaid and Haleem (2020). However, there will always be certain variations between online learning and traditional classroom environments. Let's examine these variations.

1.4.a. Time and Location of the Learner

In traditional learning, both the teacher and the student must be present at the same time and same place (Hwang and Chien 2022). The flexibility of learning from any location is made possible via remote learning or screen-based learning. Teachers and students cannot, however, have flexible schedules.

With a smart wearable and strong internet connectivity, Metaverse, on the other hand, offers complete flexibility in studying from anywhere, at any time. This enables educators to experiment with brand-new teaching techniques in both synchronous and asynchronous learning settings (Dionisio et al. 2013).

1.4.b. Learner Identity

Conventional classrooms with screens can only address the learners' true identities.

Regardless of race or creed, the metaverse enables you to build your identities as avatars in a fun, imaginative, and immersive way (Park and Kim 2022). Further, Metaverse technology can be customized to suit the unique needs and preferences of individual learners (Alhonkoski 2021; Rakshasbhuvankar and Patole 2014). For example, a student can customize their avatar and environment to match their learning style, creating a more personalized and engaging experience (Williams et al. 2018).

1.4.c. Interaction of Learners

The learners interact in person with teachers and peers in a traditional classroom setting. Due to its limitations, which cause differences, social difficulties, and other difficulties, screen-based learning makes this challenging (Zhong and Zheng 2022).

The limitations of both of the aforementioned teaching strategies are overcome by Metaverse. The avatars of the students can communicate with those of the teachers and their peers (Palvia et al. 2018), allowing for real-time feedback, social interaction, professional assistance with concept learning, individualized support, and much more. Metaverse technology enables the creation of interactive content that students can engage with directly (Fitria and Simbolon 2022). For example, a biology student can use metaverse technology to explore a virtual cell, interact with its components, and gain a deeper understanding of its functions (Lin et al. 2022).

1.4.d. Scenarios for Learning

The traditional learning environment, which includes labs, roleplays, etc., serves to create a space with restrictions for practical learning (Wu 2022; Tlili et al. 2022). The fact that screen-based learning mostly supports theoretical learning techniques makes it drab and tedious. On the other hand, metaverse can produce realistic scenarios, enabling the students to take part in genuine circumstances and study in a useful but secure setting (Guo and Gao 2022). Metaverse technology allows educators to create immersive experiences (Kye et al. 2021) that can simulate real-world environments and scenarios, enhancing the overall learning experience. For example, a medical student can use metaverse technology to practice performing surgery in a simulated virtual environment, gaining valuable experience and skills that can be applied in the real world (Jovanović and Milosavljević 2022).

1.4.e. Resources and Activities for Learning

In static situations, conventional and screen-based learning typically takes the shape of textbooks, images, videos, and other comparable learning materials (Phakamach et al. 2022). By giving individuals the resources they need to develop and learn through participation in activities, the metaverse provides learners with realistic learning scenarios. The use of metaverse technology could give students a more interesting and immersive educational experience (Ning et al. 2021; Thomason 2021). Metaverse can improve student performance and motivation by offering interactive materials and activities, which will ultimately result in higher learning results (Diaz et al. 2020).

1.4.f. Learning Assessment

Assessments can be done primarily in a summative fashion in traditional and screen-based learning in the form of tests and grades. Giving useful real-time input becomes difficult with these techniques (Popescu et al. 2022).With the aid of learning analysis, the metaverse supports both formative and summative assessments in the educational field, where thorough evaluation and prompt feedback promote improved student (Kaddoura and Al Husseiny 2023) development (Parmaxi 2020). Healthcare that incorporates learning assessment For pupils to achieve the necessary learning goals and acquire the abilities and information required to succeed in their future occupations, metaverse education is crucial (Mistretta 2022). Teachers may give students a more interesting and productive learning experience by employing metaverse technology to produce immersive and interactive evaluations (Alvarez-Risco et al. 2022).

2 Literature Review

The characteristics of the metaverse, not to mention its potential uses, might not be known to most educators. Authors (Avilas et al. 2017), want to define the new term "metaverse" in this context and to give it a precise meaning. They also offered research questions on the metaverse's potential applications (Almarzouqi et al. 2022). Also covered are the functions of AI in the metaverse and metaverse-based education. Authors made an effort to explain the metaverse and how it may be utilised for education so that academics in computer science and educational technology would have a thorough understanding of what it is. Luca 2022 says that the "metaverse," one of the inescapable technological developments, started to quickly enter modern life (Kye et al. 2021). Applications of the metaverse in education have already been embraced, although not everywhere, and there is still room for development. Virtual reality is the metaverse's most widely used technology in a learning environment (Javaid et al. 2020). Virtual reality has the benefit of being accessible from everywhere, regardless of location or space. This instructional approach can be used by a professor at a prestigious university, who can instruct students using it in virtual reality and for training (its application in surgery, cardiology, and neurology). Binbin Zhou (2022) in his article focused conceptually structuring on the smart ecosystem with four ecological integration- resource, interaction, space and collaboration ecology accelerating the organic fusion of both metaverse and smart education and also suggested new application for future smart education. He opined that the study in this area is still in the nascent stage and there is lot of scope for future research as Meta based smart education is student centric and delivers vibrant teaching experience by edifying numerous education scenarios. Xinli Zhang et al. (2022), made an in-depth discussion and proposed a framework on metaverse in education describing with reasons and cases four potential applications blended and language learning, competence and inclusive education in the field of education and further proposed different topics of research. Ahmed Tlili et al. (2022) conducted a SLR on metaverse in education using content and bibliometric exploration aiming at identifying the trends, focus and gap in the area of research on metaverse and education. The findings provide a roadmap providing insights that metaverse in education have evolved over generations and tagged Gen Z with artificial intelligence (IA) when compared to other generations. Mustafa eta al. (2022) examined the usage of metaverse technology in education sector, analysed the transition in education over years and investigated the conceptual background of metaverse in education through a systematic literature review (SLR), also identified the gap for future research. Mariapina Trunfio and Rossi (2022) aimed to build a thematic map of metaverse research through systematic literature review (SLR) on metaverse in academics using bibliometric analysis and proposed different streams of research in future like metaverse area of application, metaverse technologies, consumer and market behaviour and sustainability. Gwo-Jen Hwang and Shu-Yun Chien (2022) in his paper discussed conceptually the concept of metaverse, issues pertaining to its potential application and the role of AI in metaverse based education. Raghad Alfaisal et al. (2022) evaluated research in metaverse education using an SLR on information system models used to measure the acceptance and adoption of metaverse systems. He identified that TAM was the most used model forecasting user's intention to use, PLS-SEM was used as an analytical tool, and also studies were students ready to adopt/accept technologies to support them.

2.1 Research Gap

Metaverse in education is not a new concept, there are several studies from educators and researchers discussing the implication of metaverse in learning. Studies on metaverse include investigation of Mixed reality (MR) to deliver experience of engaging learning. Studies were conducted to know about the students' learning outcomes with metaverse using AR and mobile learning, Reyes (2020); and few articulated the various types of metaverse in education. An author, conducted the literature review pertaining to metaverse in education and synthesized it into a coherent interpretation highlighting key issues. However, the review of literature disclosed insufficient studies that could provide insights in the area of metaverse in education. Hence the present study aims at understanding the student's opinion about the metaverse in healthcare education, adoption stage of the metaverse and further the study focuses on the challenges than can be faced by them when they swim in the metaverse virtual reality environment.

3 Methodology of the Research

Current research consists of both qualitative and quantitative research method. This mixed method allows a better understanding of research problem by enjoying both techniques. For the study purpose, questionnaire was developed to measure the students as a part of quantitative analysis. The study conducted to know the student's opinion about the metaverse perspective in health care education. The study was conducted among various college students. The sample of 214 respondents was considered for the study has given their voluntary responses.

This research is an effort to understand the student's perceived expectation towards Metaverse education in healthcare sector, to know this TAM model (Davis 1989) is used to find out the attitude of the students towards its usability and usefulness and intention to use the same (Yang et al. 2022). The following framework is developed to examine the study objective (Fig. 1).

3.1 Hypotheses

Based on the above conceptual framework, the following hypotheses were developed.

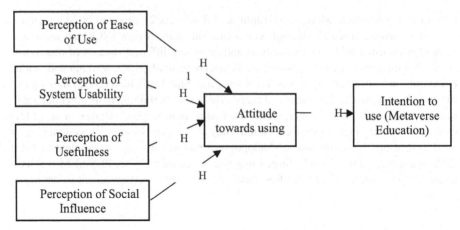

Fig. 1. Metaverse Education in Healthcare - Conceptual framework

H1. The ease of metaverse usage in healthcare education increases the student's attitude toward using the technology.

H2: The system's usability in metaverse education increases the student's attitude toward using the technology.

H3: The usefulness of metaverse education increases the student's attitude toward using the technology.

H4: The social influence on metaverse education increases the student's attitude toward using the technology.

4   Survey Data Analysis and Discussion

4.1   Demographical Characteristics of Respondents

The first part of the data collection is to know the demographic characteristics of the students who participated and given their responses with respect to metaverse in healthcare education. The demographical characteristics of the students are plotted in Table 1.

A total of 214 respondents are participated in the study, most of them are female (54%). In terms of age group, 22% of them are below 19 years old, most of them are fall in the age group of 19 to 23 years (41%), 25% of them are falling under the age group 24 to 26 and 11% of them are above 26. In terms of level of education, most of them are doing their graduation(46%) in the college, 25% of them from postgraduates level, 26% of them are doing diploma and 12% of them are doing above post graduate level.

4.2   Awareness Among the Respondents

Medical Students were asked about the metaverse, to know about their awareness level. The following table shows their knowledge about metaverse an virtual reality-based education of the students (Table 2).

Table 1. Demographical information of the respondents

Information	Type	F	%
Gender	Male	98	46
	Female	116	54
Age	Less than 19	47	22
	>18, <= 23	88	41
	>23, <= 26	56	26
	>26	24	11
Level of Education	Diploma	55	26
	Graduation level	98	46
	Post Graduate	54	25
	Others	26	12

Table 2. Awareness about Metaverse in Medical education:

Answer for the question "Do you know about metaverse in Medical education"	Description of Adopter type	F	%
I never heard about it	Unaware about the Technology	18	8
I heard the name but don't know much about it	Partially aware about the technology	32	15
I am familiar about that but not used it	Aware about the technology	58	27
I am familiar about that and planning to use it in the future	Positive decision towards the technology	81	38
I am familiar about it but planning to not to use it the future	Negative decision towards the technology	21	10
I am current using it	Implementation of the technology	4	2

Source: Primary Data

Augmented and Virtual reality based metaverse education is new technology for them, 8% of them are not aware about it those are generally doing their diploma. Students are the early adopters for any technology and always look for changes in learning environment. They are (15% of the respondents) aware about the word "Metaverse" but they don't have the complete knowledge about it. 27% of them are aware about the new learning platform metaverse but not used it, Most of them (38%) have positive attitude towards it and showed their interest to use the technology as soon as possible. Few of them (10%) are afraid to use the technology as they feel that it is difficult for them/ it may not suitable for them. Very few of them 2% them are current using it. Overall the study found that people are aware and not experience about the role of metaverse in education.

Table 3. Student's adoption status

Opinion on Student's Interest	Type of Adopter	Description	F	%
Very Likely & Likely	Early adopter / Early Majority	seek to adapt to new technology acquire competitive advantages seek input/information from reliable sources before accept	96	45
Undecided	Late Majority	conservative, extremely risk-averse, tech-averse, and price-sensitive frequently rely on a solitary	81	38
Unlikely & Very Unlikely	Laggards	Possessing almost no opinion leadership Find difficult to accept the fresh ideas and innovations fixated on the past	36	17

Table 4. Various Indicators of CHATBOT acceptance Model

Fit Indices	CMIN/DF	P	GFI	AGFI	NFI	CFI	RMSEA	TLI
Model Value	2.19	0.08	0.931	0.942	0.902	0.962	0.048	0.952

Source: Primary data

Table 5. Regression Weights of Estimated Model

DV	INF	INDV	Beta	SE	CR	Sig.	Result
Student's Attitude	←	Perception of Ease of Use	.57	.079	2.170	0.022	Accepted
	←	Perception of System Usability	.48	.061	2.527	0.041	Accepted
	←	Perception of usefulness	.52	.090	4.452	0.035	Accepted
	←	Perception of Social Influence	.49	.060	2.507	0.048	Accepted
Student's Intention to use	←	Student's Attitude	.58	.104	2.403	0.01	Accepted

* p < 0.05, ** p < 0.01

Table 4. Challenges on Metaverse Healthcare Education

Item construct	%
Metaverse make the learning more difficult	5
It is more distractive environment	7
Inability to maintain disciple in the classroom and could not concentrate	8
May create health issues	10
Restricted privacy and cybercrime risk	2
Lack of technology knowledge	5
Negative impact on social life	3
Hating technology dependency	3

4.3 Student's Adoption Status

To know the respondents interest towards use of the metaverse in their education and learning process, respondents were asked to answer the question "are you interested in working in the metaverse?". Based on their response, students were segregated as early adoption, early majority, later majority and laggards (Rogers 2003). The following table shows the respondent's type adoption based on their opinion about metaverse an virtual reality-based education (Table 3).

Early adopters seek to adapt to new technology and use it to bring about revolutionary change in order to acquire competitive advantages. People in the early majority are pragmatic and seek out evolutionary change in order to increase output. They seek input from dependable sources (other pragmatists) before deciding whether or not to accept the new technology (Rogers 2003). They adhere to three criteria in an effort to minimise risk in the adoption of new innovations and make a quick shift, look to the market leaders, and move as a group. This study found that 45% of the respondents are early adopters and early majority to accept the metaverse in their healcare education.

The bulk of people today are conservative, extremely risk-averse, tech-averse, and price-sensitive. They want preassembled, impenetrable, turn-key solutions. To stay competitive with their rivals or the majority, they are driven to adopt new advances. Furthermore, they frequently rely on a solitary, reliable source to assist them in understanding the innovation and its implementation. It is found that 38% of the respondents are not year decided about the acceptance of metaverse in their education.

Laggards are the sceptics who want to keep things as they are. They find it difficult to accept that fresh ideas might raise production (Rogers 2003). They will probably resist new developments in science and technology and only purchase if the alternatives are shown to be worse.. This study, inferred that 17% of the respondents are afraid of the technology and are not ready to imagine the virtual reality will be help them in their education.

4.4   Technology Acceptance of Metaverse in Education

The suggested measurement model was tested using the data collected through questionnaire from the respondents. Structural equation modelling was used to measure and prove the hypotheses framed using AMOS. First step in the SEM is to measure the model fit comparing the various model fit indices (Chuan and Chuan 2006). The following table shows the various model indices of the proposed model (Table 4).

The result shows that all the indicators of model fit attain the threshold limit. Hence the developed model is considered fit. The first fit is the minimal fit, i.e. Chi-Square. For the model, the Chi-Square data is 351.045 with 154 degrees of freedom is 2.19 which shows an adequate fit. The GFI (Goodness of Fit Index) achieved is 0.931 while the AGFI (Goodness of Fit Adjusted Index) is 0.942, above the required 0.90. The CFI and NFI (Normal Fit index) values computed are more than 0.90, indicating that the model fits perfectly with the data. It was discovered that RMSEA is 0.048, which is lower than 0.08, and that it confirms the model fit. SEM was employed to examine the proposed model. The following figure and table shows the result of the hypotheses and their relationship clearly (Table 5).

The Regression estimates and their significance for the entire path are calculated. The results of the model show all the independent variable has an impact on dependent variable.

- The metaverse is very simple to use, and having technological knowledge is not difficult, which has a significant and positive impact on students' attitudes toward using technology (estimator = 57% – 0.057), as the p value is less than 0.05 (p = 0.022). This result is similar to the result as the elementary school students are comfortable in using the metaverse in their education (Suh nd Ahn 2022). Further this result consistant with the literature conducted (Eeuwen 2017)
- The system usability of the Metaverse has a significant influence on students' attitudes toward using it in their healthcare education, as its p value is less than 0.05 (p = 0.02) with an estimator of 0.48. This result is supported by the literature (Yu 2022; De gagne et al. 2022)
- With the estimator value of 0.52, the students are of the opinion that the usefulness of the metaverse may increase their attitude toward using that technology, as the p value of this hypothsis is less than 0.05 (0.035), which is significant at the 5% level of significance. This result is supported by the research conducted (Kim et al. 2022) on student's perception on intention to use metavers learning.
- All are connected socially and do not live individually; society influences people to adopt new technology. The regression weight shows that the estimator is 0.49 and the p value is 0.048 (less than 0.05), which is significant at the 5% level of significance.
- The path analysis of the regression weight shows that the estimator is 0.58 (SE is 0.104) with a CR of 2.403 and a p value of 0.016 (less than 0.05), which is significant at the 5% level of significance. Finally, the attitude of the students towards the usage of the metaverse in their education indicates that they intend to use it.

4.5   Disadvantages of Metaverse Education in Classroom

Regarding the disadvantage or challenges of metaverse education are plotted in the above table, it is found that maximum of them are feeling that it may cause health issues especially eye problems, and it diverts them from learning to surfing other things in the internet. Few of them are afraid of the technology as they are not comfortable with the technology dependency (Table 6).

Even though people are facing many problems in using metaverse, the following can be followed to get rid of these issues.

1. While integrating metaverse technology in the classroom, educators can reduce the chance of eye strain and other health problems. Also, in order to prevent eye strain and other health issues brought on by continuous use of digital devices, it's crucial to teach students and teachers the value of taking breaks, practising proper posture, and adjusting screen settings (Garavand and Aslani 2022).

2. By creating a structured environment, using interactive and engaging activities, providing immediate feedback, and addressing behavioral issues can help maintain discipline in the metaverse classroom. It's essential to encourage students to participate actively and keep them motivated by providing rewards and incentives (Wang et al. 2022).

3. Metaverse education involves a combination of technical solutions and instructional initiatives to safeguard privacy and minimise cybercrime risks. It's critical to adhere to laws and regulations, as well as to teach students about cybersecurity and privacy best practises, to prevent data breaches and cyberattacks (Chen et al. 2022; Dwivedi et al. 2022).

4. Overcoming technology dependency in metaverse education requires a balanced approach that integrates technology with a variety of teaching methods and emphasizes critical thinking, problem-solving, and digital literacy. By doing so, educators can ensure that technology is used as a tool to support and enhance learning, rather than as a substitute for it (Filiz 2022; Wang and Zhao 2022).

5. Metaverse education, like any other form of online education, has the potential to negatively impact social life if students become isolated (Mystakidis 2022) and disconnected from their peers (Stanoevska 2022). In order to avoid detrimental effects on social life, networking possibilities, and a supportive learning environment must all be actively encouraged in metaverse schooling. Educators can assist students in doing so in order to help them form connections, develop business partnerships, and keep a good work-life balance (Kye et al. 2021; Allam et al. 2022).

5   Conclusion

The present study has used a combination of qualitative and quantitative research methods to take advantage and gain a better understanding of the research problem. After an extant review of literature on metaverse and education the scope and relevance of study was identified. The study aimed at measuring student's opinion about the metaverse perspective in healthcare education. The study's findings demonstrated that pupils are open to new learning innovations and that they actively seek out change. Regarding the status of adoption among students, the study found that 38% of respondents can be persuaded to utilise the technology, while 45% of respondents are early adopters and early majority to accept the metaverse in education. Students' opinions on how using the metaverse in the classroom can benefit learning revealed that students have a favourable view of how it can broaden their knowledge and help them understand concepts more clearly. However, when it comes to the difficulties of doing so, some students are worried about their health, such as eye problems, while others worry that using technology will distract them from their studies and make them uncomfortable. It has become possible to realise the experience and applications of the metaverse platform thanks to the use of internet speed. People will reportedly spend more time in the metaverse in the near future for a variety of purposes, including employment, leisure, games, education, and socialising. Although yet in its infancy, the concept of the metaverse in education offers enormous prospects and breakthroughs. This opens up the possibility for future study in the field of education to forecast students' active and engaged participation. The advent of the metaverse may also bring up contentious issues like safety, addiction, and ethical concerns that will need to be addressed in the future.

Implications of the Study

Research on the effects of student adoption of the Metaverse in their schooling is accumulating. Students who view the Metaverse favourably are more likely to be interested in what they are learning. Better learning results and greater levels of student satisfaction may result from this. Collaboration between students and educators from many countries can be facilitated by this study. As a result, a more dynamic and diversified learning environment that encourages creativity and innovation may be created. Positive metaverse attitudes among students are more likely to be associated with better levels of academic satisfaction. Higher levels of student performance and better retention rates may result from this. In this study, users can see how Metaverse may extend access to education, stimulate collaboration, improve learning results, and produce tailored learning experiences, all of which can raise student satisfaction levels. Yet, as the Metaverse develops and is incorporated into educational settings, it is crucial to keep looking into its potential downsides and restrictions. Current research can be useful to identify the possible advantages of employing this technology, such as improved student engagement, better information retention, and better performance on exams, by comprehending the teacher's perspective on the usage of the metaverse in medical education. This study also aids in understanding student opposition, technological obstacles, and doubts regarding the usefulness of the technology. By assisting educators in better anticipating and addressing these difficulties, the program's overall success may be increased. The study's findings on instructors' opinions of the metaverse in medical education can also be used to guide institutional or governmental policy and decision-making.

Limitations and Future study:

Metaverse healthcare education is a relatively new area of study, and there are several limitations to the existing research. This research is conducted on metaverse healthcare education, and most of the studies conducted so far have focused on the use of metaverse environments in medical education. The adoption of metaverse environments in healthcare education is still relatively low, and there are many obstacles, such as financial constraints, lack of technical know-how, and cultural resistance. Additionally, because of the study's small sample size, self-report measures were used to gauge adoption.

There are various areas that require more research in the future, including the following:

Effectiveness: More thorough research is required to determine whether metaverse healthcare education is effective in raising patient safety, improving clinical proficiency, and improving patient outcomes.

Implementation: Further investigation is required to pinpoint the critical elements that either support or obstruct the application of metaverse healthcare education in clinical settings.

User experience: More research is required to comprehend the usability, accessibility, and acceptability of metaverse environments among healthcare professionals and students, as well as the user experience of metaverse healthcare education.

The potential of metaverse environments to facilitate interprofessional education and collaboration between healthcare professionals has to be further investigated.

Cost-effectiveness: More investigation is required to assess how cost-effective metaverse healthcare education is.

References

Abdellatif, S., Eltahir, M., Al Salhi, N., Al Qatawneh, S.: Distance learning in emergencies: social and pedagogical relations in the context of the COVID-19 pandemic. Inform. Sci. Let. **12**(1), 243–250 (2023)

Alhonkoski, M., Salminen, L., Pakarinen, A., Veermans, M.: 3D technology to support teaching and learning in health care education–a scoping review. Int. J. Educ. Res. **105**, 101699 (2021)

Allam, Z., Sharifi, A., Bibri, S.E., Jones, D.S., Krogstie, J.: The metaverse as a virtual form of smart cities: opportunities and challenges for environmental, economic, and social sustainability in urban futures. Smart Cities **5**(3), 771–801 (2022)

Alvarez-Risco, A., Del-Aguila-Arcentales, S., Rosen, M.A., Yáñez, J.A.: Social Cognitive Theory to Assess the Intention to participate in the Facebook Metaverse by citizens in Peru during the COVID-19 pandemic. J. Open Innov. Technol. Market Complexity **8**(3), 142 (2022)

Avila, S.: Implementing augmented reality in academic libraries. Public Serv. Q. **13**(3), 190–199 (2017)

Almarzouqi, A., Aburayya, A., Salloum, S.A.: Prediction of user's intention to use metaverse system in medical education: a hybrid SEM-ML learning approach. IEEE Access **10**, 43421–43434 (2022)

Amor, R.B.: Emergency Distance Education (EDE), urgent transition to distance learning from the perspective of UAE university teachers. Inform. Sci. Let. **12**(5), 1923–1934 (2023)

Casino, F., Dasaklis, T.K., Patsakisa, C.: Systematic literature review of blockchain based applications: current status, classification and open issues. Telematics Inform. **36**, 55–81 (2019)

Chen, Z., Wu, J., Gan, W., Qi, Z.: Metaverse security and privacy: an overview. arXiv preprint arXiv:2211.14948 (2022)

Ning, H., Wang, H., Lin, Y., Wang, W., Dhelim, S., Farha, F., ... & Daneshmand, M. (2021). A Survey on Metaverse: the State-of-the-art, Technologies, Applications, and Challenges. arXiv preprint arXiv:2111.09673

Rogers, E.M.: Diffusion of innovations/everett m. rogers. vol. 576. Simon and Schuster, NY (2003)

Davis, F.D.: Perceived usefulness perceived ease of use and user acceptance of information technology. MIS Quart. **13**, 319–340 (1989)

Sonnenwald, D.H., Maglaughlin, K.L., Whitton, M.C.: Using innovation diffusion theory to guide collaboration technology evaluation: work in progress. In: Proceeding of the 10th IEEE International Workshop Enabling Technology Infrastructure Collaborative Enterprises. (WET ICE), pp. 114–119 (2001)

Chuan, C.L., Penyelidikan, J.: Sample size estimation using Krejcie and Morgan and Cohen statistical power analysis: A comparison. J. Penyelid. IPBL **7**(1), 78–86 (2006)

De Gagne, J.C., Randall, P.S., Rushton, S., Park, H.K., Cho, E., Yamane, S.S., Jung, D.: The use of metaverse in nursing education: an umbrella review. Nurse Educ. 10–1097 (2022)

Díaz, J., Saldaña, C., Avila, C.: Virtual world as a resource for hybrid education. Int. J. Emerg. Technol. Learn. **15**(15), 94–109 (2020)

Dionisio, J.D.N., Burns, W.G., Gilbert, R.: 3D virtual worlds and the metaverse: current status and future possibilities. ACM Comput. Surv. **45**, 1–38 (2013). https://doi.org/10.1145/2480741.2480751

Dwivedi, Y.K., et al.: Metaverse beyond the hype: Multidisciplinary perspectives on emerging challenges, opportunities, and agenda for research, practice and policy. Int. J. Inf. Manage. **66**, 102542 (2022)

Eeuwen, M.V.: Mobile conversational commerce: messenger chatbots as the next interface between businesses and consumers (Master's thesis, University of Twente) (2017)

Fitria, T. N., & Simbolon, N. E. (2022). Possibility of metaverse in education: opportunity and threat. SOSMANIORA: Jurnal Ilmu Sosial dan Humaniora, 1(3), 365–375

Filiz, M.: Metaverse and a swot analysis of Turkish health system. Turkish Res. J. Acad. Soc. Sci. **5**(1), 61–68 (2022)

Garavand, A., Aslani, N.: Metaverse phenomenon and its impact on health: a scoping review. Inform. Med. Unlocked 101029 (2022)

Hwang, G.-J., Chien, S.-Y.: Definition, roles, and potential research issues of the metaverse in education: an artificial intelligence perspective. Comput. Educ. Artific. Intell. **3**, 100082 (2022). https://doi.org/10.1016/j.caeai.2022.100082

Guo, H., Gao, W.: Metaverse-powered experiential situational English-teaching design: an emotion-based analysis method. Front. Psychol. **13** (2022)

Hwang, G.J., Chien, S.Y.: Definition, roles, and potential research issues of the metaverse in education: an artificial intelligence perspective. Comput. Educ. Artific. Intell. **3**, 100082 (2022)

Javaid, M., Haleem, A.: Virtual reality applications toward medical field. Clin. Epidemiol. Global Health **8**(2), 600–605 (2020)

Jovanović, A., Milosavljević, A.: VoRtex Metaverse platform for gamified collaborative learning. Electronics **11**(3), 317 (2022)

Kaddoura, S., Al Husseiny, F.: The rising trend of Metaverse in education: challenges, opportunities, and ethical considerations. PeerJ Comput. Sci. **9**, e1252 (2023)

Kim, K., Yang, E., Ryu, J.: Work-in-progress—the effect of students' perceptions on intention to use metaverse learning environment in higher education. In: 2022 8th International Conference of the Immersive Learning Research Network (iLRN), pp. 1–3. IEEE (2022)

Kye, B., Han, N., Kim, E., Park, Y., Jo, S.: Educational applications of metaverse: possibilities and limitations. J. Educ. Eval. Health Prof. **18**, 32 (2021). https://doi.org/10.3352/jeehp.2021.18.32

Lin, H., Wan, S., Gan, W., Chen, J., Chao, H.C.: Metaverse in education: vision, opportunities, and challenges. arXiv preprint arXiv:2211.14951 (2022)

Muammar, M.O., Alnaim, F.M.: Post-COVID education: factors that attribute to effective online training. J. Stat. Appl. Probabil. **12**(3) (2023). https://doi.org/10.18576/jsap/120318

Rabbani, L.M., AlQuwaitaei, R.S., Alarabi, K.S., Alsalhi, N.R.: Feedback revisited: definitional, structural, and functional issues. J. Stat. Appl. Probabil. **12**(3), 1039–1044 (2023). https://doi.org/10.18576/jsap/120313

Mesko, B.: The promise of the metaverse in cardiovascular health (2022)

Mistretta, S.: The metaverse—an alternative education space. AI, Computer Science and Robotics Technology (2022)

Mustafa, B.: Analyzing education based on metaverse technology. Technium Soc. Sci. J. **32**(1), 278–295 (2022). https://doi.org/10.47577/tssj.v32i1.6742

Mystakidis, 2022. Mystakidis, S.: Metaverse. Encyclopedia **2**(1), 486–497 (2022)

Palvia, S., Aeron, P., Gupta, P., Mahapatra, D., Parida, R., Rosner, R., et al.: Online education: worldwide status, challenges, trends, and implications. J. Glob. Inf. Technol. Manag. **21**, 233–241 (2018). https://doi.org/10.1080/1097198x.2018.1542262

Park, S.M., Kim, Y.G.: A metaverse: taxonomy, components, applications, and open challenges. IEEE Access **10**, 4209–4251 (2022)

Parmaxi, A.: Virtual reality in language learning: a systematic review and implications for research and practice. Interact. Learn. Environ. **3**, 1–13 (2020). https://doi.org/10.1080/10494820.2020.1765392

Phakamach, P., Senarith, P., Wachirawongpaisarn, S.: The Metaverse in education: the future of immersive teaching & learning. RICE J. Creative Entrepren. Manage. **3**(2), 75–88 (2022)

Popescu, G.H., Valaskova, K., Horak, J.: Augmented reality shopping experiences, retail business analytics, and machine vision algorithms in the virtual economy of the metaverse. J. Self-Govern. Manage. Econ. **10**(2), 67–81 (2022)

Alfaisal, R., Hashim, H., Azizan, U.H.: Metaverse system adoption in education: a systematic literature review. J. Comput. Educ. (2022). https://doi.org/10.1007/s40692-022-00256-6

Rakshasbhuvankar, A.A., Patole, S.K.: Benefits of simulation based training for neonatal resuscitation education: a systematic review. Resuscitation **85**(10), 1320–1323 (2014)

Ramesh, P.V., et al.: Holographic elysium of a 4D ophthalmic anatomical and pathological metaverse with extended reality/mixed reality. Indian J. Ophthalmol. **70**(8), 3116–3121 (2022)

Reyes, C.E.G.: Perception of high school students about using Metaverse in augmented reality learning experiences in mathematics. Pixel-Bit: Media Educ. Magazine **58**, 143–159 (2020)

Mousa, S., Ayman, A., Mohammad, A., Ahmad, A.M., Basem, A., Iqbal, J.: Using virtual tours as a university campus guide: al- zaytoonah university case study. Inform. Sci. Let. **12**(9), 2961–2970 (2023)

Stanoevska-Slabeva, K.: Opportunities and challenges of metaverse for education: a literature review. In: EDULEARN22 Proceedings, pp. 10401–10410 (2022)

Suh, W., Ahn, S.: Utilizing the metaverse for learner-centered constructivist education in the post-pandemic era: an analysis of elementary school students. J. Intelligence **10**(1), 17 (2022)

Thomason, J.: Metahealth-how will the metaverse change health care? J. Metaverse **1**(1), 13–16 (2021)

Tlili, A., et al.: Is Metaverse in education a blessing or a curse: a combined content and bibliometric analysis. Smart Learn. Environ. **9**(1), 1–31 (2022)

Trunfio, M., Rossi, S.: Advances in metaverse investigation: streams of research and future agenda. Virtual Worlds **1**, 103–129 (2022). https://doi.org/10.3390/virtualworlds1020007

Wang, M., Yu, H., Bell, Z., Chu, X.: Constructing an Edu-metaverse ecosystem: a new and innovative framework. IEEE Trans. Learn. Technol. **15**(6), 685–696 (2022)

Wang, Y., Zhao, J.: A Survey of Mobile Edge Computing for the Metaverse: Architectures, Applications, and Challenges. arXiv preprint arXiv:2212.00481 (2022)

Williams, J., Jones, D., Walker, R.: Consideration of using virtual reality for teaching neonatal resuscitation to midwifery students. Nurse Educ. Pract. **31**, 126–129 (2018)

Wu, H.-K., Lee, S.W.-Y., Chang, H.-Y., Liang, J.-C.: Current status, opportunities and challenges of augmented reality in education. Comput. Educ. **62**, 41–49 (2013). https://doi.org/10.1016/j.compedu.2012.10.024

Wu, T.C., Ho, C.T.B.: A scoping review of metaverse in emergency medicine. Australasian emergency care (2022)

Yang, F., Ren, L., Gu, C.: A study of college students' intention to use metaverse technology for basketball learning based on UTAUT2. Heliyon **8**(9), e10562 (2022)

Yu, J.E.: Exploration of educational possibilities by four metaverse types in physical education. Technologies **10**(5), 104 (2022)

Zhang, X., Chen, Y., Hu, L., Wang, Y.: The metaverse in education: definition, framework, features, potential applications, challenges, and future research topics. Front. Psychol. **13**, 1016300 (2022). https://doi.org/10.3389/fpsyg.2022.1016300

Zhong, J., Zheng, Y.: Empowering future education: learning in the Edu-Metaverse. In: 2022 International Symposium on Educational Technology (ISET), pp. 292–295. IEEE (2022)

Zhou, B.: Building a Smart Education Ecosystem from a Metaverse Perspective, Mobile Information Systems, Hindawi, 1574–017X (2022). https://doi.org/10.1155/2022/1938329

Performance Evaluation of Electric Vehicle Stocks: Paving a Way Towards Green Economy

Ajay Mishra[✉], Pooja Talreja, and Amit Shrivastava

Symbiosis University of Applied Sciences, Indore, India
ajay2708@gmail.com

Abstract. Transportation contributes 24% of worldwide fossil fuel combustion carbon (IEA 2020). Electric vehicles (EVs) will help in decarbonizing the transportation industry to promote climate action globally (Coignard et al 2018, Taljegard 2019, Muratori 2021, Dioha 2022). Battery EVs (BEVs) led the rise from practically zero in 2010 to over 16 million in 2021. (IEA 2022). The IEA's 2021 Global EV Outlook estimates that by 2030, 145 million EVs will make up 7% of the global vehicle pool (IEA 2021) As part of the EV30@30 Campaign, India has set a goal of reaching a 30 percent share of electric vehicles (EVs) by the year 2030. EVs would have the following effects: a) a decrease in the amount of petroleum fuel used for road transportation; b) a change in consumer demand away from automobiles with internal combustion engines and toward EVs; and c) a need for an increased amount of energy and a charging infrastructure. These changes will impact many stakeholders. This study attempts to encapsulate India's EV transition and its players. Over the past 5–10 years, EVs have grown in popularity and market share. Pure electric vehicle firms are increasing. This review article also examines the significance of the factor and the expected return rate for the AEV industry based on the study of selected EV businesses and found that EV stock prices are significantly affected.

Keywords: Electric Vehicle · Performance · Stocks · Economy

1 Introduction

Electric vehicles (EVs) may reduce greenhouse gases (GHGs) and worldwide anthropogenic emissions from the energy and transportation industries. In addition to this, they provide new economic possibilities and diversify the energy sector. Cleaner energy and mobility may be achieved by synchronising these networks with low-carbon power generation, which can be accomplished by embracing renewable energy sources that have a high energy conversion efficiency. Electric vehicles rely heavily on the electric grid. Electric vehicles have a lower environmental impact compared to internal combustion engine (ICE) autos. Grid energy production and regenerative braking are more efficient. Autonomous driving, pooled mobility, and electrification are revolutionising transportation. Thus, while designing electric vehicle charging infrastructure, these three approaching revolutions must be considered. Electric vehicles increase power consumption, requiring infrastructural upgrades. Only the distribution grid transports electrical

A. M. A. Musleh Al-Sartawi et al. (Eds.): ICGER 2023, CCIS 1999, pp. 175–194, 2024.
https://doi.org/10.1007/978-3-031-50518-8_14

energy, limiting transmission line energy. Rebuilding the electrical grid for EV charging is difficult.

China, Europe, and the US have most of the world's EVs. China, Europe, and the US sold 95% of EVs in 2021, while Indonesia, India, and Brazil sold 5%. In the last decade, EVs have not succeeded everywhere. However, developing nations want EVs. Africa has the lowest EV fleet, but sales have surged in recent years (McDonnell 2022). In 2021, African EV sales rose 90%, with BEVs accounting for 85%. (IEA 2022). South Africa's 12 million vehicles included 1000 EVs in January 2022. Kenya has 350 EVs among its 2.2 million vehicles. EV deployment is planned in many developing nations. Kenya intends to import 5% of its EVs by 2025. Namibia wants 10,000 EVs by 2030, while Egypt wants to make 20,000 EVs per year by 2023. (McDonnell 2022). The majority of developed countries in Europe and North America are adopting EVs to reduce transportation-related greenhouse gas emissions, while developing countries4 may have different reasons.Socio-economic development is the top goal in Ethiopia, India, and Haiti, where many people are underserved. Thus, developing world governments' top priority is providing enough infrastructure and modern energy for necessary services to end severe poverty. To alleviate poverty, several developing nations have implemented fossil fuel and energy tariff subsidies (Groot and Oostveen 2019). Thus, to be marketed in poor countries, EVs must be able to address other pressing issues outside climate mitigation.

The International Energy Agency (IEA) reported 4.79 million battery electric cars (BEVs) globally in 2019, including 2.58 million in China. The worldwide EV stock may reach 245 million by 2030 (IEA sustainable development scenario) as it grows by 36% annually [2]. The overall battery capacity of all EVs in 2030 might reach 12.5 TWh if each has a 50 kWh battery.

Due to favorable government laws, incentives, and subsidies, dropping manufacturing and battery costs, more public acceptance, and a bigger infrastructure to support EVs, such as charging stations, the global mobility sector is rapidly adopting EVs. More than 17 countries have been working on reducing the usage of ICE vehicles by 2050 and adopting zero-emission vehicles. In 2019, EV power generated 51 Mt-CO2-eq. This is approximately 50% of the 53 Mt-CO2-eq emissions by ICE-based vehicles.

Low-carbon electric vehicles have changed several energy and public sectors. We found the best ASEAN EV portfolio using the WHO COVID-19 pandemic statement. According to Monte Carlo simulation, the optimal risky asset portfolio weights fluctuate dramatically before and during the epidemic. Before (during) the pandemic, optimal portfolio investment weights were Toyota Motor Corporation at 49.83% (42.99%), Hyundai Motor Corporation at 20.81% (10.63%), Star 8 Corporation at 23.20% (9.73%), BMW.DE at 2.79% (32.08%), Honda Motor Company at 2.56% (0.64%), Mitsubishi Motor Corporation at 0.68% (0.09%), and Nissan Motor Co. at 0.14% (3.84%). As indicated by the Sharpe Ratio, EV stock portfolios had higher returns than risks during the epidemic, from 93.55% to 250.62%. These data favour EV stock investment, particularly during the COVID-19 epidemic.

1.1 Electric Vehicle in India: An Overview

Only 1% of Indian vehicle sales are electric. Only a few thousand electric cars and 0.4 million electric two-wheelers are on India's roadways.

Indian electric vehicle sales have lagged due to many hurdles. On October 1, 2019, new EV charging infrastructure rules were announced to accelerate EV adoption in India. India wants to import 10% less oil by 2022. Delhi wants 500,000, or 25%, of new battery-powered automobiles by 2024. Two-wheeler subsidies in India are Rs. 30,000 and Rs. The government will exempt electric cars from off-road charges and registration. The India Energy Storage Alliance (IESA) forecasts 63 lakh EVs produced annually by 2027. The government also wants 30% of Indian automobiles to be electric vehicles by 2030.

In order to encourage the use of HEVs and PEVs, the government of India developed the National Electric Mobility Mission Plan in 2012 as well as the Faster Adoption and Manufacturing of Hybrid and Electric Cars (FAME) plan, all of which are comprised of two stages. The second phase of FAME will get underway in 2019 and last until 2022. By January 1, 2020, there will be 2636 electric vehicle (EV) chargers in 24 states and territories that are eligible for FAME II incentives, including 1633 fast chargers. The State Power Board has implemented fluctuating power prices in order to have an effect on the charging of electric cars. Andhra Pradesh's rate is 6.95 rupees per kilowatt-hour, whereas the rate in Delhi is between 6 and 7 rupees. In place of a flat rate, several other jurisdictions have implemented something called a "time-of-day" (ToD) rebate or fee.

Many organisations must reassess market predictions due to the 2020 COVID-19 lockout. The Auto Expo 2020 in February is expected to boost electric car sales in India. Due to economic issues, the global fuel price has dropped, making EVs more expensive to acquire than regular automobiles. However, new customers and those who desire a clear sky, pure air, and a better home for future generations are adopting EVs. The Indian government has continued to implement the EV incentive and build ambitious EV legislation.

India's EV strategy includes public–private cooperation, incentives for EV owners, legislative reforms, EV charging infrastructure development, and help for indigenous EV and supply equipment and battery production. Delhi, Kerala, Andhra Pradesh, and other Indian states offer electric vehicle incentives and restrictions.

More recently, India has been phasing out of the function of Gompertz. Due to the thriving automobile sector, the car population will continue to rise, negatively affecting the environment and public health (Wu et al. 2014). Consequently, the following regulatory frameworks are necessary to limit the number of automobiles and pollution:

- Vehicles in India use gasoline and diesel. In 2009 compressed natural gas (CNG) was introduced as a fuel for rickshaws and taxis. It has a lower carbon dioxide emission factor than either gasoline or diesel; hence, a greater proportion of CNG as a motor fuel will cut emissions in the future.
- Emissions from vehicles may also be reduced by increasing vehicle and fuel economy. In India, the vehicle fuel policy has already established measures mandating a 20% decrease by 2017 and a 40% decrease by 2020 (Chandola and Sen 2008). Such a programme aims to enhance the quality of gasoline and impose stringent pollution regulations on the vehicle industry.

- Electric cars have previously been launched, although they are not currently the market leader in India. Through plans including the National Electric Mobility Mission Plan (NEMMP) and the Faster Adoption and Manufacturing of Electric Cars (FAME), the government in India encourages market penetration of electric cars. Since electric cars produce zero emissions on the road, they are a viable alternative to gasoline and diesel automobiles.
- Improving the quality of India's public transportation may also help curb the rising automobile stock population. Better connections (to and from places), carpooling, and stringent requirements for the purchase and maintenance of private vehicles might increase the usage of public transportation in India.

1.2   Electric Vehicle: The Future Need

The battery manufacturing sector expanded due to the necessity that electric cars have battery packs that can provide for their propulsion needs, air conditioning, and auxiliary systems. Meanwhile high dependability, capacity, and energy density are retained. This growth should lower battery prices and accelerate battery development. These factors contributed to lower EV manufacturing costs over time. EVs are used for 5% of daily commutes and weekend travel.

Japanese and European power consumption are 2% and 6%, respectively, due to charging demand. In a conventional charging arrangement, electricity runs from the grid/charger to the EV battery only in one way. Unidirectional charging may cause unexpected, fluctuating, and concentrated power usage. Managing EV charging patterns is crucial to EV market adoption globally since it affects electrical grid transmission quality. The IEA predicted that uncontrolled and concentrated electric car charging would increase power demand in 2030, especially at night. Demand in the United States, the European Union, and China is 5.5%, 6.5%, and 9.5%, respectively.

With appropriate management and supervision, EVs connected to the grid may utilise their huge battery reserves for other purposes. Vehicle-grid integration (VGI) advocates a synergistic usage of G2V and V2G technology. Thus, a system like VGI may minimise the grid's load (which may increase due to EVs' charging needs) and assist it by discharging behaviors and controlling charging and. Firm-specific risk and market-wide, systematic risk affect stock performance. The first is unrelated to stocks, whereas the second is universal. Avoiding firm-specific risk by diversifying a portfolio Diversification cannot remove market-wide risk, and investors seek higher returns. Before investing, systematic risk should be assessed by identifying the fraction of return variability owing to systemic risk factors affecting the whole economy. Financial literature calls it "beta stock return sensitivity to market return." Beta is the projected percentage return change for an asset if the market portfolio returns 1%. The security tracker tracks the market when beta equals one. Stocks with a beta larger than 1 are more systematic and risky.

2   Literature Review

(EVs) are use rechargeable batteries for power by plugging them into an electrical socket (Liu & Wei 2018). These vehicles are therefore dubbed as an environmental "green" transportation choice (Sachana, Debb, & Singh 2020). Cities are crucial to achieving this goal and promoting sustainable development (Yin, Laing, Leon, and Mabon 2018). Urban sustainability requires a global plan that prioritises social inclusion, economic viability, and ecological preservation (Huang, Yan, & Wu 2016; López-Carreiro & Monzón 2018; Pardo-Bosch, Aguado, & Pino 2019). Several scholars see the social and economic dimensions of sustainability as both a problem and an opportunity in recent urban studies (Büyükozkan & Karabulut 2018; Ferrer, Thomé, & Scavarda 2018). (Addanki & Venkataraman 2017; Shealy et al. 2018; and Yin et al. 2018).

Singh et al.'s (2020) forecasts of the number of privately owned vehicles in India up to the year 2050 In India, the most common fuels for private automobiles and two-wheelers, sometimes known as motorised two-wheelers, are petrol and diesel. The expansion of the nation's economy is strongly correlated to the rise in the number of people who own private vehicles. In the current research, the Gompertz function is used to make projections about the ownership of automobiles/1000 persons in relation to per capita GDP. With India serving as the base country, the end result provides potential values for both two-wheelers and automobiles, which are obtained from growth rates of the GDP and levels for vehicle ownership/1000 people. According to the findings of our research, the total population of two-wheeled vehicles is expected to almost triple by the year 2050, reaching 420 million units, and to nearly quadruple, reaching 562 million units, under cases of both aggressive and conservative growth respectively. In a similar vein, the total population of automobiles is projected to expand by roughly 9 times (262 million) or 14 times (432 million) by the year 2050, depending on the growth scenario being considered. After the year 2030, the moment of inflection will begin for privately owned automobiles in India. This conclusion also suggests that India is at the first stage of the Gompertz curve and that its development pattern is similar to that of industrialised countries in that it follows an "S"-shaped pattern. The research provides a few policy ideas that would be ideal for a decrease in the population of vehicles, which would ultimately have an effect on the emissions from vehicles and the dependence on oil.

EV interest in ASEAN may affect their stocks. Market optimism over EVs may boost ASEAN EV stock returns. Thus, we will examine investment choices during the COVID-19 epidemic and how they impact the portfolio of EV stocks. We construct the efficient frontier of the top 7 ASEAN EV corporations using Monte-Carlo simulation: Toyota Motor Corporation (TM), Star 8 Corporation (STRH), Hyundai Motor Corporation (HYMTF), Bayerische Motoren Werke AG (BMW.DE), Honda Motor Company (HMC), Mitsubishi Motor Corporation (MMTOF), and Nissan Motor Co. (NSANY). Due to their greater Sharpe ratio, EV equities are investable, particularly during the COVID-19 epidemic.

The projected impact of India's road transport industry's automobile stock population on energy consumption, oil demand, and car emissions was investigated. The IEA/SMP model estimated small vehicle (cars and utility vehicles) and heavy vehicles (three-wheeler populations) using the Gompertz function and GDP per capita (Fulton & Eads 2004).

Abergel et al. (2020) reported 4,8 million EVs worldwide in 2019, with China accounting for 47% and Europe accounting for 25%. In spite of increase in sales, only five countries have a market share of EVs larger than 1.5%. The main barriers for EV buyers are (1) the higher initial investment, despite running costs being lower than for

ICE vehicles (Madina, Zamora, & Zabala 2016); (2) anxiety in relation to uncertainty about driving long distances without charging (Napoli et al. 2020); and, (3) most importantly, the absence of an efficient network of CSs (Needell, McNerney, Chang, & Trancik 2016).

Private transportation increased with family affluence (Wu et al. 2014). India has more private cars than affluent countries, although vehicle ownership is still lower. India had 19 passenger vehicles per 1000 persons in 2015, whereas OECD countries had 300–400. (Paladugula et al. 2018). Private car ownership will increase as India's GDP grows. The increase will worsen traffic, oil usage, pollution of the air, carbon emissions, and general public health. Table 1 shows India's GDP and travel trends throughout time (IEA 2017; WDI 2003; MORTH 2015).

According to the study, rising countries like India would choose electric vehicles over wealthier ones. EV technology seems reasonable and economically possible given India's oil shortage and driving habits (Biswas & Biswas, 1999). The electric car industry's development depends on public awareness, customer preferences, and the benefits of electric cars. The electric vehicle industry is growing, but many barriers prevent its widespread acceptance. Rezvani et al. (2015) observed various factors that impact EV purchases. Researchers have shown that adding guardrails, terminals, transitions, and crash cushions into road and highway design may enhance vehicle restraint systems (VRS) (Tahmasseby et al. 2021).

3 The Dynamics of the Market and the Opinions of Consumers

The opinions and worries of consumers in developing nations about the up-front costs, power dependability, convenience, and functionality of electric vehicles are important impediments to the adoption of EVs. The high initial cost of electric vehicles, in particular, is a significant barrier to entry in nations where the median daily income for more than half of the population is still less than $3. Birdsall and Meyer (2015) provide an example. Governments of several countries have created financial incentives in the form of subsidies and tax breaks to encourage the adoption of EVs. Nevertheless, for a variety of reasons, the effects that were hoped for from these incentives have not materialised. The most important reason is that even with tax breaks, the enormous used-vehicle market in developing nations is still relatively cost-competitive when compared to EVs. This is true despite the fact that the market is saturated with vehicles that have been previously owned.

Because of this, novel business models like pay-as-you-go, fee-for-service, and battery swapping will be very important for the widespread adoption of electric vehicles in poor nations. Thankfully, developments in fintech and digital financial services, such as mobile money in developing nations, are driving the growth of these new types of business models. In addition, governments, politicians, and other key stakeholders will need to work together to provide the appropriate political and economic climate to encourage and facilitate the local assembly of electric vehicles. It is not clear how or if this behaviour will represent the range anxiety experienced by EV adopters. It is obvious that the consumer market's willingness to embrace electric vehicles will be directly correlated to how well consumers prepare for a network of charging infrastructure that is both dependable and strategically located. Furthermore, efforts to gain insight into people's perceptions of range anxiety and electric vehicles in different contexts and electric cars in general will go a long way towards designing and making available the appropriate technology, incentives, and supporting infrastructure. This is because people's perceptions of these things are heavily influenced by their personal experiences.

3.1 Key Factors and Challenges of EV

Tech variables (vehicle performance): Electric vehicle fuel is harder to store, more costly, and takes longer to replenish. This means electric automobiles have a lower range than diesel cars and cannot be refuelled on the road (Pearre et al. 2011). Technologically important aspects follow.

Range anxiety, charging time, and EV model variety Rangephobia: Range worry prevents customers from buying electric cars, polls show (Jensen et al. 2013). Customers want 300–450 km of driving range, according to a study (Zhu 2016). This could lead to range anxiety. When driving for long periods with a low battery charge, the motorist is unable to predict the distance they can go. Electric cars' unclear range scared off long-distance drivers (Noel et al. 2020). This would diminish vehicle reliability.

Recharge: The driver's battery range selection determines the battery's recharge time. Battery charge increases range (Daziano & Chiew 2012). Due to limited refilling capacity, this increases charging time (Egbue & Long 2012). Despite being the least problematic, this factor nevertheless discourages EV purchases (Carley et al. 2013). Most drivers think charging an electric car is harder than refuelling an ICE vehicle (Brückmann et al. 2021). Since on-road drivers can't quickly refill and go, they think EV charging time may slow them down (Graham-Rowe et al. 2012). The motorist cannot undertake spontaneous trips while charging an EV at home. Reduces adaptability.

Unintelligent electric car charging may induce taxi drivers to come home and charge their vehicles when demand is high (Christensen et al. 2012). EV models: Bessenbach and Wallrapp (2013) also cite EV model variety as a barrier to adoption. Economics (financial barrier): These are the prices for batteries, gasoline, and electric vehicles. Consumer polls show that EV prices are a major deterrent (Carley et al. 2013; She et al. 2017). Electric cars cost more due to their expensive manufacturing technologies (Noel et al. 2020). As new technologies are developed to increase EV range, the lithium-ion batteries used in EVs become more sophisticated (Biresselioglu et al. 2018). Battery prices are rising (Noel et al. 2020). Thus, battery replacement would be expensive. Insufficient awareness of automobile fuel and maintenance costs also hinders this. In essence, limited economies of scale make new technologies unfavourable to current pricing strategies. This also affects the customer's EV valuation. These vehicles cost less to maintain than ICE autos. EVs' high initial purchase price deters buyers. This shows that buyers are unaware that EVs' lower operating costs may save them money (Krause et al. 2013). Infrastructure-based charging network shortage: Traveling without a charging station is another issue (Krupa et al. 2014). Long-distance travellers regularly request more public charging stations (Habla et al. 2020). Establishing these networks is costly (Brückmann et al. 2021). Thus, charging station infrastructure expansion is uncertain. Government and carmaker investments in EV infrastructure may accelerate consumer adoption (Bhalla et al. 2018).

Drivers avoid electric cars due to inconsistent charging networks. Public charging stations are still being debated as a way to boost electric car usage. Adding charging stations and making them more accessible may encourage consumers to use EVs (Noel et al. 2020). In cities with charging stations, EVs will become more visible, and therefore, public opinion will be critical (Bunce et al. 2014). Personality: The Theory of Planned Behavior states that humans make decisions based on reasonable input evaluations and expected outcomes (Ajzen 1991). Customer knowledge affects attitude (Ajzen & Fishbein 1980). Gender, age, income, education, tastes, and environmental conscience also impact EV adoption. Electric car adopters are usually educated and eco-conscious. Socially acceptable behaviour, regard for others, expressing shared ideas, and social responsibility influence people. Environmentally conscious customers choose electric cars for two reasons, according to Kahn (2007). First, driving a fuel-efficient automobile reduces one's yearly carbon footprint. The second reason is that everyone sees your automobile. Driving a fuel-inefficient automobile may embarrass and isolate environmentalists. Electric cars are bought through peer pressure.

Performance, style, size, and safety were listed as hurdles. EV adoption may be hindered by ignorance of its benefits (Wang et al. 2017). Lack of market data prevents many electric car manufacturers from innovating (Lieven et al. 2011). Electric automobiles must be designed and marketed to elicit positive emotions (Moons & Pelsmacker 2012). Information may raise environmental awareness. This increases scepticism, decreases fatalism, and increases consumer readiness to change behaviour (as anticipated by the Theory of Planned Behavior), although it is frequently a precondition (Lane & Potter 2007).

Environmental awareness and education are seldom linked. Higher education may increase knowledge of an automobile purchase's climate-reduction potential. Due to the positive association between education and employment, more educated customers tend to drive more costly cars with higher CO2 emissions (Peters et al. 2015). Green Economy: Urban heat islands are caused by population growth, urban surface materials, forest removal, man-made heat, noise, and air pollution, concrete structures, and packed roadways (Sampson et al. 2021). This suggests that few people are directly impacted by natural resource decline and care about environmental conservation (Heffner et al. 2007; Mohamed et al. 2018). Until the matter was brought up in controlled conversations, most focus group members did not notice any connection between automobile ownership and environmental values (Flamm & Agrawal 2012). Asadi et al. (2021) believe electric automobiles will solve most environmental difficulties. Consumers believe EVs will reduce pollution (Skippon & Garwood 2011). This encourages people to buy EVs to "live lighter" and utilise fewer natural resources (Ozaki & Sevastyanova 2011; Mohamed et al. 2018). This study measured respondents' environmental awareness using an Environmental Index. Electric automobiles are largely used by environmentalists, early adopters, wealthy people, young urbanites, and techies (Axsen et al. 2015; Talantsev 2017).

Skerlos and Winebrake (2010) discuss how EVs reduce greenhouse gas emissions and other air pollutants. Even with power plant emissions, EVs emit less than ICE automobiles. Whether these EVs use natural gas, coal, or renewable fuels greatly affects this disparity. Policies: Policies and consumer attitudes may prevent electric car adoption (Brückmann et al. 2021). Environment-related government policies and incentives affecting gasoline prices and fuel infrastructure development may affect electric car uptake (David Diamond, 2009). Customers may misinterpret these regulations. Frequent policy changes may cause consumer confusion. This may hinder electric car adoption (Kester et al. 2018).

To promote electric vehicle sales, policymakers should let companies test cars. Offering EVs for monitoring or removing other barriers to EV adoption may also help (Sierzchula 2014). This research examines electric vehicle innovations. The selected EV enterprises were examined to determine the factor's relevancy and the AEV business's expected return rate. NYSE, NASDAQ, and OTC-listed US electric vehicle (EV) companies were analyzed. U.S. stocks were chosen to reduce market-specific characteristics' impact on the asset pricing model's explanatory ability (Huang 2019). The paper highlights major research gaps to help researchers (Fig. 1).

4   Overview of EV Stocks Companies in India 2023

Reliance Industries Limited operates in O2C, Oil and Gas, Retail, Digital Services, and Financial Services. The 02C business includes downstream manufacturing, logistics, supply-chain infrastructure, aviation fuel, petrochemicals, fuel retailing via Reliance BP Mobility Limited, and bulk wholesale marketing. The data shows that Reliance firms' stocks have soared since electric vehicles were introduced (Fig. 2).

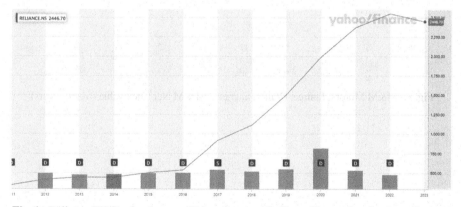

Fig. 1. Reliance EV Stocks. Source: (Yahoo finance – Reliance Net stock value over 10 years)

One of them is the TVS iQube. Customers have another option for investigating the TVS Apache series motorcycles; they may use the TVS Augmented Reality Interactive Vehicle Experience (ARIVE) smartphone app, which provides in-depth information, as well as the opportunity to schedule a test ride and make a purchase. The statistic demonstrates that TVS stock has greatly improved after the introduction of electric automobiles (Fig. 3).

The Company sells SUVs, trucks, commercial vehicles, tractors, electric vehicles, two-wheelers, and construction equipment. It is a popular Indian EV stock. Since electric cars were developed, M & M stocks have greatly improved (Fig. 4).

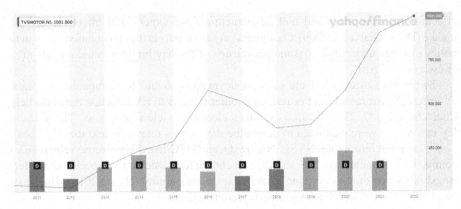

Fig. 2. TVS Motors. Source: (Yahoo finance – TVS Net stock value over 10 years)

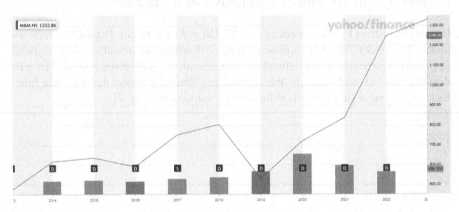

Fig. 3. M&M Motors. Source: (Yahoo finance – M& M Net stock value over 10 years)

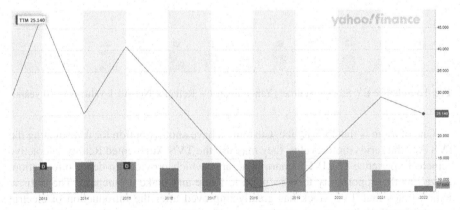

Fig. 4. TATA Motors. Source: (Yahoo finance – TATA Net stock value over 10 years)

Tata Motors Limited makes cars worldwide. The corporation sells automobiles, SUVs, trucks, buses, and military vehicles. Operations include automotive and others. IT, machine tools, and industrial automation are its services. The stock graph depicts fluctuations with insignificant impact and Since electric vehicles were released, TATA stocks have improved and found to be a stabilized (Fig. 5).

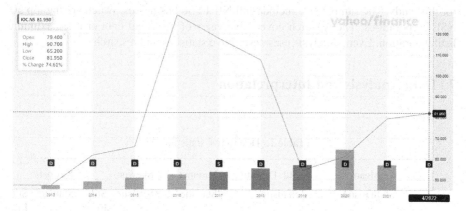

Fig. 5. IOC. Source: (Yahoo finance – IOC Net stock value over 10 years)

IOC manages many types of storage facilities, including bulk storage terminals, inland depots, aviation fuel stations, LPG bottling activities, and lubricant mixing plants. At its energy pumps around the country, it provides 257 charging stations for electric vehicles and 29 battery swapping stations. Additionally, it manages nine other refineries in India. IOC supplies have significantly increased since the first electric CHARGING POINTS were installed.

5 Objective

- To evaluate EV stock return factors and rates.
- To analyze stock values around earnings announcements.

6 Research Methodology

The growth or decline of a country's average per-capita gross domestic product is closely correlated to changes in the ownership of motor vehicles. This connection cannot be described as linear (Arora et al. 2011). This relationship takes the form of a 'S' shaped curve in developed nations, which indicates that the ownership of vehicles grows gradually at the lowest income levels, then more quickly as income rises, and then finally slows down as saturation is approached. This implies that vehicle ownership increases slowly at the lowest income levels (Dargay et al. 2007; Wu et al. 2014). The total stock is calibrated using historical data of registered passenger vehicles. The top five EV companies studied were Reliance Industries, TATA Motors, TVS Motors, Indian Oil Corporation (charging facilitator), and Mahindra & Mahindra Ltd. EV Stocks employ secondary data. NSE, CAPITALINE PLUS, RBI, and SEBI websites provided all data for this study. The sample size includes all NIFTY50 businesses, which are the top 50 NSE corporations. The research covers five years of historical data or the maximum listing duration. Event Analysis uses descriptive statistics and research.

7 Data Analysis and Interpretation

Table 1. Descriptive statistics:

	Mean	Std. Deviation	Variance	Skewness		Kurtosis	
	Statistic	Statistic	Statistic	Statistic	Std. Error	Statistic	Std. Error
TVS MOTORS	622.58918968	219.531947526	48194.276	.940	.388	.280	.759
RELIANCE	2107.11094035	425.381674967	180949.569	−.631	.403	−.357	.788
IOC	69.45450422	10.349817215	107.119	−.161	.388	−1.041	.759
MAHINDRA	806.92837932	270.726271698	73292.714	.400	.388	−.229	.759
TATA	20.09500005	9.062388471	82.127	−.280	.383	−1.247	.750
ValidN (listwise)							

EVENT STUDY- AAR and CAAR –
Hypothesis: There are efficient stock prices for Electric vehicles

EVENT	AAR VALUE	t-statistics AAR	RESULT	P- value	STATUS
−10	0.002018	1.004517	POSITIVE	.196	REJECT
−9	−3.4E-05	−0.01598	NEGAVTIVE	.940	REJECT
−8	0.003328	1.525097	POSITIVE	.085	ACCEPT
−7	0.000788	0.360873	POSITIVE	.579	REJECT
−6	−0.00192	−0.93246	NEGAVTIVE	.362	REJECT
−5	0.000851	0.420502	POSITIVE	.540	REJECT
−4	0.001839	0.853853	POSITIVE	.424	REJECT
−3	0.00458	2.175284	POSITIVE	.023	ACCEPT

(continued)

(*continued*)

EVENT	AAR VALUE	t-statistics AAR	RESULT	P- value	STATUS
−2	0.00606	2.768592	POSITIVE	.007	ACCEPT
−1	0.006386	2.103488	POSITIVE	.031	ACCEPT
0	0.001348	0.455955	POSITIVE	.047	ACCEPT
1	−0.00229	−0.59191	NEGAVTIVE	.526	REJECT
2	−0.00171	−0.69539	NEGAVTIVE	.695	REJECT
3	−0.00132	−0.57646	NEGAVTIVE	.660	REJECT
4	−0.00115	−0.51725	NEGAVTIVE	.740	REJECT
5	−0.00189	−0.89339	NEGAVTIVE	.418	REJECT
6	0.00285	1.092536	POSITIVE	.017	ACCEPT
7	−0.00127	−0.57385	NEGAVTIVE	.016	ACCEPT
8	0.001626	0.783838	POSITIVE	.586	REJECT
9	−0.00166	−0.91977	NEGAVTIVE	.395	REJECT
10	5.78E-05	0.025738	POSITIVE	.971	REJECT

If the t-statistic is more than 1.96 in absolute value, then it may be considered statistically significant at the 5% confidence level. The AAR illustrates the link between the degrees of change in wages and those of price change by comparing the two. In the event that the market operates in a semi-strong form of efficiency, it is anticipated that the AAR will equal zero. The results of this analysis indicate that the AAR is very near to zero and will continue to be very close to zero up to the announcement date. The magnitude of the AAR is around 0.016 on the sixth day of the post-announcement period. AAR value and CAAR value, together with their respective T-statistics, are shown in the table (calculated in excel) - When expressed as an AAR value, the outcome is positive for pre-event values of −10, −8, −7, −5, −4, −3, −2, and 1, and it is also positive on earning announcement day 0. In the aftermath of the incident, beneficial results were seen on days 6, 8, and 10. The negative results for the pre-event are -9 and -6, while the negative results for the post event are on days 1, 2, 3, 4, 5, 7, and 9. The hypothesis is accepted on days −8, −3, −2, −1,0, and 6/7, whereas it is denied on all other days. The fact that there was a big AAR on the day the news was made demonstrates that the AAR is caused by interest in the event. During the pre-announcement time, the AAR is found to be positive, whereas during the post-announcement period, it is found to be negative.

EVENT	CAAR	T- statistics CAAR	RESULT	P-value	STATUS
−10	0.002018	0.084897	POSITIVE	.051	ACCEPT
−9	0.001984	0.055205	POSITIVE	.052	ACCEPT
−8	0.005312	0.118773	POSITIVE	.559	REJECT
−7	0.006099	0.118079	POSITIVE	.577	REJECT
−6	0.004183	0.076944	POSITIVE	.562	REJECT

(*continued*)

(*continued*)

EVENT	CAAR	T- statistics CAAR	RESULT	P-value	STATUS
−5	0.005034	0.085828	POSITIVE	.589	REJECT
−4	0.006873	0.101938	POSITIVE	.650	REJECT
−3	0.011453	0.162556	POSITIVE	.812	REJECT
−2	0.017513	0.225403	POSITIVE	.936	REJECT
−1	0.023899	0.210389	POSITIVE	.045	ACCEPT
0	0.025247	0.217668	POSITIVE	.050	ACCEPT
1	0.02296	0.144978	POSITIVE	.308	REJECT
2	0.021254	0.203151	POSITIVE	.123	ACCEPT
3	0.019933	0.196417	POSITIVE	.023	ACCEPT
4	0.018781	0.183944	POSITIVE	.130	REJECT
5	0.016886	0.168211	POSITIVE	.219	REJECT
6	0.019736	0.155083	POSITIVE	.022	ACCEPT
7	0.018466	0.166263	POSITIVE	.275	REJECT
8	0.020091	0.187849	POSITIVE	.285	REJECT
9	0.018428	0.192587	POSITIVE	.322	REJECT
10	0.018486	0.151793	POSITIVE	.339	REJECT

A t-statistic larger than 1.96 is statistically significant with 5% confidence. Pre- and post-event CAAR results are good. CAAR is expected to be zero before the announcement day and then move to a positive (or negative) level based on good or bad news shortly after the event and stay there in an efficient market. Day −10, −9, 2, 3, 6, and all subsequent days refute hypothesis. From two days before the event, the CAAR was near to zero and exhibited no profit adjustment. The market is approximately semi-strong form efficient on event date with CAAR close to zero. After announcement, CAAR coefficient began falling and showed positive trend. Due to frequent trade watched and modified during the event window, the upward trend may be uncontaminated yet momentum maintained.

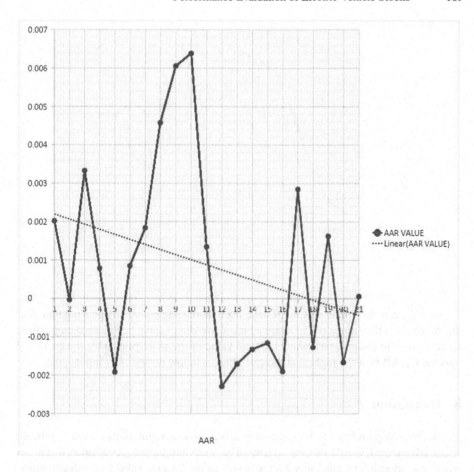

As seen in the graph, it is clearly visible that the AAR values have been increasing from the day of declaration, not at a constant rate, but increasing, proving the idea that the dividend declaration has an impact on the share prices. But they seem to drop on the 12th day as the hustle of the dividend slows down and then becomes null.

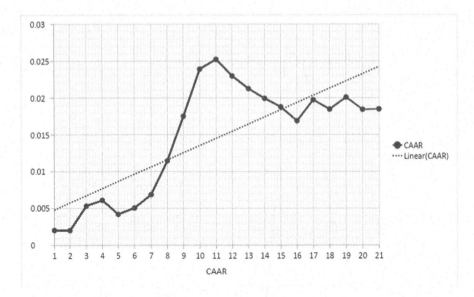

As it is seen, the values of CAAR have been increasing constantly proving that after the declaration the values of the share or the share prices have been increasing adding value to the company. CAAR show the total value of the share price after the event and thus the CAAR is at the highest at the end of the window period showing its peak.

8 Discussion

As the technology related to EVs is continually evolving, regulations have a significant role in advancing EV technologies in terms of business and societal acceptance. In nations where the adoption of electric vehicles is still in its infancy, subsidies, infrastructure, and supporting power, for balancing and supply capabilities, are deemed as essential issues to be resolved first. Fiscal incentives, such as subsidies and tax reductions, and complimentary treatments, such as road parking for free, refunding or subsidizing tolls, and priority lanes, are some illustrations of regulatory incentives that will accelerate the public's acceptance of electric vehicles.

During this time, equal attention should be paid to the construction of infrastructure to help the expanding population of electric vehicles, in addition to the placement of charging stations and provisions in building and zoning rules to facilitate installation of chargers.

Nonetheless, government support for EV use is only transitory during the first stages of adoption. These incentives are developed to ease transition from a bear to a bull market. As the community experiences the advantages of EVs and the overall cost of these vehicles can be reduced, mass adoption of EVs is anticipated, with regulatory support gradually waning. To promote a progressive move towards electric vehicles (EVs) and the accompanying V2G technology, regulators, EV companies, and the community must work together.

The following are the key findings of the Event study:

1. The event of earnings announcement declaration has a positive impact on most of the EV companies for over 3 years resulting in the increased returns, average abnormal returns and cumulative average abnormal returns.
2. . The day right after the earnings announcement declaration almost of 48% of companies have noticed an increase in the share prices or returns. This proves that the earnings announcement declaration has an impact that is positive on the stock prices of the Electric Vehicle
3. If the company is going under or realizing negative returns, the event of earnings announcement declaration helps the company to reduce the losses of the company as the prices declines but not at the same rate. Meaning that the loss reduces once the earnings announcements been declared. This is because the news of earnings announcement helps the people restore their faith in the stock of the company which are even falling down.
4. It is also seen that once the earnings announcement is declared, the prices of the shares increase for a period of 3 to 4 days and then again go down. And also, the effects of the earnings announcement declaration stay for about a period of 7 to 8 days plunging up the share prices.
5. There are a few companies whose stocks show abnormal changes in the returns or irregular changes in returns. This might be due to the improper delivery of the message that the earnings announcement are going to be declared.
6. It is also seen in a few scenarios that the prior period of the earnings announcement declaration the prices seem to rise. The meaning of which can be that the news of the earnings announcement declaration might have been received by the shareholders and thus influencing a lot of people around to buy the stocks, and after the earnings announcement is declared the prices further go up adding up to the values of the shares. This also results in increasing cumulative average abnormal returns.
7. There are also situations where the share prices seem to abruptly decline right after the earnings announcement declaration, reason being unknown.

9 Conclusion

The growth of the EV market transcends metropolitan boundaries and circumstances. The majority of cars are built for usage inside and outside of urban areas. Due to the fact that most people cannot afford separate automobiles for urban and interurban transport, electrified corridors are required to link cities. This implies that the majority of political players in urban regions must be involved in the construction of a charging station network. A city in isolation may act as a stimulant for the growth of electric vehicles (EVs), but it cannot accomplish a full development of EVs without its neighbors. A hospitable urban environment for EV adoption will aid in development since cities can generate a critical mass of the essential players who will later replicate this experience in other cities. The research duration for this work is limited to three years only. • An all-encompassing influence is considered as opposed to an industry-specific one. • Only the NIFTY50 firms are included. • The data collection is based on secondary information. • Event research was the approach utilized; the drawbacks are as follows. ONE: Calculated returns fluctuate daily, resulting in volatility. Two: The computed beta fluctuates over time. They do not accurately represent the danger involved. In a few instances, the assumptions utilized in the process of event investigation are not real. There is an issue with cross-sectional data.

10 Recommendation

With more developing nations devising domestically suitable mitigation strategies to decrease criteria pollutant emissions, replacing the oldest part of the vehicle fleet with new, lower-emitting cars might drive EV adoption and increasing the stocks of it. However, policymakers should recognise that although EVs are an obvious contender, their inclusion as a solution relies on grid cleanliness. Since the automobile fleet accounts for 50% of Bogota's particulate matter inventory, the central government has been implementing policies to centralise mobility (Rodríguez et al. 2016). EVs could only help underdeveloped nations meet their climate and air quality targets. EVs may also increase energy security, economic growth, and grid dependability for some. Thus, these characteristics are not complete, but they may help policymakers in poor nations that want to introduce EVs to their fleets. Thus, each developing nation might benefit from a complete requirements assessment to see how EV integration could assist them.

11 Limitations of the Research

Since the result analysis is based on the secondary data, as it may not answer the researcher's specific research questions, the time period is restricted to five years, the study may not be representative of time period and also of the wider population. The data is collected from Official statistics – the way things are measured may change over time, making historical comparisons difficult, hence may result in lack of relevance and accuracy.

Future Research: Although there is a large literature related to the EV stocks, the research could be carried out in other areas considering primary data analysis public view/ perspective aim on investing on the EV Stocks, challenges, trends and demographic analysis, government policies and schemes..etc.

References

Aguilar Lopez, F., Billy, R.G., Müller, D.B.: A product–component framework for modeling stock dynamics and its application for electric vehicles and lithium-ion batteries. J. Ind. Ecol. **26**(5), 1605–1615 (2022)

Alhazmi, Y.A., Mostafa, H.A., Salama, M.M.: Optimal allocation for electric vehicle charging stations using Trip Success Ratio. Int. J. Electr. Power Energy Syst. **91**, 101–116 (2017)

Aziz, M., Oda, T., Mitani, T., Watanabe, Y., Kashiwagi, T.: Utilization of electric vehicles and their used batteries for peak-load shifting. Energies **8**, 3720–3738 (2015)

Benysek, G., Jarnut, M.: Electric vehicle charging infrastructure in Poland. Renew. Sustain. Energy Rev. **16**, 320–328 (2012)

Birdsall, N., Meyer, C.J.: The median is the message: a good enough measure of material wellbeing and shared development progress Glob. Policy **6**, 343–57 (2015)

Cervigni, R., Rogers, J.A., Dvorak, I.: Assessing Low-Carbon Development in Nigeria: An Analysis of Four Sectors. In: Cervigni, R., Dvorak, I., Rogers, J.A. (eds.) The World Bank, Washington, DC (2013)

Bossche, P.V.D.: Electric Vehicle Charging Infrastructure, pp. 517–543. Amsterdam, Netherlands, Elsevier BV (2010)

Bräunl, T., Harries, D., McHenry, M., Wager, G.: Determining the optimal electric vehicle DC-charging infrastructure for Western Australia. Transp. Res. Part D: Transp. Environ. **84**, 102250 (2020)

Cai, H., Jia, X., Chiu, A.S., Hu, X., Xu, M.: Siting public electric vehicle charging stations in Beijing using big-data informed travel patterns of the taxi fleet. Transp. Res. Part D Transp. Environ. **33**, 39–46 (2014)

Clemente, M., Fanti, M.P., Ukovich, W.: Smart management of electric vehicles charging operations: The vehicle-to-charging station assignment problem. IFAC Proc. **47**, 918–923 (2014)

Coignard, J., Saxena, S., Greenblatt, J., Wang, D.: Clean vehicles as an enabler for a clean electricity grid Environ. Res. Lett. **13**, 054031 (2018)

Collett, K.A., Hirmer, S.A., Dalkmann, H., Crozier, C., Mulugetta, Y., McCulloch, M.D.: Can electric vehicles be good for sub-Saharan Africa? Energy Strategy Rev. **38**, 100722 (2021)

Dawood, F., Anda, M., Shafiullah, G.M.: Hydrogen production for energy: an overview. Int. J. Hydrogen Energy **45**, 3847–3869 (2020)

Delmonte, E., Kinnear, N., Jenkins, B., Skippon, S.: What do consumers think of smart charging? Perceptions among actual and potential plug-in electric vehicle adopters in the United Kingdom. Energy Res. Soc. Sci. **60**, 101318 (2020)

Domínguez-Navarro, J., et al.: Smart charging of electric vehicles considering photovoltaic power production and electricity consumption: a review. eTransportation **4**, 100056 (2020)

Gavranović, H., Barut, A., Ertek, G., Yüzbaşıoğlu, O.B., Pekpostalcı, O.T.: Önder Optimizing the Electric Charge Station Network of EşArj. Procedia Comput. Sci. **31**, 15–21 (2014)

Global EV Outlook2020—Analysis—IEA. https://www.iea.org/reports/global-ev-outlook-2020. Accessed on 6 Dec 2021

Goel, S., Sharma, R., Rathore, A.K.: A review on barrier and challenges of electric vehicle in India and vehicle to grid optimisation. Transport. Eng. **4**, 100057 (2021)

González, L., Siavichay, E., Espinoza, J.: Impact of EV fast charging stations on the power distribution network of a Latin American intermediate city. Renew. Sustain. Energy Rev. **107**, 309–318 (2019)

Greene, D.L., Kontou, E., Borlaug, B., Brooker, A., Muratori, M.: Public charging infrastructure for plug-in electric vehicles: what is it worth? Transp. Res. Part D Transp. Environ. **78**, 102182 (2020)

Guo, S., Zhao, H.: Optimal site selection of electric vehicle charging station by using fuzzy TOPSIS based on sustainability perspective. Appl. Energy **158**, 390–402 (2015)

Heilmann, C., Friedl, G.: Factors influencing the economic success of grid-to-vehicle and vehicle-to-grid applications—a review and meta-analysis. Renew. Sustain. Energy Rev. **145**, 111115 (2021)

J. Design of an electric vehicle fast-charging station with integration of renewable energy and storage systems. Int. J. Electr. Power Energy Syst. **105**, 46–58 (2019)

Kempton, W., Tomić, J.: Vehicle-to-grid power implementation: from stabilizing the grid to supporting large-scale renewable energy. J. Power. Sources **144**, 280–294 (2005)

Knezovic, K.; Martinenas, S.; Andersen, P

Kumar, R.R., Alok, K.: Adoption of electric vehicle: a literature review and prospects for sustainability. J. Clean. Prod. **253**, 119911 (2020)

Lutsey, N., Nicholas, M.: Update on electric vehicle costs in the United States through 2030. Int. Counc. Clean Transp **12** (2019)

Mariana, C.D., Patria, H.: Are electric vehicle stocks in ASEAN countries investible during the Covid-19 pandemic?. In: IOP Conference Series: Earth and Environmental Science, vol. 997, no. 1, p. 012002. IOP Publishing (2019)

Raveendran, V., Nair, M.G.: Power factor corrected level-1 DC public green-charging infrastructure to promote e-mobility in India. IET Power Electron. **13**, 221–232 (2020)

Sanchez-Sutil, F., Hernández, J., Tobajas, C.: Overview of electrical protection requirements for integration of a smart DC node with bidirectional electric vehicle charging stations into existing AC and DC railway grids. Electr. Power Syst. Res. **122**, 104–118 (2015)

Sathaye, N., Kelley, S.: An approach for the optimal planning of electric vehicle infrastructure for highway corridors. Transp. Res. Part E: Logist. Transp. Rev. **59**, 15–33 (2013)

Singh, N., Mishra, T., Banerjee, R.: Projection of private vehicle stock in India up to 2050. Transport. Res. Procedia **48**, 3380–3389 (2020)

Sortomme, E., El-Sharkawi, M.A.: Optimal scheduling of vehicle-to-grid energy and ancillary services. IEEE Trans. Smart Grid **3**, 351–359 (2012)

Tan, K.M., Ramachandaramurthy, V.K., Yong, J.Y.: Integration of electric vehicles in smart grid: a review on vehicle to grid technologies and optimization techniques. Renew. Sustain. Energy Rev. **53**, 720–732 (2016)

Wolbertus, R., Jansen, S., Kroesen, M.: Stakeholders' perspectives on future electric vehicle charging infrastructure developments. Future **123**, 102610 (2020)

Website

A Behind the Scenes Take on Lithium-Ion Battery Prices BloombergNEF. https://about.bnef.com/blog/behind-scenes-take-lithium-ion-battery-prices/. Accessed on 6 Dec 2021

US EPA. Climate Change Indicators: Greenhouse Gases. https://www.epa.gov/climate-indicators/greenhouse-gases. Accessed 5 Sept 2020

Statista. Worldwide Number of Electric Cars. https://www.statista.com/study/11578/electric-vehicles-statista-dossier/ .Accessed 7 Oct 2020

Ritchie, H., Roser, M.: Emissions by Sector-Our World in Data. https://ourworldindata.org/emissions-by-sector. Accessed 5 Sept 2020

NASA.Causes.Facts–ClimateChange:VitalSignsofthePlanet.   https://climate.nasa.gov/causes/. Accessed 5 Sept 2020

Power to the People: Nissan and ENEL Launch First Smart Grid Trials. https://europe.nissannews.com/en-GB/releases/release-140287-power-to-the- people-nissan-and-enel-launch-first-smart-grid-trials. Accessed 6 Dec 2021

Data & Statistics-IEA. https://www.iea.org/data-and-statistics?country=WORLD&fuel=CO2 emissions&indicator=CO2 emissions by sector. Accessed 5 Sept 2020

BureauofEnergyEfficiency.E-Mobility. https://beeindia.gov.in/content/e-mobility. Accessed 7 Oct 2020

Mordor Intelligence, "ASEAN Electric Vehicle Market | 2021 - 26 | Industry Share, Size, Growth - Mordor Intelligence," MordorIntelligence.com (2021). https://www.mordorintelligence.com/industry-reports/asean-electric-vehicle-market. Accessed 05 Sept 2021

A Review of Job Postings in India Concerning Artificial Intelligence and Machine Learning Skills

Hemraj Shobharam Lamkuche[1]([📧])([ID]), Jolly Masih[2], Abhijit Bhagwat[3], Shakti Morya[4], Vandana Onker[5], and Krishna Kumar Singh[6]

[1] School of Computing Science and Engineering, VIT Bhopal University, Kothrikalan, Sehore 466114, Madhya Pradesh, India
hemraj.lamkuche@gmail.com
[2] School of Management, BML Munjal University, Gurugram, Haryana, India
[3] Symbiosis Centre for Management and Human Resource Development, Pune, India
[4] Sai Developers, Indore, India
[5] Symbiosis International (Deemed University), Pune, India
[6] Symbiosis Centre for Information Technology, Pune, India

Abstract. In order to effectively communicate, keep records, make decisions, and evaluate data, businesses require access to information. Recently, jobs in data science domain have skyrocketed in popularity thanks to abundant data and cheap processing power. Degree programmes in Information Technology strive to keep up with the industry's rising demand. The authors looked at a large number of job listings from different sites to determine what skills and experiences are necessary for positions involving artificial intelligence and machine learning. The author also analyses the necessary abilities for each vocation and provides an evaluation. Furthermore, they compared the locations of ML and AI head-to-head. Data engineering, exploratory data analysis, programming, statistics, the internet of things, applied mathematics, neural network architectures, language, multimedia processing, and big data were all found to be more highly valued by employers in roles requiring ML and AI. Instead, communication skills and a generalist mindset are valued more highly in AI positions. Having these clearly defined abilities could also aid in the job search and in adapting existing course material to match the growing needs of the market.

Keywords: Text analysis · skills requirements · critical analysis · machine learning · artificial intelligence

Datasets: Naukri.com · Glassdoor.com · Shine.com · Monster.com

1 Introduction

82% of the Indian workforce is optimistic about their future prospects in the labor market, and jobs in data science domain are seen as some of the most promising in the coming year, according to a new study of job-seekers conducted by professional

© The Author(s), under exclusive license to Springer Nature Switzerland AG 2024
A. M. A. Musleh Al-Sartawi et al. (Eds.): ICGER 2023, CCIS 1999, pp. 195–209, 2024.
https://doi.org/10.1007/978-3-031-50518-8_15

networking platforms [1]. Due to the rapid development of new technologies and the explosion of big data, employment in these fields has increased by 74% annually over the past four years. A Gartner study backs these findings, claiming that AI/ML will cause widespread disruption in all markets. That there is a lot of interest in AI and ML jobs is a common theme in both polls. Despite the growth in demand, many industries, including IT, marketing, finance, healthcare, and supply chain, are suffering from a lack of qualified workers. Since this is the case, the need for people with expertise in AI and ML is widespread and can be found in a wide variety of sectors. Domain-level expertise is provided in a variety of sectors, including healthcare and digital marketing, by the business-related competencies. Additionally, we note that graduates in statistics are more in demand for ML jobs. This demonstrates the increased technical skill required for ML roles, particularly in data-driven banking, finance, and SCM applications. The purpose of this research is, in part, to use the revised taxonomy of abilities to distinguish between the two [2, 3].

Private sector hiring for AI/ML positions can be difficult if candidates lack formal training in the area. For the purpose of preparing workers for the contemporary economy, new training modules are especially required. Universities are often the first places where people acquire new abilities and start using new technologies. In light of this information, more and more analytics packages are including AI/ML expertise development options for their users. Due to the dynamic nature of technological standards, universities are required to regularly revise existing curricula to ensure that graduates are equipped to meet the needs of the workforce [4, 5].

The need for more precise definitions of various occupations associated with AI and ML is also growing. This research aims to solve this problem by analyzing the various categories of related abilities. To that end, we look into how skill sets for AI and ML jobs compare and contrast with one another. We were able to establish the frequency of particular skills associated with each skill group by retrieving keywords from web job postings using a content analysis technique. This allowed us to rank the importance of various skills required for AI/ML jobs and determine which categories those skills fell under. The results can also be used to shape analytics curriculum around the most in-demand skills. Courses in artificial intelligence and machine learning can be updated to include the most up-to-date resources for developing and using those tools [6, 7].

The jobs analyzed here are those associated with artificial intelligence and machine learning. There is a connection between the two regions mentioned above. These terms are currently used interchangeably in the literature and their precise meanings are unclear. The AI is a branch of CS, which aims to develop intelligent systems that imitate human behavior using predetermined rules and algorithms [8, 9]. Without the application of ML and Deep-Learning (DL) [10] techniques, there is no AI application. In ML domain, which is frequently used interchangeably with artificial intelligence, is a subfield of AI that practices automatic erudition without human input to improve data understanding. In most cases, machine learning models are used on massive datasets to find patterns, categories them, and make predictions based on those classifications and predictions. Most of the time, this is achieved by minimizing some kind of loss or error function. On the basis of whether or not the labels for the desired outputs are known beforehand, ML can also be categorized as either supervised or unsupervised ML. In contrast to less precise ML models, which can be run on inexpensive hardware like a computer's graphics processing unit, DL models require more expensive hardware for computation. In order to perform its many useful tasks, DL relies on neural networks for its algorithmic components. In addition, we stress that AI doesn't constitute the same thing as data/business analytics. The descriptive statistics based on existing data are typically the starting point for data analytics projects. Consequently, this torrent is also known as descriptive analytics. On occasion, we might even be able to utilise past events as a guide for what lies ahead. These forecasts require human interaction to comprehend data, recognize trends, and generate and evaluate hypotheses. This branch is referred to as prescriptive analytics. AI/ML systems, on the other hand, are self-sufficient and often require minimum oversight. There has been a rising need for specialists in artificial intelligence (AI) and machine learning (ML), therefore businesses would do well to evaluate their own AI and ML education requirements. The following are the questions that will hopefully be answered by this research: Firstly, what skills are needed by those who work in the domain of data sciences? then can we compare and contrast the two roles and explain how they are similar and different.

In this research, we combed through Indian job postings to identify the specific skillsets most in demand in the artificial intelligence and machine learning industries. By adopting this stance, we offer a new perspective on the standards set by businesses. With the ranked list of skills in hand, educators can refocus current informatics programmes on the area's most in demand by the workforce. Nonetheless, we leave the specifics of curriculum design to future study and do not offer any recommendations in this regard. For this study, we will focus solely on "demand side" employer-posted job advertisements in India. The gaps on the "supply side" could be investigated in future studies by looking at relevant university programmes; this might entail analyzing course descriptions and syllabi, or conducting a survey of the administrators and professors who are in charge of creating these courses. The implications of localization and the alterations in requirements across a number of countries could be the subject of further study.

Our core objectives for this study involves following:

1. To start, we highlight their similarities and contrasts while comparing and contrasting the primary technologies required for AI and ML employment. This makes sense because our competency framework classifies the abilities that companies in the two industries value at a high level.
2. Second, our viewpoint can be useful to human resources professionals when crafting job ads. It may also lead to the creation of sector-specific training programmes.
3. Third, our results can be incorporated into existing curriculum at educational institutions. The findings could be used to develop brand-new instructional materials or improve existing ones. Those who are interested in a similar career should highlight their familiarity with these sought-after competencies when applying for jobs.

By identifying the most in-demand skills for two of the most common occupational domains, this research adds to the body of knowledge on curriculum design in informatics programmes. The findings of this study can be used by companies looking to hire skilled AI/ML professionals, as well as by universities looking to better cater their curricula to current industry needs. By highlighting necessary skills, the information may also be utilized to standardize and clarify job descriptions.

This paper will be organized as follows: To begin, we take a look at how AI and ML have changed various fields of study. The literature on how businesses feel about employees' special requirements for the workplace is the next topic we cover. The educational perspective is also studied because it can shed light on the connection between job demands and degree programmes. Next, we'll take a look at the classification scheme, research approach, and data set, and then we'll talk about the findings, with an emphasis on how much each skill is worth in different jobs. In addition, we look into the shared and unique perspectives of AI and ML. This study concludes with a discussion, findings and recommendations for future research.

2   Background Work

The development of technology, which has resulted in higher industry production, has been greatly aided by AI and ML. These authors thoroughly cover the expected magnitude of AI use cases, the impact on employment, and the level of global merger and acquisition activity. Their results suggested that AI could facilitate administrative, marketing, and financial processes. They also learned that reorganizing the existing business process is necessary for the proper deployment of AI technology. The Intelligent EdTech System is just one of the potential use cases and uses of AI in education [11, 12]. They emphasized that the use of artificial intelligence extensively in the classroom might be detrimental. Through a review of the literature, the acceptance of AI technology in the classroom was investigated. It was proposed that incorporating AI into the learning environment might make it easier to complete different tasks and achieve process-oriented goals [13]. Similar to this, four different application streams were found: novel training method, improved evaluation tool, and improved communication channel [14, 15]. Both positive and negative effects of the adoption of AI in education were found in a survey-based study of students' views. Individual performance and adoption of AI were found to be influenced by factors such as age and gender.

As per the author, Industry 4.0 has arisen from the technological advancements in artificial intelligence (AI). To integrate AI into the certification program of the Association to Advance Collegiate Schools of Business (AACSB), expert systems were suggested [16]. This should result in a dependable and efficient process, cutting down on time, costs, and mistakes. [17, 18].

Text mining has been utilized to study the effect of Industry 4.0 on employment-roles and competencies. By analyzing work descriptions from Whirlpool, a multinational company, roles and skills were categorized using a glossary of tools and procedures. The authors developed tools for evaluating staff readiness for Industry 4.0, and used text mining to analyze job descriptions for Industry 4.0 positions in order to create a work profile emphasizing the most important competencies. These job descriptions initially focused on intelligent manufacturing design and management and the Internet of Things. The second group included enterprise software application domains, supply chain domains, and customer support domains. [19, 20].

Using a combination of content analysis and text mining, the authors delved into job advertisements to uncover the essential competencies needed for various roles such as business analyst, business intelligence analyst, data analyst, and data scientist. Their findings indicated that these positions require individuals with exceptional skills in planning, communication, decision-making, and data management. Moreover, the authors conducted recent research on the competencies necessary for professions like business development and sales, software engineering and development, and data science and engineering, showcasing their technological and managerial expertise to excel in these roles [21–24].

This research expands the existing knowledge base by classifying AI and ML jobs within the analytics industry. Due to the insufficient attention given to AI and ML careers, a comprehensive analysis of the necessary skills is imperative. Furthermore, the study compares the locations of AI and ML and examines how they differ and intersect. As a result, this research aims to provide insight into a substantial professional class in the Industry 4.0. By adopting a skill classification approach, the study enriches the available knowledge by introducing a restructured skill categories for these two professions [24–27].

3   Methodology: Classification Substructure

A classification substructure was developed, consisting of a collection of skill categories and corresponding skill sets, to link each job role with the appropriate competencies. The comprehensive list of competencies for various business and data analytics careers was utilized, and additional skill categories and capabilities were included to more accurately reflect the current AI/ML job market. To validate our categorization system, 100 job postings from each category were thoroughly reviewed, and three impartial evaluators were enlisted to classify skills into the appropriate skill categories. The skills and related skill categories, along with sample keywords, are presented in Table 1, enabling the identification of the skills necessary for each position. By aggregating this information across similar job roles (AI or ML), the study identified the most important skills required for each job type. The complete procedure is comprised of multiple processes, including data gathering, data parsing, data pre-processing, and data statistics.

3.1   Data Collection

Python, Maltego, and the R package were used as the main data gathering tools for web scraping. We searched for titles such as data science on Naukri.com, Glassdoor.com, Shine.com, and Monster.com using its open-source API, which takes search phrase, location, and time period as input inputs. Between March 2022 and December 2022, we focused on employment possibilities in the India area. Jobs URL and other details similar its title, summary, and position are all included in the API's output. An overview of the work description is provided in this field. We used Python and R scripts to extract the job URLs and record them in a local database in CSV and JSON format because we would like to see the full work description.

Table 1. Proposed Cataloguing Substructure for various Skills

Skill_Category	Core-Skills	Sub-Skills
Communication Skills	Composing	content, crafting copy, proofreading, blog posts, generating creative content, and brainstorming story concepts
	Verbal	Soft communication, Professionalism in communication
	Presentation	Delivering a presentation and preparing a report
	General	Accountable, determined, driven, and concentrated
	Impetus	Enthusiastic, aspiring, eager, and open to dynamic learning
Candidate Attributes	Time Supervision	Efficient time management, completing tasks in a timely manner, prioritizing tasks, tasks driven by deadline
	Brashness	Solution-oriented, proactive, self-motivated, self-directed
	Liberation	Self-sufficient, able to work
	Malleability	Flexible, adaptable, able to multitask
	Poise	Confident in decision-making, decisive in actions
	Miscellaneous	Humorous, cheerful, high-energy, dependable, proactive
Occupational	Initiative System	SaaS, CRM, SCM, SAP, ERP, Oracle, IaaS and others
	Imagining Tools	Tableau, Lumira, Crystal Reports
	Software design	Scala, Python, C#, VB.NET, JavaScript, ASP.NET, jQuery, R, D
	Exhibiting Tools	Linear programming, integer programming, dynamic programming, backtracking
	Web Grating	Web scraping, crawling, web crawling
	Core Networking Tools	Client-server, distributed computing, network security, ubiquitous computing
	Statistical-tools	SPSS, SAS, Excel, Wolfarm Mathematica, MATLAB, pandas, statistical programming
	Functional Mathematics	SciPy, Spotfire, scikits.learn, Splunk, R

(continued)

Table 1. (*continued*)

Skill_Category	Core-Skills	Sub-Skills
	Information Mining	Text mining, web mining, stream mining, knowledge discovery, anomaly detection, associations, outlier, classification
	DBMS	SQL, MongoDB, Oracle, SQL Server, DB2, R-DBMS, MS-Access
	Large Data	Semi-Structured data, V's, Hadoop, Hive, Pig, Spark, MapReduce, Presto, Mahoot, NoSQL, shark, Oozie, ZooKeeper, Flume
	Cloud-Computing	SaaS, IaaS, PaaS, Kinesis, Elastic BS, Core-Services, VMs, green computing
	Report Construction	Report Writing, Core-Analysis, Constructive-Modeling, design, problem-solving, Strategic-thinking
	Analytical-Tools	Weka, Orange-DM, TensorFlow, SPSS, Cloud Analytics
Problem Solving	Intellectual Skills	Analytical thinking, Problem-solving, Conflict management, Troubleshooting, Critical reasoning
	Originality	Storytelling, Brainstorming, Idea generation, Innovation, Imagination
	Progression Design	Process improvement, Continuous process improvement, Operations optimization, Streamlining
Administrative Analytics	Governing	Issue resolution, Social media scheduling, Product launch management, Project management
	Analytics	Finding summarization, Trend analysis, Information synthesis, Conclusion drawing, Solution proposal, Google Analytics, Live-analytics, Business-Analytics
Research	Investigation skills	Data gathering, Data collection, Data reporting, Trend monitoring
Financial Management	Financial advice	financial advice, accountancy and keeping records

3.2 Data Parsing

The standardized web pages of the supplied datasets make use of their data advantageous. As a result, a particular HTML tag is always where the relevant job description material is located. The requirements of the employer for a particular position are thoroughly covered in this portion of the job description. As a result, you can find knowledge here that is skill-based. Our Python parser accurately extracted the appropriate tag for the employment description field, and as a result, we were able to save all job descriptions that matched an AI or ML category for each position [28, 29].

3.3 Data Pre-processing

Each section of the work description is made up of a number of sentences broken up into distinct keywords. To provide perspective, these terms combine unigrams, bigrams, and trigrams. Two consecutive syllables in a sentence are represented by a bigram, whereas a unigram indicates a single word. For this, each phrase is divided into separate words. The analysis is then done without terms like a, an, the, and, in, for, etc. For the final individual words, unigrams are found. Bigrams and trigrams are created based on how close or far apart adjacent unigrams are from one another. Our analysis heavily relied on bigrams, trigrams, and unigrams as they allowed us to easily identify the relevant keywords for each skill. By making a connection between these keywords and a job posting, we were able to determine which specific talents were necessary for the position.

3.4 Data Statistics

We compiled statistics on the required skills for job openings in AI/ML. We compared the n-grams from the previous stage to the keywords listed in Table 1 for each skill, allowing us to determine the necessary qualifications for each job posting. By matching these qualifications, we were able to connect specific job postings to talent categories and related skills. This process was applied to all job postings in the AI/ML job classification, and we counted the number of jobs linked to each skill for a specific job title. To determine the relative frequency of each talent, we divided the total number of job listings for each skill by the total number of job postings for each category. The resulting converted relative frequency was expressed as a percentage in Table 4. These statistics will be utilized in the subsequent part of our analysis to classify abilities based on their relative importance across various job categories.

4   Results and Findings

We looked for employment descriptions that mentioned "artificial intelligence" and "machine learning" on Naukri.com, Glassdoor.com, Shine.com, and Monster.com, and we found 980 and 1,350 entry-level openings, respectively, from March to December 2022. It is a sufficient sample size for text analysis study. Table 2 below shows the geographic breakdown of the core-five states for each place. Majority of these professions are situated in Bangalore, Pune, Delhi, Hyderabad, and Mumbai. Demand for skilled AI/ML employees in the IT sector has dramatically increased, particularly in the cities of Bangalore, Pune, Delhi, Hyderabad, and Mumbai.

Table 2. City distribution of data science jobs

#	City (AI jobs %)	City (ML jobs %)
1	Bangalore (31.30%)	Bangalore (33.25%)
2	Pune (23.75%)	Pune (20.60%)
3	Mumbai (17.50%)	Mumbai (15.75%)
4	Delhi (12.75%)	Delhi (14.80%)
5	Hyderabad (14.70%)	Hyderabad (15.60%)

We employed regular expressions to facilitate pattern matching in strings and retrieve crucial qualifications listed in job postings. By utilizing words from each job description, we were able to associate them with various academic disciplines such as computer science, data science, artificial intelligence, machine learning, and information technology. Our findings are presented in Table 3 below.

Table 3. Major Skills required for data science jobs

#	Core Skills (AI)	%	Core Skills (ML)	%
1	Machine Learning	65.00%	Machine Learning	79.00%
2	Deep Learning	34.50%	Deep Learning	32.65%
3	Data Engineering	54.70%	Data Engineering	52.50%
4	Computer Science	58.75%	Computer Science	56.95%
5	Artificial Intelligence	51.50%	Statistics	26.50%
6	Mathematics	38.95%	Mathematics	41.55%
7	Data Science	28.50%	Data Analytics	28.25%
8	Software Engineering	17.25%	Software Engineering	18.95%

Following this, we will present a comprehensive analysis of the necessary skills required for different job classifications within the realm of Artificial Intelligence (AI) and Machine Learning (ML). Table 4 outlines the top five skill sets necessary for each employment category, listed in descending order based on the number of job listings that mention at least one related talent. Additionally, we present the top five abilities in each skill category. Our evaluation of these skills is based on the proportion of job postings for a particular job category that specifically mention each skill in relation to the total number of job listings.

In order to determine whether there is a significant statistical difference between two occupations, a hypothesis test was conducted. The percentage count of a specific talent in relation to data science professionals can be examined using a combined two-sample t-test. We examined the percentage of every skill's relevance to AI versus ML employment based on this supposition. The assumption that there was no mean difference between the two observation groups was tested. Due to a low p-value that we noticed, we came to the opinion that there is a 5% significant difference between the job categories for AI and ML.

Table 4. Results for data sciences job positions

Category	Skills	% of keywords (AI Jobs)	% of keywords (ML Jobs)
Occupation	Decision Making	86.50	87.85
	Data Mining	71.25	98.50
	Text Mining	69.55	96.75
	Programming	45.75	75.50
	Statistics	37.50	65.50
	Big Data	32.55	58.95
	Cloud Computing	39.95	42.65
Employee	Attitude	75.50	98.05
	Time Management	65.25	52.75
	Motivation	45.55	42.75
	Independence	35.80	35.50
	Attention	22.25	18.50
Communication	General	73.35	61.95
	Verbal	59.95	41.65
	Written	30.35	34.55
	Presentation	19.95	18.95
	Active	21.25	16.50
	Clarity	23.35	24.25
Inter-Personal	Team	47.25	46.50
	Personal	13.35	11.45
	Networking	13.75	07.25
Problem Solving	Active Listening	22.55	23.65
	Analysis	32.50	31.75
	Critical Thinking	36.75	43.35
	Research	22.75	45.50
	Creativity	29.95	33.75
	Team Building	28.75	26.65
	Dependability	14.50	17.45

It is important to note that the percentage columns do not sum up to 100% as a single job posting may require multiple majors such as a Bachelor's in both data science and engineering or a Master's in either data science or engineering. While traditional degrees in engineering, mathematics, and computer science are still a requirement for AI/ML positions, there is a growing demand for specialized areas such as data science, artificial intelligence, and machine learning. In addition, expertise in domain-specific areas is also required for many of these roles, indicating a need for business degrees. This is particularly evident in the case of ML jobs, which are highly specialized and require domain expertise, and holds true for AI positions as well.

The viewpoints of AI and ML are compared and contrasted, with a detailed examination of the necessary skills in Tables 4. In both AI and ML positions, work abilities are critical requirements, including strong decision-making skills and the ability to analyze data from various sources. The ability to connect different pieces of information and draw conclusions is essential in today's data-driven digital economy. ML jobs require expertise in data mining techniques, including traditional methods such as regression, classification, outlier detection, and forecasting, as well as more specialized techniques such as web mining, text mining, and stream mining. Big data and statistical knowledge are also crucial for ML jobs, as shown in Fig.1. Probability and hypothesis testing remain important, but the field is dominated by specialized software such as NumPy, Scikit-learn, Pandas, as well as more conventional software like R, SPSS, SAS, and others. The volume, variety, and speed of big data have necessitated the development of new modeling paradigms, leading to interest in programs like Hadoop, MapReduce, and JSON. When it comes to ML jobs, possessing hard skills such as programming, data modeling, statistics, data mining, and structured data are more critical. Additionally, more positions in machine learning (ML) demand expertise in neural networks, such as convolutional, deep, and recurrent neural networks (modeling skills). Python and R are popular computer languages, in addition to C, C, and Java. You also need to be familiar with design tools like Pytorch, Tensorflow, etc. for these positions. So it appears that ML positions are more technically oriented. Contrarily, AI positions place more value on having a wide perspective on system design through familiarity with enterprise systems like Oracle, SAP, etc. Therefore, AI jobs are more generic in that success depends on a knowledge of the entire process.

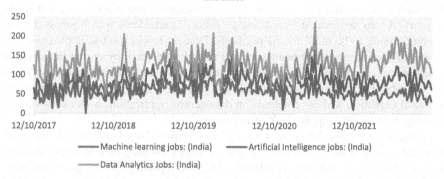

Fig. 1. Artificial Intelligence, Machine Learning and Data Analytics jobs trends in India

Employee qualities are becoming more and more significant at work. A positive mindset is the most crucial qualification for both of these positions. Successful professionals must have a "can-do" or "go-getter" mentality as well as a strong drive to learn. More than anyone else, millennials need to learn how to organize their time. Employees who can establish priorities and complete them on time are valued in today's fast-paced, ever-changing business environment. Independent thought and drive are the following two crucial soft skills. Self-starters, independent employees are able to complete their tasks with little to no assistance from others. They assume full ownership of the projects they work on and are also very proactive. They must be extremely driven, enthusiastic, and impassioned about this. You need these qualities to succeed in any work. The next trait that is considered a sign of a meticulous and organized individual who can add value to any organization is attention to detail. These findings should be discussed in the classroom in terms of employee characteristics, and universities should modify their curricula appropriately [30, 31].

Organizational skills, like how to communicate with others, are also important for both types of jobs. They are done as a team and require working together. High-value skills include being a leader and making connections with clients and other important people inside and outside the company. In the problem-solving skill category, the focus is on people who can think logically and use good judgement to troubleshoot and solve business problems. These skills are very helpful when planning a business strategy for a company's long-term growth. The employee's aptitude for innovation and creativity demonstrates their entrepreneurial character. Outside-the-box thinking also encourages workers to advance their knowledge and develops new revenue streams for the company. The final subtype of problem-solving, "process design," exemplifies the value of combined processes at the corporate level. The goal of process design and improvement is to lower expenses, effort, and errors.

5 Discussion

Our research revealed that 32 abilities, which we divided into seven categories, are needed for data science professions (see Table 1 above). We examine the situation from the perspective of the employer by examining the employment advertisements. The IT sector has recently shown the most interest in AI and ML technology. Due to this, the major cities of Bangalore, Pune, Delhi, Hyderabad, and Mumbai are where the majority of jobs are located. According to Table 3, individuals with business degrees are more likely to be hired for AI positions. Domain-level expertise is provided in a variety of sectors, including healthcare and digital marketing, by the business-related competencies. Additionally, we note that graduates in statistics are more in demand for ML jobs. The aforementioned reveals that ML roles necessitate a greater degree of technical expertise, with an emphasis on data-centric applications in domains such as banking, finance, and supply chain management.

Job ads for AI and ML shared a lot of similarities. They both have similar business and Technical skills. It is well recognized that by knowing their business, strategic decision-makers can enhance AI solutions. Skills in reporting, visualization, and technical data analysis are very highly regarded. The main concepts in both supervised and unsupervised learning are categorization and prediction. Forecasting and outlier detection abilities are valued by employers as well. In the past, data mining has been used to extract patterns from structured data. The quantity, diversity, and speed of data are driving an increase in the popularity of web and stream mining. Specialized software and unstructured database administration are required. These decisions are being made through text-mining, web-mining, and social-network analysis. The findings demonstrate the growing demand for skills like Hadoop, MapReduce, Hive, and others. Skills in SQL and Oracle are also less in demand. About 60% of ML employment required strong software development and statistical expertise, compared to only 20% of AI jobs. ML professions also require skills in data analysis, regression, classification, and outlier detection. Such language is rarely found in job postings for AI. More "open-source" tool abilities are currently sought for in job postings. There are fewer requirements for entry into certain fields. The employment market does not give large providers' analytic products like SAS, SPSS, SAP, etc. a priority.

6 Conclusion

To begin with, institutions can consider expanding their existing management information systems, data science, data analytics, and business intelligence programs to incorporate AI/ML. Therefore, our study can assist in creating undergraduate and graduate degree programs that align with current market demands. Furthermore, hiring managers can benefit from the study findings by identifying AI/ML professionals with the requisite expertise. By employing the suggested skills, the hiring team can create well-crafted and consistent job descriptions. So, the hiring team could get the most out of their employees. In our most recent survey, we ranked the abilities required for AI/ML positions. With what we have learned, two things can be done. So, creating degree programmed that include undergraduate and graduate study could benefit from our research. Second, hiring managers might utilize the outcomes to identify AI/ML specialists with the necessary qualifications. The hiring team might create job descriptions that are well-written and consistent by employing the specified abilities. The hiring team may then make the most of its staff members. Overall, the objectives of this research is to provide job seekers a broader aspect in choosing appropriate skillsets for machine learning and artificial intelligence jobs in India.

References

1. Akanksha Jaiswal, C., Arun, J., Varma, A.: Rebooting employees: upskilling for artificial intelligence in multinational corporations. Int. J. Hum. Resource Manage. 33(6), 1179–1208 (2022). https://doi.org/10.1080/09585192.2021.1891114
2. LinkedIn. LinkedIn Job Search: Find US Jobs, Internships, Jobs Near Me. LinkedIn (2022)
3. Bonsay, J., Cruz, A.P., Firozi, H.C., Peter, J.C.: Artificial Intelligence and labor productivity paradox: the economic impact of AI in China, India, Japan, and Singapore. J. Econ. Finan. Account. Stud. 3(2), 120–139 (2021). https://doi.org/10.32996/jefas.2021.3.2.13
4. Gonzalez, M., Capman, J., Oswald, F., Theys, E., Tomczak, David: "Where's the I-O?" artificial intelligence and machine learning in talent management systems. Person. Assess. Dec. 5(3) (2019). https://doi.org/10.25035/pad.2019.03.005

5. Gonzalez, M. F., et al.: Allying with AI? Reactions toward human-based, AI/ML-based, and augmented hiring processes. Comput. Human Behav. **130** (2022). https://doi.org/10.1016/j. chb.2022.107179

6. Dsouza, P.K.: Absolute answerability in the Era of Artificial Intelligence and Machine Learning: a talent management perspective. In: Proceeding of 2019 International Conference on Digitization: Landscaping Artificial Intelligence, ICD 2019 (2019). https://doi.org/10.1109/ICD47981.2019.9105675

7. Murthy, H., Lamkuche, H.: Harnessing the power of ML and NLP for decision making in education sector from social media data. Cardiometry **22**, 415–420 (2022). https://doi.org/10. 18137/cardiometry.2022.22.415420

8. Osman, N.A., Alshammar, M.M., Mohamed, T.I.: AI techniques for combating electronic crimes and enhancing cybersecurity: Kuwaits security services as a mode. Inf. Sci. Lett. **12**(7), 3339–3345 (2023)

9. Alazzam, B.A., Alkhatib, M., Shaalan, K.: Artificial Intelligence Chatbots: a survey of classical versus deep machine learning techniques. Inf. Sci. Lett. **12**(4), 1217–1233 (2023)

10. Samah, W.F., Suresh, S., Moaiad, A.K.: Customer churn prediction in telecommunication industry using deep learning. Inform. Sci. Let. **11**(1), 185–198 (2022). https://doi.org/10. 18576/isl/110120

11. Vinichenko, M.V., Rybakova, M.V., Chulanova, O.L., Kuznetsova, I.V., Makushkin, S.A., Lobacheva, A.S.: Using natural and artificial intelligence in the talent management system.Int. J. Recent Technol. Eng. **8**(3) (2019). 10.35940/ijrte.C6152.098319

12. Hrehová, D., Teplická, K.: Harmonization of skills and needs of the global labour market. In: International Multidisciplinary Scientific GeoConference Surveying Geology and Mining Ecology Management, SGEM, vol. 3 (2016). https://doi.org/10.5593/SGEM2016/B53/S22.108

13. Shehata, S.O.: Saudi journalists employing artificial intelligence algorithms to detect fake news. J. Statist. Appl. Probabil. **12**(3), 877–896 (2023). https://doi.org/10.18576/jsap/120302

14. Bayan, A.A., Manar, A., Khaled, S.: Artificial intelligence chatbots: a survey of classical versus deep machine learning techniques. Inform. Sci. Let. **12**(4), 1217–1233 (2023). https://doi.org/10.18576/isl/120437

15. Saad, D., Abdulsalam, D., Venus, B.: New aspects on using artificial intelligence to shape the future of entrepreneurs. Inform. Sci. Let.**1**, 39–50 (2020). https://doi.org/10.18576/isl/090106

16. Chedrawi, C., Howayeck, P.: Artificial intelligence a disruptive innovation in higher education accreditation programs: expert systems and AACSB. In: Lecture Notes in Information Systems and Organisation, vol. 30 (2019). https://doi.org/10.1007/978-3-030-10737-6_8

17. Halwani, M.A., Amirkiaee, S.Y., Evangelopoulos, N., Prybutok, V.: Job qualifications study for data science and big data professions. Inf. Technol. People **35**(2) (2022). https://doi.org/10.1108/ITP-04-2020-0201

18. Garcia-Arroyo, J., Osca, A.: Big data contributions to human resource management: a systematic review. Int. J. Hum. Resour. Manag. **32**(20) (2021). https://doi.org/10.1080/09585192. 2019.1674357

19. Zhou, R., et al.: Online scheduling algorithm for heterogeneous distributed machine learning jobs. IEEE Trans. Cloud Comput. (2022). https://doi.org/10.1109/TCC.2022.3143153

20. Shashi Anand, S., Francis Saviour Devaraj, A., Kanniga Devi, R., Bala Subramanian, C., Raja Subramanian, R., Nagaraj, P.: Effective design and implementation oF B.Tech (CSE) curriculum with industry tie-ups. J. Eng. Educ. Transform. **34**(no. Special Issue) (2021). https://doi.org/10.16920/jeet/2021/v34i0/157140

21. De Mauro, A., Greco, M., Grimaldi, M., Ritala, P.: Human resources for Big Data professions: a systematic classification of job roles and required skill sets. Inf. Process. Manag. **54**(5), 807–817 (2018). https://doi.org/10.1016/j.ipm.2017.05.004

22. Gaikwad, D., Lamkuche, H.: Segmentation of services provided by E-commerce platforms using PAM clustering. J. Phys. Conf. Series **1964**(4), 042036 (2021). https://doi.org/10.1088/1742-6596/1964/4/042036
23. Jhanwar, H., Goel, N., Lamkuche, P.: Telecommunication stocks prediction using long short-term memory model neural network. In: Computing, Communication and Learning. CoCoLe 2022. Communications in Computer and Information Science, vol. 1729, pp. 300–310 (2023). https://doi.org/10.1007/978-3-031-21750-0_26
24. Agarwal, H.S., Gurele, D., Lamkuche, S.: SAILFISH-I: a lightweight block cipher for cloud-enabled fog devices. In: The 6th International Conference on Information and Communications Technology. (CICT), IEEE Access, pp. 1–6 (2022)
25. Akyazi, T., Goti, A., Oyarbide, A., Alberdi, E., Bayon, F.: A guide for the food industry to meet the future skills requirements emerging with industry 4.0. Foods **9**(4), 492 (2020). https://doi.org/10.3390/foods9040492
26. Pramod, D., Lamkuche, H.S.: CSL: FPGA Implementation of Lightweight Block Cipher for Power-constrained devices. Int. J. Inform. Comput. Secur. **12**(2/3), 1 (2020). https://doi.org/10.1504/IJICS.2020.10023595
27. Lamkuche, K., Singh, H.S., Shirkhedkar, K.: A lightweight block cipher for cloud-based healthcare systems. In: Computing, Communication and Learning. CoCoLe 2022. Communications in Computer and Information Science, vol. 1729, pp. 3–14 (2023). https://doi.org/10.1007/978-3-031-21750-0_1
28. Pouliakas, K.: Determinants of automation risk in the EU labour market: a skills-needs approach. SSRN Electron. J. (2021). https://doi.org/10.2139/ssrn.3253487
29. Grant, M.: Aligning skills development with labour market need (2016)
30. Holmes, M.: Jobs, trades, skills, and the profession. Computer (Long. Beach. Calif). **35**(9) (2002). https://doi.org/10.1109/MC.2002.1033038
31. Meyer, M.A.: Healthcare data scientist qualifications, skills, and job focus: a content analysis of job postings. J. Am. Med. Informatics Assoc. **26**(5) (2019). https://doi.org/10.1093/jamia/ocy181

Semiparametric Score-Driven Exponentially Weighted Moving Average Model

Randa A. Abdelkarim[1]([⊠]) [iD] and Ibrahim A. Onour[2]

[1] Faculty of Mathematical Science and Informatics, University of Khartoum, Khartoum,
Sudan
randamakki@gmail.com
[2] School of Management Studies, University of Khartoum, Khartoum, Sudan

Abstract. Measuring volatility is used in many important financial and economic models. This paper proposes a new semiparametric score driven exponentially weighted moving average (SP SD-EWMA) model to improve the efficiency of the parametric score driven exponentially weighted moving average (SD-EWMA) model when residuals are fat-tailed and possibly skewed. We experimented the efficiency performance of our model on S&P 500 sample daily data. Implementing in-sample and out-sample analysis it is shown that the proposed model outperforms the other competing models (SD-EWMA and Standard EWMA models) as it renders higher log-likelihood function and smaller Akaike Information Criterion as well as smaller prediction errors. To validate further the outperformance of the proposed model we checked the forecast error of one, two and three days-ahead of value-at-risk (VaR) measure over the out-of-sample period to ensure that proposed model renders the smallest rate of violations and close to the expected level. This paper highly recommends using the proposed model to reduce the statistical efficiency loss of the classical/score-driven parametric volatility models and that could help investors and asset managers better adjusting their trading strategies.

Keywords: Time-varying Volatility · Generalized Autoregressive Score Model · Kernel Density Estimator

1 Introduction

Higher-order moments as well as time-varying volatility is becoming more substantial in an empirical econometric analysis. Empirical studies such as (Harvey & Siddique 1999) and (Harvey & Siddique 2000) have proven that the financial series distribution is skewed and has fat-tailed, and if the normality assumption assumed for the error terms of the financial series that leads to unreliable results in models of risk management, option pricing, hedging activities, portfolio selection, asset allocation.

During the past years, several researchers, (Sun & Yan 2003), (Prakash et al. 2003), and (Ganouati et al. 2006) indicated that models incorporating higher moments have more predictive power in portfolio allocation. (Burns 2003), (Wilhelmsson 2009), (Angelidis et al. 2007) and (Onour 2010), among others, explain the usefulness of incorporating skewness and kurtosis in risk management to compute superior VaR estimates. (Heston & Nandi 2000) and (Christoffersen et al. 2003) provide an improvement in pricing by proposing option pricing models with conditional skewness. (Apergis & Gabrielsen 2012) propose a hedge ratio model that improves the performance of the hedges by incorporating skewness and kurtosis.

Generalized Autoregressive Score (GAS) model based on the score driving mechanism encompasses other standard observation driven models such as GARCH, autoregressive conditional duration (ACD) models and most of the Poisson count models. Furthermore, this approach is applied to different densities, nonlinear models and nonstandard multivariate models. The primary benefits of this method, the probability evaluation is straightforward and simple such as the GARCH model. Furthermore, the GAS model can be extended to asymmetric, long memory, regime-switching, including exogenous variables, and other complicated dynamics (Creal et al. 2011) and (Creal et al. 2013).

Parametric distribution models might not have the flexibility to effectively capture some distributional characteristics such as skewness and kurtosis, which motivates the use of one of the nonparametric methods, see (Hardle et al. 2004). (Engle & GonzalezRivera 1991) illustrated that, estimating the error density by assuming a nonparametric density, one can estimate the model parameters more efficiently nevertheless some efficiency loss remains. (Sun & Stengos 2006) and (Drost & Klaassen 1997) developed a semiparametric model using kernel density estimator for the error term and achieved the semiparametric efficiency bounds for parameter estimation.

Until now, all GAS models are fully parametric, the only one research to extend them to the semiparametric method was done by (Blasques et al. 2016). They produced a semiparametric model under the GAS framework using the nonparametric kernel density estimator for the residual same as (Drost & Klaassen 1997) and (Sun & Stengos 2006). The semiparametric GAS model of (Blasques et al. 2016) outperforms GARCH type models as well as parametric GAS models.

The main aim of this study is to propose new model that extends the parametric score-driven EWMA model to become semiparametric score-driven model using the non-parametric kernel density estimator as in (Blasques et al. 2016; Singh et al., 2016), to improve the statistical efficiency of the parametric score-driven EWMA model when the residuals are fat-tailed and skewed. The main difference between our proposed model and that of Blasques et al.'s (2016), is that the proposed model is score-driven EWMA not score-driven GARCH model.

The rest of the paper is organized as follows: Sect. 2 presents our proposed model and presents the algorithm to estimate its unknown parameters. The formula of the nonparametric Kernel density estimator and its consistency theorem was established. Section 3, is an application section, testing the performance of our proposed model using in-sample and out-of-sample empirical study, and the proposed model performance when forecasting Value at Risk is evaluated. Section 4 gives conclusions about our overall work and makes suggestions for future work.

2 Methodology

2.1 Semiparametric SD-EWMA Model (SP SD-EWMA)

To improve the efficiency of the SD-EWMA model we will estimate the error density q(.) in two steps. First, estimate it using the standard normal distribution. Second step estimate q(.) using the nonparametric kernel density estimation same as (Blasques et al. 2016). Our new semiparametric SD-EWMA model is given by the equation:

$$y_t = \mu + \xi_t = \mu + \sigma_t \epsilon_t, \ \epsilon_t \sim q(\epsilon_t)$$

and the dynamics of the volatility driven by the equation:

$$\tau_{t+1} = \lambda \tau_t + (1 - \lambda)s_t \tag{1}$$

$$s_t = \frac{\partial \ln p(y_t | \tau_t)}{\partial \tau_t} = -\frac{1}{2}(\epsilon_t . \nabla q(\epsilon_t) + 1) \tag{2}$$

where $\tau_t = \ln\sigma_t^2$ is the log variance, which is initialized with a fixed point $f_1 \in R$ (σ_t can written as $e^{\frac{\tau_t}{2}}$), $\lambda(0 < \lambda < 1)$ is a static parameter which is the decay factor, $\nabla q(\epsilon_t)$ is the derivative $\nabla q(\epsilon_t) = \frac{\partial \ln q(\epsilon_t)}{\partial \epsilon_t}$ can written as $\xi_t e^{-\frac{\tau_t}{2}}$.

From Eq. 2 the conditional variance of the score is given by:

$$\mathbb{E}_{t-1}\left[s_t^2\right] = \mathbb{E}_{t-1}\left[\left(-\frac{1}{2}[\epsilon_t \cdot \nabla q(\epsilon_t) + 1]\right)^2\right]$$

$$\mathbb{E}_{t-1}\left[s_t^2\right] = \mathbb{E}_{t-1}\left[\frac{1}{4}(\epsilon_t^2 \cdot (\nabla q(\epsilon_t))^2 + 2\epsilon_t \cdot \nabla q(\epsilon_t) + 1)\right]$$

$\mathbb{E}_{t-1}[\epsilon_t] = 0$, therefore:

$$\mathbb{E}_{t-1}\left[s_t^2\right] = \frac{1}{4}\mathbb{E}_{t-1}\left[\epsilon_t^2 \cdot (\nabla q(\epsilon_t))^2 + 1\right] \tag{3}$$

(Lucas & Zhang 2015) developed Score-Driven EWMA (SD-EWMA) model under the GAS framework based on the parametric Student-t distribution for the error term and drive the dynamics of volatility parameter by the score function. Their volatility equation is different from the Eq. 1 which uses the log variance instead of the variance to obtain a positive variance, see (Nelson 1991) and the conditional variance of the score is shown in Eq. 3 which is independent of τ_t, so we don't need to choose a convenient scaling of the score function. For more detail see (Harvey 2013) and (Creal et al. 2013).

In addition, the Eq. 1 is different from the equation of the standard exponential weighted moving average (S-EWMA) model that is given by:

$$y_t = \mu + \xi_t = \mu + \sigma_t \epsilon_t, \ \epsilon_t \sim q(\epsilon_t)$$

$$\sigma_t^2 = \lambda \sigma_{t-1}^2 + (1 - \lambda)\xi_{t-1}^2$$

where λ is the decay factor ($0 < \lambda < 1$), μ is the conditional mean, ϵ_t is the standardized error term, σ_t^2 is the variance and q(.) is the standardized error density.

The score function s_t of Eq. 1 is used instead of the squared lagged error term ξ_t^2. Therefore, if ϵ_t is asymmetric or fat-tailed it directly translated into Eq. 1 through using the score function s_t in contrast to using the squared lagged error term ξ_t^2.

2.2 Derivation of the Score Function

Here, we will follow (Blasques et al. 2016) work to derive the score function s_t (in Eq. 2).

$$s_t = \frac{\partial \ln p(y_t|\tau_t)}{\partial \tau_t} = \frac{\partial \ln \left[\frac{q(\epsilon_t)}{e^{\frac{\tau_t}{2}}} \right]}{\partial \tau_t}$$

$$= \frac{\partial \left[\ln q(\epsilon_t) - \ln e^{\frac{\tau_t}{2}} \right]}{\partial \tau_t} = \frac{\partial \ln q(\epsilon_t)}{\partial \tau_t} - \frac{\partial \ln e^{\frac{\tau_t}{2}}}{\partial \tau_t}$$

$$= \frac{\partial \ln q(\epsilon_t)}{\partial \epsilon_t} \cdot \frac{\partial \epsilon_t}{\partial \tau_t} - \frac{\partial \ln e^{\frac{\tau_t}{2}}}{\partial \tau_t}$$

Let $\nabla q(\epsilon_t) = \frac{\partial \ln q(\epsilon_t)}{\partial \epsilon_t}$ and $\epsilon_t = e^{-\frac{\tau_t}{2}} \xi_t$, therefore:

$$s_t = \nabla q(\epsilon_t). \frac{\partial (e^{-\frac{\tau_t}{2}} \xi_t)}{\partial \tau_t} - \frac{1}{2} \cdot \frac{e^{\frac{\tau_t}{2}}}{e^{\frac{\tau_t}{2}}}$$

$$s_t = \nabla q(\epsilon_t). - \frac{1}{2} e^{-\frac{\tau_t}{2}} \xi_t - \frac{1}{2}$$

$$= -\frac{1}{2} \epsilon_t . \nabla q(\epsilon_t) - \frac{1}{2}$$

Thus:

$$s_t = -\frac{1}{2} \left[\epsilon_t . \nabla q(\epsilon_t) + 1 \right]$$

2.3 Kernel Density Estimator (KDE)

Volatility models (Yu et al. 2023) with the parametric distribution for the error term might not have the flexibility to effectively capture some distributional characteristics such as skewness and kurtosis. This reason motivates the use of one of the nonparametric methods which are an easy and clear techniques to let the model more flexible to capture skewness and kurtosis, see (Hardle et al. 2004). (Engle & Gonzalez-Rivera 1991) illustrated that, estimating the error density by assuming nonparametric density, one can estimate the model parameters more efficiently. Our proposed model uses the nonparametric kernel density estimator of (Sheather & Marron 1990; Siloko et al. 2023) to product more flexible and efficient score driven EWMA model rather than using the parametric densities such as student t distribution as in (Lucas & Zhang 2015).

Identifying the probability density function of the random variable ϵ_t as $q(\epsilon_t)$ then the kernel estimator of the pdf of random variable ϵ_t is given by:

$$\hat{q}(\epsilon_t) = \frac{1}{nh} \sum_{i=1}^{T} K\left(\frac{\epsilon_t - \epsilon_i}{h} \right) \tag{4}$$

where K(.) is the kernel function, the parameter h is the bandwidth of the kernel density, ϵ_t is a point at which the pdf is to be estimated, ϵ_i is a value from the data and n is the sample size.

We adopt the common kernel function K(.) which is the Gaussian kernel function.

$$K(\epsilon_t) = \frac{1}{\sqrt{2\pi}} e^{-\frac{\epsilon_t^2}{2}}$$

Therefore Eq. 4 become as:

$$\hat{q}(\epsilon_t) = \frac{1}{nh\sqrt{2\pi}} \sum_{i=1}^{T} e^{-\frac{(\epsilon_t-\epsilon_i)^2}{2h^2}} \tag{5}$$

(Parzen 1962) presented the consistency theorem of kernel density estimators, the kernel estimate $\hat{q}(.)$ can approximate actual q(.) to any precision degree if q(.) is a bounded density. When K(.) and q(.) are Gaussian, the value $1.06n - 1/5\sigma$ for h will reduce the Asymptotic Mean Integrated Squared Error (AMISE), where σ is the empirical standard deviation of q(.) since the actual standard deviation is usually unknown (Silverman 1986).

2.4 Algorithm of the Semiparametric SD-EWMA Model

The parameters estimation of our new semiparametric SD-EWMA model performed by the following procedure:

1. Assume q(.) is the standard normal distribution with zero mean and unit variance.
2. Estimate the model parameters (μ, λ) using maximum likelihood estimator.
3. Use the estimated parameters to compute the standardized residuals $\hat{\epsilon}_t = \frac{y_t - \hat{\mu}}{\hat{\sigma}_t}$.
4. Estimate the nonparametric kernel density estimator $\hat{q}(.)$ using the standardized residuals $\hat{\epsilon}_t$.
5. Re-estimate the model parameters (μ, λ) using the semiparametric maximum likelihood estimator (based on the estimated nonparametric density $\hat{q}(.)$).

Step 1 and 2 build the Standard EWMA model using the standard normal distribution for the error term. Then the next steps 3, 4, and 5 produce the semiparametric SD-EWMA using the estimations of the parameters from step 2 and the kernel density estimator (Eq. 5) for the error term to maximize the semiparametric likelihood and re-estimate the model parameters.

2.5 Parameter Estimation

As other common volatility models, the model parameters estimation is conducted by maximizing both parametric and semiparametric likelihood function assuming the error term follows a standard normal density or nonparametric kernel density.

In our proposed model, the log-likelihood function for the observation t and error density q(.) can be written as:

$$l_t(\theta, q) = -\frac{1}{2}\tau_t(\theta) + \log q\left(\xi_t . e^{-\frac{\tau_t(\theta)}{2}}\right)$$

where θ is the static parameters and $ft(\theta)$ is defined recursively through Eq. 1. (Blasques et al. 2014) establish the properties of the maximum likelihood estimator for the score driven model.

Our proposed model first assumes q(.) is a standard normal distribution then from the above equation we obtain the parametric likelihood function. Second assume q(.) is a kernel density estimator (Eq. 5) then again from the above equation we obtain the semiparametric likelihood function for our model.

Note that, using the estimated parameters $\hat{\theta}$ and simulated from the estimated density $\hat{q}(.)$, can forecast the conditional volatility $\hat{\tau}_t$ easily by iterating the volatility through Eq. 1.

3   Empirical Study

This section compares the performance of the new proposed model semiparametric score-driven EWMA (SP SD-EWMA) model with the competing standard EWMA (S-EWMA) and score-driven EWMA (SD-EWMA) models. We use the daily prices of Standard & Poor's 500 (S&P 500) stock market index, which measures the performance of about 500 largest companies in the United States. R program is used to estimate the model parameters via a Newton-Raphson algorithm to maximize both parametric and semiparametric log-likelihood function.

3.1   Data and Descriptive Statistics

We apply the models on the daily prices of Standard & Poor's 500 (S&P 500) equity index over the period from September 1, 2010 to August 13, 2018. We have 2000 observations of the daily close price of S&P 500 that can be freely obtained from the website (https://finance.yahoo.com) which is credible and reliable website with daily international stock price.

The daily return y_t of our stock market index is given by $y_t = \log\left(\frac{p_t}{p_{t-1}}\right)$ where p_t is the daily index closing price. Table 1 presents the descriptive statistics of the daily return of Standard & Poor's 500 (S&P 500) equity index. It is obvious that the distribution of our returns are so far from the normality, the p-value of (Jarque & Bera 1980) test for our returns is equal to zero. The skewness is negative, which indicates a bias towards downside exposure and the kurtosis is very large, therefore the returns distribution is leptokurtic.

3.2   In-sample Analysis

We take the first 1600 observations which is the 80% of the overall data to present the in-sample data that is used to estimate the static parameters for the proposed model semiparametric score driven EWMA model (SP SD-EWMA), parametric score-driven EWMA model (SD-EWMA) and the standard EWMA model (S-EWMA). For the S&P 500 daily return the in-sample data is taken over the period from September 1, 2010 to January 10, 2017.

Table 1. Descriptive statistics of the daily return of the Standard & Poor's 500 (S&P 500) over the period from September 1, 2010 to August 13, 2018 with 2000 observations.

Descriptive statistics	S&P 500
Minimum	−0.06895
Maximum	0.04631
Mean	0.00048
Median	0.00057
Variance	0.00008
Standard deviation	0.00895
Skewness	−0.5735
Kurtosis	8.278521
Jarque-Bera	0.000

According to the Log-Likelihood Function (LLF) and Akaike Information Criterion (AIC) in Table 2, the SP SD-EWMA model outperforms the SD-EWMA model and the S-EWMA for the in-sample period because it renders the higher LLF value and the smaller AIC value. Since the log-likelihood value for the S&P 500 daily return is about 1500, 1561 points higher than the SD-EWMA model and S-EWMA model, respectively. The AIC for the proposed model is smaller by 1.88, 1.95 points than the SD-EWMA model and the S-EWMA model, respectively.

Table 3 shows the standard error, t value and it's probability value for the estimated parameters of our three models: S-EWMA, SD-EWMA, and SP SD-EWMA models. Through the simple t-test, the volatility coefficient $(\hat{\lambda})$ of the three models are all very significant, suggesting the presence of the conditional time-varying variance and the ability of the models to capture its dynamic.

Table 2. Estimated parameters, Log-Likelihood Function (LLF) estimates and Akaike Information Criterion (AIC) of the SP SD-EWMA, SD-EWMA and the S-EWMA models for the in-sample data. AIC $= -2.(LLF/T) + 2.(m/T)$ where m denotes the number of parameters and T is the number of observations.

Est. Parameter	S-EWMA	SD-EWMA	SP SD-EWMA
$\hat{\mu}$	0.00056	0.0008	−0.0387
$\hat{\lambda}$	0.92001	0.8707	0.67725
$\hat{v}$	–	5.13	–
LLF	5349.7188	5411.0514	6910.6228
AIC	−6.684648	−6.760064	−8.635779

Table 3. Standard error, t value and it's probability value for the estimated parameters for the three models: S-EWMA, SD-EWMA and SP SD-EWMA models.

Model	Est. Parameter	Std. Error	t value	Pr (> ltl)
S-EWMA	$\widehat{\mu}$	0.0002	2.74	0.0006 **
	$\widehat{\lambda}$	0.0114	50.51	<2.22 e^{-16} ***
SD-EWMA	$\widehat{\mu}$	0.0017	4.61	3.8797 e^{-06} ***
	$\widehat{\lambda}$	0.01918	45.39	<2.22 e^{-16} ***
	$\widehat{v}$	0.69137	7.42	1.13 e^{-16} ***
SP SD-EWMA	$\widehat{\mu}$	0.15002	−2.57	0.0098 **
	$\widehat{\lambda}$	0.1953	3.46	0.00052 ***

Signif. Codes: 0 '***' 0.001 '**' 0.01 '*' 0.05 '.'

3.3 Out-of-Sample Analysis

The out-of-sample performance is the true test of any estimated model. Therefore, we evaluate the model's forecast adequacy using the Root Mean Squared Error (RMSE) and Mean Absolute Error (MAE) for the last 600 observations from my sample data.

Letting σ_t be the observed values of the square root of the conditional variance, and the predicted values for them is the estimated $\widehat{\sigma}_t$, then the error term e_t is given by ($\sigma_t -\widehat{\sigma}_t$), therefore:

$$RMSE(RootMeanSquaredError) = \sqrt{mean\left(e_t^2\right)}$$

$$MAE = mean\ |e_t|$$

From Table 4 the proposed SP SD-EWMA model outperforms the other competing models (S-EWMA and SD-EWMA models) because it renders the smallest prediction error recording to both RMSE and MAE values. Since the RMSE and MAE values of the proposed model are smaller than the S-EWMA model by 0.0051 and 0.00476, respectively. In addition, they are also smaller than the competing SD-EWMA model by 0.0062 and 0.00446, respectively.

We use the t-test for two independent means to determines whether there is a statistically significant difference between the means of the error term e_t of the competing models S-EWMA and SD-EWMA models with respect to the proposed SP SD-EWMA model. Results show substantially significant difference between the means of the error term e_t, since the p-value is equal to $2.2e^{-16}$.

3.4 Value at Risk (VaR)

This section assesses the VaR forecasts through (1) unconditional coverage (LR$_u$) of (Kupiec 1995) and (2) conditional coverage (LR$_c$) of (Christoffersen 1998) likelihood ratio tests for the S&P 500 index at the confidence level 95%. For the three models,

Table 4. RMSE, MAE, t-value and p-value for the out-of-sample S-EWMA, SD-EWMA and SP SD-EWMA models.

Model	RMSE	MAE	t-value	p-value
S-EWMA	0.0061	0.0050	33.1	$2.2e^{-16}$
SD-EWMA	0.0063	0.0047	24.9	$2.2e^{-16}$
SP SD-EWMA	0.001	0.00024	–	–

we use one, two and three day-ahead VaR forecasts over the out-of-sample period from January 10, 2017 to August 13, 2018.

Table 5 presented the rate of violations (V) and the likelihood ratio tests (LR_u) and (LR_c) at 5% significance level for the three models and for the one, two and three day-ahead VaR forecasts of the S&P 500 index. The LR_u is distributed as chi-square with one degree of freedom, the 5% critical value for $\chi2(1)$ and $\chi2(2)$ are 3.841 and 5.99, respectively.

The findings illustrate that the newly proposed model attains the smallest rates of violations, and they are close to the expected level. For the one-day-ahead VaR forecasts, it decreases by 18 and 14 times from the violations rate of S-EWMA and SD-EWMA models respectively. And for the two-day-ahead VaR forecasts, it decreases by 4 and 7.5 times from the violations rate of S-EWMA and SD-EWMA models respectively. Also, for the three-day-ahead VaR forecasts, it decreases by 2.75 and 5 times from the violations rate of S-EWMA and SD-EWMA models respectively.

Table 5. Rate of violations (V), unconditional coverage (LR_u) and conditional coverage (LR_c) likelihood ratio tests at 5% significance level for the three models and for the one, two and three day-ahead VaR forecasts of the S&P 500 index.

		S-EWMA	SD-EWMA	SP SD-EWMA
One-day-ahead VaR	V	0.36	0.28	0.02
	LRu	366.2	238.3	5.05
	LRc	366.3	242.2	9.78
Two-day-ahead VaR	V	0.16	0.3	0.04
	LRu	35.7	129.5	1.05
	LRc	37.48	133.79	2.53
Three-day-ahead VaR	V	0.11	0.2	0.04
	LRu	8.26	38.43	0.46
	LRc	8.32	39.22	2.47

The null hypothesis of (LR_u) has been rejected at a 5% significance level for the S-EWMA and SD-EWMA models for the one, two and three day-ahead VaR forecasts and is rejected for the SP SD-EWMA model for the one day-ahead VaR forecasts, the only two cases that it hasn't been rejected are the SP SD-EWMA for the two and three day-ahead VaR forecasts. We can notice that, for the one, two and three day-ahead VaR forecasts the proposed model achieves substantial decreasing in the LR_u values in comparison with SD-EWMA and S-EWMA models.

In addition, the (LR_c) null hypothesis is rejected for the S-EWMA and SD-EWMA models for the one, two and three day-ahead VaR forecasts and is rejected for the SP SDEWMA model for the one day-ahead VaR forecasts, the only two cases that it hasn't been rejected are the SP SD-EWMA for the two and three day-ahead VaR forecasts. Again, for the one, two and three day-ahead VaR forecasts the proposed model achieves substantial decreasing in the LR_c values in comparison with SD-EWMA and S-EWMA models.

Summary of the previous results, as expected the proposed model substantially outperforms the S-EWMA and SD-EWMA models for the one, two and three day-ahead VaR forecasts at a 5% significance level over the out-of-sample period.

4 Conclusion and Future Work

One of the early observation-driven approaches widely used to capture time varying volatility is the exponentially weighted moving average (EWMA) model. Several parametric extensions of the EWMA model have been considered based on assuming one of the parametric distributions for the error term.

In this paper, we proposed a new semiparametric score driven EWMA (SP SD-EWMA) model. By assuming the nonparametric kernel density for the residuals and at the same time using the score function to capture the volatility dynamics, to improve the efficiency of the parametric score driven EWMA model. We presented the formula of our proposed model, derivation of the score function of the nonparametric Kernel density estimator, formula of the nonparametric Kernel density estimator and its consistency theorem, and the algorithm to build our model. Finally, we introduced the log-likelihood function that used to estimate the parameters of the proposed model.

According to Log-Likelihood Function (LLF) and Akaike Information Criterion (AIC), the SP SD-EWMA model outperforms the SD-EWMA model and the S-EWMA for the in-sample period because it renders the higher LLF value and the smaller AIC value. We evaluate the model's forecast adequacy using the Root Mean Squared Error (RMSE) and Mean Absolute Error (MAE) through the out of sample data. Since the RMSE and MAE values of the proposed model are smaller than the SD-EWMA and the S-EWMA model. Using the common t-test, results show substantially significant difference between the means of the error term.

Finally, we evaluate the one, two and three day-ahead VaR forecasts through unconditional coverage and conditional coverage likelihood ratio tests for the S&P 500 index at the confidence level 95% over the out-of-sample period. As expected, the proposed model obtains the smallest rates of violations and they are close to the expected level and substantially out-performs the S-EWMA and SD-EWMA models for the one, two and three day-ahead VaR forecasts at a 5% significance level.

The study of volatility has long been a hotly debated topic among experts, especially in these uncertain times. The impact of COVID-19 and the Russia-Ukraine war on capital markets was immediate, appearing first on the world's largest stock prices before spreading to smaller markets. This paper highly recommends using the proposed model rather than the classical/score-driven parametric volatility models, since it is expected to detect and forecast the volatility more effectively and that could assist investors and asset managers better adjusting their trading strategies.

To improve this work, we propose the following: First, future work can be done, by using the back-transformed kernel density estimator of (Wand et al. 1991) for the error term. Second, one can use the nonparametric density of (Tapia & Thompson 1978), also see (Engle & Gonzalez-Rivera 1991). Lastly, the sample size can be extending to include the daily data of S&P 500 for the period of COVID-19 and the Russia-Ukraine war.

References

Angelidis, T., Benos, A., Degiannakis, S.: A robust var model under different time periods and weighting schemes. Rev. Quan. Financ. Acc. **28**(2), 187–201 (2007). https://doi.org/10.1007/s11156-006-0010-y

Apergis, N., Gabrielsen, A.: Optimal hedge ratio estimation during the credit crisis: an application of higher moments. Front. Financ. Econ. **21**(9), 64–84 (2012)

Blasques, F., Ji, J., Lucas, A.: Semiparametric score driven volatility models. Comput. Stat. Data Anal. **100**, 58–69 (2016)

Blasques, F., Koopman, S., Lucas, A.: Maximum likelihood estimation for generalized autoregressive score models, Tinbergen Institute (2014)

Burns, P.J.: The quality of value at risk via univariate garch. SSRN Electron. J. (2003). https://doi.org/10.2139/ssrn.443540

Christoffersen, P.F.: Evaluating interval forecasts. Int. Econ. Rev. 841–862 (1998)

Christoffersen, P., Heston, S., Jacobs, K.: Option valuation with conditional skewness option valuation with conditional skewness (2003)

Creal, D., Koopman, S.J., Lucas, A.: A dynamic multivariate heavy tailed model for time-varying volatilities and correlations. J. Econ. Bus. Stat. **29**(4), 552–563 (2011)

Creal, D., Koopman, S.J., Lucas, A.: Generalized autoregressive score models with applications. J. Appl. Economet. **28**(5), 777–795 (2013)

Drost, F., Klaassen, C.: Efficient estimation in semiparametric garch models. J. Econometrics **81**(1), 193–221 (1997)

Engle, R., Gonzalez-Rivera, G.: Semiparametric arch models. J. Bus. Econom. Statist. **9**, 345–359 (1991)

Ganouati, J., Essid, H., Vigeant, S.: Optimal portfolio allocation under higher moments: Dea-cross efficiency framework. Eur. Financ. Manag. **12**(1), 29–55 (2006)

Hardle, W., Muller, M., Sperlich, S., Werwatz, A.: Nonparametric and Semiparametric Models. Springer Series in Statistics (2004)

Harvey, A.C.: Dynamic Models for Volatility and Heavy Tails. Cambridge University Press (2013)

Harvey, C., Siddique, A.: Autoregressive conditional skewness. Economet. J. **12**(1), 465 (1999)

Harvey, C., Siddique, A.: Conditional skewness in asset pricing tests. J. Financ. **55**(3), 1263–1295 (2000). https://doi.org/10.1093/rfs/13.3.585

Heston, S.L., Nandi, S.: A closed-form garch option valuation model. Rev. Financ. Stud. **13**(3), 585–625 (2000). http://www.eurojournals.com/JMIB.htm

Jarque, C.M, Bera, A.K.: Efficient tests for normality, homoscedasticity and serial independence of regression residuals. Econ. Lett. **6**(3), 255–259 (1980). https://doi.org/10.1016/0165-1765(80)90024-5

Lucas, A., Zhang, X.: Score-driven exponentially weighted moving averages and Value-at-Risk forecasting. Int. J. Forecast. **32**(2), 293–302 (2015)

Nelson, D.: Conditional heteroskedasticity in asset returns: a new approach. Econometrica **59**, 347–370 (1991). http://dx.doi.org/10.2307/2938260

Onour, I.A.: Global food crisis and crude oil price changes: do they share common cyclical features? Int. J. Econ. Policy Emerg. Economies **3**(1), 61–70 (2010). https://www.inderscie nce.com/info/inarticle.php?artid=32795

Parzen, E.: On estimation of a probability density function and mode. Ann. Math. Statist. **33**(3), 1065–1076 (1962). https://doi.org/10.1214/aoms/1177704472

Prakash, A.J., Chang, C.H., Pactwa, T.E.: Selecting a portfolio with skewness: Recent evidence from us, European, and Latin American equity markets. J. Bank. Financ. **27**(7), 1375–1390 (2003). https://doi.org/10.1016/S0378-4266(02)00261-3

Yazdanian, A.R.: On Tikhonov regularization method in calibration of volatility term-structure. Inf. Sci. Lett. **2**(2), 93–100 (2013)

Sheather, S.J., Marron, J.S.: Kernel quantile estimators. J. Am. Stat. Assoc. **85**, 410–416 (1990)

Siloko, U.I., et al.: A new multivariate product kernel functions of the beta polynomial family. J. Stat. Appl. Probab. **12**(3), 1385–1398 (2023). https://doi.org/10.18576/jsap/120340

Silverman, B.W.: Density estimation for statistics and data analysis (1986)

Singh, R.J.A., Khanday, M.: Economic design of X control chart for DEWMA under non-normal population. J. Stat. Appl. Prob. **5**(2), 321–328 (2016). https://doi.org/10.18576/jsap/050213

Sun, Q., Yan, Y.: Skewness persistence with optimal portfolio selection. J. Bank. Financ. **27**(6), 1111–1121 (2003). https://doi.org/10.1016/S0378-4266(02)00247-9

Sun, Y., Stengos, T.: Semiparametric efficient adaptive estimation of asymmetric garch models. J. Econometrics **133**(1), 373–386 (2006)

Tapia, R., Thompson, J.: Nonparametric Probability Density Estimation. Johns Hopkins University Press, Baltimore (1978)

Yu, L., Yaacob, H.M., Buqi, D.: Multiscale Spillover transmission in chinas investment preferences using dynamic stochastic volatility framework. Inf. Sci. Lett. **12**(7), 3283-3298 (2023)

Wand, M.P., Marron, J.S., Ruppert, D.: Transformations in density estimation. with discussion and a rejoinder by the authors. J. Am. Stat. Assoc. **86**(414), 343–361 (1991)

Wilhelmsson, A.: Autoregressive conditional skewness. J. Financ. Quan. Anal. **34**(4), 82–104 (2009)

Impact of Social Media Marketing, Innovation, and Effective Management on SMEs Performance: A Conceptual Study

Zahra Al-Hooti[1], Abrar AL Alawi[2]([✉]), Zunaith Ahmed[1], and Talal Al-Busaidi[1]

[1] College of Economic, Management, and Information System, University of Nizwa, Nizwa, Oman
{5585145,04716066}@uofn.edu.om, zunaith@unizwa.edu.om
[2] Entrepreneurship Center, University of Nizwa, Nizwa, Oman
abraralalawi@unizwa.edu.om

Abstract. Recently, the social media phenomenon has spread widely across the globe, resulting in the creation of new opportunities to influence individuals in a variety of fields. In addition, social media have become forcefully imposing themselves on our reality, as they are an integral part of a lifestyle, especially regarding SMEs. Small and Medium Enterprises (SMEs) performance is an essential and powerful factor determining the business venture position in the competitive environment. Effective management is associated with the SMEs active and competitive performance. This paper aims to develop a framework that shows the social media impact on SMEs performance with a mediating variable that has effective business management. Also, this paper is interested to understand the link between innovation and social media to the performance of SMEs. This study develops a conceptual framework relying on reviewed recent literature. The study revealed that innovation, social media marketing, and effective management predicts SMEs performance. Besides of that, the recommendations and suggestions are provided in this paper to help decision-makers in regulating and taking corrective actions.

Keywords: Effective Management · Innovation · Marketing · Performance · SMEs · Social Media · Oman

1 Introduction

Social media is one of the most fundamental e-marketing platforms that had a significant impact on traditional marketing operations and promotional efforts. Social media has emerged as a major challenge to both traditional and broadcast media as a tool for promotions, and newspapers and television channels have suffered as a result. SMEs are a primary consideration of each economy of countries, having the greatest potential for growth and impact on economic stability (Hitka et al. 2021). A significant portion of society, prompting many small businesses to use these networks for marketing, communication, and integration between the marketer and the consumer, recognizing and communicating with them. Even though social media is rapidly being used for business objectives, the operational consequences are still unknown.

A. M. A. Musleh Al-Sartawi et al. (Eds.): ICGER 2023, CCIS 1999, pp. 222–232, 2024.
https://doi.org/10.1007/978-3-031-50518-8_17

Firms' social media initiatives may improve firm-customer contact and internal and external collaboration by facilitating information flow and knowledge exchange within and across enterprises. (Lam et.al 2016). Recently, social media and online customer relations are reimagining how organizations conduct business (Harazi et al. 2023; Maki 2023). (Berger & Thomas 2016). So, marketers are taking advantage of the growing demand for social media to market their activities, as well as the desire to create positive trends for the products they offer to large segments of the population, paving the way for small businesses to invest in marketing and advertising their goods and services as platforms.

Social media encourages the formation of networks in the complex and dynamic environment in which businesses operate (Martín-Rojas et al. 2021). In addition, marketing is a crucial activity that plays currently played as the most difficult aspect of any SMEs success, survival, growth, and prosperity because it allows them to plan and design items that meet the wants and desires of their target market, as well as distribute them effectively. In this respect, the paper aims to develop a conceptual study that examined variables of social media impact and will rapidly affect SMEs performance. Furthermore, the framework proposed is recognized to have effective business management as a mediating variable. The paper also may contribute an interesting implication for SMEs managers to understand the social media impact and its reflection on innovativeness and performance.

2   Literature Review and Construct Development

2.1   Firms Innovativeness (FI) and Effective Business Management (EBM)

Tuominen, Rajala and Möller (2004) Many aspects of adjustment differ significantly between firms who are high or low performers, as measured by their innovativeness, according to their empirical findings. The type of business logic and the nature of environmental dynamism have a significant impact on the innovativeness relationship through the firms. Given the positive and long-term relationships between adaptability and innovation, managers should identify innovation, business market, and organizational factors concurrently. (Folan et al. 2013) defined business as an organization that creates the services and products that individuals desire to purchase. According to Bart (1996) many management practices identified as promoting innovation were widely used by the companies, according to the findings. It was discovered that these procedures had a significant impact on new sales revenue. Surprisingly, these practices were not well outlined in the firms' mission statements. Nonetheless, the study discovered a strong and positive relationship between the content of mission statements and the extent to which innovativeness practices were used. Accordingly, the empirical study Chen, Huang and Hsiao (2010) tested the influence of organizational commitment and the management of knowledge format and the innovation level in which the firm standpoints both the social capital and networks and discovered that knowledge management is significantly associated with firm innovativeness. Furthermore, a supportive environment and a decentralized, integrated, and less formalized structure mitigate the impact of knowledge management on innovation. The study also investigates the effects of climate and structure of the organization on knowledge management, with the findings indicating that an innovative and supportive environment is associated with better knowledge management.

2.2 Firms Innovativeness (FI) and SMEs Performance (SMEP)

SMEs are sometimes defined numerically or expressly to include businesses with a workforce of 1 to 100 employees, with the highest limit occasionally being 250 employees. It can also be classified according to qualitative standards as having a limited share market, being personally managed by the owner, or even not having a formalized bureaucratic structure (Inyang 2013). Marketing capabilities, specifically branding, and innovation, were found to mediate the relationship positively and significantly between social media use and firm performance. However, some researchers when investigated the impact of firm innovativeness on business performance varies depending on market turbulence and competitive intensity, according to Tajvidi & Karami (2021) findings. Moreover, the performance effect of firm innovativeness is most positive during times of high turbulence in the market and increased competitive intensity. However, when there is lower turbulence in the market and low competitive intensity, it is least positive. Some studies examined marketing capability through the lens of multiple capabilities: branding and innovation (Merrilees et al. 2011). Furthermore, the ability to innovate and brand is critical for competitiveness and delivering outstanding results (Hogan & Coote 2014).

The research paper of Hult, Hurley and Knight (2004) addressed the factors that contribute to some industrial firms being more innovative than others, investigate if innovation affects business performance, and study the relationship between innovativeness and business performance. So, they confirm that the innovativeness' of the firm is affected the firm's performance with a high relationship, and the implications of the causes and consequences of organizational innovativeness are provided. Empirical information suggests that business performance is closely related to innovation. Many papers have been conducted to investigate the relationship between innovation and business performance, either directly or as part of a bigger study. The results of these studies appear to point to a relationship between innovation and business performance. Generally, there is overwhelming proof that innovation is critical to a company's profitability and growth in the long-run. (Geroski et al. 1992; Cosh and Hughes 1996).

Sandvik and Sandvik (2003) the findings of a study on the impact of business strategy on business performance were presented in this paper. New product development is proposed as a moderator of market orientation's impact on the performance of the entrepreneurial venture. Product innovativeness is measured in two ways: through the use of new-to-the-firm and new-to-the-market product lines. It supported the significant influence of market orientation on both measurements of the innovativeness of products or services. Just the use of new-to-market products appears to have a positive impact on business performance. Neely and Hii (1998) and Alpay et al. (2012) paper investigates how various aspects of innovativeness, such as product, industry, process, corporate strategy, and cognitive innovativeness, affect marketing effectiveness and firm performance. Also, this supported the marketing effectiveness's role as a moderator in the relationship between firm performance and product and strategic innovativeness dimensions. Innovation is the commercialization of novel creation of ideas. A firm's innovativeness refers to the application of new ideas through new products, services, or processes (Freixanet et al. 2021; Kwon et al. 2021; Ramdani et al. 2022; Zhang & Zhu 2021). However, a firm's innovative practices including creative and innovative marketing activities affect the SMEs performance. Innovative ideas are the generators for better employee and organizational performance (Freixanet et al. 2021; Rozak et al. 2021; Sikandar Ali Qalati et al. 2022; Tajvidi & Karami 2021; Zhang & Zhu 2021).

Several studies demonstrated that effective business management is induced by the firm's innovativeness in operating the business activities that best match the dynamic evolution in the marketplace (Amoah et al. 2021; Basri 2020; Djakasaputra et al. 2021). On the other hand, multiple scholars pay considerable attention to investigating the different firms' management approaches to business performance. Traditional approaches of managing SMEs sought as one of the significant factors that led to performance regression especially in the case of SMEs. Meanwhile, sophisticated and innovative management system evidence substantial ability in enhancing overall business performance (Oyewobi 2020; Sikander Ali Qalati et al. 2021; Rozak et al. 2021; Tajvidi & Karami 2021; Trawnih et al. 2021).

The sustainability of SMEs under the intensive market competitiveness resulted mainly from the continuous customer preferences and desire for adaptation. One of the major means to meet customers' needs and wants is through the employment of the appropriate channels such as social media applications (Basri 2020; Sikander Ali Qalati et al. 2021; Zhang & Zhu 2021). Firms' innovative practices promote the business image and represent the organization's overall culture. This can be achieved via employee motivation towards the accomplishment of business goals and objectives which is consequently reflected on SMEs overall performance and sustainability (Amoah et al. 2021; Sikander Ali Qalati et al. 2021; Rozak et al. 2021; Trawnih et al. 2021; Zhang & Zhu 2021).

2.3 Firms Innovativeness (FI) and Social Media Marketing (SMM)

The term social media is known as the electronic technologies that emphasize and facilitate user-generated content or interaction e.g., (Kaplan & Haenlein 2010); (Terry 2009);(Bader et al. 2022); (Ismaeil 2023). Social media are "those which facilitate online contact, networking, and collaboration," according to Russo et al. (2008). The theory of dynamic capability state that firm's advantage in the intensive competitive environment lies in the collection of overall firm and their employee skills, their planned and implemented process, and the routine operations and practices that ultimately differentiate the firms from other competitors in the market. As per the dynamic capability theory, the differentiation and uniqueness of firms or any institution are measured through the innovative practices in products or services, research, and development, as well as patterns the firm performs (Drydakis 2022; Freixanet et al. 2021; Rozak et al. 2021; Zhang & Zhu 2021). In this respect, innovation is a major requirement to satisfy the increasingly changing customers' needs and wants. In light of the substantial technological evolution, marketing activities must be supported with developed technological tools such as social media platforms (Djakasaputra et al. 2021; Kwon et al. 2021; Ramdani et al. 2022; Trawnih et al. 2021). Moreover, marketing through social media tools plays an essential role in enhancing the efficiency of firms goals as well as it mitigates the risk associated with business different activities (Djakasaputra et al. 2021; Drydakis 2022; Kwon et al. 2021; Zhang & Zhu 2021). Accordingly, the utilization and application of marketing activities through social media platforms facilitate better opportunities for idea generation and innovation to adapt to the customer's preferences (Amoah et al. 2021; Djakasaputra et al. 2021; Freixanet et al. 2021). From another perspective, the empirical implication of innovative ideas under uncertain circumstances is promoted due to the features the social media enjoy and the digital technologies developed ability in marketing and collecting information required for marketing-related decision purposes (Djakasaputra et al. 2021; Drydakis 2022; Selvarajan et al. 2018; Tajvidi & Karami 2021; Trawnih et al. 2021). Susanto et al. (2023) examined the mediating and moderating effects of marketing skills and social media use. Marketing expertise, according to the empirical results, greatly mediates the link between entrepreneurial orientation and SME success. Social media use also mediates and moderates the link between entrepreneurial orientation and SME performance in part.

2.4   Social Media Marketing (SMM) and SMEs Performance (SMEP)

Qalati (2021) made an empirical investigation paper to measure social media's mediating role adoption and used a close-ended questionnaire. 423 responses were observed and found that small and medium enterprises became important sectors of the world economy. Businesses have been very dynamic and therefore SME owners must interact with stakeholders more actively. Technology can play a very important role in better SME performance. Social Media platforms help specifically to connect organizations or SMEs and their owners with clients and suppliers. Erlangga (2021) this study conducted in Indonesia and collected 210 samples, to determine the social media's influence on the purchasing decision of SMEs by using random sampling techniques. The study concluded that social media marketing positively impacts the purchasing decision of SME products.

A study was made in Dhaka to explore empirically the role of social media as an effective factor in the marketing of SMEs performance (Sumona Salam 2019). According to this study, social media is a good technique for establishing simple and easy contact with various stakeholders in order to sustain SMEs. Relationship Marketing is an important marketing strategy that small and medium enterprises should adopt as clients don't only purchase according to the price and quality but also based on the relationship between client and organization.

A theoretical model used a survey of 310 firms in India to analyze the impact of social media on business performance, sales, connecting with buyers, identifying consumer needs, and employee creativity. The study concluded that the use of social media by SMEs and customers provided opportunities for both parties. SME could improve products and customers were able to reach the right product they were looking for. This mechanism improved the way how to use CRM and improved the customer service of SMEs (Sheshadri Chatterjee 2020). Also, during Covid-19 a study was made and collected a number of 254 from micro, SMEs and found that the use of social media marketing like Facebook, Instagram, and WhatsApp by enterprises has a positive impact on their performance. This had a positive impact on sales, customer relationships, productivity, and creativity. If the leadership of the social media market improves, SMEs' performance will improve as well (Syaifullah & Syaifudin 2021). A study conducted by Martín-Rojas et al. (2023) examine Spanish SMEs and investigate the role of social media use as a predictor of entrepreneurship and SME success. They further investigated the mediating role of organizational resilience. The findings indicate that social media usage improves SMEs' entrepreneurial abilities. The results further highlight the significance of organizational resilience for strategy, which has an excellent mediating influence on performance of SMEs.

2.5 Social Media Marketing (SMM) and Effective Business Management (EBM)

Facebook usage improves SMEs' non-financial performance by lowering marketing and customer service costs, improving customer relations, and increasing information accessibility, according to the study of Ainin et. al (2015). Compatibility and effectiveness of cost have also been identified as variables that influence SMEs' use of Facebook. Meanwhile, research done by Musa et al. (2016) studies the impact of social media marketing techniques on the performance of firms in Malaysian small and medium businesses. Three types of correlations are investigated reputation and image of the brand, engagement of customers, and customer attitudes through the brand. The independent variables were found to be significant, and there was a significant relationship with online SMEs. Research findings are expected to aid and stimulate SMEs in their use of social media for marketing. However, Berger, & Thomas (2016) discovered that, in practice, the timing of social media marketing implementation in a small business might not be the most critical aspect, and the emphasis is instead on the time and cost apparent. In addition, social media marketing is a subset of digital marketing that utilizes the use of the influence of well-known social media platforms to advance corporate goals. To build brands and attract the appropriate audience, people in this sector create profiles and share images and videos (Wadhwa et al. 2023).

2.6 Effective Business Management (EBM) and SMEs Performance (SMEP)

Ates, Garengo, Cocca and Bititci (2013), Identified and analyzed the gap between theory and practice in performance management in SMEs, taking into account specific SME characteristics and needs, to determine how SMEs can improve their managerial practice for effective performance management. The study discovered that SMEs use four different management methods, but there are some gaps between what they do and what the literature recommends. SMEs appear to be more concerned with internal and short-term planning than with long-term planning, which improves performance management approach through the use of balanced and appropriate strategic and operational methods and relevant measures. Also, strategic control should be improved through a structured method to assessing performance in SMEs. Current approaches, on the other hand, have proven insufficient for the special needs of the SME sector. The procedure's goal is to come up with metrics that will help push operational performance toward strategic goals. The case study's findings show that the approach has the potential to increase corporate strategy control and the encouragement of ongoing development in SMEs (Hudson, Lean, & Smart 2001).

Adopting and measuring business performance management can help a company's long-term attractiveness and sustainability. The researcher tried to is to present a framework for implementing BPM in Slovak SMEs based on transportation industry studies. The study's findings show that SMEs are generally confused with BPM and how it is applied. While the BPM system may help small businesses improve their competitiveness, SMEs are divided on the benefits of BPM (Gruenbichler et al. 2021).

2.7 Conceptual Framework

Firms' innovativeness and their employment of social media marketing mean to influence the business management effectiveness and as a result SMEs performance. To reach on better understanding of the factors affecting SMEs performance and based on the above literature review which paves the way for the authors to draw the following conceptual framework. This framework is drawn relying on Kohli and Jaworski (1990) who declared that marketing is essentially a statement of a company's viewpoint, ideals, or policies. The business philosophy and how it is positioned into practice, as seen in an organization's actions and behaviors, can be contrasted (Fig. 1).

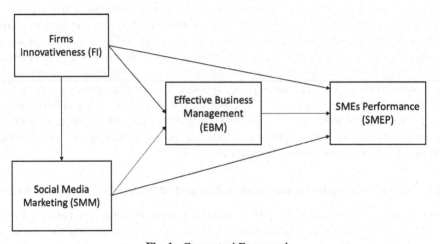

Fig. 1. Conceptual Framework

*FI: Firms Innovativeness; EBM: Effective Business Management; SMEP: SMEs Performance; SMM: Social Media Marketing.

* The conceptual framework was developed after reviewing the literature that mainly related to the topic.

3 Conclusion and Recommendation

Small and Medium Enterprises (SMEs) performance is a critical determinant of their existence and survival in today's increasing competitiveness. However, SMEs performance is driven by multiple internal and external factors that strengthen or weaken the business's ability to survive and sustain its competitive advantage. Customers are the fundamental drivers of SMEs developed strategies, plans, and actions. Therefore, business continuous innovative practices towards increasing customer demand and changing preferences demonstrate pivotal influencers of SMEs social media platform selection as a marketing channel. Moreover, firm's innovativeness and social media marketing leads remarkably to effective management of business ventures. This suggests an ultimate impact on SMEs performance and the perceived image from the perspective of current and future firm customers. SMEs performance is the key to their sustainable success, thus, emphasizing the role of how effective management of business reinforce their success in term of efficiency, productivity, and sales. Therefore, SMEs adopting innovative marketing and management approaches adhere to advanced progress in the marketplace. Accordingly, to promote the SMEs performance and sustain the venture capabilities as well as its sustainability, business owners must place induced efforts to train and improve business employee skills, abilities, and knowledge in order to be capable to adapt and promote various sophisticated innovative media for the SMEs marketing activities purposes.

4 Practical Implication

This conceptual paper will add to the existing knowledge pertaining SMEs and social media's impact on innovative and effective business management. That will provide the marketers and managers with an improved knowledge of the social media effective tools in improving SMEs performance and management strategies. In addition, practitioners and SMEs owners suggested using the insights concluded based on the attained results to design their innovative and sophisticated management practices and marketing media that in turn will enhance their capability to leverage their performance within the intensive market conditions.

5 Limitations and Suggestions for Future Research

Like any other research this paper has limitations, this one has flaws that could be utilized in future studies. Other elements may play a role in obtaining better results. Further research into the social media effect on the performance of Oman SME is suggested in this paper. Furthermore, SME can be found in many industries. The impact of social media applications varies depending on the industry. Future researchers could evaluate the social media impact of marketing on SMEs by focusing on a specific industry.

References

Ainin, S., Parveen, F., Moghavvemi, S., Jaafar, N.I., Shuib, N.L.M.: Factors influencing the use of social media by SMEs and its performance outcomes. Ind. Manag. Data Syst. 115(3), 570–588 (2015)

Ali Qalati, S., Li, W., Ahmed, N., Ali Mirani, M., Khan, A.: Examining the factors affecting SME performance: the mediating role of social media adoption. Sustainability 13(1), 75 (2020)

Alpay, G., Bodur, M., Yilmaz, C., Büyükbalci, P.: How does innovativeness yield superior firm performance? Role Mark. Effectiveness Innov. 14(1), 107–128 (2012)

Ates, A., Garengo, P., Cocca, P., Bititci, U.: The development of SME managerial practice for effective performance management. J. Small Bus. Enterp. Dev. (2013)

Bader, M.D., Aityassine, L.F., Khalayleh, A.M., Al- Quran, A.Z.: The impact of e-marketing on marketing performance as perceived by customers in Jordan. Inf. Sci. Lett. **11**(6), 1897–1903 (2022)

Bart, C.K.: The impact of the mission on firm innovativeness. Int. J. Technol. Manage. **11**(3–4), 479–493 (1996)

Berger, H., Thomas, C.: SMEs-social media marketing performance. Int. J. Web Eng. Technol. **11**(3), 215–232 (2016)

Chatterjee, S., Kar, A.K.: Why do small and medium enterprises use social media marketing and what is the impact: empirical insights from India. Int. J. Inf. Manage. **53**, 102103 (2020)

Chen, C.J., Huang, J.W., Hsiao, Y.C.: Knowledge management and innovativeness: the role of organizational climate and structure. Int. J. Manpower **31**(8), 848–870 (2010)

Cosh, A., Hughes, A.: The Changing State of British Enterprises. ESRC Centre for Business Research, Cambridge (1996)

Erlangga, H.: Effect of digital marketing and social media on purchase intention of SMES food products. Turk. J. Comput. Math. Educ. (TURCOMAT) **12**(3), 3672–3678 (2021)

Geroski, P.A., Machin, S.: Do innovating firms outperform non-innovators?. Bus. Strat. Rev. Summer 79–90 (1992)

Gruenbichler, R., Klucka, J., Haviernikova, K., Strelcova, S.: Business performance management in small and medium-sized enterprises in the Slovak republic: an integrated three-phase-framework for implementation. J. Competitiveness **13**(1), 42–58 (2021)

Folan, P., Browne, J., Jagdev, H.: Performance: its meaning and content for today's business research. Comput. Ind. **58**(7), 605-620 2007

Harazi, M.N., Farghly, D.M.: Impact of social media ads on unhealthy food concepts and adolescent health in Jazan region. Inf. Sci. Lett. **12**(7), 3069–3076 (2023). https://doi.org/10.18576/isl/120733

Hitka, M., Schmidtová, J., Lorincová, S., Štarchoň, P., Weberová, D., Kampf, R.: Sustainability of human resource management processes through employee motivation and job satisfaction. Acta Polytech. Hung. **18**(2), 7–26 (2021)

Hogan, S.J., Coote, L.V.: Organizational culture, innovation, and performance: a test of Schein's model. J. Bus. Res. **67**(8), 1609–1621 (2014)

Hudson, M., Lean, J., Smart, P.A.: Improving control through effective performance measurement in SMEs. Product. Plann. Control **12**(8), 804–813 (2001)

Hult, G.T.M., Hurley, R.F., Knight, G.A.: Innovativeness: Its antecedents and impact on business performance. Ind. Mark. Manage. **33**(5), 429–438 (2004)

Inyang, B.J.: Defining the role engagement of small and medium-sized enterprises (SMEs) in corporate social responsibility (CSR). Int. Bus. Res. **6**(5), 123–132 (2013). https://doi.org/10.5539/ibr.v6n5p123

Ismaeil, A.: Electronic marketing and digital transformation for culture heritage. Inf. Sci. Lett. **12**(6), 2451–2456 (2023)

Kaplan, A.M., Haenlein, M.: Users of the world, unite! the challenges and opportunities of social media. Bus. Horiz. **53**(1), 59–68 (2010). https://doi.org/10.1016/j.bushor.2009.09.003

Kichatov, V., Mihajlovski, N.: Social media as a promotional tool: a comparison between political parties and companies (2010)

Kohli, A.K., Jaworski, B.J.: Market orientation: the construct, research propositions, and managerial implications. J. Mark. **54**(2), 1–18 (1990)

Lam, H.K., Yeung, A.C., Cheng, T.E.: The impact of firms' social media initiatives on operational efficiency and innovativeness. J. Oper. Manag. **47**, 28–43 (2016)

Laforet, S., Tann, J.: Innovative characteristics of small manufacturing firms. J. Small Bus. Enterp. Dev. **13**(3), 363–380 (2006)

Martín-Rojas, R., García-Morales, V.J., Garrido-Moreno, A., Salmador-Sánchez, M.P.: Social media use and the challenge of complexity: evidence from the technology sector. J. Bus. Res. **129**, 621–640 (2021)

Martín-Rojas, R., Garrido-Moreno, A., García-Morales, V.J.: Social media use, corporate entrepreneurship and organizational resilience: a recipe for SMEs success in a post-Covid scenario. Technol. Forecast. Soc. Chang. **190**, 122421 (2023)

Merrilees, B., Rundle-Thiele, S., Lye, A.: Marketing capabilities: antecedents and implications for B2B SME performance. Ind. Mark. Manage. **40**(3), 368–375 (2011)

Musa, H., Ab Rahim, N., Azmi, F.R., Shibghatullah, A.S., Othman, N.A.: Social media marketing and online small and medium enterprises performance: perspective of Malaysian small and medium enterprises. Int. Rev. Manag. Mark. **6**(7S), 1–5 (2016)

Neely, A., Hii, J.: Innovation and Business Performance: a Literature Review, p. 65. University of Cambridge, The Judge Institute of Management Studies (1998)

Salam, S., Hoque, A.S.M.M.: The role of social media and effect of relationship marketing on SME performance in Bangladesh: multi-group CFA. Asian People J. (APJ) **2**(1), 12–31 (2019)

Sandvik, I.L., Sandvik, K.: The impact of market orientation on product innovativeness and business performance. Int. J. Res. Mark. **20**(4), 355–376 (2003)

Susanto, P., Hoque, M.E., Shah, N.U., Candra, A.H., Hashim, N.M.H.N., Abdullah, N.L.: Entrepreneurial orientation and performance of SMEs: the roles of marketing capabilities and social media usage. J. Entrepreneurship Emerg. Econ. **15**(2), 379–403 (2023)

Syaifullah, J., Syaifudin, M., Sukendar, M.U., Junaedi, J.: Social media marketing and business performance of MSMEs during the COVID-19 pandemic. J. Asian Financ. Econ. Bus. **8**(2), 523–531 (2021)

Tajvidi, R., Karami, A.: The effect of social media on firm performance. Comput. Hum. Behav. **115**, 105174 (2021)

Tsai, K.H., Yang, S.Y.: Firm innovativeness and business performance: the joint moderating effects of market turbulence and competition. Ind. Mark. Manage. **42**(8), 1279–1294 (2013)

Tuominen, M., Rajala, A., Möller, K.: How does adaptability drive firm innovativeness? J. Bus. Res. **57**(5), 495–506 (2004)

Amoah, J., Belás, J., Khan, K.A., Metzker, Z.: Antecedents of sustainable SMEs in the social media space: a partial least square-structural equation modeling (PLS-SEM) approach. Manag. Mark. **16**(1), 26–46 (2021). https://doi.org/10.2478/mmcks-2021-0003

Basri, W.: Examining the impact of artificial intelligence (Ai)-assisted social media marketing on the performance of small and medium enterprises: toward effective business management in the Saudi Arabian context. Int. J. Comput. Intell. Syst. **13**(1), 142–152 (2020). https://doi.org/10.2991/ijcis.d.200127.002

Djakasaputra, A., Wijaya, O.Y.A., Utama, A.S., Yohana, C., Romadhoni, B., Fahlevi, M.: Empirical study of Indonesian SMEs sales performance in digital era: The role of quality service and digital marketing. Int. J. Data Netw. Sci. **5**(3), 303–310 (2021). https://doi.org/10.5267/j.ijdns.2021.6.003

Drydakis, N.: Artificial intelligence and reduced SMEs' business risks. a dynamic capabilities analysis during the COVID-19 pandemic. Inf. Syst. Front. 0123456789 (2022). https://doi.org/10.1007/s10796-022-10249-6

Freixanet, J., Braojos, J., Rialp-Criado, A., Rialp-Criado, J.: Does international entrepreneurial orientation foster innovation performance? the mediating role of social media and open innovation. Int. J. Entrepreneurship Innov. **22**(1), 33–44 (2021). https://doi.org/10.1177/1465750320922320

Kwon, W.S., Woo, H., Sadachar, A., Huang, X.: External pressure or internal culture? an innovation diffusion theory account of small retail businesses' social media use. J. Retail. Consum. Serv. **62**(May), 102616 (2021). https://doi.org/10.1016/j.jretconser.2021.102616

Maki, E.Y.Z.: The impact of social media advertising on womens purchasing decision and its economic repercussions. J. Stat. Appl. Probab. **12**(3), 8 (2023). https://doi.org/10.18576/jsap/120308

Oyewobi, L.: Impact of social media usage on performance of construction business (CBs) in Abuja-Nigeria. J. Financ. Manag. Property Constr. **26**(2), 257–278 (2020)

Qalati, S.A., Ostic, D., Shuibin, G., Mingyue, F.: A mediated–moderated model for social media adoption and small and medium-sized enterprise performance in emerging countries. Manag. Decis. Econ. **43**(3), 846–861 (2022). https://doi.org/10.1002/mde.3422

Qalati, S.A., Yuan, L.W., Khan, M.A., Anwar, F.A.: mediated model on the adoption of social media and SMEs' performance in developing countries. Tech. Soc. **1**(64), 101513 (2021). https://doi.org/10.1016/j.techsoc.2020.101513

Ramdani, B., Raja, S., Kayumova, M.: Digital innovation in SMEs: a systematic review, synthesis and research agenda. Inf. Technol. Dev. **28**(1), 56–80 (2022). https://doi.org/10.1080/02681102.2021.1893148

Rozak, H., Adhiatma, A., Fachrunnisa, O., Rahayu, T.: Social media engagement, organizational agility and digitalization strategic plan to improve SMES 2019; performance. IEEE Trans. Eng. Manag. 1–10 (2021).https://doi.org/10.1109/TEM.2021.3085977

Selvarajan, T.T., Singh, B., Solansky, S.: Performance appraisal fairness, leader-member exchange and motivation to improve performance: a study of US and Mexican employees. J. Bus. Res. **85**, 142–154 (2018). https://doi.org/10.1016/j.jbusres.2017.11.043

Tajvidi, R., Karami, A.: The effect of social media on firm performance. Comput. Hum. Behav. **115**, 1 (2021). https://doi.org/10.1016/j.chb.2017.09.026

Terry, M.: Twittering healthcare: social media and medicine. Telemed. e-Health, 507–510 (2009). https://doi.org/10.1089/tmj.2009.9955

Trawnih, A., Yaseen, H., Al-Adwan, A.S., Alsoud, A.R., Jaber, O.A.: Factors influencing social media adoption among SMES during Covid-19 Crisis. J. Manag. Inf. Decision Sci. **24**(6), 1–18 (2021)

Wadhwa, R., Bansal, R., Chakir, A., Katyal, R.: Exploring social media adoption and SME performance: role and challenges. In: Strengthening SME Performance Through Social Media Adoption and Usage, pp. 189–200. IGI Global(2023)

Zhang, F., Zhu, L.: Social media strategic capability, organizational unlearning, and disruptive innovation of SMEs: the moderating roles of TMT heterogeneity and environmental dynamism. J. Bus. Res. **133**(May), 183–193 (2021). https://doi.org/10.1016/j.jbusres.2021.04.071

Students Intention Towards Digital Entrepreneurship – Industry 5.0

C. Nagadeepa[1] , K. P. Jaheer Mukthar[1] (✉) , Edwin Asnate-Salazar[2] ,
Jorge Castillo-Picon[2] , Rosario Yslado Méndez[2] , and Sandra Mory-Guarnizo[3]

[1] Kristu Jayanti College Autonomous, Bengaluru, India
jaheer@kristujayanti.com
[2] Universidad Nacional Santiago Antunez de Mayolo, Huaraz, Peru
[3] Universidad Señor de Sipán, Chiclayo, Peru

Abstract. Abstract Entrepreneurship provides economic growth for the nation in various ways. Entrepreneurs are contributing new ideas to the world and presently with help of digitalization introducing some innovation and technology-driven startups. Educational Institutions plays a significant role to develop entrepreneurial skill among students. There are various factors affecting the students for their intention towards Digital Entrepreneurship. Family background, Environment, Society needs are the important factors affecting the students to move towards entrepreneurs and since the present world coping with technology and digitalization, entrepreneurship also moving towards digitalization. This research aims to study the student's intention towards digitalized entrepreneurship and its effect.

Keywords: Digital Entrepreneurship · Self-efficacy · Innovation · EDP education

1 Introduction

The entrepreneurship concept is a significant interest among developing countries. Entrepreneurship has a pivotal role in a country's economic development. With the emergence of technology and digitalization, entrepreneurship also focuses towards digitalization and moving to digital entrepreneurship. Most youngsters have become entrepreneurs after their graduate studies. The government also provides support to entrepreneurs and new start-ups. Traditional entrepreneurship intention changed these days to digital and technological entrepreneurship. Innovation and technology are important factors to consider in entrepreneurship.

The entrepreneurial skill developed among youngsters by various factors. Traditional entrepreneurship changed digital entrepreneurship because of technological innovation, development and digitalization. There are various factors influencing students to become digital entrepreneurs like Digital Literacy, their creative ability, entrepreneurial education from the educational institution and form the society, Innovative technologies etc.

The original version of the chapter has been revised. The affiliation assignments have been corrected. A correction to this chapter can be found at
https://doi.org/10.1007/978-3-031-50518-8_19

The digital literacy rate is high for college students because of the usage of electronic devices and education also transferring knowledge through digital media. Educational institutions, the Environment and society play a significant role in digital literacy. Digital literacy helps students to be creative and to become entrepreneurs. Universities and colleges provide entrepreneurial courses to students and entrepreneurship education helps them to be creative and the digital entrepreneurial self-efficacy. Entrepreneurial education helps students to create and to make innovative ideas in digital entrepreneurship.

2 Need for the Study

Entrepreneur's contribution is helpful for the growth of the nation. Entrepreneurial skills are developed at a younger age and various factors affect to move towards entrepreneurship. The present world is technologically driven and entrepreneurs also step forwards in digitalized innovation in various fields. Universities and colleges have an important role to play in entrepreneurial skills training among youngsters. Therefore, this research is needed in this present situation to know the intention of students towards digital entrepreneurship.

3 Theoretical Background

Digital entrepreneurship has been defined in numerous research studies from a variety of angles. Digital entrepreneurship can be defined as the "process of entrepreneurial creation of digital value through the use of various socio-technical digital enablers to assist successful acquisition, processing, dissemination, and consumption of digital information" by Sahut, Iandoli, and Teulon (2021). DE was also described by Le Dinh, Vu, and Ayayi (2018) as the combination of conventional entrepreneurship with more innovative and clever ways to do company using digital resources. Digital Entrepreneurship is also defined by Bailetti (2012) as a project investment using technologically and scientifically specialised individuals and assets for the value creation of the firm.

According to Beckman (2012), digital entrepreneurship is the process of making use of opportunities in the realm of cutting-edge research and engineering. Digital entrepreneurs, as defined by Nambisan (2016), also include business owners whose ventures are centred around technology.

Esmaeeli (2011) asserts that because the literature on digital entrepreneurship is just getting started, it is essential to create a typology of a company's digitalization. According to him, the degree of business digitalization may be determined by 1) the digital nature of a firm's good or service, 2) the potential for distribution of a good or service via digital channels, 3) the possibility of digital engagement with significant external stakeholders along the value chain, and 4) the possibility for internal activities which are virtual in nature related to the operations of a firm. This is to be performed via digital channels (p.165). Consequently, "digital entrepreneurship" refers to the production of new value through the adoption of a novel model of business in terms of digital products or services, a digital office environment, a digital marketplace, digital distribution, or some mixture of these (Esmaeeli 2011).

Based on Hull et al. (2007), there are three different forms of digital entrepreneurship. One is called "mild digital entrepreneurship," whereby the term "digital" is used to supplement traditional entrepreneurship. The "click and mortar" business model is comparable to this one. The second is referred to as "moderate digital entrepreneurship," in which the business spends a sizeable quantity of resources on the elements of the value chain such as digital products, digital services and delivery. The final one is described as "extreme digital entrepreneurship," or pure-player in more recent times. In the final type, the business is entirely digital, from production to clients.

Definition of Digital Entrepreneurship: Digital entrepreneurship has been defined as "the process of using digital technologies to start or grow a business, create new products or services, or disrupt existing industries" (Kane 2016, p. 1). It involves leveraging digital tools such as social media, mobile devices, and cloud computing to innovate and compete in the market. The creation, development, and management of digital and innovative products or services with the purpose of generating value and growth through the use of digital technologies" (Gómez et al. 2021, p. 2).

Drivers of Digital Entrepreneurship: Several factors have been identified as drivers of digital entrepreneurship. These include advances in digital technology, the availability of capital, and changes in consumer behavior. According to Hatak et al. (2020), the most significant drivers of digital entrepreneurship are the increasing access to the internet, the proliferation of mobile devices, and the emergence of new digital platforms.

Challenges of Digital Entrepreneurship: Digital entrepreneurship also poses unique challenges, such as the need for technical skills, cybersecurity risks, and fierce competition. Scholars have noted that digital entrepreneurs face several barriers to success, including limited resources, inadequate digital infrastructure, and a lack of trust in online transactions (Ferreira et al. 2019; Rashid et al. 2020).

Digital Entrepreneurship Strategies: To overcome these challenges, digital entrepreneurs employ various strategies, such as leveraging social media, collaborating with other entrepreneurs, and adopting agile methodologies. For example, research by Kim and Lee (2019) suggests that social media can be used to build brand awareness, connect with customers, and conduct market research.

Digital Entrepreneurship Ecosystem: Finally, scholars have explored the role of the digital entrepreneurship ecosystem in supporting the growth and success of digital ventures. This ecosystem includes a range of actors, such as venture capitalists, accelerators, and government agencies. According to Stam (2015), the quality of this ecosystem can impact the ability of digital entrepreneurs to access resources, find mentors, and build networks. Definition of Digital Entrepreneurship (Haase et al. 2018).:

Characteristics of Digital Entrepreneurship

Scholars have also identified several key characteristics of digital entrepreneurship. These include the usage of technologies to create and distribute products, the emphasis on agility and speed in decision-making, and the ability to scale rapidly (Le et al. 2021; Nambisan & Baron 2019).

Intersection of Digital and Traditional Entrepreneurship

Finally, scholars have explored the intersection of digital and traditional entrepreneurship, highlighting the ways in which digital technologies are transforming traditional business models and industries (Ratten 2017). This intersection has created novel opportunities for entrepreneurs to create value and disrupt existing markets.

Digitally literate entrepreneurs can adapt to changes in technology and use media for marketing, communication, trend analysis, and gauging consumer demand. Because individuals are constantly connected via cell phones, social media is a crucial component today. It is quite simple to manage enterprises and broaden the internet market thanks to a variety of applications (Nambisan & Baron 2019). Following various communities, topical themes, and organizations are crucial for business entrepreneurs. Such skills, which were developed with online administration into electronic commerce and reinforced by coding and big data analytics, are prerequisites for starting a start-up where technology-driven entrepreneurs may engage with and reach a larger market.

Creativity/Innovativeness

Innovation is a crucial aspect of digital entrepreneurship. Scholars have noted that digital entrepreneurs must continuously innovate to stay ahead of competition and remain relevant in the market (Le et al. 2021). A student's inventiveness has a big impact on their ability to be an entrepreneur and leads to it. Educational institutions are crucial in helping students develop their creativity (Rahman 2019). The student's ability to think creatively and innovatively is enhanced. To be a successful entrepreneur in the modern world, innovation is necessary (Guzmán & Trujillo 2018). The creativity of the students make them entrepreneur and empowered to take new initiatives.

Miller (1983) recently claimed that successful organisations often exhibit an aptitude for innovation, initiative, and risk-taking. This concept was given the moniker entrepreneurial orientation by him (Vial 2016). Companies with an entrepreneurial attitude consistently seek and seize new opportunities, develop novel values, and establish themselves as market leaders (Guzmán & Trujillo 2018). Innovation in digital entrepreneurship is closely tied to technology. Digital entrepreneurs leverage emerging technologies such as artificial intelligence, blockchain, and the Internet of Things to create innovative products and services (Le et al. 2021). These technologies enable entrepreneurs to create new and unique products and services that were not possible before.

Entrepreneurial Education

McGrath (1999), students can learn about the elements that cause failure in business and can prevent the same errors by taking part in entrepreneurship education (Craig et al. 2006; Kuratko, 2003). Entrepreneurial education is becoming increasingly important for students in the 21st century. Scholars have noted that entrepreneurial education can help students develop important skills such as creativity, critical thinking, problem-solving, and risk-taking (Tang et al., 2020; Deamer 2004) discovered that students' prior experience with entrepreneurship has a detrimental impact on the impact of entrepreneurship education on entrepreneurial ambition. The phrase "entrepreneurship education" suggests that people can learn and be trained for entrepreneurship, and research on this premise has been widely used. Entrepreneurial education is becoming increasingly important for students in the 21st century. Scholars have noted that entrepreneurial education can help students develop important skills such as creativity, critical thinking, problem-solving, and risk-taking (Tang et al. 2020). Entrepreneurial education also prepares students to be more resilient and adaptable to changes in the job market (Dana 2001; Henry et al. 2005;)

Entrepreneurial education can take many forms, including formal education programs, experiential learning programs, and entrepreneurship incubators (Choi & Kim 2020). Scholars have explored the effectiveness of entrepreneurial education in developing important skills and fostering entrepreneurship among students. A meta-analysis by Tang et al. (2020) found that entrepreneurial education has a positive effect on developing entrepreneurship-related knowledge, skills, and attitudes among students. Entrepreneurial education also has a positive effect on students' intentions to start a business and on the actual creation of new ventures.

Despite the benefits of entrepreneurial education, there are also challenges in implementing effective programs. These include a lack of qualified instructors, a lack of resources, and a lack of support from parents and policymakers (Choi & Kim 2020). Additionally, there is a need for more research to identify the most effective approaches to entrepreneurial education.

Self-efficacy

The social cognitive viewpoint of Bandura (1999) is where the idea of self-efficacy originates ((Bandura 1997). The conviction that one can effectively carry out an activity is known as self-efficacy, and it has been said that "Efficacy beliefs influence how people feel, think, motivate themselves, and conduct" (Bandura 1993; Chen et.al. 1998). It is usual to practice when discussing self-efficacy to distinguish between generalized self-efficacy and other types of the task- or domain-specific self-efficacy (Chen et al. 2018).

Rauch and Frese (2007) discovered generalized self-efficacy and proactive personality as significant predictors of the likelihood of business startup and venture success in a meta-analysis of practicing entrepreneurs. They concluded that individuals with greater levels of generalized self-efficacy were more likely to start new firms, and those who also possessed a proactive personality and high levels of generalized self-efficacy were more likely to succeed in those endeavors. This study emphasizes the recurring findings that these two constructs have an impact on entrepreneurship success.

Individuals with higher levels of self-efficacy are more likely to perceive opportunities, take risks, and persist in the face of failure (Kautonen et al. 2015). Several factors have been identified as influencing self-efficacy in digital entrepreneurship. These include prior entrepreneurial experience, education and training, social support, and access to resources and networks (Vasilenko et al. 2017; Bae et al. 2018). Prior experience in starting and running a digital business can increase an individual's self-efficacy, as can education and training in digital entrepreneurship. Social support from family, friends, and mentors can also boost self-efficacy, as can access to resources such as funding and networks. These interventions aim to provide individuals with the skills, knowledge, and support necessary to succeed in digital entrepreneurship, thereby increasing their self-efficacy (Vasilenko et al. 2017; Bae et al. 2018).

4   External Factor

4.1   Industrial Development Towards Innovation

Industrial development influences people to become an entrepreneur. Industries are moving towards innovation based on the requirements of society and the environment. Competitive industries introduce new ideas and technology to survive in the market. Industrial development can create opportunities for entrepreneurship by creating new markets, providing access to resources and infrastructure, and generating demand for new products and services (Zahra et al., 2019). Entrepreneurship, in turn, can contribute to industrial development by fostering innovation, creating jobs, and promoting economic growth. Entrepreneurial ecosystems include access to finance, mentorship, education and training, and networking opportunities (Stam et al. 2018).

The Emergence of Digital Entrepreneurship in Industrial 5.0
Industrial 5.0 is driving the emergence of new forms of digital entrepreneurship, which leverage advanced technologies to create innovative products and services. These digital entrepreneurs are often focused on developing new business models that are based on the integration of physical and digital systems (Cegarra-Navarro et al. 2019).

Technical skills such as programming and data analysis, as well as soft skills such as creativity and adaptability (Chen et al. 2020). The development of digital skills is essential for individuals and organizations that want to succeed in the rapidly evolving landscape of Industrial 5.0 entrepreneurship.

Policies to Promote Industrial 5.0 Entrepreneurship
Governments and other stakeholders can implement policies to promote entrepreneurship in the context of Industrial 5.0. These policies can include investment in digital infrastructure, support for digital skills training programs, and incentives for the development of new digital businesses (Brynjolfsson et al. 2018). Further, these policies can include investment in infrastructure, tax incentives for businesses, and support for entrepreneurship education and training programs (Gindling & Newhouse 2017; Kimuyu et al. 2018; Leng et al. 2017). China have shown how digital platforms are enabling new forms of entrepreneurship that leverage the power of big data and artificial intelligence. Other studies in Europe have explored how the integration of physical and digital systems is creating new opportunities for entrepreneurship in industries such as manufacturing and logistics (El Khatib et al. 2018).

5 Technology Innovation

Technology is the skill of transforming raw materials into products and services that benefit society more. New products, new industrial methods, new raw materials, and new scientific research are all promoted as a result of technological development (Brynjolfsson et al. 2018). The knowledge economy, which is composed of knowledge producers and is driven by fundamental research, and the commercial economy (Chen et al. 2020)., which is composed of knowledge users and is driven by the market, together make up an innovation ecosystem.

Technology innovation with digitalization moving forward each day. Technological in novation happens in all areas of the world. Knowledge of digital skill and technology helps people to make innovative technology and this influence people to become entrepreneurs (Zahra et al. 2019).

6 Incentives

One of the vital drivers of entrepreneurship is incentives. If supporting loans, regulations, and organisations are developed, entrepreneurship will grow rapidly. The usage and use of quickly developing information and communication technologies (ICT), such as machine learning, internet of things (IoT), cloud computing, big data analytics, etc., and their enhanced utilisation are what digitalization is all about (Parviainen et al. 2017).

Fisch (2019) and Ahrens et al. (2019), entrepreneurs are using digital technology to finance innovation and support business development. Entrepreneurs frequently employ digital technologies to develop new digital goods and services as well as new business models that are focused on the digital economy.

India, a rising nation in South Asia, has also seen a rise in the number of digital start- ups and entrepreneurs. With an average yearly growth rate of 12 to 15%, India is the country with the greatest start-up ecosystem worldwide. In 2018, 50,000 start-ups dominated the Indian economy. What's more, more than 9000 of these start-ups are technology-driven ventures, which is interesting to note. Additionally, as evidenced by the approximately 1200 new technology start-ups scheduled to begin in 2019, the country's tech-oriented start-up scene is continuously expanding (Start-up India 2021).

Additionally, it is asserted that start-up incentives like Make in India, Start-up India, STEP, JAM, and Digital India are fueling this rise in digital entrepreneurship. Sen (2019) asserts that start-up India has been one of the most effective government-led initiatives introduced by the Indian Government to create a digital entrepreneurship platform. The achievement of an annual growth rate of 108% in 2018 and total funding that exceeds US $4.2 billion are considered indicators of the scheme's success.

Financial Enhancement Towards Better Economic Status

Digital entrepreneurship has the potential to enhance financial inclusion and promote better economic status for individuals and communities. Digital platforms, such as e-commerce and mobile banking, can facilitate access to financial services and provide new opportunities for entrepreneurship (Klein et al. 2019). Financial management skills are critical for the success of digital entrepreneurs. Effective financial management practices, such as budgeting and cash flow management, can help entrepreneurs to manage their finances and grow their businesses (Salmi et al. 2019). Digital entrepreneurship education programs can play a key role in promoting financial management skills and enhancing the financial literacy of entrepreneurs. Crowdfunding has emerged as a popular financing option for digital entrepreneurs, provide a mechanism for entrepreneurs to raise capital from a large number of individuals, often with relatively small investments (Belleflamme et al. 2019). By leveraging crowdfunding, digital entrepreneurs can access new sources of capital and expand their businesses. Digital startups are often highly innovative and can disrupt traditional industries, creating new opportunities for growth and development (Al-Tit et al. 2018). By fostering a culture of digital entrepreneurship and supporting the growth of digital startups, policymakers can help to promote economic development and enhance the economic status of individuals and communities.

Research Gap

By referring and reviewing a variety of prior literature and studies, the researchers have determined the variables under the current study. These variables are catagorised into independent variables and dependent variables. Various researches were conducted by various researchers on entrepreneurship, impact of entrepreneurship on GDP, success story of entrepreneurship and factors influencing entrepreneurship. Consumer purchasing patterns of millets. Additionally, a number of aspects of intention to become entrepreneurship are investigated, including awareness and attitude, ethical self-efficacy, motivation, knowledge of entrepreneurship and their intention. Various national and international studies on entrepreneurship are reviewed. Based on the relevant literature, there are a few studies that examine digital entrepreneurship intention, particularly the future of world that is student's intention. This paper is considering two important aspects which are the motivating factors of the young blood students who are intended to start their digital entrepreneurship.

Research Objective:

- To measure the internal factors of the student's intention towards digital entrepreneurship.
- To measure the external factors of the student's intention towards digital entrepreneurship

7 Methodology

This study adopts both qualitative and quantitative approaches. The first stage of the study was exploratory in nature which involved a thorough review of the relevant literature. The second phase of the study involved the survey method to conduct a descriptive study. After moving past a review of the literature, the researcher concentrates on methodology, developing goals with the statement of the problem and choosing the best research design for the study.

Context and Sample Size: Two hundred students were included in the study. The students were chosen from parts of Karnataka. The students were selected from various cities of Karnataka are Bangalore, Mysore, Shivamogga, Mangalore, Manipal. Survey was conducted using social media and google form. Questionnaire were circulated among the students to get their responses regarding their intention towards digital entrepreneurship.

Sampling Method: For a purposeful sampling strategy, students who are interested towards entrepreneurship especially students of EDP club were chosen. Primary data was gathered via a survey questionnaire. The survey was sent via Google Forms, emails, WhatsApp, and social media. The opinions of several of the participants were recorded in the face-to-face interview. By utilizing the proper econometric and statistical tools, the collected data is tested and interpreted. The current study uses the frequency approach, percentage analysis as well as Correlation and Regression tests to prove the hypothesis. To prove the hypotheses Structural equation modelling was used with the help of SPSS AMOS.

Research Framework and Hypotheses Development
The following presents the research framework which has been developed to prove the hypothesis. It is based on the research gap (Fig. 1).

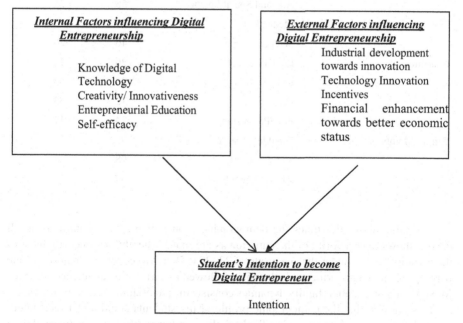

Fig. 1. Research Framework and Hypothesis

According to the objectives of the study, the following hypothesis were framed:

H1: There is a significance influence of student's internal factors on their intention to become digital entrepreneur.
H2: There is a significance influence of external factors on student's intention to become digital entrepreneur.

Data Analysis:
The collected data were analysed using SPSS and interpreted as follows. The first section of the analysis includes the demographic data of the study sample and their influence on student's intention to become digital entrepreneur (Table 1).

Table 1. Percentage Analysis on demographic Profile of the Respondents

Demographic Element	Groups	N	%
Gender	Male	122	56
	Female	78	44
Age	Below 20	21	10
	21–23 years	77	35
	23–25 years	81	36
	Above 25years	41	19
Stream of Education	Engineering	98	45
	Arts and Social Science	55	25
	Medical	21	10
	Science	46	20
Education	Pre University	26	12
	UG	98	45
	PG	72	33
	PhD/Professional	24	11
Family Members	2 and less than 2	85	39
	3- 5 members	98	45
	Above 5 members	37	17

The table above illustrates the demographic profile of the survey participants. It clearly shows that majority of the participants are male, whereby the majority most of the participants fall under the age group of 23–25 (35%). Moreover, the majority of the participants are engineering students (45%) followed by Arts& Social Science students. Most of the participants' family dynamics consists of 2 to 5 family members (Table 2).

It is inferred that the demographic profile of the students could affect their intention to become digital entrepreneur. To check the significant differences between digital entrepreneur - intention and the demographic elements, the chi square test was undertaken. The test result showed a p value of 0.003 for gender, stream of education 0.017, level of education 0.030 which is less than 0.05 at 5% significance hence the null hypothesis is not accepted/rejected. These factors are positively associated with the student's intention to become digital entrepreneurs. The rest of the factors have higher p value. As such, the null hypothesis is accepted, and this indicates that age and family does not have significance association with student's intention to become digital entrepreneur.

Table 2. Demographic influence on Intention towards Digital Entrepreneurship

Particulars – Factors	Sig
Gender	0.003
Age	0.227
Stream of Education	0.017
Level of Education	0.030
Family Members	0.206

To prove the proposed hypotheses SEM analysis was used and AMOS software helped to draw the equation to prove the hypothesis. The SEM equation was used to analyse the data collected. The model was fit and the model fit indices were above the accepted standards. The following table shows the results of indices value of the proposed model (Tables 3 and 4).

Table 3. Student's intention to become digital entrepreneur - Model Fit Indices

Indices	Values
X2	440.14
DF	352
p	0
CMIN/DF	1.236
RMSEA	0.058
GFI	0.821
CFI	0.921
AGFI	0.885

Table 4. SEM – Model Regression Weights

Proposed Path	Direct Effect of the Path	S.E	C.R	P
Intention <– Internal Factor	0.42	0.081	2.087	0.037
Intention <– External Factor	0.57	0.052	1.977	0.042

The above table shows the path result of the model. All the calculated values are more than the table value ie. 1.968 (Fig. 2).

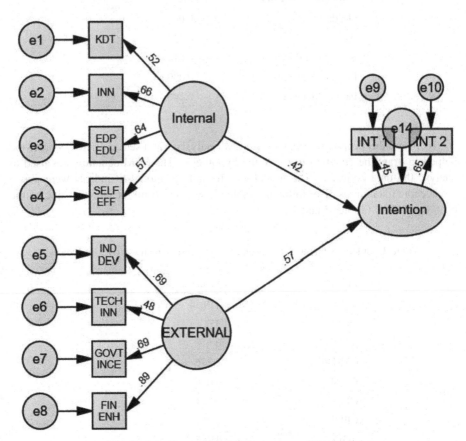

Fig. 2. Intention – Digital Entrepreneur – SEM Model

Abbreviation Used in the Model:
KDT - Knowledge of Digital Technology
INN - Creativity/ Innovativeness
EDP EDU - Entrepreneurial Education
SELF EFF - Self-efficacy IND DEV - Industrial Development towards innovation
TECH INN - Technology Innovation
GOVT INCE - Incentives
FIN ENH - Financial enhancement towards better economic status

Results: Internal Factors and Student's Intention to Become Digital Entrepreneur
The null hypothesis is rejected because the p value of the proposed path (0.037) is less than the acceptable value of 0.05. There are various internal factors within the students are motivating them to become entrepreneur further various factors influencing

towards digital world also. In today's digital era, students are having Knowledge of Digital Technology and they are thinking creatively and so innovative. All the institutions are providing entrepreneurial education and they are well focused towards their goal. Students are influenced by their own internal factors to become digital entrepreneurs. Digital entrepreneurship relies heavily on the use of technology, so students should be introduced to a range of digital tools and technologies that can support entrepreneurship, including website design, digital marketing, and e-commerce platforms. One of the most effective ways to prepare students for entrepreneurship is through experiential learning opportunities, such as internships, co-op programs, and entrepreneurship competitions. These experiences provide students with practical competencies, capabilities and experiences that can help them to develop the confidence and resilience required for entrepreneurship.

External Factors and Student's Intention to Become Digital Entrepreneur
The null hypothesis is rejected because the p value of the proposed path (0.042) is less than the acceptable value of 0.05. Not only their internal motivators, there are various external factors also motivating them to become entrepreneurs. Industry 5.0, the Industrial Development towards Digital technology, Artificial Intelligence and innovation, Technology Innovation are the triggering factors towards digital entrepreneurs. There various government Incentives attracts the students to start their own digital business. Further, Financial enhancement towards better economic status is also one of the influencing factors. Students should be more aware about the Indian government's initiative schemes which will support students and young entrepreneurs in the digital space. Startup India, Digital India, a program to support digital entrepreneurship, such as digital skills training, funding support, and incubation facilities; Atal Innovation Mission- a programs to support student startups, including funding support, mentorship, and incubation facilities; Pradhan Mantri Yuva Yojana provides entrepreneurship education and training to young people. Indian government has launched several initiatives to support digital entrepreneurship among students and young people. These schemes provide funding support, mentorship, training, and incubation facilities to help students and young entrepreneurs to start and grow their businesses.

8 Conclusion

The purpose of the study is to determine the factors influencing the **student's intention to become digital entrepreneur** in important cities of Karnataka. The study proved that the students are now a days very focused about their goal and knowledgeable also. Further the COVID-19 pandemic situation taught them a great lesson and the importance of digital technology. The world is moving towards digital technology. Industry 5.0 created a great demand for Technology innovations. Technology provides up to date information to everyone in their fingertips. These technology developments attract the students toward digital innovations and students are motivated to become digital entrepreneur. A curriculum that prepares students to become successful digital entrepreneurs should combine theoretical knowledge with practical skills and experiences, and should incorporate opportunities for networking, mentorship, and experiential learning. By providing students with a well-rounded education that covers all aspects of entrepreneurship, we can help to prepare the next generation of digital entrepreneurs to succeed in a rapidly-changing digital landscape.

Implications of the Study for Students Are:
With the rise of digital technologies, there is a growing demand for professionals with skills in areas such as e-commerce, social media marketing, and data analytics. By studying digital entrepreneurship, students can develop skills that are relevant for the digital economy and enhance their employability. Further this study, encouraging entrepreneurial mindset among the students to develop an entrepreneurial mindset, which can be valuable in a variety of settings. This mindset includes a willingness to take risks, a focus on innovation and creativity, and an ability to identify and pursue opportunities. This study, helps to create positive social impact, such as promoting financial inclusion and reducing poverty. By studying digital entrepreneurship, students can learn how to develop socially responsible business models and contribute to social welfare.

Implications of the study for Researchers, Policy Makers (University) and Business: By studying the factors that influence students' intention to become digital entrepreneurs, researchers can gain a better understanding of the factors that drive entrepreneurship in the digital age. This can help policymakers and educators design programs and initiatives to promote entrepreneurship. Further, this study help identify barriers such as lack of access to funding or resources is found to be a barrier, policymakers and educators can develop initiatives to address these challenges.

This study expects that Educators and policymakers design effective entrepreneurship education programs that address the needs and interests of students. By understanding what motivates students to become digital entrepreneurs, educators can develop programs that are engaging, relevant, and effective. Policymakers can use this research to develop policies that support entrepreneurship and create an environment that is conducive to entrepreneurship.

9 Future Study

There are several areas of further study in students' intention towards digital entrepreneurship that could be explored. The role of education and training, The impact of social and cultural factors, the impact of personal characteristics such as risk tolerance, and creativity on students' intention to become digital entrepreneurs, the role of technology such as 2artificial intelligence, blockchain, and the Internet of Things, are impacting students' intention to become digital entrepreneurs, and how these technologies are being used in new business models and ventures. Further, there can be a study on the impact of entrepreneurship ecosystems, such as access to funding, networking opportunities, and supportive government policies, in shaping students' intention to become digital entrepreneurs.

References

Al-Tit, A.A., Bontis, N., Chaker, N.: The impact of digital entrepreneurship on economic growth and job creation. J. Small Bus. Manage. **56**(4), 626–638 (2018)

Ahrens, A., Lund, K.D, Marschall, M., Dau, T.: Sound source localization with varying amount of visual information in virtual reality. PLoS ONE, **14**(3), e0214603 (2019). https://doi.org/ 10.1371/journal.pone.0214603

Bae, T.J., Qian, S., Miao, C., Fiet, J.O.: The relationship between entrepreneurship education and entrepreneurial intentions: a meta-analytic review. Entrep. Theory Pract. **42**(2), 273–309 (2018)

Bailetti, T.: Technology entrepreneurship: overview, definition, and distinctive aspects. Technol. Innov. Manag. Rev. **2**(2), 5–12 (2012)

Bandura, A.: Perceived self-efficacy in cognitive development and functioning. Educ. Psychol.duc. Psychol. **28**(2), 117–148 (1993). https://doi.org/10.1207/s15326985ep2802_3

Bandura, A.: Social cognitive theory: an agentic perspective. Asian J. Soc. Psychol. **2**, 21–41 (1999). https://doi.org/10.1146/annurev.psych.52.1.1

Beckman, C.M., Eisenhardt, K., Kotha, S., Meyer, A., Rajagopalan, N.: Technology entrepreneurship. Strat. Entrepreneurship J. **6**(2), 89–93 (2012)

Belleflamme, P., Lambert, T., Schwienbacher, A.: Crowdfunding: tapping the right crowd. J. Bus. Ventur. **34**(1), 1–21 (2019)

Bosma, N., Levie, J.: 2009 Executive Report. Global Entrepreneurship Research Association (GERA) (2010). http://www.gemconsortium.org/docs/download/666

Brynjolfsson, E., Hu, Y.J., Simester, D.: The Future of Work: How the New Order of Business Will Shape Your Organization, Your Management Style and Your Life. John Wiley & Sons (2018)

Cegarra-Navarro, J.G., Soto-Acosta, P., Wensley, A.K.P.: Digital entrepreneurship in the industry 4.0 era. J. Bus. Res. **98**, 365–371 (2019)

Chen, C.C., Chen, W.C., Chen, C.Y.: Skills, competencies and innovation in the fourth industrial revolution. J. Bus. Res. **106**, 13–22 (2020)

Chen, C.C., Greene, P.G., Crick, A.: Does entrepreneurial self-efficacy distinguish entrepreneurs from managers? J. Bus. Ventur. **13**(4), 295–316 (1998). https://doi.org/10.1016/S0883-902 6(97)00029-3

Chen, Y., Li, H., Yue, X.: Entrepreneurial self-efficacy, entrepreneurial orientation, and firm performance: a meta-analysis. J. Bus. Ventur. **33**(5), 658–674 (2018)

Choi, S.J., Kim, Y.: Entrepreneurial education for high school students: a systematic review of the literature. J. Entrepreneurship Educ. **23**(1), 1–14 (2020)

Craig, J.B.L., Johnson, D.: Establishing individual differences related to opportunity alertness and innovation dependent on academic-career training. J. Manag. Dev. **25**(1), 28–39 (2006)

Dana, L.P.: The education and training of entrepreneurship in Asia. EducationnTraining. **43**(8/9), 405–415 (2001)

Deamer, I., Earle, L.: Searching for entrepreneurship. Ind. Commer. Train. **36**(3), 99–103 (2004)

El Khatib, Y., Aouad, G., Rankouhi, B.: Industry 4.0: A bibliometric review of its operationalization and implications on supply chain management. J. Ind. Inf. Integr. **12**, 67–81 (2018)

Esmaeeli, H.: The study of effecting factors on digital entrepreneurship (a case study). Interdisc. J. Contemp. Res. Bus. **2**(12), 163–172 (2011)

Ferreira, J.J., Fernandes, C.I., Raposo, M.L.: Digital entrepreneurship: a systematic literature review and research agenda. J. Bus. Res. **98**, 365–376 (2019)

Fisch, C.: Initial coin offerings (ICOs) to finance new ventures. J. Bus. Ventur. **34**, 1–22 (2019). https://doi.org/10.1016/j.jbusvent.2018.09.007

Gindling, T.H., Newhouse, D.L.: Industrial Policy and Development in the 21st Century. Oxford Research Encyclopedia of Economics and Finance (2017)

Gómez, J., Roig-Tierno, N., Llopis, J.: The definition of digital entrepreneurship: a literature review. Sustainability **13**(2), 596 (2021)

Guzmán, A.M., Trujillo, M.A.: The role of innovation in digital entrepreneurship. Int. J. Entrepreneurship **22**(1), 1–8 (2018)

Haase, H., Schief, M., Skorupinski, P.: Entrepreneurship for social and environmental impact: an introduction and review of current literature. Int. J. Entrep. Ventur. **10**(1), 1–20 (2018)

Hatak, I., Harms, R., Fink, M., Traut-Mattausch, E.: The impact of entrepreneurship education and entrepreneurial intention on entrepreneurial orientation. J. Bus. Res. **109**, 101–113 (2020)

Henry, C., Hill, F., Leitch, C.: Entrepreneurship education and training: can entrepreneurship be taught? Part II. Educ. + Train. **47**(3), 158–169 (2005)

Hull, C.E., Hung, Y.-T.C., Hair, N., Perotti, V., DeMartino, R.: Taking advantage of digital opportunities: a typology of digital entrepreneurship. Int. J. Netw. Virt. Organ. **4**(3), 290–303 (2007)

Kane, G.C.: The rise of digital entrepreneurs. MIT Sloan Manag. Rev. **57**(4), 1–6 (2016)

Kautonen, T., van Gelderen, M., Fink, M.: Robustness of the theory of planned behavior in predicting entrepreneurial intentions and actions. Entrep. Theory Pract. **39**(3), 655–674 (2015)

Kim, B., Lee, J.: Social media use in digital entrepreneurship: a systematic literature review and future research agenda. Int. J. Entrep. Behav. Res. **25**(2), 366–383 (2019)

Kimuyu, P.K., Misati, R.N., Were, M.: Industrial parks, innovation and entrepreneurship in East Africa: a review of the literature. J. Entrepreneurship Innov. Emerg. Econ. **4**(1), 62–75 (2018)

Klein, S., Mayer, C., Urbach, N.: Digital entrepreneurship, access to finance, and economic development. Entrep. Theory Pract. **43**(1), 176–201 (2019)

Kuratko. Entrepreneurship Education: Emerging Trends and Challenges for the 21st Century. Coleman White Paper Series (2003). www.usasbe.org

Le Dinh, T., Vu, M.C., Ayayi, A.: Towards a living lab for promoting the digital entrepreneurship process. Int. J. Entrepreneurship **22**(1), 1–17 (2018)

Le, V., Nguyen, H.N., Nguyen, N.T.H., Le, T.: The role of digital entrepreneurship in the fourth industrial revolution: a review of literature. Sustainability **13**(1), 72 (2021)

Leng, T., Wong, P.K., Chen, Y.: Industrial policy, entrepreneurship, and economic growth: evidence from Southeast Asia. J. Bus. Res. **70**, 396–401 (2017)

Miller, D.: The correlatives of entrepreneurship in three types of firms. Manag. Sci.. Sci. **29**(7), 770–791 (1983)

Nambisan, S.: Digital entrepreneurship: toward a digital technology perspective of entrepreneurship. Entrep. Theory Pract. **414**, 1–27 (2016)

Nambisan, S., Baron, R.A.: Digital entrepreneurship: Toward a digital technology perspective of entrepreneurship. Entrep. Theory Pract. **43**(2), 314–338 (2019)

Parviainen, P., Kääriäinen, J., Tihinen, M., Teppola, S.: Tackling the digitalization challenge: how to benefit from digitalization in practice. Int. J. Inf. Syst. Proj. Manag. **5**, 63–77 (2017)

Rahman, M.M., Hossain, M.S., Alam, M.S.: Digital entrepreneurship and innovation. J. Innov. Entrepreneurship **8**(1), 1–14 (2019)

Rashid, M.M., Islam, S.M.S., Ahmad, B., Hossain, M.S.: Understanding digital entrepreneurship: a systematic literature review and future research agenda. J. Small Bus. Manage. **58**(4), 778–803 (2020)

Ratten, V.: Digital entrepreneurship: a research agenda. J. Small Bus. Manage. **55**(4), 544–549 (2017)

Rauch, A., Frese, M.: Let's put the person back into entrepreneurship research: a meta-analysis on the relationship between business owners' personality traits, business creation, and success. Eur. J. Work Organ. Psy. **16**(4), 353–385 (2007). https://doi.org/10.1080/13594320701595438

Rauch, A., Hulsink, W.: Putting entrepreneurship education where the intention to act lies: an investigation into the impact of entrepreneurship education on entrepreneurial behavior. Acad. Manag. Learn. Educ. **14**(2), 187–204 (2015)

Sahut, J.-M., Iandoli, L., Teulon, F.: The age of digital entrepreneurship. Small Bus. Econ. **56**(1), 1–19 (2021)

Salmi, A., Jylhä, T., Jarvinen, J.: The impact of financial management skills on the success of digital entrepreneurs. J. Small Bus. Manage. **57**(3), 1012–1032 (2019)

Stam, E.: Entrepreneurial ecosystems and regional policy: a sympathetic critique. Eur. Plan. Stud. **23**(9), 1759–1769 (2015)

Stam, E., Spigel, B., Acs, Z.J.: Entrepreneurial ecosystems. Small Bus. Econ. **51**(1), 1–14 (2018)

Tang, J., Kacperczyk, A.J., Fei, Y.: The effectiveness of entrepreneurship education: a meta-analysis. J. Bus. Ventur. **35**(1), 106088 (2020)

Timmons, J.A.: New Venture Creation: Entrepreneurship for the 21st Century. Irwin, Burr Ridge (1994)

Urban, B., Bratina, T., Horvat, D.: Student perceptions of entrepreneurship education: a cross-national study. J. Entrepreneurship Educ. **22**(6), 1–15 (2019)

Vasilenko, M., Vasileva, V., Kolvereid, L.: Entrepreneurial self-efficacy in the context of digital entrepreneurship. J. Small Bus. Manage. **55**(1), 132–147 (2017)

Vial, G., Stettner, U.: Innovation and entrepreneurship in the digital economy. J. Innov. Econ. Manag. **3**(20), 11–22 (2016)

Zahra, S.A., Wright, M., Abdelgawad, S.G.: Entrepreneurship and innovation in emerging economies. J. Bus. Ventur. **34**(3), 1–12 (2019)

Zampetakis, L.A., Beldekos, P., Moustakis, V.: Entrepreneurship education and entrepreneurial intention: do female students benefit? Int. Entrepreneurship Manag. J. **14**(3), 623–641 (2018)

Correction to: Students Intention Towards Digital Entrepreneurship – Industry 5.0

C. Nagadeepa⑩, K. P. Jaheer Mukthar⑩, Edwin Asnate-Salazar⑩,
Jorge Castillo-Picon⑩, Rosario Yslado Méndez⑩,
and Sandra Mory-Guarnizo⑩

Correction to:
Chapter 18 in: A. M. A. Musleh Al-Sartawi et al. (Eds.):
Global Economic Revolutions: Big Data Governance
and Business Analytics for Sustainability, **CCIS 1999,**
https://doi.org/10.1007/978-3-031-50518-8_18

In the originally published version of chapter 18, the author affiliations were incorrectly assigned. This has been corrected.

The updated version of this chapter can be found at
https://doi.org/10.1007/978-3-031-50518-8_18

Author Index

A. M. A. Musleh Al-Sartawi et al. (Eds.): ICGER 2023, CCIS 1999, pp. 251–252, 2024.
https://doi.org/10.1007/978-3-031-50518-8

Printed in the United States
by Baker & Taylor Publisher Services

Printed in the United States
by Baker & Taylor Publisher Services